CRADLE OF FLAVOR

CRADLE

OF

FLAVOR

HOME COOKING FROM THE SPICE ISLANDS OF
INDONESIA, MALAYSIA, AND SINGAPORE

James Oseland

FOOD PHOTOGRAPHS BY CHRISTOPHER HIRSHEIMER
GLOSSARY AND BLACK-AND-WHITE PHOTOGRAPHS BY JAMES OSELAND

W. W. NORTON & COMPANY   NEW YORK   LONDON

For information about permission to reproduce selections from this book, write to Permissions,

W. W. Norton & Company, Inc., 500 Fifth Avenue, New York, NY 10110

Manufacturing by The Maple-Vail Book Manufacturing Group

Book design by Iris Weinstein

Cartography by Justin Morrill

Production manager: Andrew Marasia

Library of Congress Cataloging-in-Publication Data

Oseland, James.

Cradle of flavor : home cooking from the spice islands of Indonesia, Malaysia, and Singapore / James Oseland.

p. cm.

Includes bibliographical references and index.

ISBN-13: 978-0-393-05477-4 (hardcover)

ISBN-10: 0-393-05477-2 (hardcover)

1. Cookery, Southeast Asian. I. Title.

TX724.5.S68O84 2006

641.5959—dc22

2006003532

W. W. Norton & Company, Inc., 500 Fifth Avenue, New York, N.Y. 10110

www.wwnorton.com

W. W. Norton & Company Ltd., Castle House, 75/76 Wells Street, London W1T 3QT

1 2 3 4 5 6 7 8 9 0

To my Indonesian family, the Alwis

CONTENTS

COLOR PHOTOGRAPHS FOLLOW PAGES 64 AND 96.

Tak kenal maka, tak sayang.
If you don't know it, you can't love it.

—INDONESIAN FOLK SAYING

CRADLE OF FLAVOR

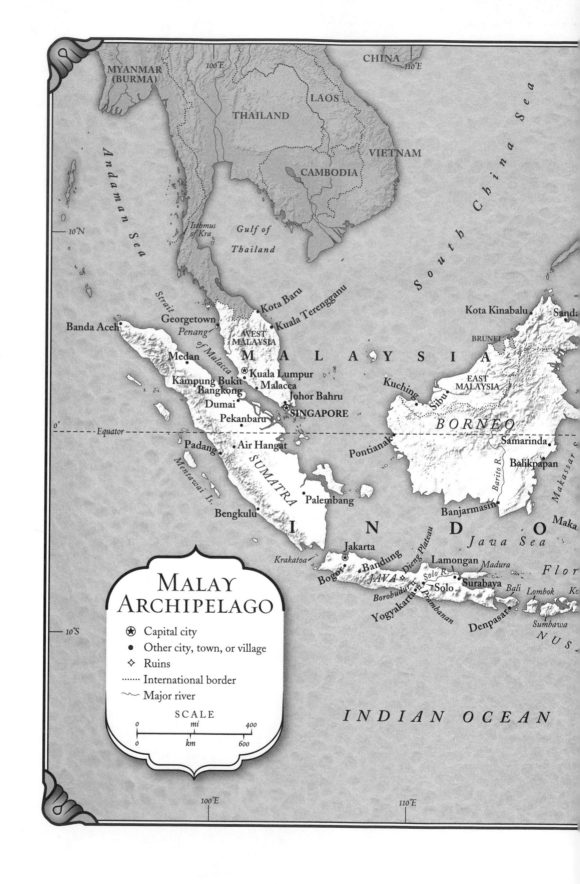

MYANMAR
(BURMA)

100°E

CHINA
110°E

LAOS

THAILAND

VIETNAM

CAMBODIA

A n d a m a n   S e a

S o u t h   C h i n a   S e a

10°N

*Isthmus
of Kra*

*Gulf of
Thailand*

Kota Baru

Kota Kinabalu   Sanda

Georgetown
Penang

Kuala Terengganu

BRUNEI

Banda Aceh

WEST
MALAYSIA

M A L A Y S I A

Medan

S t r a i t   o f   M a l a c c a

⊛ Kuala Lumpur
Malacca

Kuching

EAST
MALAYSIA

Kampung Bukit
Bangkong

Johor Bahru

Sibu

B O R N E O

Dumai

⊛ SINGAPORE

Pekanbaru

0°

Equator

Samarinda

Padang

• Air Hangat

Pontianak

Barito R.

Balikpapan

M e n t a w a i   I s.

S U M A T R A

M a k a s s a r

Palembang

Banjarmasin

Maka

Bengkulu

I N D O

N

D   O

J a v a   S e a

Jakarta

Krakatoa

Bandung

Dieng Plateau

Lamongan

Madura

Flor

Bogor

JAVA

Solo R.

Surabaya

Bali

Lombok   Ko

Solo

Borobudur

Yogyakarta ✧ *Prambanan*

Denpasar

Sumbawa

N U S

10°S

I N D I A N   O C E A N

100°E

110°E

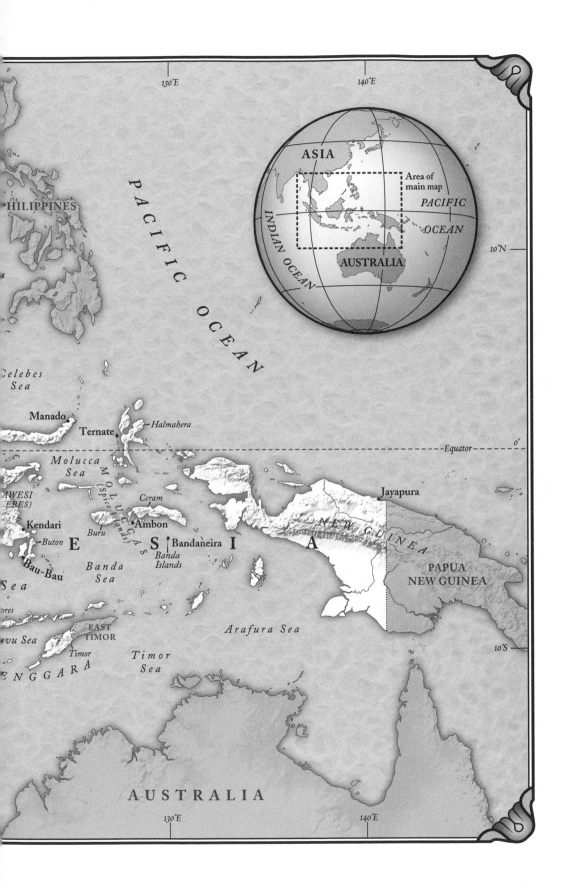

130°E   140°E

ASIA
                                    Area of
                                    main map
PACIFIC
INDIAN OCEAN
                                    OCEAN
                              10°N
AUSTRALIA

PHILIPPINES

P A C I F I C

Celebes
Sea

Manado
Ternate   Halmahera

O C E A N

Molucca
Sea

Ceram
Buru   Ambon
Kendari
Buton   E   S   Bandaneira   I   A
Bau-Bau   Banda
           Banda   Islands
Sea

Jayapura

NEW GUINEA

PAPUA
NEW GUINEA

10°S

AWESI
EBES)

Sea

ores
avu Sea
            EAST
            TIMOR
ENGGARA   Timor

Arafura Sea

Timor
Sea

Equator   0°

M O L U C C A S (Spice Islands)

AUSTRALIA

130°E   140°E

ABOVE LEFT: *Siti, beloved cook for the Alwi family, in Jakarta, Indonesia.*

ABOVE CENTER: *The island of Gunung Api, an active volcano, part of the Banda Islands chain in Indonesia.*

ABOVE RIGHT: *A typical home covered in ornate ceramic tiles in Georgetown, Malaysia.*

1. INTRODUCTION

One rainy spring day in 1982, while walking to catch the 30 Stockton bus home from school, I bumped into Tanya Alwi, a fellow classmate at the San Francisco Art Institute. I was nineteen years old, a second-year student in the film-studies program. At that point, all I really knew about Tanya was that she was about the same age and had the most contagious laugh I had ever heard. It was big and comforting and seemed to make everyone warm up to her. I wanted to get to know her better, so I asked her to join me for coffee. As we sat down in a crowded North Beach café, one of those smoky tin-ceilinged places off Columbus Avenue, I asked her where she was from.

"Indonesia," she answered in an accent that sounded almost British. "More or less." The two concrete details I knew about the country rushed into my mind: I knew that it was the world's fourth most populous nation and that it was the backdrop of more than one Joseph Conrad novel that I'd read. Over the course of several espressos, Tanya told me about herself. She explained that her father, Des, was the descendant of an aristocratic Muslim family of nutmeg and pearl traders from Banda, part of the Spice Islands, or Moluccas, which lie in eastern Indonesia and have lured the world's spice seekers for centuries. The Alwi bloodline, Tanya said, bore traces of all the peoples who had come to Banda during the last thousand years: She was part Malay (an ethnic group originally from Central Asia), part Arab, part Indian, part Chinese, part Portuguese, and part Dutch.

When Des was a boy, Tanya went on, he was taken under the wing of Bung Hatta, who had been exiled to Banda for his political beliefs by the Dutch colonial government (which had ruled Indonesia for nearly four hundred years) and who would eventually become the nation's first vice-president. Through his affiliation with Bung Hatta and, later, with Sukarno, the first president of Indonesia, Des was active in combat against the Dutch, and was regarded as a national hero following Indonesia's independence in 1942. Several years later, Des (Tanya, I learned, always refers to her father by his first name) became a member of Indonesia's diplomatic corps and served in Hong Kong (where Tanya was born) and

Geneva. "Now we're back in Jakarta," Tanya said, finishing another espresso. "All's well that end's well. Isn't that what they say, yes?" Her laughter filled the café.

"It sounds like you're the princess of the Spice Islands," I said. Tanya asked me about my background. After hearing about her exotic past, mine seemed especially boring. I told her that my dad was an office-products salesman and that I had grown up in a suburban California tract house watching *The Brady Bunch* and eating frozen chicken potpies. "To tell you the truth," I said, "my life so far has been classic middle-American."

Tanya studied me. "Have you ever been to Asia?" she asked. I shook my head. My only travels had been a few cross-country road trips in the family's Dodge station wagon and a three-week journey to Mexico when I was seventeen. "Why don't you come to Indonesia after the semester is over?" she continued. "You can stay at our house in Jakarta over the summer vacation." I looked at her apprehensively. I had been taught to be wary of things that sounded too good to be true. As we were saying good-bye, I made up my mind to forget Tanya's offer. But that night at home I couldn't get it out of my head. I was dying to travel. I whispered the word *Jakarta* a few times as though I could will myself into being there just by saying it. I called Tanya before I went to sleep.

"No, I wasn't joking. You can come," she confirmed. "You'll love it there."

A few weeks later, thanks to my dad giving me a round-trip ticket, I was on a flight high above the Malay Archipelago, the vast expanse of Southeast Asian islands that includes Indonesia, Malaysia, and Singapore. (It also sometimes includes the culturally distinct islands of the Philippines, a country not covered in this book.) As the plane lowered, I saw hundreds of small, lush islands, many not more than half a mile in diameter, dotting the Java Sea. Soon we were over Java itself, Indonesia's most densely populated island and, according to the reading I had done in the weeks leading up to my departure, home to its most storied civilizations. I saw red-tile-roofed villages interspersed with coconut palms and neatly laid out rice paddies. In the distance, three volcanoes rose to perfect cones, like a trio of Mount Fujis. Steam was escaping from the tallest one. I held my breath, not wanting the moment to pass.

Tanya and Johnny, a driver for the Alwi family, were standing in the shade just off the tarmac at the Jakarta airport. I beamed, happy to see a familiar face after the nearly thirty-hour journey. "Welcome to the other side of the world," Tanya said, as we inched our way through the long customs line toward the car. Once we were outside, the foreignness of everything hit me head-on: the sticky heat, the dust, the pervasive sweet aroma of *kretek-kretek* (Indonesia's clove-laced cigarettes), and the vivid colors of everything I saw, including Day-Glo sarongs, glossy green tropical plants, a bloodred sunset—my first glimpse of the sun from this side of the world. As we drove down bumpy streets in Tanya's fortresslike Toyota Land Cruiser, I felt like I was dreaming. There were rickshaws and horses and

carts competing for road space with honking trucks. There were old Dutch colonial man-
sions, their stucco facades covered with pink bougainvillea vines. But most memorable,
down every street and alley were canvas-covered food stalls. Each stall, or *warung*, was a
self-contained miniature restaurant, with small tables for diners and a makeshift kitchen
centered around a wood-burning stove. They were like no fast-food places I knew back
home. Hand-painted illustrations hanging outside each *warung* announced what was being
sold. One offered fried noodles, another chicken satay, another fresh coconut juice.

We arrived at the Alwi home about an hour later. It was a large, newish house, the front
yard dotted with tall mango trees. In sharp contrast to the hot, noisy Jakarta streets, the
interior was cool and quiet. Everywhere I looked, shiny teak and mahogany furniture
stood, each piece carefully arranged to create visual harmony. A breeze ruffled a length of
turquoise silk curtains. Farther inside, I saw a screened-off aviary filled with pale gray
doves. Their soft cooing filled the room.

"It's time to meet the big man himself," said Tanya, guiding me to the master bedroom
just off the living room. She knocked, and then opened the door. Des sat at the foot of a
large bed, reading a newspaper. He was in his fifties, a truly big man, like an Asian Francis
Ford Coppola, with a gray batik shirt, a shock of unruly black hair, and thick eyebrows. I
nervously approached him, feeling a bit like the Cowardly Lion approaching the Wizard of
Oz. "You must be James," he said in a basso voice that fit his appearance perfectly. "Tell
me, is it your first time in Asia?" I nodded. "Well, I hope you didn't leave your heart in San
Francisco." He chuckled, proud of his joke, and returned to his paper.

Ann, Tanya's mother, also in her fifties, sat at a dressing table at the other end of the
room. A fine-boned woman with long, black hair pulled into a neat bun, she was sketching
on her eyebrows in a careful arch with a makeup pencil. Stopping and turning toward me,
she said softly, "My husband and I have a dinner to go to, but welcome. I hope that you
will remember your stay in Indonesia always." I smiled, grateful for her words.

Tanya led me into the dining room and introduced me to the household staff. There
was Mat, a lanky young fellow from East Java; Siti, a shy, pretty girl in her early twenties;
and Inam, the cook, a woman with a wide, apparently ever-present smile. Inam handed me
a tall glass.

"Drink it," Tanya said. "It's *stroop*, a lime-syrup cordial. It's a traditional welcome beverage." I took a sip, letting the cool, sweet drink trickle down my dry throat. I knew at once
that I was going to like it there.

About a week after I arrived, my jet lag—not to mention the dislocation I felt from
being in such a radically different environment—was finally starting to fade. I slowly
began to settle into the rhythm of life in the Alwi home. Everyone, from Inam to Ann,

helped ease me into things, offering me everything from fluffy new pillows to a small Indonesian dictionary that I quickly became addicted to for translating all the unfamiliar words I was hearing. Over time I was to learn that unfailing hospitality is a hallmark of the people of this part of the world. Anything less is taboo.

Every morning at eight-thirty I would go downstairs to the dining room, where Inam would have the day's first meal laid out on the table. At each place setting was a glass of sweet orange pekoe tea scented with cinnamon—a Bandanese touch—and a plate of chile fried rice topped with a just-fried egg. A few coconut-milk curries left over from the previous day's dinner sat at the center of the table. As Tanya and I ate, we would listen to Des recite his agenda. Some days he would be having lunch with Suharto, Indonesia's president; others he would be off to a board meeting in Singapore, ninety minutes away by plane. Ann would come down to breakfast a little later than everyone else. Before she ate, she would lean over and inhale the fresh-plucked jasmine—her favorite flower—that Inam set out in a small cloisonné bowl at her place every morning. The fragrance was Ann's first course.

After breakfast one morning, Tanya told me about a party that her mother would be hosting the following Saturday. It was to be a *selamatan*, or feast, in honor of a charity group that Ann had founded. "The food is going to be really wonderful," Tanya explained, drawing out her words for dramatic emphasis. "All of the guests will be providing the dishes. It's our version of a potluck."

In the week leading up to the party, I watched Inam, Siti, and Mat scrub, dust, fluff, and polish everything in sight. Saturday, the day of the party, it was hotter than usual, with a bright, cloudless sky that made the plants in the backyard droop. From my room, I could hear a gamelan quartet (the traditional musicians of Java). I walked downstairs into the living room. Smartly dressed guests, most of them women in orange, pink, yellow, and red batik silk and cotton sarongs, were greeting one another and sipping tea and iced *stroop*. A few ladies smiled at me as I walked past.

Not seeing anybody that I recognized, I made my way to a large banquet table. Inam was doing some last-minute fine-tuning, carefully adjusting platters of food to suit her sense of visual balance. I counted thirty-two dishes on the silk tablecloth. There were glistening coconut-milk curries, pickled vegetables tinted yellow with turmeric, vegetable stir-fries, whole grilled fish adorned with lemon basil, and sticky-rice sweets in every color of the rainbow.

"Are you hungry?" someone asked in heavily accented English. I turned around to see an elegant Indonesian woman in her fifties wearing an orange batik dress. She placed on the table a platter of grilled chicken whose perfectly charred skin smelled of coriander and smoke.

"I'm not hungry," I joked. "I'm starving." I eyed the chicken and asked her about it.

"It's a recipe from my family's home on the island of Sulawesi, from the town of Manado," she said. "Where are you from?" San Francisco, I told her. "I have been there, once," she responded. "It's very nice. You even have palm trees. Do you speak Indonesian?"

"No, not yet," I answered, "unless you count *ya* [yes]; *tidak* [no]; and *satu, dua, tiga* [one, two, three]."

"Don't worry," she said, laughing. "That's better than most. How do you like our food so far?"

"What I've had in the last week has been incredible," I told her. "I never knew how amazing the food was here."

She smiled and said, "People usually don't. We're the best-kept secret in Asia. Too few of us are living abroad to share our cuisine, and what you get in our fancy hotels here is, well, not so authentic. My name is Ibu Suzan." She extended her hand. "I am an old friend of Ibu Ann's. Tell me, do you know any of these foods?" (*Ibu* means "mother" in Indonesian and Malay, but it is also used as a term of respect for older women.)

"A few," I answered. "I know that's some kind of curry." I pointed toward a bowl full of what looked like a coconut-milk curry with vibrant orange swirls of oil on top. "And I know that's stir-fried bok choy over there. But I'm not really sure about the rest."

"Let me take you on a tour," Ibu Suzan said. "The food on the table is a map of the nearby region, not only Indonesia. The guests who have brought these dishes come from all over Indonesia, Malaysia, and Singapore, but now all live in Jakarta. Each dish is a specialty of where the guest comes from."

She pointed to an antique blue-and-white delft bowl that held fresh tuna braised with tomatoes and whole spices. "This one is called *ikan bumbu rujak*," Ibu Suzan said. "It was brought by Tanya's aunt from Banda, in the Spice Islands of Indonesia. They use cloves and nutmeg in everything there. Here, have some." She served me a small portion on top of some warm, fluffy rice, then handed me a spoon, the eating utensil of choice when fingers aren't used. The dish was sublime, gently sweet and savory at the same time, with tantalizing hints of nutmeg and cloves—the native fruits of Banda—in the background.

"Now try these," Ibu Suzan said, pointing to four dishes that had been brought by a woman from Padang, in West Sumatra, Indonesia. "The city of Padang is one of the most famous places in Southeast Asia for food. They love chiles there more than anybody on earth." I was especially drawn to a beef dish topped with finely shredded fresh lime leaves; Ibu Suzan told me it was called *rendang*. I tried a piece. It was meltingly tender, with delicate layers of flavor I could only begin to identify. It reminded me of dishes that I had tasted in Thai restaurants in San Francisco, but it was even more complex, more bold.

By now other guests were coming over and fixing plates for themselves. Some sat down, while others remained standing as they ate. "*Rendang* is Padang's best-known dish," Ibu Suzan continued. "Every good cook in Malaysia, Indonesia, and Singapore can make it—even the local Chinese people have their own version, made with pork. We Muslims are not allowed to take pork. We make it with water buffalo instead."

Next, Ibu Suzan had me try a few dishes from Java. As she explained each one, I sampled small portions of *opor ayam*, a subtle chicken curry seasoned with cinnamon sticks and coriander seeds; *tempe kering*, crisp, thin strips of fried tempeh (the nutty-tasting soybean cakes native to Java) with a sweetish, sticky sauce of palm sugar, chiles, and shallots; and a *tumpeng*, a two-foot-high cone of fragrant yellow coconut rice surrounded by a patchwork of colorful condiments. Thanks to its lime leaves and lemongrass, the rice was intensely fragrant.

We moved on from the Javanese dishes to some that were from Singapore and Malaysia. "These were brought by Ibu Teresa—that lady over there," said Ibu Suzan, pointing to a woman who wore a smart lilac suit instead of a sarong. "She's a Nyonya, or Straits Chinese, from Kuala Lumpur, in Malaysia. That means her ancestry is part Chinese, part Malay. Nyonya food is a combination of both." Though Ibu Teresa's stew, curry, and salad contained some obviously Chinese ingredients, such as dried plums and salted mustard greens, they tasted unlike any Chinese food I was familiar with—the flavors were more untamed, with a liberal use of spices, coconut milk, and fresh tropical fruit. I caught Ibu Teresa looking at Ibu Suzan and me from across the table. I smiled. "Your food is beautiful," I said. Ibu Teresa smiled back, pleased.

As I sampled more dishes, including Ibu Suzan's richly seasoned grilled chicken, I understood her point. This food, all of it, *was* a culinary map. It represented cuisines that were, I was to learn, deeply connected in spite of the miles separating them. Just then, Tanya, who was wearing a pink and gold sarong that glittered in the light, nudged her way between Ibu Suzan and me. "James," she said, picking up a spoon. "I see you've already discovered the secret to life in Indonesia. Pretty good for just a week."

"The secret?" I asked.

"That eating is the only thing that really matters here!" she answered with her signature laugh. I moved in for seconds.

Weeks passed, and I continued to settle into Jakarta life. When I wasn't wandering on foot through the winding streets behind the Alwis' home, I would join Tanya on her social rounds. One morning, she asked me to accompany her on a visit to a special family friend. "Bebe Huwei is her name," she said. "She was a famous Indonesian film star when she was younger. Now she's supposed to be the best psychic in Jakarta. She should do a reading for you. Do you believe in such things?"

I shrugged. I wasn't sure.

Soon we arrived at Bebe Huwei's home, a grand nineteenth-century mansion. A servant signaled our car to enter the grounds. Inside the house, we were led into a candlelit room cluttered with dusty antiques. On the walls were five-foot-high oil paintings of, I assumed, a much younger Bebe Huwei. In one, she wore a gown, and in another, a formfitting sarong, her hair teased into a sixties' bouffant. Everywhere were mementoes of her life as a celebrity: framed newspaper clippings, awards, old black-and-white film stills.

A few minutes later, Bebe Huwei entered the room. She was now in her sixties but lived up to the majesty of the portraits. She was elegantly dressed in a sarong and a long, tight-fitting traditional blouse—a *kebaya*—with a fine gold brooch pinned to it. "Please, come to the dining room," she said. Tanya and I followed. We took seats at a large table covered with pads of paper and stacks of old newspapers. I sat there silently as Bebe Huwei and Tanya chatted away for a few moments in Indonesian. Another servant brought a plate of butter cookies and a pot of hot tea.

"Please, take a biscuit," Bebe Huwei said, offering me one of the cookies. I bit into one. It was as crisp as a cracker and buttery sweet.

"I learned to make these in Amsterdam. I lived there once," she said, straightening her hair. "But I could never live in Europe again. They have no belief there."

With that, she reached for a pen and slowly began to draw small concentric circles on a blank piece of paper. Tanya shot me a look. I suppressed a smile. The circles soon became a wild, erratic spiral that ran over the edges of the paper onto the newspaper underneath. Finally, Bebe Huwei stopped and stared at me. Her eyes were as black as night.

"Your life has changed by coming here," she said. "Everything you knew about the world will never be the same."

I was silent for a few seconds. "How do you mean?" I asked.

"You came here for three months, but you will stay for a year," she answered. "Then you will keep coming back for the rest of your life. Look." She pointed to what she had drawn. "This is you at the outside of the spiral. As the years pass, you will move more closely to the center, which represents the part of the world you're in now, and you will find what you are looking for. A revolution has begun inside of you. You must accept it."

Tanya and I went to our next appointment that morning without saying a word.

Bebe Huwei had been right. There was indeed a revolution going on inside me, but not the kind I'd expected. Several weeks later, I woke during the night in a drenching sweat. My head throbbed as if it were being pierced by a drill. I knew at once that something was seriously wrong. The next morning I paid a visit to the Alwis' family doctor. The diagnosis came quickly, and was not at all what I wanted to hear: I had dengue fever, the doctor said, a mosquito-borne virus that, though not usually fatal, would cause the high fever and severe headache to last for several weeks. There was no cure or treatment except for traditional herbal remedies—called *jamu* in Indonesian—and bed rest. Lots of it.

I recuperated for a few miserable days in a crowded hospital and then at the Alwis' home, staring at the constantly whirring ceiling fan that hung directly over my bed. I sweated and trembled, imagining big, oily mosquitoes dive-bombing my head. Three times a day, Inam brought food to my room, usually thick rice porridge flavored with ginger, which is thought to have restorative powers, and a glass of bitter *jamu* followed by sweet lime *stroop* to clear my palate. In my delirium, I watched the only two English-language videotapes I could find in the house, *Chinatown* and *Logan's Run*, at least twenty times each. When it got to the point that I could recite long stretches of dialogue from *Logan's Run*, I knew it was time to get out of bed.

So one day I gathered my strength and ventured downstairs for one of Inam's lime drinks. I walked into the kitchen—the *dapur*, in Indonesian—a small half-indoor, half-outdoor room that extended into a backyard garden. In contrast to the grandeur of the rest of the house, the kitchen was spare. There was a modest four-burner gas range with a few woks and some pots hanging on hooks above it. Two open shelves held staple ingredients like sweet soy sauce and spices bundled into small paper bags. Perishable aromatics—shallots, chiles, garlic, fresh turmeric—were stored inside wire-mesh baskets hanging from the ceiling. (There was no need for other storage space or even a refrigerator, I learned, since shopping was done daily and ingredients were cooked soon after Inam bought them.) Interestingly, there was no counter space. Food preparation—peeling, cutting, grinding—was done on cutting boards and in mortars placed directly on the spotlessly clean tile floor.

And that's where I found Inam, gently crushing fresh red chiles in a flat granite mortar. She looked up and smiled. "You're not sick anymore?" she asked in Bahasa Indonesia, the national language. I'd started to pick up the basics of it in the past few weeks, enough to carry on simple conversations. I squatted on the floor next to her and gave a hand gesture for so-so. "What are you making?" I asked.

"*Bumbu-bumbu*," Inam said, "flavoring paste"—the foundation of dishes. I asked her what it was for. "*Sambal goreng buncis*," she replied. I knew what that was—a simple green bean dish with coconut milk—because it was one of my favorites. "Do you want to watch me make it?"

"Yes," I said, nodding. It would be much better than another viewing of *Logan's Run*. Inam moved from the mortar and pestle to a wooden cutting board, also on the floor, where she began to slice a few garlic cloves and small, purple shallots into thin, lacy pieces. She placed the slices in a bowl and then cut into a cylindrical block of hard, brown palm sugar. Though I knew the ingredient was responsible for sweetening many of the dishes I'd eaten in Indonesia, I had yet to taste it on its own.

"May I?" I asked. Inam shaved a piece of the sugar off with her knife. It was delicious, a combination of caramel and honey, with a touch of smokiness.

Next, she pressed a small piece of dried shrimp paste—a salty, pungent ingredient made from tiny fermented shrimp—onto the tip of a bamboo skewer. I leaned in closer. Over a low flame on the stove, she twirled the skewer so that the fire touched all sides of the shrimp paste. Soon a sharp, burning odor permeated the air. I recoiled. Inam burst into laughter.

"The smell is no good, but the taste is delicious," she said, still laughing.

"Why grill it?" I asked.

"It makes it more *halus*," she told me. I grabbed the paperback dictionary that Tanya's mother had given me. *Halus* meant "subtle." I continued to watch, admiring the relaxed, unhurried way Inam went about her cooking. It was as though she were meditating with her eyes open.

"Are you from Jakarta?" I asked. She shook her head from side to side.

"*Ngak*," she said, no. "I'm from East Java." She slid the grilled shrimp paste off the skewer and placed it in the mortar with the chiles. "It's a small, quiet place, very different from Jakarta. I come from a rice-farming family. You want to go there and visit?"

"I hope to someday," I replied. "Is *sambal goreng buncis* an East Java specialty?"

Inam nodded, then removed a small iron wok, blackened from years of use, from the wall. She poured a stream of coconut oil into the wok and let it heat up. In a single motion, she eased the shallots, garlic, chiles, and shrimp paste into the oil. As they sizzled around frantically, their aromas combined in a spicy invisible cloud. I sneezed. Inam smiled.

A few minutes later, she added a few fistfuls of green beans she had cut into pretty diagonal slices, followed by some freshly made coconut milk. Soon after, the dish was ready. Inam handed me a spoon. It was mellow and delicious, with a sauce that was strong as well as subtle.

For the next few weeks, as often as I felt up to it, I spent my time in the kitchen with Inam. I'd never really taken a great interest in cooking before, but watching everything that happened in the Alwis' kitchen, from the calm focus Inam gave to cleaning a whole fish to the way she and Siti would carry on lively conversations as they pounded flavoring pastes, captivated me. It was my entry not only into Indonesian cuisine, but also into Indonesian culture.

The cooking for lunch and dinner began every morning at nine, seven days a week, usually after a trip to the nearby vegetable market or a visit from the traveling vegetable man, Ali, who signaled his arrival from the street with a low-pitched gong. He pushed a creaky wooden cart bursting with freshly picked vegetables, including cabbages, carrots, and bamboo shoots, along with such unfamiliar (to me) produce as water spinach, which resembled long bunches of thick, just-cut grass. Inam would approach the well-worn cart, purse her lips, and assess what looked good. She was part scientist, part mystic. After she had finished gently squeezing and poking, she would make her selections—a kilo of tofu, a coconut, a few bunches of long beans, a head or two of garlic. She chose whatever seemed especially vibrant, not just what she needed, and I'd help her carry it all back to the kitchen. Then I'd silently watch from a stool in the corner as she and Siti and whoever else was around that particular morning began preparing the day's lunch and dinner. One day Inam would make Indonesian-style fried chicken, the next day *rendang* and *gado-gado*, a Javanese mixed-vegetable salad with peanut dressing.

I started jotting down recipes. I didn't want any of what I was observing to slip away. I wrote down how Inam extracted tamarind pulp, how she carefully coaxed coconut milk from grated coconut flesh and warm water, how she balanced the spices that would go into her curries so they wouldn't overwhelm one another. It began to dawn on me that cooking a meal didn't have to be what I'd experienced in my mom's kitchen: a chore performed on a schedule. What I saw instead in the Alwis' kitchen was a soulful, relaxed act more akin to painting. And Inam, for her part, seemed to find my interest amusing. In spite of the fact that men are rarely seen in Indonesian kitchens, she always did her best to make me feel welcome, never shooing me away or discouraging me. "You're strange," she said once with a wink, "but it's good for a man to learn to cook."

Another prediction that Bebe Huwei, the psychic film star, had made turned out to be true. Though I was supposed to have stayed in Southeast Asia only for the duration of my summer vacation, I remained much longer. Tanya returned to school in San Francisco at the end of August, but I decided to stay on and put my studies on hold. Exploring the sights, smells, and tastes of Indonesia seemed like a far more exciting learning experience. The Alwis, endlessly gracious hosts that they were, didn't seem to mind. I think they were amused by the food-obsessed young American in their midst.

After fully recovering from my bout of dengue fever, I came down with a major case of itchy feet. Alone and with no particular route in mind, I started venturing into other parts of Indonesia. First, I left Jakarta by train for Bandung, a city tucked high away on the slopes of a green volcanic mountain range. It had been founded by Dutch settlers trying to escape the sweltering heat of low-lying Jakarta. On my second day in town, a young, friendly bus conductor named Radja invited me to join his family for supper. I ended up staying two weeks. Though the family was of modest means, the Pulungans were as hospitable as the Alwis. In their two-room flat, I quickly adapted to sleeping on a bed that sagged like a hammock and bathed publicly, in an open-air facility a hundred yards away. I ate *very* well: Radja's mother was an excellent West Javanese cook. After discovering my interest in food, she made several local specialties every day, including lemongrass-scented coconut rice, mixed-vegetable salads with fresh lemon basil and grated coconut, and ginger-infused curries. Each dish was more delicious than the one before it.

Intrigued by stories that Tanya had told me, I traveled east from Bandung by a combination of bus, train, and thumb to see the Hindu and Buddhist temple ruins of Central Java. One of these, Borobudur, not far from the city of Yogyakarta, had been completed in the ninth century by the Sailendra dynasty—an ancient Javanese kingdom. This vast and tall Buddhist monument rose from rice paddies like a mountain and stirred my soul. But what I responded to even more deeply were the foods I ate in the region in street stalls, markets, and people's homes. I gorged on *gudeg*, a braise of young jackfruit and palm sugar; garlic-marinated deep-fried tempeh; and *nasi liwet*, rice served with an array of spiced side dishes, fresh herbs, and vegetable pickles. I went by rickety bus through East Java and discovered *soto*, a spiced chicken soup topped with bean sprouts and finely chopped celery greens. I was beginning to be able to pick up on the regional differences in the foods I ate: Central Javanese dishes, for example, usually contained large quantities of palm sugar, while those of East Java got most of their sweetness from subtle combinations of spices such as coriander and cinnamon.

With my dog-eared copy of one of the few Indonesian guidebooks available in 1982 (Bill Dalton's out-of-print *Indonesia Handbook*), I made my way just a few miles east of East Java to the small island of Bali, with its ancient Hindu culture and moss-covered temples. The foods in Bali, rich in coconut milk and flavored with herbs, echoed those I'd eaten in East Java, a reflection of the fact that Balinese culture had descended from the kingdoms of ancient Java. I journeyed by boat to the Spice Islands, Des's nutmeg paradise, and was as mesmerized by the foods I ate there as I was by the old spice groves I strolled through. Nutmeg and cloves, as Ibu Suzan had told me months before at the *selamatan* in Tanya's home, appeared in nearly every dish I ate, from the richly spiced fish stews to the salads, which were laced with crisp, tart slivers of fresh nutmeg fruit.

With Karma, Tanya's older brother, I traveled by plane to Kalimantan, which covers the southern two-thirds of the vast island of Borneo and is governed by Indonesia (the northern third belongs to Malaysia and the small nation of Brunei). Together we explored Banjarmasin, a steamy port with Dutch-built canals crisscrossing it—an Amsterdam of the tropics. Later, without Karma, I went up the Barito River, deeper into Borneo, and traveled, mostly on foot, into what was during those years still the isolated home of the Dayaks, the indigenous tribal people of Borneo's rain forests whose simple culture had probably not changed much since the Stone Age. I slept in tribal houses without electricity, and one morning at two o'clock I watched a harvest ceremony in which wild boars were sacrificed to local gods, then slow-roasted over huge fires. I thought about my life in California and wondered if I could ever go back.

Five times during my travels, my Indonesian visa expired, requiring me to leave the country to renew it. I flew to Singapore each time and checked into the same small hotel for week-long stays in the heart of the city's Little India neighborhood. I reveled in the sweet smell of the spice shops, the air-conditioning (which was often nonexistent in Indonesia), and, of course, the food. If Indonesia had awakened my palate, my journeys into Singapore and neighboring Malaysia—a country of twenty-four million people just to the north of Singapore—helped refine it. Though many people think of Singapore and Malaysia as separate from Indonesia, they are, in fact, a part of the same web of cultures.

Until several hundred years ago, the political borders that separate these three nations didn't exist. Indonesia, Malaysia, and Singapore share the same languages, peoples, and histories of trade and conquest. They also have the same culinary traditions, give or take a few ingredients and cooking methods. In the maze of open-air food stalls across the street from my Little India hotel, I tasted fried noodle dishes that were closely linked to those I'd eaten in Indonesia. I snacked on tropical-fruit salads that were called *rujak* in Indonesia but known as *rojak* in Singapore and Malaysia. I devoured *kare kepala ikan*, a gingery, chile-hot Singaporean fish curry that was a close relative of the *gulai ikan* (coconut-milk fish curry) I knew from West Sumatra.

A four-week train journey up peninsular Malaysia, from the country's hot, flat south to its hilly, jungly north, allowed me to start clearly seeing the influences that Chinese, Indian, and Arab spice traders had made on the region's cuisines during the last two thousand years. I ate dishes in Malacca, an ancient spice-trading port on the country's west coast, that combined Chinese and Indian ingredients with Malay cooking sensibilities. I was entranced by *popiah*, jicama-stuffed Chinese spring rolls drizzled with a typically Malay-style peanut-chile sauce. I also tasted *assam laksa*, a rice-noodle soup that was Chinese in concept but contained tamarind, fresh mint, shallots, chiles, and pineapple, favorite Malay ingredients. I ate *nasi kemuli*, a Nyonya rice dish seasoned with nutmeg, cloves, cinnamon, star anise, cumin, fennel, and poppy seeds that called to mind Indian *biriyani* (spiced rice) but whose soul was wholly Malaysian. I watched spellbound as street-food hawkers made Chinese-style stir-fries with local greens.

I ended my travels that year in Georgetown, a city on the small Malaysian island of Penang that had been settled by the British. One late afternoon under a neon pink sunset, as I sipped sweet milky tea in a noisy Chinese coffee shop, I realized in an instant that I'd found my home.

But San Francisco was still technically home, and so I returned, almost a year to the day after I left. I was happy to see my family again, happy to see the Bay Area hills from my bedroom window. As the months passed, though, I began to long for all the friends I'd made in Southeast Asia and for the delicious foods they'd introduced me to. Hoping to recapture the flavors I'd come to love, I made repeated visits to the handful of Indonesian and Malaysian restaurants I could find in the Bay Area. I was continually disappointed. Where was the sophisticated layering of flavors I'd known in true Indonesian beef *rendang,* or the unabashed use of nutmeg and cloves that was the hallmark of the Spice Islands? It was time to start cooking some of the recipes I'd written down.

For my first dish, I decided to make *opor ayam,* a Javanese chicken curry of coconut milk, coriander seeds, cinnamon, galangal, and ginger. I went to Chinatown for the ingredients that I didn't already have. I bought candlenuts (used for thickening), a can of coconut milk (oh, how I wished I had the courage to make my own by hand!), a nub of frozen galangal, and imported dried *daun salam* leaves (a Javanese herb that lends an earthy undertone to a dish). As I cooked, I followed my notes closely. I took care to grind the flavoring paste to the proper smoothness ("like creamy mashed potatoes," I'd written). I cut the chicken into sixteen pieces, the way I'd seen it done many times before in Southeast Asia.

I wanted this dinner to be a celebration of my travels, and invited Tanya and Mike, a professor of ours, to sample my efforts. I laid out a piece of yellow silk as a tablecloth. I set the table as carefully as Inam might have.

The dinner wasn't bad—but it wasn't wonderful, either. Although I'd used all the right ingredients, the *opor ayam* had none of the depth that I knew it should. Despite my misgivings, Tanya and Mike ate what I'd cooked heartily. "Inam would be proud," Tanya said, as I cleared the table. But I resolved to do better.

During the next few weeks, I prepared several other dishes. None satisfied me. I convinced myself that I couldn't be a good cook without some Indonesian, Malaysian, or Singaporean cook looking over my shoulder, guiding me through the process. Then I came up with a new plan: I would make one dish over and over again until I got it right. I chose the relatively easy *sambal goreng buncis,* the green bean curry that I'd first watched Inam make. My initial try was acceptable, but the coconut milk curdled slightly because I had let it boil too vigorously. (Why hadn't I remembered Inam's quiet admonitions to prevent this?) My second try was only marginally better—the green beans were undercooked and made the dish taste inappropriately raw.

By my third try, I was more determined than before. I didn't just automatically grab the first green beans I saw in the supermarket. I waited until I found really fresh, radiant beans from the farmers' market near my home and carefully picked through them, one by one. I made doubly sure that the canned coconut milk I was using was the right thickness and sweetness, tasting it a few times after I opened it before adding it to the curry—it was as good as any I'd had in Asia, I was happy to learn. And perhaps most important, I remained calm as I cooked, tuning out the rest of the world as I had seen many cooks in

Indonesia, Malaysia, and Singapore do. I forged a connection with what I was doing. I paid close attention to what was happening with each ingredient at each step of the way. How was the shallot in the flavoring paste reacting to the heat as I sautéed it? At what point was the lemongrass beginning to infuse the broth? Had Inam somehow taught me all this? I was sure she had, but I couldn't remember when.

After the dish simmered for twenty-five minutes, I anxiously dipped a spoon in the pot. The curry tasted bright and direct, with just the right balance of pungency and sweetness. I smiled. My second journey had begun.

In the two decades since, I've traveled to Indonesia, Malaysia, and Singapore more than twenty-five times, learning, exploring, seeing old friends and making new ones, and gathering recipes. I've studied the Nyonya dishes of Singapore and Malaysia, the chile-hot foods of West Sumatra, and the sweet ones of Central Java. I've trekked through hundreds of the region's markets, vegetable farms, tempeh factories, and rice paddies. I've learned its main languages, Bahasa Malaysia and Bahasa Indonesia (actually, they're almost identical, so I'm bragging when I say I know both). I've come to understand how the spices native to each region are used in its dishes. (Nutmeg, for example, is sometimes added whole or cracked, not ground, to season stocks and curries.) And I've become an expert at making these dishes in my own home. Many food lovers have gone to France and Italy and discovered the spectrum of flavor that lies beyond the food they have been raised on. I ended up in Indonesia, Malaysia, and Singapore instead. This book is the result.

A comprehensive look at the foods of these countries could fill a ten-volume set. Here, I can only present a collage of some of the dishes, people, and places I've grown to love from my visits. There are entire islands and regions, such as Borneo and Nusa Tenggara (the vast expanse of Indonesian islands that includes Lombok, Flores, and Sumbawa), that I haven't included. I've also purposefully omitted certain difficult-to-make dishes, such as *roti canai*, one of my favorite Malaysian street foods, an Indian-style bread that requires a tricky, multistep sequence of letting the dough rise and then kneading it to achieve the correct croissant-like texture. Instead, I've focused primarily on classic, easy-to-make home dishes, the heart and soul foods of Indonesia, Malaysia, and Singapore. The majority of these recipes have come from cooks like Inam or Radja's mother in Bandung. Each reflects the cook's own expertise, her intimate interpretation of a dish. Most are fairly simple to make. There is no intricate method for slicing herbs, no razzle-dazzle technique for stir-frying vegetables. Nearly all dishes go from the cutting board to the table in less than an hour. And, like your favorite aunt, they readily forgive mistakes. I've yet to make a dish in this book that didn't *taste* good, even if I've made a misstep in the process of cooking it.

In translating these dishes for the Western kitchen, I made only the smallest changes.

While Inam slowly grinds the flavoring pastes for her curries with an old stone mortar and pestle, I use a food processor, which can reduce the preparation time of a dish by twenty minutes. While Jimi, my favorite roaming satay vendor in Java, uses a fire of coconut shells to grill his satay, I've given you the easier option of oven broiling in addition to grilling over charcoal fire. Still, I've remained true to the origin of each recipe, respecting its essence and integrity. I encourage you to read At the Market: Ingredients (pages 38 to 93) to familiarize yourself with the few ingredients you may not know—and to learn more about those you already do. Then go on to read In the Kitchen: Techniques and Equipment (pages 94 to 109) for a detailed look at some methods that will broaden your cooking experience.

This book is not intended to be the final word. It's simply my way of helping food lovers gain an appreciation of little-known—and supremely delicious—cuisines. But the real reason I wrote it is to honor the hundreds of women and men who shared their recipes, their lives, and, indeed, their souls with me over the years, like Tamalia, the mother-in-law of a friend in Central Java. One hot July afternoon, she invited me to watch her make lunch and then to feast on it. "Take this recipe," she said as she drizzled fresh coconut milk into the curry she was making, "and whenever you make it, remember me." And I do, every time.

ABOVE LEFT: *An old man traveling to Sulawesi, Indonesia, by small ferry on the Java Sea.*

ABOVE CENTER: *A Chinese opera singer performing on the streets of Georgetown, Malaysia.*

ABOVE RIGHT: *Harvesting nutmeg in Indonesia's Banda Islands*

2. CUISINES AND GEOGRAPHY

THE FOODS OF INDONESIA

ACEH (pronounced ah-CHAY) earned worldwide attention from the earthquake and tsunami that devastated its northwestern coastline in 2004. But in the seventeenth century, when Aceh was the capital of a spice empire ruled by Sultan Iskandar Muda, the region was celebrated for its cuisine. During his reign, traders from Arabia and India brought shiploads of exotic spices to Aceh, and cooking advanced to a high art. Aceh's modern-day home cooks adore spices as much as their ancestors. Locally grown cinnamon, cloves, nutmeg, fennel, and star anise are the featured ingredients in local curries, such as *kari kambing* (Acehnese Goat Curry, page 314), a rich coconut milk–based dish served at wedding feasts. Another favorite is *masam jing* (Hot-and-Sour Fish Stew with Bamboo Shoots, page 247), a brash dish with lime juice and chiles that's best eaten with white rice to tame its heat. The Acehnese are fond of cooking with a variety of wild herbs that grow in the region, including *ampan* (a type of nettle) and marijuana, which imparts an earthy kick—and a narcotic buzz—to many dishes.

The mountainous province of **WEST SUMATRA** is home to the Minangkabau, an ethnic group known for their distinctive architecture. The curving rooftops of Minangkabau buildings mimic the horns of their mascot, the water buffalo. The Minangkabau are also known for their sophisticated but earthy cuisine, usually called *nasi Padang* (Padang rice) outside of West Sumatra, and which takes its name from the province's capital city, Padang. Cooks make use of the ingredients that flourish in local rain forests, including tiny wild eggplants and aromatic kaffir lime leaves. The most celebrated local dish is *rendang daging sapi* (Beef Rendang, page 304), a braised dry beef curry seasoned with ginger, galangal, nutmeg, and cinnamon. But dishes cooked using the same method—which is

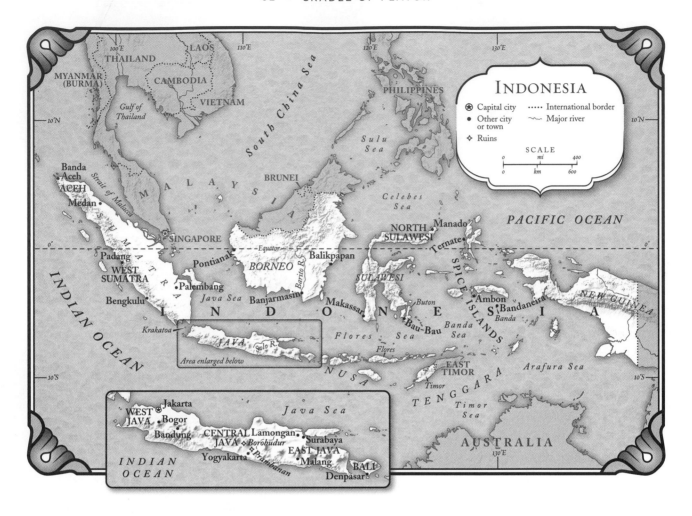

collectively called "rendang"—are seemingly endless: in addition to beef rendang, there are delicious rendangs made of potatoes (Potato Rendang, page 223), tuna, unshelled shrimp, and the young local ferns called *paku.* Long, red fresh chiles, known as *lado merah,* often take the forefront in Minangkabau cooking. *Kentang balado* (Rohati's Crisp-Fried Potatoes with Chile and Shallot Sambal, page 221) is a classic example of the local passion for fiery foods.

The foods of **WEST JAVA** and of its primary ethnic group, the Sundanese, are more delicately spiced than those of other parts of Indonesia. Spare grilled meats, flavored with little more than smoke and served with bunches of herbs such as *kemangi* (lemon basil), are popular, as are *sate ayam* (Chicken Satay, page 147) and *nasi goreng* (Javanese Fried Rice, page 183), a classic Indonesian dish in which rice is stir-fried with a flavoring paste made of red chiles, dried shrimp paste, and palm sugar. West Java is often thought of as the salad bowl of the country, since many of Indonesia's finest vegetables are grown there. Bundles of blanched long beans and crisp stir-fries of such Asian greens as bok choy and *kangkung* (water spinach) are essential elements of every meal. Jakarta, the capital of Indonesia, is located in coastal West Java, but because its residents hail from all over the country, the city cannot be considered truly Sundanese. Instead, the Sundanese count Bandung, a Dutch-built city that is rich in colonial architecture, as their capital. One of Bandung's most memorable stops is its huge central *pasar malam* (night market), which opens at two o'clock in the morning so cooks can get a jump on the day's shopping.

CENTRAL JAVA was home to the Sailendra, Sanjaya, and Janggala, a succession of ancient empires that ruled large areas of Southeast Asia from the eighth to the thirteenth centuries; among the monuments these empires left behind are Borobudur, a vast Buddhist stupa, and Prambanan, a Hindu place of worship. The culinary arts flourished during their reigns, with cooks vying to impress the royal court. Lavish feasts consisted of such dishes as *tumpeng* (Celebration Yellow Rice, page 178) and *urap* (Chopped Vegetable Salad with Coconut and Lime Leaf Dressing, page 156). Today, the cuisine of the region—a mixture of spicy and sweet flavors—remains true to its royal roots. Coriander, cumin, cinnamon, and signature aromatics, such as lemongrass and shallots, provide the spiciness for *opor ayam* (Javanese Chicken Curry, page 275) and other curries; the sweetness can be attributed to palm sugar, or *gula jawa* (Javanese sugar). Though cooks in Central Java take pride in balancing sugar with spice, sometimes the former wins out. Exuberantly sweet dishes such as *tempe kering* (Caramelized Tempeh with Chiles, page 325) and *tahu goreng bacem* (Twice-Cooked Tofu with Coriander, page 330) exemplify this. Another intensely sweet favorite is *gudeg,* a braise of young, unripe jackfruit and palm sugar that's popularly eaten in Yogyakarta and Solo, Central Java's main cities.

EAST JAVA and its nearby neighbor, the small island of **BALI**, boast mythic landscapes of cloud-covered volcanic peaks and pristine coastal plains. The Majapahit Empire, the last great Hindu realm of the Indonesian islands before their Islamification in the sixteenth century, was based in East Java, and modern-day Balinese culture, which remains Hindu, is a relic of this empire. Although the foods of East Java and Bali echo those of Central Java, they have distinctive characteristics. Both celebrate dramatic flavor combinations. *Soto ayam lamongan* (The Soto King's Chicken Soup, page 271) is a favorite soup enlivened with warm layers of cumin, coriander, ginger, and kaffir lime leaves, all grown locally. The Java and Flores seas provide the fresh fish that go into classic fare like *pepes ikan* (Grilled Whole Fish with Lemon Basil and Chiles, page 256), a whole fish steamed then grilled in a vibrant flavoring paste. A delicious Balinese sambal is Lemongrass and Shallot Sambal (page 122), an unusual dish in which the ingredients are finely chopped rather than being pulverized in a mortar and pestle.

NORTH SULAWESI (formerly Celebes) is noted for the fiery foods of its residents, the Minahasans. Primarily Christian, they are culturally connected to the people of the nearby Philippine island of Mindanao. Minahasan food is almost always seasoned with large quantities of ginger, lemongrass, lemon basil, and fresh red chiles, an aromatic combination that creates one of the most joyous-tasting cuisines in Southeast Asia. A signature dish is *ayam panggang sulawesi* (Grilled Coconut Chicken with Lemon Basil, page 292): in this rich concoction, chicken is cooked in a flavorful coconut-milk curry before it's grilled, then basted with the thickened curry. Another favorite dish in the region is a slow-simmered curry made of young papaya leaves, coconut milk, chiles, and, of course, loads of ginger and lemongrass.

The **SPICE ISLANDS** are scattered like green gems in the Banda Sea. This archipelago of more than a thousand culturally linked islands, also known as the Moluccas, is where spice seekers from around the globe have come since ancient times to make their fortunes from the native nutmegs and cloves that grew—and continue to grow—in profusion. (And it is the part of the world that Columbus was seeking when he bumped into the Americas instead.) The most famous of the Spice Islands is the cluster known as Banda. Immense nutmeg trees grow there under the nearly ever-present equatorial sun. During harvest, in May and November, the fruits fall to the ground like rain, and local cooks use their seeds year-round for the fragrance they impart to dishes. As with all the other cuisines of Indonesia, curries and stews are king in Banda. Lavish dishes featuring whole cloves and cracked nutmegs, such as *ikan bumbu rujak* (Spice-Braised Tuna, page 242), attest not only to the skill of local cooks with spices, but also to their love of their staple food, fish. A homey classic is *tuna goreng* (Pan-Seared Tamarind Tuna, page 254), a simple-to-make dish in which tuna is marinated in tamarind extract, then panfried until caramelized.

THE FOODS OF WEST MALAYSIA AND SINGAPORE

The capital city of Penang, **GEORGETOWN** (also known, confusingly, as Penang), was founded in 1786 by Francis Light, a British subject who had been looking for a strategic trading port midway between India and China. The virtually uninhabited island of Pinang (the Malaysian spelling of the word for betel nut) proved an ideal location. The British brought indentured servants from China and southern India to farm the spice plantations they planted on Georgetown's jungly outskirts (the descendants of nutmeg trees smuggled centuries ago from the Spice Islands continue to thrive here). The Chinese and Indian workers eventually settled down, living side by side (and often intermarry-

ing) with the Muslim Malays who already called the island home. The cuisine that resulted is a bold mix of Chinese, Indian, and Malay cooking styles. *Char kuey teow* (Penang-Style Stir-fried Kuey Teow Noodles, page 193) is a famous Chinese-style noodle stir-fry with chiles and garlic, while Kevin's Spiced Roast Chicken with Potatoes, Penang Style (page 287), is a British-inspired dish that blends the European love of roasting poultry with the Asian love of spices. Street foods reach their Southeast Asian apogee in Georgetown: There is seemingly not one square inch of public real estate not taken over by vendors (or hawkers, as they're called locally) offering their tempting fare.

The Malays established the first great civilizations of Malaysia, and **KELANTAN**, a devoutly Muslim state on the country's northeast coast, is one of their strongholds. Most of

Kelantan's Malays can trace their lineage to the Indonesian island of Sumatra, and their cuisine reflects that fact. Sumatran-influenced coconut-milk curries flavored with complex seasonings, such as *kari terung* (Asiah's Eggplant Curry, page 229, an eggplant dish with ginger and cumin), are regional favorites. As in Sumatra, sambals, the salsalike condiments made of chiles, accompany almost every meal. But the Kelantanese have also created dishes that are uniquely their own, such as the gutsy pickle *paceri nenas* (Malaysian Spiced Pineapple Pickle, page 136), which is seasoned with cinnamon and star anise.

KUALA LUMPUR is Malaysia's largest city. The culinary identity of its three million residents is shaped by the three ethnic groups that call it home: the Malays, the Chinese, and the Indians. Stroll through Chinatown and enjoy excellent Hokkien and Hainanese fare. Take a trip to Kampung Baru, one of the city's Malay enclaves, and sample *nasi lemak* (Ginger-Scented Coconut Rice, page 178), Malay-style coconut rice, fragrant with ginger. Visit Brickfields for an authentic taste of south India. Or savor elements of all three cuisines in such uniquely Kuala Lumpur dishes as *kare laksa* (Chicken Curry Noodle Soup, Kuala Lumpur Style, page 195), which uses Chinese egg noodles and tofu, Malay coconut milk, and an abundance of warm Indian spices. Served with blanched mung bean sprouts, it's one of Southeast Asia's—if not the world's—most delicious noodle dishes.

Seven hundred years ago, **MALACCA** was a quiet fishing village overlooking the tranquil Straits of Malacca. It became the premiere hub for the Malay Archipelago's spice trade and was transformed into the richest, most cosmopolitan Southeast Asian city of its day with sixteenth-century Europe's increasing demand for spices. Ships from as far away as Arabia, India, and China docked in its port, exchanging spices and cultural traditions. The distinctly Malaccan cuisine that developed was based on native ingredients, such as lemongrass and ginger, and imported ones, such as black mustard seeds from India. The Nyonyas (the term used for women of the culture; a male is known as a *baba*), also called the Straits Chinese or Peranakans (which means "born here"), were—and are—the culinary stars of the city. They trace their ancestry to the Chinese seafarers who arrived five centuries ago and married local Malay women. Nyonya classics include the soulful *ayam pong teh* (Nyonya Chicken and Potato Stew, page 281) and *udang masak nenas* (Nyonya Shrimp Curry with Fresh Pineapple and Tomatoes, page 260), which combines chiles, coconut milk, and lemongrass to make a bold dish that is wholly Malaccan.

SINGAPORE and Malaysia were one nation until 1965, when Singapore, a tiny tropical island not much larger than San Francisco, became independent. Since then it has grown into one of the world's economic success stories: high-rises and slick housing blocks now dominate what was a backwater British trading port two centuries ago. In spite of all the progress, Singapore's culinary traditions, a blend of Malay, Chinese, and Indian influences, like those of Penang and Malacca, live on. Spicy, warm flavors dominate in dishes such as *ketam lada hitam* (Black Pepper Crab, page 264), a street-hawker specialty flavored with ginger, fresh turmeric, and black peppercorns. A favorite streetside breakfast hints at Singapore's English past: soft-boiled eggs (Kopi Tiam Soft-Boiled Eggs, page 333) and thick slices of toasted white bread. But the city-state's best foods are found in its home kitchens: *kacang panjang belacan* (Ching Lee's Braised Lemongrass Long Beans, page 218) is a Singaporean dinner-table classic seasoned with lemongrass and chiles—key ingredients in both Indonesia and Malaysia—that highlights the connection these three countries share.

ABOVE LEFT: *A durian vendor in Georgetown, Malaysia.*

ABOVE CENTER: *Chiles in West Sumatra.*

ABOVE RIGHT: *A fisherman and his catch at a market in the Spice Islands, Indonesia.*

3. AT THE MARKET: INGREDIENTS

When I came to Indonesia in 1982, I was captivated by the huge open-air food markets, or *pasar-pasar* (from the word *bazaar*, handed down by Arab spice traders), that were the centerpiece of every village, town, and city I visited. To my new-to-Asia eyes, these bustling places, with their mountains of colorful vegetables and baskets of locally harvested spices, were right out of a Somerset Maugham account of old Asia.

Inam, the Alwi family cook in Jakarta, taught me an invaluable lesson the first time we shopped together at the local market, the Pasar Ampera, not far from home. "In my cooking, I always look for ingredients that are *hidup*," she said, using the Indonesian word for "alive," as we made our way down a crowded aisle filled with vegetable vendors. I naively asked her if she meant ingredients that were still breathing. "No, I mean ingredients that are filled with life and flavor," she said, laughing, "not old, tired ones that should be thrown away. See how these long beans look and feel?" She handed me a bunch of long beans. They were firm and taut and seemed like they had been picked from the vine that morning. Next, she grabbed a handful of dried red chiles and smelled them as though they were fresh. "Even dried ingredients should be *hidup*," she said. "It's the secret to cooking."

Inam's advice has had a tremendous impact on how I cook. Even without the sprawling markets of Indonesia, Malaysia, and Singapore at my disposal, over the years I've figured out ways to stay true to what she taught me. Just a few miles from my New York City apartment, I've discovered sources that sell foods that are every bit as *hidup* as those found in Southeast Asia. I pinch, prod, squeeze, and smell the green beans, tomatoes, and Asian greens at my local farmers' market to find out which will taste the best. I study the whole red snappers at my favorite Asian fish merchant and ask him where they were caught. Did they come that morning from the cool waters off Long Island, just a hundred miles from my apartment? Or were they frozen and airfreighted days ago from parts unknown, perhaps thousands of miles away? I have located the butchers in Chinatown who sell plump, locally raised free-range chickens the same day that they're killed, finding them sweeter and more tender than their mass-produced counterparts.

Inam taught me that the concept of *hidup* also applies to bottled, canned, and packaged ingredients, such as soy sauces, coconut milk, and dried shrimp paste. I've come to learn which would pass her test. For instance, which canned coconut milk tastes most like milk just pressed from sweet, fresh coconut meat? Which contains the fewest additives? When I shop I avoid bottled, canned, and packaged products with unnecessary preservatives and flavorings. They can affect the character of an ingredient—and the dish in which it is used. I carefully study the ingredients lists on labels for such preservatives as disodium guanyalate, potassium sorbate, and sodium bisulfite and the misleadingly named "natural flavorings" that are actually chemically engineered flavors originally derived from natural sources, not the true flavorings themselves. I also religiously read expiration dates on bottles and packages, making sure to keep the products on my shelf for no more than a week or two longer than the date given.

WHERE TO SHOP

Shopping for Asian ingredients is considerably easier today than it was two decades ago when I first started cooking Indonesian, Malaysian, and Singaporean dishes. Back then, making a meal required a long drive from my Bay Area home to the handful of Asian specialty grocers that stocked key ingredients such as lemongrass. Nowadays, due to the surging numbers of Chinese, Vietnamese, Thai, Filipino, Laotian, and Cambodian immigrants in North America (sadly, very few expatriate Indonesians, Malaysians, and Singaporeans currently populate our shores), once-rare items are almost as common as extra-virgin olive oil. In farmers' markets, Chinese and Southeast Asian food stores, and even your favorite Western supermarket, you'll find virtually all the ingredients you need to make the recipes in this book. Even if you live outside a large metropolitan area without a sizable Asian community, you shouldn't encounter much difficulty. I intentionally did much of the recipe testing for this book away from New York City, at a friend's house in the small city of Binghamton, New York, about 180 miles northwest of Manhattan. As it turned out, there were three excellent small Asian markets just a few miles away that offered all the specialty ingredients that I needed. Everything else was readily available at the local Western supermarket.

Always consider your local farmers' market first when shopping for the vegetables, aromatics, and meats you'll need for these recipes. What is sold there will usually be more *hidup* than what you'll find in any supermarket or Asian grocery. As a bonus, many of these ingredients, including shallots, garlic, chiles, lemon basil, lemongrass, carrots, Kirby cucumbers, Asian greens, potatoes, chicken, eggs, beef, and pork, are organic, or, at the very least, raised in an environmentally responsible fashion. Make friends with vendors to learn what their vegetable-growing schedules are and to make special requests. I have, for instance, a favorite vendor at the small farmers' market a few blocks from my Brooklyn apartment who alerts me when he's bringing in fresh water spinach.

But farmers' markets are useful sources for only some ingredients. Your usual supermarket will likely carry many of the other essential items you'll need, such as meats, soy sauces, peanut oil, tofu, fresh Chinese egg noodles, canned coconut milk, coconuts, dried chiles, and bean sprouts. For all of the ingredients that you can't find at your usual supermarket, visit the Chinatown or Chinese or Southeast Asian groceries nearest your home. (Unfortunately, Korean and Japanese markets usually aren't good sources, as northern Asian foodstuffs rarely overlap with those of Southeast Asia.)

North America's Chinatowns are especially handy for certain ingredients, among them poultry, fish and shellfish, tofu, and impeccably fresh Asian vegetables. But in the last decade, small Chinatown vendors have encountered competition from the excellent Chinese and Southeast Asian supermarkets that have sprung up in both traditional urban Chinatowns and suburban communities with large Asian populations, such as Monterey Park, near downtown Los Angeles; the Richmond District of San Francisco; Elmhurst, in the New York City borough of Queens; and Alexandria, Virginia, across the Potomac River from Washington, D.C. These supermarkets include the wonderful 99 Ranch chain on the West Coast (and in the Atlanta area; visit www.99ranch.com for locations) and the equally good Hong Kong and Super 88 supermarkets on the East Coast. In addition to fine-quality meats, fish, and vegetables, these supermarkets have small but comprehensive sections dedicated to the ingredients of Indonesia, Malaysia, and Singapore. You may have to do some searching, as these sections are seldom clearly marked and though store employees may be fluent in Cantonese, they may not speak English well enough to help you out. But in them you'll discover important ingredients, including shrimp chips imported from Indonesia, dried *daun salam* leaves (an herb), and usually a few brands of dried shrimp paste.

You can find these supermarkets (and smaller Chinese and Southeast Asian grocers, including those inside Chinatowns and out) in your local yellow pages under "Ethnic Grocers," "Grocers," or "Supermarkets." Also visit www.thaitable.com and www.vietworld kitchen.com, which include listings for southeast Asian markets in many American metropolitan areas. An Internet search engine, such as Google or Yahoo, is another great tool for locating sources. I find that I get the best results by placing quotation marks around the name of the vicinity I'm searching for, followed by a plus sign, followed by Chinese grocer or Southeast Asian grocer, again in quotation marks. For example, type in "Evanston"+ "Chinese grocer." Another option is to visit Web sites that have food-related message boards on which you can post a query about where to find Asian food purveyors in your area. Two good sites are www.chowhound.com and www.craigslist.com.

Yet another avenue for buying ingredients, especially useful if you live far from a Chinatown or an Asian market, or are simply too busy to shop in person, is online vendors, such as those listed in Sources (page 363). Online merchants offer a variety of excellent fresh and nonperishable ingredients, such as fresh and dried chiles, Asian greens, and sweet soybean paste, which they will ship to your door overnight or within a few days. But there is one hitch: you will have to trust the vendor's ability—not your own wisdom—to judge how *hidup* a particular ingredient is.

Finally, both individual entries in this chapter and the companies listed in Sources offer additional information on where to find ingredients.

BUYING AND STORING SPICES

Not all of the world's great spices come from Indonesia, Malaysia, and Singapore, but an impressive number do. Nutmeg, mace, cloves, cassia, and turmeric are native to the tropical forests of the Malay Archipelago. These spices—along with star anise, pepper, fennel, black mustard seeds, cardamom, coriander, and cumin, which were introduced to the region by traders from India, Arabia, and China—create the signature flavors of local cuisines, making every dish taste as playful and *enak* (delicious) as possible. In the West, we use spices sparingly. By contrast, cooks in Indonesia, Malaysia, and Singapore are fearless. As you'll discover in the recipes in this book, they crack open whole nutmegs to flavor curries and braises, add several cinnamon sticks at a time to lend warmth to both sweet and savory dishes, and lavish heaping tablespoons of coriander seeds on their satay marinades.

My favorite places to buy spices in North America are Bangladeshi, Indian, and Pakistani food shops. Whether tiny and mysterious or as large and brightly lit as a supermarket, these fragrant stores tend to have the freshest, best-tasting spices available. They offer every variety you will need, from cloves to black mustard seeds, in bulk or plastic bags of various sizes. If no such shop exists near you, www.kalustyans.com and www.patel brothersusa.com are reliable online sources.

Though spices have protective cell structures, their volatile oils begin to diminish the moment they're harvested. Thus, the sooner you can get them from the shop and into the dish you're cooking, the better. Always buy whole spices—even cinnamon—and grind them yourself. Preground spices have only a fraction of the taste and aromatic liveliness of their whole counterparts. Buy the smallest amount possible so that you won't have to store it for long. If you do have leftover spices, keep them in tightly sealed glass jars or plastic containers in the refrigerator at a temperature of 32° to 45°F (0° to 7°C). Your refrigerator's coolness will preserve their fragile aromas and reduce the possibility of rancidity, while its darkness helps them retain their color. I take this storage technique a step further: I keep all my leftover spices in small, tightly sealed plastic and metal containers in my freezer, which I've found best preserves their flavors. I discard any spices that I have not used after a year (though I usually toss out certain highly aromatic ones, such as cardamom, after six months). For specific storage recommendations, see the entries for individual spices in this chapter.

ASAM GELUGOR (ah-SAHM guh-LU-gor)
Garcinia atroviridis; *asam gelugor* or *asam keping* (INDONESIA, MALAYSIA, AND SINGAPORE)

This sour-tasting, apple-sized, yellow fruit, native to Malaysia, is rarely eaten raw. Instead, it is thinly sliced—skin, core, seeds, and all—then left to dry in the sun. The leathery dried slices are about 2 inches (5 centimeters) wide, brown to dark brown, and have an earthy, slightly fermented aroma. They add tartness to soups, curries, braises, and stews, such as Chicken Rendang with Cinnamon and Star Anise (page 278) and Nyonya Duck Soup with Salted Mustard Greens (page 295). Nyonya cooks prize *asam gelugor* for the way it balances the natural sweetness of dishes containing coconut milk. I like it for its appealingly smoky-sour taste, which is similar to tamarind but more assertively tart. Rinse slices of *asam gelugor* under cold running water before adding them to dishes; they're not cleaned after they're dried. Discard the plumped cooked slices before serving the dish, as they're too harshly sour to eat on their own.

BUYING AND STORING: *Asam gelugor* is available in most Chinese and Southeast Asian supermarkets. Imported from Malaysia or Thailand, it's sold in plastic bags 5 or 6 inches (13 or 15 centimeters) long labeled *asam*, *assam*, or dried tamarind slices. (Some Indonesian and Malaysian cookbooks refer to *asam gelugor* as dried sliced tamarind or tamarind skin, but both are misnomers. Though it's used similarly, the *gelugor* fruit is botanically unrelated to tamarind.) Because it's also a popular ingredient in the dishes of southern Thailand, *asam gelugor* is stocked wherever Thai ingredients are sold. Ask for it by either of its Thai names, *som khaek* or *sommawon*. Store it in a sealed plastic container or glass jar inside a cool cupboard for up to 2 years.

ASIAN GREENS

Simple stir-fries of Asian greens, such as Stir-fried Asian Greens with Garlic and Chiles (page 205), appear at almost every Indonesian, Malaysian, and Singaporean meal, balancing the heartier dishes on the table with their crispness and vitality. Because of their popularity, greens are ubiquitous in local markets. Vendors in the region carry hundreds of varieties, from long, thick-stalked bok choy to thin, spring green *choy sum* fringed with pretty yellow flowers. A stroll through any open-air *pasar* (market) at dawn, when the day's fresh greens have just been laid out in a colorful patchwork of lime and emerald greens, is one of the great visual pleasures of Southeast Asia.

Thanks to the large number of Asians who now call North America home, nearly all of these greens are available here. The best places to buy them are from vendors in farmers' markets who carry Asian vegetables, vegetable stalls in Chinatowns, and from Chinese or Southeast Asian supermarkets. Even obscure varieties, such as water spinach, which was once difficult to locate, can now be easily found, especially in the late summer months. I avoid buying greens from non-Asian supermarkets, where they are likely to have been sitting on the shelf too long, losing their freshness and crunch by the minute.

BUYING, STORING, AND WASHING: Asian greens are sold one of three ways: by the individual stalk or head, in bunches of a few held together with twine or a rubber band, or in plastic bags. If you have the option, buy them by the stalk or head, picking and choosing the best of the bin one by one. Avoid buying greens in plastic bags, which make discerning freshness difficult. Additionally, plastic bags encourage rot, decreasing the already-limited shelf life of greens. The best time to buy greens in colder climates is from July to September, when they are at their sweetest and most abundant; in warmer places, such as California and Florida, the growing season is generally from March to November. Keep in mind that, like spinach, Asian greens lose at least 50 percent of their volume once they're cooked. For a side dish of stir-fried greens at a meal built around rice, I like to allow at least roughly 4 ounces (115 grams) greens per person.

Selecting good Asian greens is easy and even sensuous. As a rule, look for vivid color, a sign that the greens have been picked recently. They should have unblemished leaves without rot or yellowness. Feel the tips of the stems. They should be smooth and supple, not dried out or wrinkly (or both). If you're choosing a thick-stalked green, such as bok choy, gently press your thumb against the surface of the thickest portion of the stem: it should be firm to the touch, not mushy or pliant. If you're buying a whole bunch of greens, make sure the entire bunch is lush and perky, not just the stalks on the outside. Poke around inside the bunch to check on the condition of the leaves at the center—they should be just as fresh. Finally, smell the greens. Their aroma should be clean and grassy, not mildewy or "off."

If you have no choice but to buy greens in a plastic bag, attempt to follow the same criteria you use for selecting greens sold by the stalk or in bunches. Pay close attention to the bottoms of the stalks or bunches; they should be firm and smooth, not dried out. Also make sure that there are no waterlogged or mildewed leaves or stems.

Asian greens have the most vibrant taste if you use them the same day you buy them. Otherwise, store them in the refrigerator in a tightly sealed plastic bag—with a dry paper towel slipped inside to help inhibit moisture—for up to 2 days. Don't wash greens prior to storage. Even a fairly thorough drying can leave behind moisture that will accelerate spoilage.

Wash greens in several changes of very cold water in a wide, roomy pot, such as a Dutch oven, or in the bin of a large salad dryer. They bruise easily, so handle them gently, as you would baby lettuces. Depending on the source, greens can be quite dirty or sandy (or both) and will need up to a half dozen separate rinsings (those from farmers' markets tend to contain the most dirt because they're seldom washed after harvest). Greens can hide dirt-trapping nooks where the stems meet the stalks. I have found that slicing such greens in half lengthwise (or, if it's a large green, such as standard bok choy, in quarters or eighths) can make cleaning a lot easier. Another method that can help, though more time-consuming (especially if the greens you're using are very small), is to wash each head individually under cold running water, rather than dunking many heads at once into a pot full of water. Pull back each leaf from the base of the stem to make certain there is no hidden dirt. Gently pat greens thoroughly dry with paper towels or an absorbent kitchen towel. Alternatively, spin them a few times in a salad spinner (which is how I dry my greens). Generally speaking, greens should be as dry as possible before being cooked; wet greens can result in a watery dish.

The following greens are those you will need for the recipes in this book:

BOK CHOY *Brassica rapa; sayur sawi putih* (INDONESIA, MALAYSIA, AND SINGAPORE)
Sometimes spelled *pak choy* or *baak choy,* bok choy (the Cantonese name for this vegetable) is a delicate-tasting member of the cabbage family. It's the most popular Asian green in North America, with more than 40 commonly cultivated species. When raw, bok choy can be as piquant as a radish; cooked, it's mellow and sweet. The easiest to find (and the one generically referred to as bok choy in this book and elsewhere) is usually about 18 inches (45 centimeters) long and has ivory white stalks that taper into broad, dark green leaves. Another popular variety, often called Shanghai choy or Shanghai bok choy, is uniformly lime green and smaller and stubbier than bok choy. With both, the smaller the head, the more tender the greens. Large heads of both varieties can be unpleasantly sinewy, particularly in late summer when hot, dry weather can toughen greens.

I especially like the baby versions of both bok choy and Shanghai choy. Usually no more than 3 inches (7.5 centimeters) long, they have a wonderfully delicate, cabbagelike flavor and stir-fry to perfection within a minute or two of being added to a hot wok or pot. Bok choy and Shanghai choy are sold either in individual heads or in bunches containing a few heads. The baby varieties are usually sold in bins for shoppers to pick their own, head by head.

CHOY SUM *Brassica chinensis; sayur sawi* (INDONESIA, MALAYSIA, AND SINGAPORE)

This variety of bok choy (also called *yu choy*) is identifiable by its straight stalks measuring 6 to 8 inches (15 to 20 centimeters) long (and lightly grooved from tip to base); its thin, longish lime- to deep-green leaves; and its bright yellow flowers. (I'm singling it out from the other varieties because its appearance and taste are so different.) *Choy sum* (the Cantonese name for the green) has a sweeter, mellower taste than bok choy. Be on the lookout for stalks with flowers that haven't completely opened. The greens will be younger and taste sweeter. *Choy sum* is sold either in bulk or in bunches of many stalks.

KAI LAN *Brassica alboglabra*

Also known as Chinese broccoli, *kai lan* (the Cantonese name for the green, sometimes spelled *gai lan*) is yet another member of the bok choy family. It has thick, stout, round stems (which should be peeled if they are thicker than 1/2 inch/12 millimeters) and deep green leaves (they resemble small, elongated collard green leaves) covered with a white haze. Stalks of *kai lan* often have a cluster of white flowers that extend from the central stem; they are edible and, I think, delicious.

Mature *kai lan* (stalks longer than 4 inches/10 centimeters) should be cooked until crisp-tender in boiling water, a technique that emphasizes its robust taste; it's usually too woody to be stir-fried. Tender, immature stalks (called baby *kai lan*, its slim stems don't need peeling), which are usually no longer than 3 inches (7.5 centimeters), stir-fry beautifully and are readily available throughout the year, though they are sweetest in the late summer months. Both mature and immature *kai lan* are sold in bulk; mature *kai lan* is also sold in bunches of many stalks.

WATER SPINACH *Ipomoea aquatica; kangkung* (INDONESIA, MALAYSIA, AND SINGAPORE); *ong choy* (CANTONESE)

Cooks in Indonesia, Malaysia, and Singapore (and neighboring Thailand, Laos, Cambodia, Myanmar, and the Philippines) prize this green above all others. Often known in North America as morning glory (its leaves vaguely resemble the flowering ornamental vine) or water convolvulus, it's available in two varieties, both identifiable by their hollow, strawlike stems. One grows in watery ditches and swamps and has pale green, wide, arrowhead-shaped leaves. The other grows on land and has darker, more slender leaves. Both varieties are now cultivated in Florida and California and are quite similar in taste, though loyal fans of either might disagree. Both are rarely available in bulk; instead, they come in thick bunches of many stalks. Because of its high water content, water spinach tends to spoil rapidly once harvested; try to use what you buy the same day.

BEAN SPROUTS

Vigna radiata; *taoge* (INDONESIA); *taugeh* (MALAYSIA AND SINGAPORE); *sai dau nga choy* (CANTONESE)

The bean sprouts called for in this book are mung bean sprouts, the crunchy seedlings of mung beans. Small and tender, they are not to be confused with bigger, tougher soybean sprouts, which have seedpods that are double the size (the seedpods of mung bean sprouts are no larger than 1/8 inch/3 millimeters long; those of soybean sprouts are roughly 1/4 inch/6 millimeters long). Though mostly recognized as an ingredient in Chinese cooking, bean sprouts are indispensable in Indonesian, Malaysian, and Singaporean cuisines, both as a component in stir-fries and salads and as a crunchy addition to noodle soups. Always wash bean sprouts thoroughly in cold water (as you would Asian greens) and gently pat them dry with paper towels or spin them in a salad spinner before using. Wet bean spouts can make for a waterlogged dish, especially when it's a stir-fry.

BUYING AND STORING: Look for perky, bright ivory bean sprouts in supermarkets and Asian markets. The best sprouts are available in bulk in clean, moisture-free bins, though I've bought good prebagged bean sprouts from Chinatown vegetable vendors. Don't buy bean sprouts that seem limp, are slightly amber, or have an "off" smell—all sure signs that they aren't fresh. Fresh bean sprouts give off a clean, pleasantly earthy aroma, not a sweaty, dank odor. Avoid sprouts sitting in a tub of water in the produce section, a ploy some vendors use to camouflage old specimens. Store bean sprouts in an airtight plastic bag in the refrigerator, and use them within 1 or 2 days, as they spoil quickly.

BLACK MUSTARD SEEDS

Brassica nigra; *biji sawi* (MALAYSIA AND SINGAPORE)

Don't confuse black mustard seeds with yellow (or white) mustard seeds (*Brassica alba*), the variety used to make mustard. Although they are about the same size (roughly 1/16 inch/2 millimeters in diameter), black mustard seeds are silvery black, not golden yellow. They taste different, too, with an earthy, pleasantly bitter quality and none of the horseradish-like pungency of yellow mustard seeds. (On rare occasions, mustard seeds that are slightly more brown than black are available in Bangladeshi, Indian, or Pakistani grocery stores. Their taste is almost identical to black mustard seeds.) A staple in their native India, black mustard seeds have been adapted by cooks in Malaysia and Singapore for such Indian-influenced dishes as Indian-Style Fish Stew with Okra (page 249). To intensify their taste, you need to sauté them in a small amount of very hot oil until they pop open, a process that usually takes no more than a few seconds. To accomplish this, you'll require very hot oil—if it's not at least 350°F (180°C) the seeds will just sit inert in the pan rather than sputter and pop. Be sure to let the oil cool for a few moments before adding additional ingredients, or the new ingredients are likely to scorch.

BUYING AND STORING: Look for black mustard seeds in small plastic bags or jars in any Bangladeshi, Indian, or Pakistani grocery store. Avoid seeds that are shriveled or dusty, a sign that they are old. Store them in a tightly sealed jar or plastic container in the refrigerator or freezer. Since they're not particularly aromatic, they keep longer than more powerfully fragranced spices such as cloves, though I recommend discarding them after a year.

CANDLENUTS

Aleurites moluccana; *kemiri* (INDONESIA); *buah keras* (MALAYSIA AND SINGAPORE)

Candlenuts, which are native to Indonesia, are distantly related to macadamia nuts. They closely resemble their more famous kin, though they're slightly larger and have a rougher, waxier exterior. Candlenuts aren't eaten as a snack, nor are they used to flavor foods. Instead, they're ground up finely in flavoring pastes to lend body and thickness to dishes, serving roughly the same purpose as flour in Western sauces. They appear with equal frequency in coconut milk–based curries, such as Nyonya Shrimp Curry with Fresh Pineapple and Tomatoes (page 260), and water-based stews, such as Fragrant Fish Stew with Lime and Lemon Basil (page 240). There's another difference between candlenuts and macadamia nuts: candlenuts are mildly toxic when raw, and must be cooked before they're eaten. I realize this sounds alarming. It certainly was to me the first time Inam grabbed my wrist to prevent me from popping a whole one into my mouth. "*Jangan* [Don't]!" she said, laughing. "It's not food!" But raw candlenuts, I later learned, aren't seriously poisonous. Eating one can cause a brief bout of nausea, not much more. When they're finely ground (as they will be when you use them), they lose their toxicity within a few seconds of exposure to heat. All of the recipes in this book require cooking candlenuts for at least 20 minutes—plenty of time to lay any concerns you may have to rest.

BUYING, STORING, AND SUBSTITUTING: Candlenuts are typically sold in 7-ounce (200-gram) plastic bags in Chinese and Southeast Asian markets, usually in sections devoted to Indonesian, Malaysian, and Singaporean ingredients. The most common brand in North America is Rotary, distributed by Empire International, a Pomona, California–based Indonesian food importer. Look for shiny, dust-free nuts. Older candlenuts have a dry, powdery exterior. Store them in the freezer in a jar or tightly wrapped in the package in which they came, where they'll keep for up to a year. They'll likely become rancid if kept in a cupboard for longer than 6 months. If you have difficulty finding candlenuts, unsalted raw or roasted macadamia nuts can be substituted. Though macadamias don't have the same thickening properties of candlenuts, they do lend dishes a similar (very) subtle nutty taste.

CARDAMOM

Elettaria cardamomum; *kapulaga* (INDONESIA); *buah pelaga* (MALAYSIA AND SINGAPORE)

Cardamom, which is native to the Malabar Coast of south India (what is now northern coastal Kerala), was brought to the Malay Archipelago by Indian spice traders. An intensely aromatic ingredient with a peppery-floral taste, cardamom shows up in such strongly spiced dishes as Chicken Rendang with Cinnamon and Star Anise (page 278) and Malaysian Spiced Pineapple Pickle (page 136). While in India it often flavors milk-based sweets, in Indonesian, Malaysian, and Singaporean cooking it's primarily used in savory dishes. Whole cardamoms—squat, papery pods about 1/4 inch (6 millimeters) long that encase tiny black seeds—are called for in most recipes in this book. (The West Sumatran Chicken Curry variation on page 277 calls for the seeds only.) When you're asked to crack a whole pod with the flat side of a knife, gently press down while rocking the knife back and forth for a few seconds over the pod to break it open. You want to crack the hull, not smash it. Add the whole cracked pod to the dish; remove it when serving, if you like.
BUYING AND STORING: Look for whole green cardamom pods, which have more fragrance than white, black, or brown cardamom (white cardamom is merely bleached green cardamom), but any whole cardamom is fine for the recipes in this book. All are easy to find in jars or small plastic bags in Bangladeshi, Indian, and Pakistani shops and in the spice sections of better Western supermarkets. Don't buy hulled cardamom seeds, since the longer the seeds are out of their pods, the less flavorful they'll be. Store cardamom in a tightly sealed jar or plastic container in the refrigerator or freezer for up to 6 months.

CHICKEN

Ayam (INDONESIA, MALAYSIA, AND SINGAPORE)

Like good cooks here, good cooks in Indonesia, Malaysia, and Singapore insist on free-range chicken, known as *ayam kampong* (village chicken). Typically weighing no more than 3 pounds (1.4 kilograms), an *ayam kampong* tastes sweeter and richer than its commercially raised counterpart. If a cook doesn't have a flock of *ayam kampong* in her backyard, she will likely choose a live bird at her local market, to be killed and plucked on the spot. Already-slaughtered birds are also available from butchers, but they're always a cook's second choice, since their freshness can't be guaranteed.

Back home, I buy whole, small, free-range fryer chickens from poultry butchers in the nearest Chinatown or at Chinese or Southeast Asian supermarkets. They come closest to the deep taste and supple texture of the chickens available in Southeast Asia. Chickens at Chinese butchers usually come from small, family-run poultry farmers, such as Bo Bo

Poultry in the New York area. Unlike commercially raised chickens, they are literally whole: they include the head and feet, which I often use for stock. Chinese butchers usually have chickens displayed in open cold-storage bins for customers to select their own. If not, indicate to the butcher the chicken that appeals to you from the other side of the display-case glass. My second choice for chickens in America is the whole "organic," "natural," or "naturally raised" free-range fryer or roaster chickens available from select farmers' markets and quality supermarkets such as Whole Foods. These are excellent, flavorful birds, though they're often too large—even the fryers usually weigh over 4 pounds (1.8 kilograms)—for my taste. Feel free to substitute free-range-chicken parts (thighs, drumsticks, and breasts) for most of the chicken recipes in this book, as long as the weight is equivalent to that of the whole chicken.

BUYING AND STORING: I never buy chickens that weigh more than 3 1/2 pounds (1.6 kilograms), even for roasting. Smaller fryer chickens are more flavorful and retain their rich flavor better than muscle-bound roasters. Also, because a small fryer means a young chicken, its flesh is juicier and more tender than its older relatives, whose flesh tends to be bland and tough. Seek chickens with clear, moist skin and full, plump flesh. Avoid those with dry skin and mushy flesh. Avoid frozen chickens, too. Freezing breaks down the bird's flesh and can cause the cooked meat to have an unappealing, spongy texture, especially in a slow-cooked dish like Chicken Rendang with Cinnamon and Star Anise (page 278). Before you make your purchase, take a good whiff. Fresh fowl should give off no odor. Store whole chickens (and parts) in the rear of your refrigerator—the coldest part—and use them within a day of purchase if possible.

CUTTING UP A WHOLE CHICKEN: Cooks in Indonesia, Malaysia, and Singapore cut whole chickens into 10 or 16 bone-in pieces for curries, stews, and frying. A chicken cut into 10 pieces (best for frying) yields 4 breast pieces, 2 wings, 2 drumsticks, and 2 thighs; the 16-piece version (best for curries and stews) results in 6 breast pieces, 2 wings, 4 drumstick pieces, and 4 thigh pieces. Cut either way, the meat cooks more evenly (which means you won't have overcooked breasts and undercooked thighs), and the pieces can be eaten more efficiently with your fingers, the eating utensil of choice in the region. Also, the collagen that leaks out from cut bones and joints imparts a richer flavor and silkier texture to stocks and curries than whole chicken thighs, legs, or breasts. If you're familiar with the traditional Chinese method of cutting up chicken for soups or stews, you'll be acquainted with the method I describe below. Most Chinatown or Chinese-market butchers will gladly cut up the chicken for you when you buy it whole. Just ask them to cut it into pieces for Chinese soup or stew, indicating 2 inches (5 centimeters) with your fingers, and specifying the number of pieces you want. A tip of a dollar or two will show respect for his or her skill and help establish a relationship for the future.

If you buy chicken from a merchant who is not familiar with cutting birds into such small pieces, you can easily do it yourself. Here's how:

First, choose your cutting tool. A sharp chef's knife, a sharp Chinese cleaver, or heavy-duty kitchen or poultry shears will work best. Select the one that you are most comfortable with. I like to use the sturdy, wonderfully sharp kitchen shears made by J.A. Henckels, widely available in kitchen-supply shops. You may experiment, however, perhaps even trying a combination of all three tools for different aspects of cutting. For instance, a pair of shears or a cleaver is especially handy for cutting directly through bone, while a sharp chef's knife is excellent for severing joints.

Next, rinse your whole chicken under cold running water, taking special care to clean the cavity well of blood and tissue, which can make a dish taste bitter. Pat the chicken thoroughly dry inside and out with paper towels. A well-dried chicken will be much easier to grip as you cut. With your knife, cleaver, or shears, remove any of the clumps of fat inside the cavity and underneath the neck flap. Discard the fat.

If you bought your chicken from an Asian market, the head and feet will probably still be attached. Although they are traditionally added to curries and stews in Indonesia, Malaysia, and Singapore (for flavor and, in the case of the feet and neck, to be eaten), most North Americans will find the idea unappealing. Using a cutting board as your work surface, stretch the neck out and lop it off at its base with a firm chop (or snip, if you're using shears). Next, find the center of the knee joints by bending the knees back and forth a few times. I like to feel around with my fingers for the center of each joint, which will be bumpier and yield more to the touch than the surrounding bony area. Gently cut (or snip) through the center of each joint, removing both feet with a swift, straight cut. The cut will be easy—as will all cuts through all poultry joints—if you've located the center of the joint. If you like, you can reserve the head, neck, and feet to make stock later on. Otherwise, discard them.

Now, find the joint that connects the wing to the chest by bending the wing back and forth a few times. Cut both wings from the chest through the center of each joint with a clean slice. If you like, remove and discard the wing tips (I usually leave them attached, but it's up to you).

Next, locate the joint that connects the leg (the thigh and the drumstick) to the body by bending the whole leg back and forth a few times. Cut through the center of each joint and remove both legs with a clean slice.

All that remains is the whole chest, including the breast and back. Turn the bird so that the breast side is facing down and carefully slice (or snip) in a straight line about 1/2 inch (12 millimeters) away from the backbone, cutting through the ribs down the length of the back. Repeat with the other side. You may discard the backbone (or save it for stock), if you wish, or cut it into 3 pieces, though they'll yield scant meat. With the breast skin side down, visually locate the center of the breastbone. Gently cut the breast into halves. Don't worry if the skin bunches up and pulls away from the flesh; it will still cook just fine. (On that note, I never recommend skinning chicken before cooking it—except when making satay—as you lose considerable flavor if you do.)

Next, feel around with your fingers to locate the joints between each drumstick and thigh. Cut each drumstick from the thighs at the joints with a clean cut. If you ultimately want 10 pieces, leave the drumsticks and thighs as whole pieces. If you want to end up with 16 pieces, cut each thigh and each drumstick in half. To do this, visually locate the halfway mark. With your knife or shears, cut directly through the middle of the bone with a firm chop (or snip). This takes a bit of practice if you're not accustomed to doing it. It may help to first cut through the meat until you reach the bone before trying to cut through the bone itself. This way you can better orient yourself for the cut you're about to make. Above all, try to *cut* the bone, not break or shatter it, which will result in jagged edges. Finally, if it is 10 pieces you're after, cut each breast half crosswise in two, through the yielding, gelatinous bone. For 16 pieces, cut each half into 3 equal chunks.

Be careful to remove any bone shards that may have resulted from the cutting before you proceed with cooking. I sometimes like to give the cut-up chicken a final cold-water rinse (then thoroughly pat dry) to ensure that no errant shards remain.

CHILES
Capsicum spp.

Ever since chiles were first brought to Indonesia, Malaysia, and Singapore by Portuguese traders in the fifteenth century, they've been embraced as though they were a native ingredient. You'll nearly always find them on the table in one form or another: crushed into a flavoring paste, sliced into a curry, even whole and raw in a small serving dish, as a condiment to nibble on cautiously throughout the meal. Hundreds of different types, hybridized by local farmers over the last five centuries, enliven curries, stews, soups, salads, and sambals, the chile-based condiments popular throughout the region. In addition to the floral flavor they impart, it's commonly believed that their pungency lowers your body temperature, a plus, whether real or imagined, in the pervasive equatorial heat. But cooks never allow chile heat, known as *pedas*, to overpower food. Heat in dishes is always balanced by sweetness, sourness, and saltiness. Keep in mind that foods that include chiles are always eaten along with plenty of steamed rice, which helps lessen their fire.

Cooks in Indonesia, Malaysia, and Singapore rarely seed chiles, as they believe that much of the nuanced flavor of a chile lives in its seeds and the surrounding cottony membranes, the hottest parts. To remove both deprives the chile (and the dish it's used in) of its full potential. If the number of chiles called for in a recipe seems excessive, simply use fewer chiles, rather than seeding them. (In most recipes, I've offered a range; if you enjoy heat, use the maximum amount.) When deciding whether or not to reduce the number, take into consideration the heat level of the chiles. Some varieties have a reputation for being very piquant, but chiles can also vary in heat from batch to batch. The only way to know the heat level of a particular batch is to sample a few chiles while they are still raw. Taste a portion that contains a seed or two (the milder, seedless tip won't be a good indicator of pungency), and keep in mind that a chile's heat diminishes slightly as it cooks.

When cutting chiles, I follow the lead of my friends in Southeast Asia: I eschew the rubber gloves popular in Western kitchens—I find that they distance me from the intimacy of the cooking process. Instead, I'm careful not to rub my eyes or touch any other sensitive areas until I've washed my hands thoroughly with soapy lukewarm water. If you feel more comfortable wearing rubber gloves, which help keep volatile capsaicin, the compound that makes chiles hot, away from skin, do so.

Never substitute jarred chile paste for fresh chiles. Instead, if chiles are hard to find in your area or you use them rarely, find a nice batch, wrap them in a protective cocoon of plastic wrap or aluminum foil, and freeze them for up to a few months. Although frozen chiles darken and lose their crispness, they're a far better option than an overly salty, chemical-laden jar of ground chiles, which also often contains vinegar that can further skew the taste of a dish.

Many of the chiles used in Indonesia, Malaysia, and Singapore are commercially available in North America; those that aren't have close counterparts. Here are the ones you'll need for the recipes in this book:

FRESH RED HOLLAND CHILES *Capsicum annum* var. *longum; cabe merah* (INDONESIA); *lada merah, cili merah* (MALAYSIA AND SINGAPORE)
Also known as Dutch or finger chiles, Holland chiles are ruby red, glossy skinned, and have a narrow, fingerlike body that ends in a sharp point. They're usually at least 4 inches (10 centimeters) long and are about 1/2 inch (12 millimeters) in diameter at their thickest point. They have juicy, sweet flesh and tight, waxy skin that keeps them from spoiling quickly. Holland chiles vary from mildly hot to scorching, though they lose much of their pungency when cooked. A hybrid of Indonesian and Malaysian chiles, they were developed in the Netherlands by Dutch botanists eager to reproduce Indonesian food at home. Most Holland chiles in North America are grown in hothouses in the Netherlands, from which they are shipped year-round.
BUYING, STORING, AND SUBSTITUTING: Holland chiles can be found in many Asian and specialty markets, usually in bulk but sometimes wrapped in plastic. Vegetable merchants

often like to stock Holland chiles more than many other varieties because of their long shelf life. Seek the firmest, brightest chiles you can find, with no soft, wrinkly, or dark, mildewy spots. They should have a sweet, clean aroma. Store small quantities (no more than 25) for 10 days to 2 weeks in a closed paper bag in the refrigerator (plastic bags trap moisture, encouraging spoilage). Keep larger quantities wrapped securely in plastic or foil in the freezer, where they'll keep for up to 3 months.

If you can't find Holland chiles, Fresno, cherry bell, cayenne, Anaheim, Huachinango, jalapeño, or serrano chiles make excellent substitutes. Many of them are available in Latin American markets. Use only the ripe, red fruits, not immature green ones, which have an inappropriately grassy flavor and lack sweetness. If using chiles no longer than 3 1/2 inches (9 centimeters), such as Huachinango, jalapeño, or serrano, add 1 or 2 more to compensate for their small size. If using chiles longer than 5 inches (13 centimeters), such as Anaheim, reduce the number by 1 or 2. Small red Thai chiles and habanero chiles are too fearsomely hot to use as substitutes.

FRESH THAI CHILES *Capsicum frutescens*; *cabe rawit* or *cabe burung* (INDONESIA); *cili padi* (MALAYSIA AND SINGAPORE)

What are generically referred to as Thai, bird, or bird's-eye chiles in North America are the best stand-ins for the hundreds of varieties of small chiles used in Southeast Asian cooking. Narrow and intensely hot, Thai chiles, which are about 1 1/2 inches (4 centimeters) long and 1/8 inch (3 millimeters) in diameter at their widest point, provide a lovely grassy pungency to dishes. The Thai chiles available in North American markets are generally green, though occasionally you'll see both red ones and ones that are a red-green mix. Use only the green ones in recipes calling for green Thai chiles. Indonesians often nibble on whole Thai chiles as part of a meal for their pure, unrestrained heat.

BUYING, STORING, AND SUBSTITUTING: Look for Thai or bird's-eye chiles in all Asian and South Asian markets, either in bulk or in small plastic bags. Seek firm, smooth, glossy chiles with a clean, sweet smell. Handpick them from a bulk bin, if possible, to ensure better-quality chiles. Store them in a closed paper bag in the refrigerator for up to 2 weeks, or freeze them, well wrapped in plastic or aluminum foil, for up to 3 months.

The serrano, a small, stubby green chile (usually 2 inches/5 centimeters long) with a gently rounded tip, can be substituted. Serranos, which are favorites of Mexican cooks, are not as hot, so you should add 2 or 3 additional chiles to a recipe to compensate for their mildness. I don't like to substitute jalapeños—they take on a sweet taste as they cook, changing the character of a dish.

SMALL DRIED RED CHILES *Cabe kering* (INDONESIA); *lada kering* (MALAYSIA AND SINGAPORE)

Dried red chiles, which have a ruddier, more caramelized taste than fresh ones, are used by cooks in Indonesia, Malaysia, and Singapore to lend earthiness and heat to dishes. They appear frequently in the flavoring pastes and sambals of Malaysia and Singapore, but are used less often in Indonesia. Hundreds of varieties of dried chiles are eaten in the Malay Archipelago. For the recipes in this book, virtually any variety of small dried red chile no more than 3 inches (7.5 centimeters) long will work, including two popular Mexican varieties, árbol and japones, or Thai. Sample various kinds, seeing how they vary in flavor and heat, to determine which you like the best (I'm partial to chile de árbol). Don't use ancho, chipotle, or pasilla chiles, which are imported from Mexico and are too aromatic and smoky. As with fresh chiles, don't be tempted to seed dried chiles; instead, use fewer chiles if they're too hot for you.

BUYING AND STORING: Look for small dried red chiles in all Asian, South Asian, Latin American, and well-stocked supermarkets. They're usually sold in small plastic bags, though they're occasionally available in bulk. Store them tightly sealed in a plastic bag in the freezer, where they'll keep for up to 1 year.

CHINESE CELERY GREENS
Apium graveolens; *seledri* (INDONESIA); *daun sop* (MALAYSIA AND SINGAPORE); *kunn choy* (CANTONESE)

Chinese celery greens are used as an herb, not a vegetable, and are the opposite of the familiar thick-stalked, scant-leaved celery heads found in Western markets. They instead have thin, reedy stalks topped with a flourish of bushy, pale green leaves. Their taste is similar, however, though a little more concentrated. Cooks in Indonesia, Malaysia, and Singapore chop or mince the leaves, discarding the sinewy stalks, and add them to stir-fries, stews, and soups, which accounts for their Malaysian and Singaporean name, *daun sop*, or "soup leaf."

BUYING, STORING, AND SUBSTITUTING: Chinese celery greens are available year-round in Chinese and Southeast Asian markets, but they're at their best from July to October. They're sold in small bunches of a few stalks. Choose bunches that are uniform in color and pert, not limp. Store them as you would conventional celery: in a closed paper bag (to inhibit moisture). They'll keep for about a week. The leaves of conventional celery can be substituted, though their taste is not as intense.

CHINESE CHIVES
Allium tuberosum; *daun bawang* (INDONESIA, MALAYSIA, AND SINGAPORE); *gow choy* (CANTONESE)

Members of the garlic family, Chinese chives are used to brighten soups, salads, and stir-fries in Southeast Asia. You'll find a variety of Chinese chives in Asian markets. Look for those that resemble thick, long blades of deep green grass, rounded at the top and with a blunt end. Their taste is more subtle than that of scallions, with aromatic, oniony notes (*daun bawang* means "onion leaf"). Don't confuse Chinese chives with garlic chives, which have thick stems and come crowned with tiny, bulbous flower heads.

BUYING, STORING, AND SUBSTITUTING: Chinese chives are easy to find in Chinese and Southeast Asian markets. They should have uniformly dark green leaves; the shorter—and hence, younger—chives will be less sinewy and milder tasting. Store them in a closed paper bag in the refrigerator (the paper bag fosters a drier environment, slowing spoilage) for no more than 3 or 4 days. The white and green parts of scallions can be substituted for Chinese chives, though they lack the complex taste.

CINNAMON
Cinnamomum cassia; kayu manis (INDONESIA, MALAYSIA, AND SINGAPORE)

The cinnamon grown and used in Southeast Asia is primarily cassia, or *kayu manis* (literally sweet wood), the bark of a tree native to the Malay Archipelago, rather than true cinnamon (*Cinnamomum zeylanciaum*), native to Sri Lanka. Its peppery-sweet taste is a popular accent in countless savory and sweet dishes, and I find that it's almost identical in flavor to true cinnamon, though more concentrated and thus better suited to intense-tasting Indonesian, Malaysian, and Singaporean foods. Lush cassia groves, their lofty trees topped with fiery pink leaves, are a feature of landscapes from Sumatra to the Spice Islands. The bark is peeled from the tree after 2 to 5 years—the older the tree, the more potent the bark's taste—and sun dried, where it curls within a few days into the familiar thick, reddish brown quill-like cylinders. Should you travel through highland Sumatra and Java, where cassia is commonly grown, you may well see entire villages whose streets are carpeted year-round with drying cassia quills—a vision straight out of Oz!

BUYING AND STORING: It's easy to tell the difference between cassia and true cinnamon. Cassia sticks are darker, thicker, and coarser than true cinnamon, whose sticks are paler, thinner, and relatively brittle. Most of what is available in our markets is falsely labeled cinnamon, when it's actually cassia, so you should have no problem finding it. Whole cassia sticks, which vary in length from 3 to 12 inches (7.5 to 30 centimeters), are widely available in Western supermarkets and in Asian and South Asian markets. Always buy the stick form of cassia, as opposed to ground cinnamon, which has a weaker flavor. The most vibrant tasting comes from Sumatra (the packages at spice shops usually clearly label the origin), though Vietnamese cassia is also excellent. For best results, store cassia sticks in the refrigerator (or freezer) in a tightly closed container. They'll keep for 3 or 4 months before their taste starts to fade.

CLOVES

Eugenia caryophyllata; Syzygium aromaticum; cengkeh (INDONESIA);
bunga cengkeh (MALAYSIA AND SINGAPORE)

Cloves, the dried flower buds of a tropical evergreen tree, are native to Ternate and Tidor, two small islands in the Moluccas chain of Indonesia. Countless battles were waged over their ownership by the people who lived on the islands and European colonialists, as cloves were one of the old world's most revered spices. In ancient times, they were coveted by the Chinese and Egyptians for their use in food as much as for their analgesic properties (the oil of cloves is still widely used to relieve aches and pains). Although Westerners typically think of cloves as a dessert ingredient, cooks in Indonesia, Malaysia, and Singapore use them almost exclusively in savory dishes. They lend an enchanting, spicy-sweet perfume to many meat and fish curries and pickles. Another use is in the *kretek*, the popular Indonesian cigarette made of tobacco and ground cloves. The cigarettes are believed to have been invented in the nineteenth century by Haji Jamahri, a Javanese man who thought that the addition of cloves to his tobacco cigarettes negated their unhealthiness. Their aroma is the signature scent of Indonesia, for rare is the Indonesian man (women seldom smoke) who doesn't enjoy a *kretek* at least on occasion.

BUYING AND STORING: Most of the cloves available in the West come from Zanzibar and Madagascar. They are comparable in taste and appearance to what grows in Indonesia. Look for cloves that are a deep, uniform brown and have round, puffy centers. The freshest, best-quality cloves are available in specialty or South Asian markets, where their turnover will be highest. Cloves store well in a tightly sealed jar in the refrigerator or freezer for up to 6 months, at which point they start to lose their potency.

COCONUTS

Coconuts are believed to be native to the Malay Archipelago, so it's no surprise that they are so basic to its cooking. Westerners most often think of coconut as a topping for cakes or puddings, but in Indonesia, Malaysia, and Singapore it shows up in one form or another at nearly every meal. Its grated meat adds sweetness to raw salads, and, perhaps most significantly, the luscious milk extracted from its flesh enriches fiery curries and dry-braised *rendang* dishes, such as Beef Rendang (page 304), Chicken Rendang with Cinnamon and Star Anise (page 278), and Potato Rendang (page 223). Coconut milk also adds flavor and substance to sweets and steamed rice dishes.

GRATED FRESH COCONUT

The finely grated meat of fresh mature coconuts contributes richness and a gentle, mellow taste to salads and, when pan toasted until golden, gives body to curries, particularly those of Aceh, Indonesia. Though store-bought grated dried coconut might seem like a convenient option, it lacks the suppleness and natural sweetness of freshly grated. Learning to grate your own coconut may at first seem daunting, but you'll be well rewarded for your efforts.

The first step is to find a good-quality mature coconut. Don't confuse the pale beige young coconuts available in many Chinese, Southeast Asian, and specialty supermarkets with the more compact chocolate brown mature coconuts. (Identifiable by their pithy exterior, which is often carved into a point at the top, young coconuts have a soft, pud-dinglike flesh. They're usually whacked open and eaten as a refreshing snack, rather than used as an ingredient in cooking.) Mature coconuts in North America are generally prod-ucts of Mexico and the Caribbean and are available year-round at Western, Asian, and Latin supermarkets. They are likely to be fresher at the latter two because of greater turnover. Look for a heavy, firm, evenly brown coconut with an unblemished exterior; it should weigh 1 to 3 pounds (455 grams to 1.4 kilograms). The size of the coconut doesn't matter as much as its heft: a light coconut indicates dried or thin flesh. Give the coconut a vigorous shake. You should be able to hear the liquid slosh around. Avoid coconuts with weepy or damp "eyes" (the three ovoid shapes on the rounded end). Take a sniff of the eyes. They should give off no mildewy odor. The coconut is spoiled if they do.

CRACKING AND REMOVING MEAT: I was intimidated by this process for years. How, I won-dered, was it possible to crack open such a stonelike object without the benefit of a sharp Southeast Asian cleaver or hatchet? I overcame my fear by learning a few easy steps.

To avoid spilling the liquid when you crack the coconut open, you need to drain it first. Gripping the coconut firmly between your knees, and using a hammer, carefully pound a thick nail or ice pick into 2 eyes until you have poked a hole that pierces the flesh. Invert the coconut and let the liquid (which is not coconut milk, but rather coconut water) drain into a glass. Take a sip. It should taste clean and subtly sweet. (Feel free to drink it all if you like the taste!) If the liquid is even remotely sour or mildewy tasting, the coconut has gone "off," and you'll need to use another one. (I buy 2 or 3 coconuts at a time, in case I end up with a spoiled one—sometimes even my own coconut-selecting rules don't work.)

Now, holding the bottom of the coconut firmly in one hand with the eyes pointing down, slowly rotate the coconut and whack the upper third with a hammer 5 to 10 times, or until a thin fissure begins to form. (Be sure to hold the coconut from its bottom, so you can avoid hitting your fingers with the hammer.) Continue rotating and hitting the coconut until you can easily break and peel away a few large pieces of the shell. Just keep whacking until this happens (it might take a few more whacks than you think). Separate the meat from the shell with a strong paring knife, prying any stubborn pieces loose with a firm digging, scraping motion. You don't need to peel off the thin, brown skin that surrounds the white flesh. Although purists dislike the color it adds to dishes, I like its subtle earthy taste.

GRATING: The best way to grate coconut is with the finest grating surface of a box grater or single-sided hand grater, such as a Microplane, exactly as you would grate Parmigiano-Reggiano cheese, yielding lacy shreds. Another method is to cut the coconut meat into 1-inch (2.5-centimeter) pieces and grind them in a large food processor until they are light and fluffy, 30 seconds to 1 minute. Make sure that you don't overprocess the coconut, or it will become sticky.

STORING: Store grated coconut and extra whole pieces in the freezer in a sealed zip-lock bag, tightly wrapped plastic wrap or aluminum foil (or both), or an airtight plastic container. They will keep for up to 3 months.

•

TOASTED GRATED COCONUT

Indonesian, Malaysian, and Singaporean cooks use pan-toasted grated coconut, called *keresek* (or *kresik*), to thicken curries and to add an irresistible caramelized taste to the vegetable salads called *kerabu*. It will keep in an airtight plastic container in the refrigerator for up to 1 week. I like to make extra to store in the freezer, where it will last for up to 3 months in a tightly sealed jar or plastic container or a zip-lock bag.

MAKES ABOUT 1 1/2 CUPS (4 1/2 OUNCES/130 GRAMS)

Meat from 1 medium-sized coconut, cut into 1-inch (2.5-centimeter) pieces

1. Fill the work bowl of a regular-sized food processor one-third full with the coconut meat. (Be sure the pieces are no larger than 1 inch/2.5 centimeters; larger ones will get caught in the processor blades.) Pulse until fluffy and light, 30 seconds to 1 minute. Don't over-process, or the coconut will become gluey. Repeat until all of the coconut is grated.

2. Heat a 12-inch (30-centimeter) skillet (nonstick works best) over medium-low heat. When it's hot, add the grated coconut and toast slowly, stirring often with a spatula and gently rotating the pan to disperse the coconut evenly around its surface. Continue until

the coconut is the color of light caramel and pleasantly fragrant. (The coconut will color fairly evenly but some bits won't noticeably change color.) This will usually take 10 to 20 minutes, depending on how dry the coconut is and the intensity of the heat. Resist the temptation to raise the heat. It's easy to overbrown the coconut, which will make it taste bitter. (Conversely, if it's underbrowned, it will taste bland.) If the coconut begins to burn or overbrown, immediately remove the pan from the heat, allow to cool for 1 minute, stirring the coconut constantly, and then return to low heat to continue cooking.

3. Transfer the toasted coconut to a bowl and set it aside for a few minutes to cool.

4. Place the cooled toasted coconut in the food processor, and pulse until it resembles fine sawdust, about 1 minute. Use immediately, or store as directed in the headnote.

COCONUT MILK

Making coconut milk in North America from scratch that tastes the same as the milk made in Southeast Asia is difficult, if not impossible. The problem lies with the coconuts that are available to us, which rarely have a high enough fat content to yield a properly rich extraction. The result instead is a thin, weak-bodied milk that makes dishes taste pallid. Happily, much of the canned coconut milk available to us is of excellent quality.

Before I explain the specifics of canned coconut milk, I want to clear up a common misconception. Coconut milk is the creamy liquid that results when finely grated meat from a mature coconut is mixed with warm water. It is not the clear liquid inside a coconut, which is coconut water. Cooks in Indonesia, Malaysia, and Singapore nearly always make their own milk from coconuts they buy at the market or gather from trees behind their house. They crack them open, finely grate the flesh, and then massage it by hand in warm water for a minute or two. Then they strain it, either by hand or through a colander. What's left behind is coconut milk, a thick, snow white, creamy liquid. Cooks repeat this process up to 5 times, each extraction yielding progressively thinner milk with a lower fat content. Thicker extractions are generally reserved for meat curries, while thinner ones are added to fish and vegetable curries, steamed rice dishes, and sweets.

Two important notes about cooking with coconut milk: First, always stir canned coconut milk well before you measure it for a recipe. Otherwise, you may end up using milk that's too thick or too thin. When coconut milk reaches temperatures below 70°F (20°C), it begins to coagulate. If your pantry is cold enough, the milk may seize up into a solid mass. If it doesn't seize up completely, the richer (and thicker) portion may have risen to the top, which means that it will need to be thoroughly mixed with the thinner liquid underneath. Second, never allow coconut milk to come to an aggressive boil for more than a few seconds, or it may curdle. If it does come to a strong boil (or anything beyond a simmer, really), immediately reduce the heat, or remove the pot from the fire altogether and allow it to cool for a minute or two before returning it to the stove.

BUYING AND STORING: The best place to buy canned coconut milk is in Chinese and Southeast Asian supermarkets, where you'll find many different brands. Purchase unsweetened coconut milk or cream. (They're usually almost identical, despite the label.) Never buy the sweetened coconut milk or cream available in Western supermarkets, which is used for making desserts and sweet drinks. Most unsweetened coconut milk comes from Thailand or the Philippines, generally in cans holding 15 to 19 fluid ounces (470 to 590 milliliters), and is very affordable, costing no more than a dollar and a half or so in Asian markets. (Cans sold in Western supermarkets are often priced significantly higher.)

Choosing the best coconut milk is like choosing what kind of pot to cook in—it's a highly personal choice. Once you get to know the brands available in your markets, decide which ones you like. Avoid coconut milk labeled lite, which has been diluted with extra water and is too weak for the recipes in this book. Look for brands that contain the least amount of additives. Generally speaking, the higher the price, the fewer the additives. Try a couple of brands in a blind taste test to see what their characteristics are. The better-quality ones will have a thick, coagulated cap of rich coconut milk, with thinner, liquidy coconut milk underneath (the thick milk will liquefy when heated). The milk will smell sweet and coconutty. It will taste succulent, with pronounced coconut notes. Inferior brands will be thin and uniformly mixed, with no cap of thick milk, a sure sign of chemical stabilizers; their taste will be bland and watery.

After much experimentation, I find myself relying more and more on Mae Ploy brand coconut milk, imported from Thailand. It has everything I want in coconut milk—richness, sweetness, and a smooth, supple texture—and it's easy to find in Chinese and Southeast Asian supermarkets. Another good brand is Chaokoh, also from Thailand. (Be sure not to confuse it with the less expensive, similarly named Chaokroh brand, which is of poorer quality.) Yet another good brand is Thai Kitchen's organic coconut milk, widely available even in non-Asian supermarkets.

Canned coconut milk will keep in a cool pantry for up to 2 years. Store leftover opened canned coconut milk in a sealed plastic container for up to 3 days in the refrigerator or 3 months in the freezer.

CORIANDER SEEDS

Coriandrum sativum; *ketumbar* (INDONESIA AND MALAYSIA)

Coriander seeds were first brought to the Malay Archipelago by Indian spice traders and soon became a keystone ingredient, especially in the earthy, zesty flavoring pastes and marinades of Java. Javanese Grilled Chicken (page 289) and Chicken Satay (page 147) are two recipes that call for a large quantity of the spice.

Two types of coriander seeds are available: One is round and light brown to tan and has a lemony taste. The other is egg shaped and has a green-yellow tint. It offers a fresher, grassier taste. Though it's true of all spices, it's even more important to use whole coriander seeds rather than the preground spice, as the latter has little taste. Indonesian cooks often toast the seeds before grinding them to bring out their flavor; individual recipes will let you know when this is necessary. The green leaf of the coriander plant, what we usually call cilantro in North America, is rarely used as an ingredient or garnish in traditional local foods.

BUYING AND STORING: The freshest, best-tasting coriander seeds come from Bangladeshi, Indian, and Pakistani spice shops, which usually carry both the round and egg-shaped varieties and have a high turnover, ensuring aromatic seeds. Store them in a tightly sealed jar or plastic container in the refrigerator or freezer for up to 6 months.

CUCUMBERS

Cucumis sativus; *ketimun* (INDONESIA); *timun* (MALAYSIA AND SINGAPORE)

The thick-skinned, big-seeded cucumbers that we know in the West are unknown in Indonesia, Malaysia, and Singapore. The vegetable found in markets there is shorter and stubbier, with tender yellowish skin and easy-to-chew seeds. The Kirby, a pickling cucumber readily available in U.S. markets, comes close, though it's generally a bit smaller. In late summer, look for the sweetest, most tender Kirbys at farmers' markets. Choose ones that are small (3 to 5 inches/7.5 to 13 centimeters is the standard length), firm, and uniformly deep green, with no soft or wrinkly spots on the skin, especially at the tips. If you can't find Kirbys, you can substitute the long, seedless English variety, though they tend to be less crunchy and flavorful.

STORING: Store cucumbers in the refrigerator in a tightly sealed plastic bag. Use them as quickly as possible. They begin to soften and lose their vitality within 2 to 3 days.

CUMIN

Cuminum cyminum; *jintan putih* (INDONESIA, MALAYSIA, AND SINGAPORE)

After coriander, cumin is the most important spice in the cooking of Central and East Java. Cooks rely on its pungent, subtly bitter taste to offset the sweetness of coconut milk–based curries. It also plays a dominant role in The Soto King's Chicken Soup (page 271), a celebrated dish of East Java. People of south Indian descent in Malaysia and

Singapore use cumin seeds to brew up a medicinal infusion believed to purify the digestive system and drink it warm, with meals. (To make it, simmer 1 teaspoon cumin seeds in 4 cups/32 fluid ounces/1 liter water for 5 minutes, then strain.) Toasting the seeds to release extra flavor is uncommon, as cooks believe that roasting cumin results in a taste that's too heavy and dark. Sautéing them together with the other ingredients of a flavoring paste elicits the desired effect better.

BUYING AND STORING: Good-quality cumin is easy to come by. Look for seeds that are a pale dusty brown to greenish tan and about 1/4 inch (6 millimeters) long at quality supermarkets or Bangladeshi, Indian, or Pakistani spice shops. Avoid the rarer black cumin seeds, which have a different flavor. Store in a tightly sealed jar or plastic container in the refrigerator or freezer. Discard unused seeds after 6 months.

CURRY LEAVES
Murraya koenigii; daun kari (INDONESIA, MALAYSIA, AND SINGAPORE)

I'm crazy for the fresh, lemony zing of curry leaves. They make every dish they season taste more alive. These small (they're only about 1 inch/2.5 centimeters long), deep green leaves grow on an evergreen tree of the citrus family native to India and Sri Lanka. The name comes from their use in curries, not because they taste like curry. They're a mainstay in many Indian Malay, Nyonya, and Malay dishes, including Indian-Style Fish Stew with Okra (page 249), and appear less often in Indonesian recipes. Before the leaves are used in any dish, they're sautéed in hot oil until they're crispy and show translucent spots, a process that not only tenderizes them, but also heightens their taste, much as pan toasting opens up the bouquet in spices. (All the recipes that call for curry leaves give instructions for how to do this.) Western diners unfamiliar with curry leaves often relegate them to a corner of their plates, suspecting that, like bay leaves, they aren't for eating. But curry leaves, with their pleasing taste, are edible, the only exception being when they are large—say, wider than 1/2 inch (12 millimeters)—in which case they're flavorful but tough. To remedy this, cut away the thick central stem of each leaf and cut the leaf lengthwise into strips before sautéing.

BUYING AND STORING: Fresh curry leaves grown in Florida and California are sold in many Indian markets and occasionally in markets specializing in Southeast Asian ingredients. Usually packaged in sealed plastic bags, the leaves are attached to a thin branch (each branch supports roughly 20 leaves), with each bag containing 3 to 5 branches. Look for small, deep green, fresh-looking leaves with no signs of rot or dryness. Don't buy dried curry leaves, as they have absolutely no taste. If you can't find fresh leaves, omit them from the recipe. (Also, despite the vaguely similar appearance, never substitute bay or laurel leaves, which have an entirely different flavor.)

Store curry leaves in the refrigerator inside a closed paper bag (to discourage moisture), where they'll keep for up to 2 weeks. Alternatively, you can seal them well in plastic wrap or aluminum foil and store them in the freezer, where they'll last for up to 6 months. Their flavor and texture will be only slightly diminished, since the required sautéing helps bring them back to life.

DAUN PANDAN (down pahn-DAHN)
Pandanus amaryllifolius; *daun pandan* (INDONESIA, MALAYSIA, AND SINGAPORE)

Native to Indonesia's Spice Islands, *daun pandan*, also called pandanus leaf, pandan leaf, and screwpine, is a beloved aromatic in the Malay Archipelago. The large, dark green leaves, 2 to 3 feet (60 to 90 centimeters) long, resemble supersized blades of grass or, perhaps more accurately, gladiola leaves. They're used only as a seasoning, tied into a knot or torn in half lengthwise (techniques that help release their aroma) and added to dishes as they simmer, as even the cooked leaves are too tough and sinewy to eat. *Daun pandan* leaves impart a subtle, vanilla-like flavor to curries such as Fragrant Fish Stew with Lime and Lemon Basil (page 240), steamed rice dishes such as Lemongrass-Scented Coconut Rice (page 176), and traditional sticky-rice sweets such as Sweet Rice Dumplings with Palm Sugar and Coconut (page 349). A few leaves tucked into a pot of rice as it steams make the rice exquisitely aromatic. If you can't find *daun pandan* leaves, omit them from the recipe.

BUYING AND STORING: *Daun pandan* leaves are sold frozen, whole or factory trimmed into 3-inch (7.5-centimeter) pieces, at Chinese and Southeast Asian grocers, often next to frozen galangal and banana leaves. Usually imported from Thailand, packages are most often labeled *bai toey*, the Thai name for the leaves. Keep them frozen until ready to use, as they only take a minute or two to thaw. Domestically grown fresh *daun pandan* leaves are occasionally available in Chinese and Southeast Asian markets on the West Coast and in Florida; they come in bags or sealed in plastic. If you find them, buy a few bags, rewrap the leaves tightly in plastic wrap, then aluminum foil, and freeze them for up to 3 months. They'll have a much purer taste than the imported frozen leaves of unknown age.

DAUN SALAM (down sah-LAHM)
Syzygium polyantha; *daun salam* (INDONESIA, MALAYSIA, AND SINGAPORE)

Daun salam leaves are an important herb in Indonesian cooking, especially in Java, where they are native. Added fresh or dried to dishes such as Lemongrass-Scented Coconut Rice (page 176), Javanese Chicken Curry (page 275), and Caramelized Tempeh with Chiles (page 325), the leaves impart a subtle spicy, woodsy flavor that has no precedent

FRESH RED HOLLAND CHILES (PAGE 53)

TAMARIND PASTE
(PAGE 89)

FRESH GALANGAL
(PAGE 69)

DRIED SHRIMP PASTE
(PAGE 65)

FRESH THAI CHILES
(PAGE 54)

CANDLENUTS
(PAGE 48)

FRESH TURMERIC
(PAGE 92)

ASAM GELUGOR
(PAGE 43)

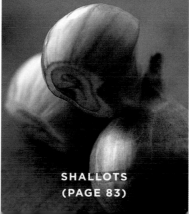

SHALLOTS
(PAGE 83)

FRESH LEMONGRASS STALKS, *LEFT* (PAGE 75);
FRESH LEMONGRASS TIED INTO A KNOT, *RIGHT* (PAGE 76)

CHINESE CELERY GREENS
(PAGE 55)

FRESH LEMON BASIL
(PAGE 74)

FRESH CURRY LEAVES
(PAGE 63)

CHINESE CHIVES
(PAGE 55)

DRIED DAUN SALAM
(PAGE 64)

FROZEN DAL
PANDAN, TIE
(PAGE 6

FRESH KAFFIR LIME LEAVES
(PAGE 73)

TEMPEH
(PAGE 90)

LONG BEANS
(PAGE 76)

BOK CHOY
(PAGE 45)

CHOY SUM
(PAGE 46)

WATER SPINACH
(PAGE 46)

TOFU
(PAGE 91)

SHANGHAI CHOY
(PAGE 45)

KAI LAN
(PAGE 46)

DRIED SPICES:
CORIANDER
(PAGE 61),

CUMIN SEEDS
(PAGE 62),

WHOLE GREEN
CARDAMOM IN
PODS (PAGE 49),

FENNEL SEEDS
(PAGE 66)

BLACK MUSTARD SEEDS
(PAGE 47)

WHOLE CLOVES
(PAGE 57)

WHOLE NUTMEG
(PAGE 77)

STAR ANISE
(PAGE 88)

CINNAMON (CASSIA) STICKS
(PAGE 56)

DRIED SHRIMP
(PAGE 65)

PALM SUGAR (PAGE 79)

SMALL DRIED RED CHILES
(PAGE 54)

CANNED UNSWEETENED
COCONUT MILK (PAGE 60)

BLE-BLACK SOY SAUCE,
7 (PAGE 87); INDONE-
N SWEET SOY SAUCE,
RIGHT (PAGE 72)

SWEET SOYBEAN PASTE
(PAGE 88)

KUEY TEOW RICE NOODLES (PAGE 189)

CHINESE EGG NOODLES, COOKED, TOP; AND
UNCOOKED, BOTTOM (PAGE 189)

NYONYA SAMBAL
(PAGE 120)

GREEN MANGO SAMBAL
(PAGE 123)

LEMONGRASS AND SHALLOT
SAMBAL (PAGE 122)

JAVANESE SAMBAL
(PAGE 119)

CHOPPED VEGETABLE SALAD WITH COCONUT AND LIME LEAF DRESSING (PAGE 156)

GADO-GADO (PAGE 154)

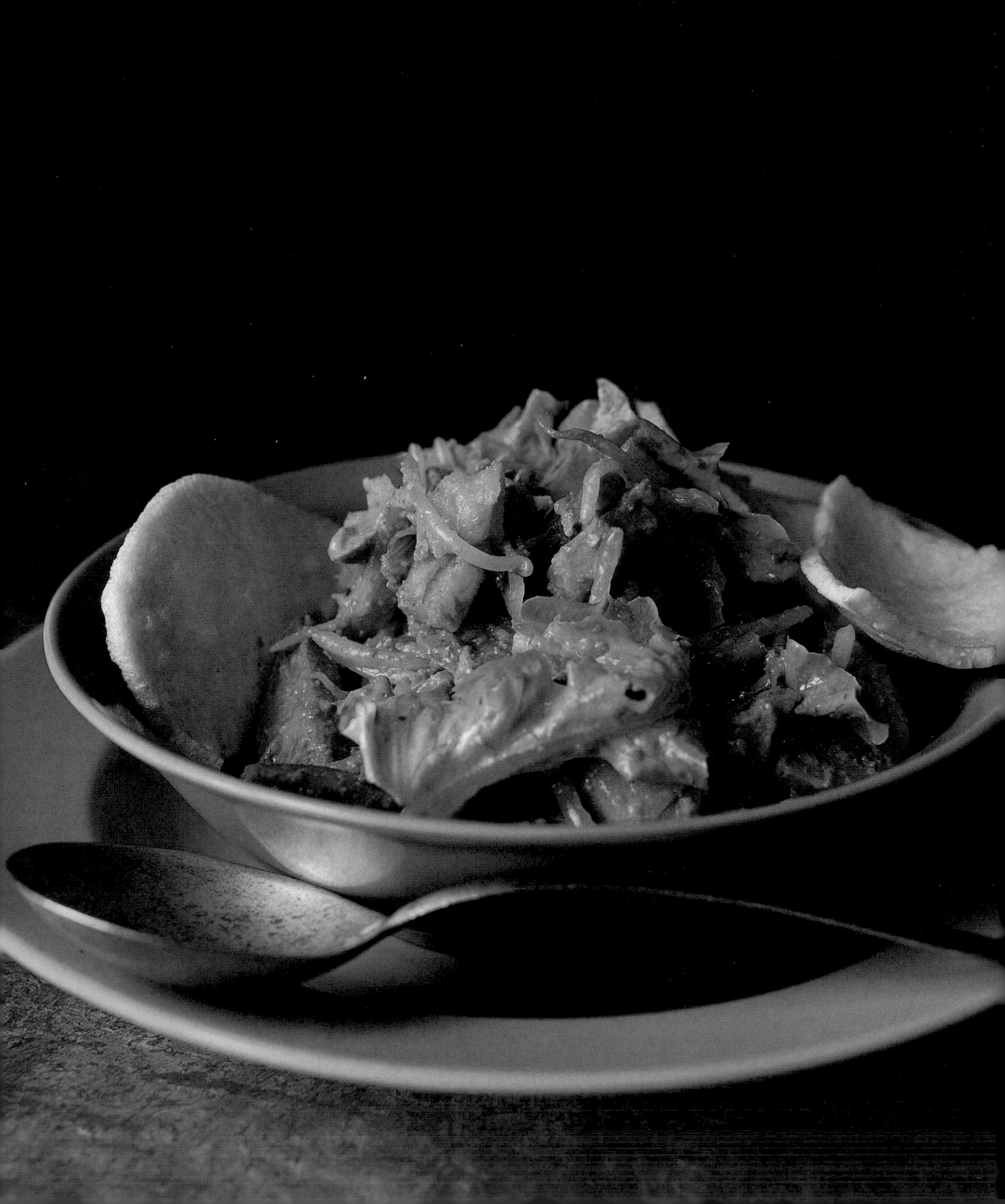

in the West. When fresh, the leaves are dark green and 3 to 4 inches (7.5 to 10 centimeters) long. When dry, they are brittle, crinkly, and a dusty silvery green. Both the fresh and dried leaves are used interchangeably in Indonesian kitchens. The *daun salam* tree is a member of the cassia family, and the spicy taste of the leaves reflects that connection. There is no substitute for *daun salam* leaves. If you can't find them, omit them from the recipe.

BUYING AND STORING: Chinese and Southeast Asian grocery stores sell dried *daun salam* leaves imported from Indonesia in small plastic bags clearly labeled Daun Salam—Indian Bay Leaves. (Don't be misled by the labeling; bay or laurel leaves are not a substitute.) Fresh *daun salam* leaves are unavailable in North America. Wayang, from Empire International in Pomona, California, is the most common brand. The leaves will keep for up to 2 years in a sealed plastic container or a glass jar in a cupboard.

DRIED SHRIMP
Udang kering (INDONESIA, MALAYSIA, AND SINGAPORE); *ha mai* (CANTONESE)

Dried shrimp are small whole shrimp harvested from the South China Sea and then sun dried. Usually headless and peeled, they're generally no larger than 1/2 inch (12 millimeters) long and provide a pleasingly briny undertone to dishes, especially those made by the Nyonyas of Malaysia and Singapore. Unless the recipe calls for finely ground dried shrimp, they need to be soaked in warm water for about 10 minutes to soften. Always thoroughly wash dried shrimp under cool running water before using them, as they're usually not cleaned before they're packaged.

BUYING AND STORING: Look for dried shrimp in all Asian markets in small plastic packages. You'll also find them sold in self-service bins in many Chinese supermarkets. Read the labels before you buy and select brands with a minimum of added colorings and preservatives. Choose shrimp that are pale pink to orange pink; bright pink indicates an excess of preservatives. As a rule, the higher the price, the purer—and the more subtle tasting—the shrimp will be. Though dried shrimp come in a range of grades and sizes, buy shrimp that are no longer than 3/4 inch (2 centimeters) for the recipes in this book. Larger specimens are likely to impart a strong fishy taste to dishes. Store dried shrimp in the freezer, tightly wrapped in plastic, foil, or inside a plastic container, for up to 1 year.

DRIED SHRIMP PASTE
Belacan (buh-LAH-chan; MALAYSIA); *trassi* (tuh-RAH-see; INDONESIA)

Dried shrimp paste is a firm, barely moist, pale pink to dark reddish brown paste made from tiny brine shrimp (not the larger-sized ones sold for eating). The shrimp are mixed with salt and allowed to ferment in earthenware crocks. The thick fermented paste that forms as the shrimp break down is then ground into a smoother paste and sun dried. The dried paste, which has the consistency of clay, is shaped into small rectangular blocks or round cylinders, which are again sun dried. Though it has a strong pungent smell and intensely "fishy" taste before it's cooked, dried shrimp paste becomes a delicate seasoning that recedes quietly into the background of dishes. It's never eaten uncooked, nor is it used in quantity. Usually no more than a teaspoon or two goes into most dishes, with the exception of some sambals.

To neutralize its strong flavor, Indonesian, Malaysian, and Singaporean cooks generally toast or sauté dried shrimp paste before they use it in flavoring pastes or sambals. Cooks in Indonesia accomplish this by placing a thin wad of the paste onto a bamboo skewer and roasting it over an open flame until its entire surface is lightly charred. An equally effective method—and the one I most often call for in the recipes in this book—is to wrap the dried shrimp paste in a small piece of aluminum foil, press it down with the palm of your hand to form a disk, and place the parcel directly onto a heat source (a gas flame works best, but an electric burner is fine). It's an easy technique, as long as you're careful to toast the paste and not burn it to a crisp. I've given detailed directions for doing this in each of the recipes that call for it.

BUYING, STORING, AND SUBSTITUTING: Small blocks of dried shrimp paste, usually 3 to 4 inches (7.5 to 10 centimeters) long and weighing 8 ounces (225 grams), are widely available in Chinese and Southeast Asian markets. They come wrapped in paper or plastic and are clearly labeled *belacan*, *belachan*, *trassi*, *terassi*, or some variation on these spellings. (Spelling can be maddeningly inconsistent on imported Asian ingredients!) The dried shrimp paste available to us in North America is usually from Malaysia. Store it tightly wrapped in plastic in the refrigerator, where it will keep for up to 6 months; its dryness and high salt content inhibit spoilage. In addition to keeping mine wrapped in plastic, I also place it in a plastic container to make sure its strong smell doesn't penetrate the other items in my refrigerator. Don't freeze dried shrimp paste, which destroys its texture.

If you can't find dried shrimp paste, the softer, moister Thai shrimp paste, *gapi*, which comes in small plastic containers clearly labeled shrimp paste, will do just fine. Toast it as you would dried shrimp paste. I'm often asked by students in my cooking classes whether they can substitute Thai or Vietnamese fish sauce. They can't. Fish sauce has radically different flavor characteristics.

FENNEL SEEDS

Foeniculum vulgare; *adas manis* (INDONESIA); *jintan manis* (MALAYSIA AND SINGAPORE)

Fennel seeds, an aromatic southern European spice with a taste that resembles licorice, found their way to Southeast Asia on the ships of ancient Arab spice traders. They're used in Indonesian, Malaysian, and Singaporean cooking to add a quietly sweet note to pickles, such as Malaysian Spiced Pineapple Pickle (page 136), and some curries. Always use whole fennel seeds, rather than ground fennel, which has none of the vivid taste. Look for greenish seeds: the greener the appearance, the fresher and more intense the flavor.

BUYING AND STORING: Purchase fennel seeds at quality supermarkets or from Bangladeshi, Indian, or Pakistani spice shops. Store them in an airtight plastic container in the refrigerator or freezer, where they'll keep well for up to 6 months.

FISH

Ikan (INDONESIA, MALAYSIA, AND SINGAPORE)

Fresh, sweet fish just harvested from the warm waters of the Pacific and Indian oceans that hug the coasts of Indonesia, Malaysia, and Singapore turn up at nearly every meal. The varieties used are myriad but nearly all of them have counterparts in North America. Among the most popular are snapper, tuna, and mackerel. Farm-raised freshwater fish, including carp, catfish, and tilapia, are also eaten, but with some reluctance, as cooks in the region don't find them as flavorful as saltwater fish. It's a matter of preference, of course, for all three fish are wonderfully succulent.

BUYING: You'll discover the freshest, cleanest, highest-quality fish in North America at the numerous fish markets tucked away on busy Chinatown streets. I'll be the first to admit that these markets can seem intimidating from the outside. With their raucous environments and wet, slick floors, they're the polar opposite of a serene trip to the fish vendor at an upscale supermarket. But the quality you'll find—and the rapid turnover that keeps that quality consistent—is worth any initial uncertainty you may feel. I tend to roam among three small New York Chinatown fish markets that are within a block of one another. One always seems to have the nicest snapper, another the best mackerel and kingfish, and the third the freshest tuna. I found the markets by accident. One afternoon I noticed that each of them was packed with shoppers, so I ventured into all three to see what was for sale. I've been going back to buy fish from these same vendors ever since.

Choosing fish in a Chinatown fish market is literally a hands-on affair. If you're a first timer, just follow other shoppers' leads, scrutinizing the colorful fish laid out on the icy display cases. Jump right in and pick through the fish as though you were selecting vegetables. Choose a whole, ungutted fish that looks as if it was just caught. The skin should be shiny and vivid, and the body should be intact and sound, without nicks, slashes, or blemishes. The eyes should be bulbous and clear, not sunken or cloudy. Lift the cheeks of the fish and peer underneath: the gills should be uniformly deep red and moist, with no signs of fading (a sure indication that the fish was caught days ago). Press your index finger into the thickest portion of the body: the flesh should feel firm and tense, not mushy. Take a deep whiff of the entire fish, head to tail: as a rule, it should smell sweet and appetizing and not the least bit fishy. Try to buy fish that hasn't been previously frozen, though it is difficult to know for sure unless you ask the vendor.

Ask your fish merchant to gut, scale, and clean the whole fish. Always make sure to request that he or she clip off the sharp, pointy fins, which can easily pierce the skin. Rinse the fish thoroughly under very cold running water as soon as you bring it home. If any scales or innards were missed, flake the scales off with a sharp knife and pull the innards out with your fingers. Cook all fish (including steaks and fillets) the same day you buy them, preferably within an hour or two after you return home, and always keep them cool before you cook them.

Whole fish are called for in most of the fish recipes in this book, though bone-in steaks and fillets can be substituted in nearly all cases (and I've given the appropriate substitutions when possible). Keep in mind, however, that using fillets may compromise the taste of the dish, as heads, tails, and bones lend deep flavor to curries, soups, and stews. Also, the freshness of steaks and fillets is harder to determine. When buying them, make sure that their surfaces are moist and not discolored. Give them the same sniff test that you give whole fish.

The following varieties will work best for the recipes in this book:

COMMON MACKEREL *Ikan kembong* (INDONESIA, MALAYSIA, AND SINGAPORE)
A stubby, silvery Atlantic and Pacific fish with green, blue, and/or gray splotches running along its length. Common mackerel are generally available whole; they're usually no more than 18 inches (45 centimeters) long, weighing roughly 2 pounds (900 grams). They have an assertively fishy taste and dark, oily flesh that works well in brightly seasoned curries.

KINGFISH *Ikan tenggiri* (INDONESIA, MALAYSIA, AND SINGAPORE)
Not to be confused with common mackerel, Atlantic and Pacific kingfish, also known as Spanish mackerel, has gorgeous silvery skin that's sometimes punctuated with a thin, yellow stripe running horizontally down the center of both sides. Most of the kingfish available are quite large—up to 3 feet (90 millimeters) long and more than 10 pounds (4.5 kilograms), sometimes even larger—so you'll usually be buying steaks or a portion of a whole fish. Whole fish weighing about 4 pounds (1.8 kilograms) are occasionally available; buy them when you see them. This fish has a sweet, delicate taste that many (including me) prefer to common mackerel.

ROCK COD
When I lived in California, these were my favorite locally harvested fish. Resembling snappers (though a bit shorter and stubbier), fish from the rock cod family thrive in the cool Pacific

waters off the West Coast. Their skin ranges in color from grayish to golden to pink (or a combination of all three colors). Another thing that easily distinguishes rock cods from snappers is their eyes: they are bulbous and surrounded by a circular air sack, not recessed into the head. The flesh of rock cods is sweet and delicate and well suited for use in curries, soups, and stews, rather than for panfrying (it tends to fall apart). Select rock cods that are about 18 inches (45 centimeters) long and weigh 2 to 2 1/2 pounds (900 grams to 1.1 kilograms).

SNAPPER *Ikan merah* (INDONESIA, MALAYSIA, AND SINGAPORE)
Snappers, which are commonly harvested from both Atlantic and Pacific waters, are often (but not always) red, have long, lean bodies, and boast sweet meat that's excellent in most of the fish recipes in this book. Look for small fish (which will be more tender) that are about 2 feet (60 centimeters) long and weigh about 3 pounds (1.4 kilograms); you'll need a slightly shorter one to make Grilled Whole Fish with Lemon Basil and Chiles (page 256).

TILAPIA
This squat, usually farm-raised freshwater fish is generally no longer than 18 inches (45 centimeters) and weighs about 2 pounds (900 grams). The varieties of tilapia available in fish markets are green and/or silver. They have light flesh and a sweet, subtle taste that's excellent in many of the fish recipes in this book. Seek whole fish, not fillets, as the freshness of the latter is more difficult to judge.

TUNA
Tuna is a word of Indonesian and Malaysian origin, and the fish is extremely popular in both countries. Pacific yellowfin is the variety most commonly available in our markets, but Pacific bluefin is by far the tastiest. Both are usually available in preskinned fillets, not as a whole fish or as bone-in steaks. Tuna fillets have almost always been in the deep freeze, so don't bother searching for fresh specimens. Look for glossy, deep burgundy fillets that contain streaks of fat. They'll taste far better than the pale, fatless tuna fillets generally used in sushi.

GALANGAL

Alpinia galanga; *laos* (INDONESIA); *lengkuas* (MALAYSIA AND SINGAPORE); *lan jiang* (CANTONESE)

Galangal, a knobby rhizome (underground stem) related to ginger, is one of Southeast Asia's most beloved aromatics. It was a popular dried ingredient in European cooking until the eighteenth century, but mysteriously fell out of favor. It has thin, pale yellow skin punctuated by brown concentric rings and pithy pink shoots erupting from its sides (cut off the shoots before using the galangal, as they have little flavor). The flesh is creamy white and very firm—much firmer than ginger. The taste is pleasantly woodsy, with subtle notes of pine-tree sap (the Latin name for the genus to which galangal belongs, *Alpinia*, alludes to this). Ground up in flavoring pastes, sliced thinly, or used whole and bruised with the bottom of a glass measuring cup, it imparts an earthy pungency to countless savory dishes. It's particularly popular in the foods of Java, where it is native, and appears in everything from Caramelized Tempeh with Chiles (page 325) to marinades for fried chicken. It has a wonderful ability to heighten and intensify the flavors of heavily spiced dishes, such as Fragrant Fish Stew with Lime and Lemon Basil (page 240).

BUYING AND STORING: Use fresh or frozen galangal, never dried, which has little taste. If fresh or frozen is not available, omit it from the recipe. Luckily, fresh galangal is increasingly easy to find in Asian and specialty-food markets. Upscale supermarkets, such as Wegman's on the East Coast and Whole Foods all over the United States, now regularly stock it in their produce sections. Look for firm, bright knobs with no dark or slimy skin, both of which indicate spoilage. Store it in the refrigerator in a closed paper bag for up to 2 weeks. If you live in an area where locating fresh galangal is a challenge, buy it in quantity when you see it and freeze it. Its quality won't be noticeably compromised. Frozen galangal, usually imported from Thailand, makes a fine substitute for fresh. It's widely available in Chinese and Southeast Asian markets in small shrink-wrapped packages, usually tucked away in frozen storage bins along with other aromatic rhizomes such as turmeric. It comes in either whole chunks or slices 1/4 inch (6 millimeters) thick and will keep for up to 6 months in the freezer. Allow it to thaw before using.

GARLIC
Allium sativum; *bawang putih* (INDONESIA, MALAYSIA, AND SINGAPORE)

Garlic is an indispensable ingredient in the cuisines of Indonesia, Malaysia, and Singapore. Cooked, it lends flavor to nearly every curry and stew in the region; raw, it heightens the taste of sambals and salads; crisply fried, it adds richness to soups. (See the shallots entry, page 83, for directions on frying garlic, and see Crisp-Fried Shallots, page 84.) Though native to Central Asia, garlic is widely cultivated in the Malay Archipelago, where local varieties are generally smaller, sweeter, and milder than those we encounter in the West. Because of this, cooks there tend to be generous with the amount they use—it's not unusual to see as many as 15 cloves go into a flavoring paste. Always use the sweetest, mildest garlic you can find. A few cloves of stale, harsh-tasting garlic can skew the taste of an entire dish.

An important note: When a recipe calls for 1 clove garlic, use a medium-sized clove about 3/4 inch (2 centimeters) long and 1/2 inch (12 millimeters) wide. If the cloves you are using are larger than that, cut them down to this size. If they are smaller, use as many as you need to make up the size required.

To make quick work of peeling a garlic clove, place the unpeeled clove on a cutting board, trim the stem end off, and, using a fast, firm whack, smash it with the flat side of a knife. The skin will slip off easily.

BUYING AND STORING: Look for the smallest, firmest garlic heads you can find. Organic varieties from farmers' markets (generally available in the late summer and fall) will taste the sweetest and most delicate. Garlic with small cloves and purple-tinged skin tends to be more subtly flavored than white-skinned varieties. Don't buy bulbs that are sprouting, a sign that they're past their prime. Also, don't use elephant garlic, which is actually not garlic but a garlicky-tasting member of the leek family. Store garlic in a dry, cool place, such as a cupboard or a metal-lined onion-storage drawer, and try to use it within 1 week.

GINGER

Zingiber spp.; *jahe* (INDONESIA); *halia* (MALAYSIA AND SINGAPORE)

Ginger, a rhizome (underground stem) believed to be native to the Malay Archipelago, is one of the region's most essential ingredients. It adds zesty freshness to countless foods, sweet and savory alike. Two commonly available but botanically different varieties can be used interchangeably in the recipes in this book: "old" and "young" ginger, names that refer not to age but type. Old ginger, the one we see in most supermarkets, is dusty beige and has thick skin, sinewy flesh, and an earthier, hotter taste. Young ginger (also known as stem ginger) is thin skinned and light yellow, with pinkish collars of leaf sheaths at the base of new shoots. It's sweeter than old ginger, and its flesh is more tender and juicy, making it easier to slice and pulverize. Both varieties should be peeled with a knife or vegetable peeler before using (some Southeast Asian cooks use the edge of a spoon to peel ginger, a technique I find ineffective). When prepping ginger, young or old, for a flavoring paste, slice it as thinly as possible against the grain of sinew that runs through it. Large chunks may result in strands of sinew that no food processor can grind up.

Many of the recipes in this book for curries, soups, stews, braises, and desserts call for bruising a piece of peeled ginger with a blunt object, such as the bottom of a glass measuring cup, until it is cracked open and juicy (a similar technique is used for galangal and lemongrass). Remove the piece of ginger before serving the dish.

BUYING AND STORING: The enormous popularity of ginger means it can be found fresh almost anywhere vegetables are sold, but the quality will be higher at markets catering to an Asian clientele. Most of the ginger in North American markets is cultivated year-round in always-temperate Hawaii, so there are no seasons for it. When buying either old or young ginger, look for a good-sized "hand" (a whole piece that extends into several smaller nubs). It should be heavy for its size and have smooth, taut skin with a subtle sheen. Never buy a lightweight, wrinkly piece, indications it has been sitting on the shelf too long. The best way to store ginger is in a closed paper bag, which will inhibit moisture from developing, in the vegetable bin of the refrigerator. It should keep for at least 2 weeks.

INDONESIAN SWEET SOY SAUCE
Kecap manis (keh-CHOP mah-NEESE; INDONESIA, MALAYSIA, AND SINGAPORE)

Sweet soy sauce is hugely popular in the cooking of Indonesia and, to a lesser extent, Malaysia and Singapore. (The word *kecap*, by the way, is derived from the Cantonese *koe-chiap*, or "sauce," from which we get the word *ketchup*. It was probably handed over by traders from southern China who long ago traveled extensively in the Indonesian islands.) This dark brown infusion of palm sugar and soy sauce has the consistency of honey and an enticing sweet-salty taste. Cooks use it in marinades and to flavor stews, but its main purpose is as a table condiment and dipping sauce. Indonesian sweet soy sauce mixed with sliced red chiles and lime juice, called *sos kecap rawit* (page 125), is a ubiquitous condiment. But even served by itself, it's delicious, especially when drizzled over fried rice and egg dishes. Because it was hard to find in North America prior to the 1980s, Indonesian cookbooks published during those years, such as Time-Life's excellent *Recipes: Pacific and Southeast Asian Cooking* from their Foods of the World series recommended making Indonesian sweet soy sauce from scratch by simmering together soy sauce and palm sugar or brown sugar until the mixture reached a syrupy thickness. (There's no tradition of this in Indonesia, where the ingredient is bought in bottles at the market.) Because of its widespread availability now, this is no longer necessary.

BUYING AND STORING: Look for 620-milliliter bottles (they are seldom marked in fluid ounces, though they hold about 20) in Chinese or Southeast Asian markets in sections that feature soy sauces or Indonesian products. The two most commonly available brands, both imported from Indonesia, are Cap Bango and ABC. Cap Bango, which has an illustration of a pelican on the label (apparently for no other reason than it is a pretty bird), is purer and more delicious. It contains no preservatives or flavorings and delivers a richer, more complex taste, with hints of smoke and honey. Store Indonesian sweet soy sauce as you would soy sauce: in a cool, dark place, such as a cupboard. It will keep indefinitely without refrigeration, but should be replaced after 2 years.

JAPANESE EGGPLANTS

Solanum spp.; *terung* (INDONESIA, MALAYSIA, AND SINGAPORE)

What we call Japanese eggplants (or, occasionally, Chinese or Asian eggplants) are actually many different species of eggplants, all native to India. They are long, slender, thin skinned, and lilac to dark purple, and vary in size from 3 to 9 inches (7.5 to 23 centimeters) long and 1 to 2 inches (2.5 to 5 centimeters) in diameter. I look for the lilac-skinned variety because it tends to have a sweeter taste, more tender skin, a more buttery texture, and fewer (and smaller) seeds. All Japanese eggplants are less bitter than their larger kin, so there's no need to salt them in advance to purge them of bitterness. In Malaysia and Singapore, eggplant is often deep-fried until tender before it's added to curries shortly before serving. Cooks believe that this step prevents the eggplants from becoming mushy.

BUYING AND STORING: Look for Japanese eggplants at farmers' markets during the summer months, as well as year-round at reliable produce vendors and all Asian markets. Select specimens that are firm and heavy for their size. The skin should be taut, shiny, and free of blemishes. Store them in a plastic bag in the refrigerator. Depending on their freshness, Japanese eggplants will keep for up to 4 days.

KAFFIR LIME LEAVES

Citrus hystrix; *daun jeruk purut* (INDONESIA); *daun limau purut* (MALAYSIA AND SINGAPORE)

Kaffir lime leaves are from a short, squat citrus tree native to Southeast Asia. They are a signature aromatic in Indonesian, Malaysian, and Singaporean dishes. Used fresh and whole (never dried), they lend citrusy undertones to stews, curries, and braises, especially those made with coconut milk, such as all the *rendang* recipes in this book and Padang Fish Curry (page 244) from West Sumatra, Indonesia. They are finely shredded or pulverized and added for their fresh taste to vegetable and rice salads, such as Herbal Rice Salad (page 186), and also used as a garnish. *Purut* (stomach), the local name for the fruit (whose juice and rind also finds its way into dishes, none of which are in this book), refers to its knobbly, bumpy skin, which resembles a stomach.

Kaffir lime leaves are easy to identify. Glossy and dark green, they are fat, oval, and have 2 lobes, which give them an hourglass shape. When a recipe calls for a "whole" kaffir lime leaf, use a leaf with both lobes intact. If the leaf is broken in half, use 2 lobes. Most home cooks in Indonesia, Malaysia, and Singapore don't bother to buy kaffir lime leaves. Almost every kitchen I've ever been in, from high-rise flats in Singapore to rural homes in the Spice

Islands, has a pot with a small kaffir lime tree growing somewhere nearby. When a dish calls for the leaves, the cook plucks as many she needs.

BUYING AND STORING: Kaffir lime trees are now cultivated in California and Florida to meet a growing demand for the leaves. Many Chinese and Southeast Asian markets stock fresh or frozen leaves; some specialty supermarkets carry them as well. Fresh leaves come in small plastic bags or containers in the vegetable section. Select leaves that look tender and are deep green and glossy; avoid those that have blemishes, bruises, or dry or yellow spots.

Frozen kaffir lime leaves are tucked away in Chinese and Southeast Asian supermarkets in the freezer compartment, near other aromatics such as galangal and turmeric. Look for leaves that aren't too encrusted with ice crystals, a sure sign that they've been in and out of the deep freeze a few times, losing flavor each time.

Fresh leaves can be stored in a tightly closed paper bag in the refrigerator for 10 days, or in a zip-lock plastic bag in the freezer for up to 6 months. When frozen, they'll retain much of their flavor, though they'll turn a deep, dull shade of forest green. Thaw them for a minute or two before using them in a recipe. When you find fresh leaves, buy more than you need and freeze the rest. It's always a game of culinary roulette as to whether your local vendor will have the leaves on hand the next time you need them.

Unless you have no choice, don't substitute dried kaffir lime leaves for fresh or frozen. They lack aroma and flavor.

LEMON BASIL

Ocimum spp.; *daun kemangi* or *daun selasih* (INDONESIA, MALAYSIA, AND SINGAPORE)

Fresh lemon basil, native to tropical Asia, has an exquisite, intensely lemony fragrance, which is why cooks in Indonesia, Malaysia, and Singapore favor it over other Asian basil varieties. It adds citrusy-floral notes to all manner of dishes, such as Grilled Whole Fish with Lemon Basil and Chiles (page 256), Fragrant Fish Stew with Lime and Lemon Basil (page 240), and Chopped Vegetable Salad with Coconut and Lime Leaf Dressing (page 156), a Javanese staple that calls for handfuls of the fresh herb. Only the leaves and flowers are used in most dishes; the stems are usually too tough to eat. Sometimes a whole stem is used to season a dish as it cooks; the stem isn't meant to be eaten, though it can remain in the dish when it's served.

BUYING, STORING, AND SUBSTITUTING: Lemon basil, distinguishable from other varieties by its citrusy fragrance, pale green leaves, and softly fuzzy stems, is becoming increasingly available. Check farmers' markets in mid- to late summer, specialty supermarkets that stock a comprehensive selection of fresh herbs, and some Southeast Asian markets. (I buy mine year-round from a Thai purveyor near my New York apartment; in Thai cooking, it is known as *bai maenglak*.) Look for young, full, perky bunches that aren't weighed down with buds or flowers (those are more mature and, hence, not as sweet and tender). Avoid wilted leaves and those with brown spots. Unfortunately, lemon basil doesn't keep well for longer than 3 days. Refrigerate it in a securely closed plastic bag filled with air gathered by swinging the bag quickly from side to side.

The dark green, anise-scented, purple-stemmed basil used in Thai and Vietnamese cooking, known, somewhat confusingly, as Asian or Thai basil, can be substituted. It is an easy-to-find herb in the vegetable sections of Chinese and Southeast Asian markets. But truthfully, all basil varieties make good substitutes, including Italian sweet basil, opal basil, and cinnamon basil. The character of the dish will differ slightly, but will be no less delicious.

LEMONGRASS

Cymbopogon citratus; *sereh* (INDONESIA); *serai* (MALAYSIA AND SINGAPORE)

Lemongrass, native to the Indonesian islands, is a staple in the cooking of the Malay Archipelago, its luscious flavor the secret behind countless savory and sweet dishes. It's used two ways: finely chopped and ground into flavoring pastes; and as a whole stalk bruised, tied into a knot, and added to a dish as it cooks, infusing its essence in the same way that a bouquet garni seasons a French braise. (See below for instructions on how to tie lemongrass into a knot.) The citrusy flavor of lemongrass comes from its high concentration of citral oil, which is also present in lemon rind. Lemongrass stalks are generally 1 1/2 to 2 feet (45 to 60 centimeters) long, pale green to ivory, and woody, with stiff bladelike leaves (though most of the leaf is usually removed by the time a stalk makes it to the market).

Always lop off the hard bottom inch (2.5 centimeters) or so of the stalk with a sharp chef's knife or cleaver before you use it, and peel away the tough and relatively tasteless 2 or 3 outer layers. If you're cutting lemongrass for a salad or plan to add it to a flavoring paste, use only the bottom 5 inches (13 centimeters) of the stalk, where most of the flavor is concentrated. In both instances, be sure to slice it as thinly (against the grain) as possible: lemongrass doesn't grind easily in a food processor, nor will it in your mouth.

BUYING AND STORING: Most Indonesian, Malaysian, and Singaporean cooks don't buy lemongrass at the market, but pluck it from a constantly replenishing plant somewhere close to their kitchen. For those of us not so lucky, whole stalks are now widely available in most upscale supermarkets, virtually all Chinese and Southeast Asian supermarkets, and often at farmers' markets, especially in late summer. Look for firm, thick, greenish white stalks with no wrinkles—the thicker the stalk, the tastier it will be. The stalks should show no signs of mildew or rot. To store, wrap the lemongrass in plastic and refrigerate for 2 to 3 weeks. If you aren't certain when you'll be using it, lemongrass can be frozen for up to 3 months. You can trim the top and bottom of the stalk so it fits more easily into the freezer.

TYING LEMONGRASS INTO A KNOT: Tying whole stalks into knots and adding them to dishes as they cook is an Indonesian technique that allows dishes to be subtly perfumed without being overwhelmed by the taste of lemongrass. To make a lemongrass knot, cut off the hard, brown bottom end of the stalk and an inch (2.5 centimeters) or so of its bristly, greenish top. Next, peel away the tough (and often discolored) outermost 2 or 3 sheaths of the stalk—just as if you were cleaning a leek of its outermost layers. Now, with a heavy, flat-surfaced object, such as the base of a knife handle or the bottom of a glass measuring cup, smack the stalk down its entire length until it is pliant and juicy but not pulverized. The goal is to bruise the stalk, not smash it to bits. Finally, tie the stalk into an overhand knot as tightly as you can without breaking it (though if you do break it, you can still use it). Remove the lemongrass knot before serving a dish, or leave it in for dramatic effect—it's up to you.

LIMES

Citrus spp.; *jeruk* (INDONESIA); *limau* (MALAYSIA AND SINGAPORE)

With scores of lime varieties grown in the region, it's no surprise that limes are used so often in Indonesian, Malaysian, and Singaporean cooking. Lime juice finds its way into marinades for fish and chicken, it's squeezed over cooked curries and stir-fries as a finishing note, and you'll encounter it as the base for sweet beverage syrups. It has an amazing ability to "de-fish" fish and seafood dishes and enliven dark, complex curries, such as Acehnese Goat Curry (page 314).

Kasturi limes (sometimes known by their Filipino name, *kalimansi*), popular in Indonesia, Malaysia, and Singapore, are occasionally available in North American Chinese and Southeast Asian markets. Green skinned and the size of large grapes, they have orange pulp and an irresistibly fragrant sour taste. Buy them when you see them and store as you would the slightly more astringent Persian limes, the most commonly available variety in North America. Or, extract the juice and store it in a plastic container in the freezer, where it will keep for up to 6 months. But for the recipes in this book, the juice of any lime variety will do.

LONG BEANS

Vigna spp.; *kacang panjang* (INDONESIA, MALAYSIA, AND SINGAPORE); *dau gok* (CANTONESE)

A relative of black-eyed peas, nutty-tasting long beans live up to their name, usually measuring about 18 inches (45 centimeters) long. While most green bean varieties are native to

Central America, long beans are native to Southeast Asia. They come in two varieties. The most common is dark green and has tight, firm flesh. The other, harder-to-find variety is pale green, with thicker, spongier flesh. (There is also a lovely purple variation of the pale green variety that's increasingly available in North American markets.) Cooks in Indonesia, Malaysia, and Singapore favor the pale green beans because they're slightly sweeter and their more porous skin absorbs flavors easier. Regular green beans are generally not a good substitute except for salads. Their skin is too thin and their water content is too high, which can result in a soggy dish. Before you cook long beans, trim off the tips with a sharp knife.

BUYING AND STORING: I find the freshest long beans in Chinese vegetable markets and from farmers' market vendors who sell Asian vegetables, especially in the late summer, when they're at the height of their North American season. Long beans are usually sold in bunches that contain 10 to 40 beans. Whether buying the pale green or dark green variety, look for plump and firm yet flexible beans without blemishes or wrinkly, soft skin. They shouldn't feel pithy or mealy; nor should the beans inside be very swollen (a mark of an overly mature long bean). Pay close attention to the tips: They should be plump, with no dryness or wrinkling, signs that they were picked some time ago. With your fingers, probe to the center of the bunch to make sure that the beans in the middle are as good as those on the outside. You don't need to consider the length of the beans when selecting a bunch. Shorter beans, perhaps only a foot (30 centimeters) long, are younger, but are not necessarily more flavorful or tender. Store them in a tightly closed paper or plastic bag in the refrigerator, where they will keep for up to 4 days.

NUTMEG
Myristica fragens; *pala* (INDONESIA); *buah pala* (MALAYSIA)

The Banda Islands of eastern Indonesia are the original home of nutmeg, the fragrant brown seed that was the focal point of centuries of global trade and conquest. Jan Huygen van Linschoten, a Dutchman who sailed with the first Portuguese expedition to Indonesia's Spice Islands in the fifteenth century, summed up the importance of this spice in his diary: "The nutmeg comforts the brain, sharpens the memory, warms and strengthens the maw, drives wind out of the body, makes a sweet breath, drives down urine, stops the laske [an old English term for mental imbalance], and to conclude is good against all cold diseases in the head, in the brain, the maw, the lice, and the matrice." He forgot to mention that it also tastes extraordinarily good.

Indonesian, Malaysian, and Singaporean cooks use nutmeg to add warmth and fragrance to curries, meat and vegetable dishes, and sweets and cakes. Even though the seeds are rock hard, they grind or grate easily. I use the finest grating surface of a cheese grater to grate mine, though you can also use a nutmeg mill or a Microplane grater. Cracked whole nutmegs are often added directly to stocks, in the style of a cinnamon stick, rather than being ground or grated, with the pieces removed before serving. (Use a nutcracker or a heavy, flat object, such as the bottom of a glass measuring cup, to crack one open.)

During Banda's nutmeg harvests (there are at least two per year that coincide with the onset of the island's rainy seasons), cooks use the firm, ripe yellow-skinned nutmeg fruit, which is intensely aromatic and tart in dishes. It's added to stews and curries for its acidity, and, best of all, it appears finely slivered in the chile-hot *sambal buah pala*. It is also candied and used to make a jam called *seleh pala*. Interestingly, mace, the vermilion webbing that encases nutmeg seeds, is rarely used in Indonesian, Malaysian, and Singaporean dishes, though it does find its way into some sweets, medicinal salves, and ointments.

BUYING AND STORING: Bandanese nutmeg—the world's most flavorful—is unavailable outside Indonesia. Most of what we find in North America has been grown in Madagascar and Grenada. Always buy whole nutmeg, never ground, for the richest flavor. The most aromatic is available from Bangladeshi, Indian, and Pakistani spice markets and specialty supermarkets. It should be stored tightly sealed in a plastic container in the refrigerator or freezer, where it will retain its flavor for up to 1 year. Store partially used nutmeg seeds the same way.

OILS

Minyak (INDONESIA, MALAYSIA, AND SINGAPORE)

Coconut oil is the traditional cooking oil in Indonesia, Malaysia, and Singapore. However, in recent years, because of health concerns about saturated fats, coconut oil is often replaced by locally produced nut and vegetable oils, such as peanut and canola. Though lacking in the rich taste of coconut oil, they have excellent properties of their own. In my own kitchen, peanut oil is my everyday favorite. It has a subtle, appetizingly peanutty fragrance and a neutral, clean taste that fades nicely into the background of dishes. Coconut oil, especially if not fresh, can taste oppressively strong and give dishes an unwanted heavy quality. Another plus with peanut oil, especially refined peanut oils such as Planters brand, is that it smokes only at very high temperatures, making it ideal for deep-frying meats, poultry, shallots, garlic, tofu, tempeh, and shrimp chips. Canola oil also has a high smoke point and subtle flavor, but I find that I'm the most consistently satisfied with peanut oil.

BUYING, STORING, AND SUBSTITUTING: Look for peanut oil in all supermarkets and Chinese and Southeast Asian markets. My favorite brand is Knife, a cold-pressed oil from Taiwan. It has a clean peanut aroma that dissipates when cooked, is of consistently high quality, and is only half the price of the more commonly available Planters and Hain brands (my second and third choices, respectively). The freshest and most pure-tasting canola and rapeseed oils are found in health-food stores and quality supermarkets. Avoid olive and corn oils; their flavors are too pronounced and can throw off the balance of seasonings in a dish, though a mild olive oil is acceptable, if inauthentic, for stir-frying Asian greens.

Store all oils in a cool, dark place and discard them after 6 months, as they can become rancid. Discard any oil that foams excessively when heated, a sign that it's not fresh. I always toss out all oils that I have used for deep-frying, with the exception of the oil used for deep-frying shallots or garlic (page 84). It has a subtle oniony taste and when used as a stir-frying oil, makes foods taste succulent. Store it in an airtight container in the refrigerator for up to 3 days.

PALM SUGAR

Gula jawa and *gula merah* (INDONESIA); *gula melaka* (MALAYSIA AND SINGAPORE)

Indonesian and Malaysian palm sugar—firm, deeply sweet, and reddish brown—is made from the boiled-down sap of the fruit of the sugar palm (*Arenga saccharifera*), a variety native to Java. In Indonesia the sugar is called *gula merah* (red sugar) or *gula jawa* (Javanese sugar), while in Malaysia and Singapore it's known as *gula melaka*, which refers to the city of Malacca, home of the most delicious Malaysian variety. This versatile ingredient is used extensively in sweets and desserts, such as Plantains with Coconut Milk and Palm Sugar (page 347), but its real appeal is in savory dishes such as Stir-fried Shrimp Sambal (page 262) and Chopped Vegetable Salad with Coconut and Lime Leaf Dressing (page 156), where its complex, caramel-like, subtly smoky taste balances saltiness, heat, and sourness. The sugar is usually sold in cylinders 2 to 3 inches (5 to 7.5 centimeters) in diameter, the shape the result of reducing the sap inside bamboo poles; it gets its smoky taste from the cooking fire used to process it. Indonesian and Malaysian palm sugar also comes in disks that are flat on one side and rounded on the other (an imprint of the halved coconut shells in which the sugar is processed).

Palm sugar is displayed in gooey, carefully arranged mounds in Indonesian, Malaysian, and Singaporean markets. I remember shopping one time with Rohati, a cooking friend in West Sumatra, Indonesia, in a market near her home. She needed palm sugar, so I thought I'd give her a hand choosing some. I found what I thought would be a good variety from a vendor—round and pure looking, each disk came wrapped in a plastic bag. "*Ado!*" Rohati said when she saw it, using an Indonesian exclamatory term. "That one is not nice. It was made in a factory in Jakarta." She immediately directed me toward a teetering pile of palm sugar in a large rattan basket. There was a small swarm of bees hovering around it. "This one is locally made in a village near here," she said. "It's the purest of all, and if it's good enough for the bees, it's good enough for me!"

Solid and with a moist but firm consistency, palm sugar is fairly easy to slice with a knife, but difficult to break apart with your fingers. Before adding it to dishes, always slice it as thinly as possible to ensure that it melts easily during cooking.

BUYING, STORING, AND SUBSTITUTING: Excellent Indonesian palm sugar can be found in Chinese and Southeast Asian markets in cylinders wrapped in paper or plastic and clearly labeled *gula jawa* or sometimes *arenga* sugar. Store palm sugar in a plastic container or tightly wrapped in plastic in a cool, dark, dry place, such as a cupboard. It will keep for up to 2 years. Over time it may lose much of its moisture and become rock hard, but you can still use it.

Palm sugars appear in markets throughout Southeast Asia and Africa but they are derived from sugar palms different from those in Indonesia and Malaysia. In India and Sri Lanka, palm sugar that comes from the *Phoenix sylvestris* sugar palm is known as jaggery. In Thailand, the sugar comes from yet another variety of sugar palm and is variously called *nam taan pep*, *nam taan bik*, and *nam taan mapraow*. As with wine, the flavors of palm vary radically with their place of origin. I'm partial to the variety from Java. With experimentation, you'll discover your own favorite.

Jaggery is probably the most readily available and the closest in taste to the palm sugar of Java. You'll find it in South Asian markets, sold in chunks of varying size and usually tightly wrapped in burlap sacks. *Piloncillo*, a minimally processed cane sugar, is also lovely. It's available in Mexican markets and comes in distinctive, easy-to-identify cylindrical cones or 4-inch (10-centimeter) disks. Other, milder-tasting Southeast Asian palm sugars, such as those used in Thailand and Vietnam, come in 2-inch (5-centimeter) disks or flat blocks the size of small chocolate bars, have a less complex flavor, and are usually light tan. A variety of moist Thai palm sugar comes in plastic jars; its taste is similar to the bar-shaped Thai sugar. Any of these sugars will work fine if Indonesian palm sugar is unavailable, and all of them should be stored in the same manner as the Indonesian sugar. In a pinch, even dark brown sugar, found in every supermarket, can be substituted for palm sugar, though it lacks its sophistication.

PALM VINEGAR

Cuka (INDONESIA, MALAYSIA, AND SINGAPORE)

Palm vinegar, made from the same fruit that yields palm sugar, shares the spotlight with tamarind and lime juice as a souring agent. West Sumatran and Malaccan cooks have a particular affinity for adding a splash of it to dishes, either toward the end of cooking or after they've been cooked. Its mild flavor adds surprising sweetness to foods such as Pan-Seared Mackerel with Chiles and Garlic (page 252).

BUYING, STORING, AND SUBSTITUTING: Most of the palm vinegar available in North America comes from the Philippines. It's available in tall, clear glass or white plastic bottles in either the vinegar section or the section devoted to Filipino foods in Chinese and Southeast Asian supermarkets. Identifiable by its cloudy, opaque appearance (at least when stored in a clear glass bottle), it resembles water with a few drops of cream added to it. My favorite brand is Datu Puti, imported from the Philippines by Southeast Asia Food, Inc. (Datu Puti sells a vinegar made from coconut water called coco vinegar, too. It's also mild tasting and milky white, comes in a clear glass bottle, and is an excellent second choice to palm vinegar.) Store palm vinegar in a cool, dark cupboard for up to 1 year.

If you can't find palm vinegar, all cider or white rice vinegars make fine substitutes. Don't substitute balsamic vinegar or any other wine vinegars, however. Their dark color (in the case of red wine vinegars) and winey, deeply fermented taste are inappropriate.

RICE

Nasi (cooked; INDONESIA, MALAYSIA, AND SINGAPORE);
beras (uncooked; INDONESIA, MALAYSIA, AND SINGAPORE)

This entry covers the kind of rice to use (and how much to buy) in North America. For a more detailed discussion of how rice is grown, cooked, and eaten in Indonesia, Malaysia, and Singapore, as well as how to use it in your own cooking, see pages 167 to 189. Of the countless types of white rice cultivated and eaten in Indonesia and Malaysia, the most favored for everyday cooking are varieties with a sweet aroma, a subtle taste, and long grains. Cooked correctly, they are pillowy and fluffy, with an unsticky surface. The grains gently hold together rather than clump, as opposed to the shorter-grained, stickier, glossy-surfaced rices of northern Thailand, Japan, and South Korea. They also soak up sauces better and are ideal for making fried rice and such salads as Herbal Rice Salad (page 186).

In North America, jasmine rice is most like the rices eaten in Indonesia, Malaysia, and Singapore. It is a fragrant, long-grain white rice primarily imported from Thailand. It's called jasmine for its mild floral scent, not its relationship to the flower. The variety I like best is Thai *hom mali*, a strongly scented jasmine hybrid developed in Thailand and widely available in Chinese and Southeast Asian markets and select supermarkets. The most fragrant, consistently high-quality brand of *hom mali* is Rice King, imported from Thailand in 10- and 20-pound (4.5- and 9-kilogram) bags. It's easy to identify: there are illustrations of two yellow-and-green rice stalks on both bags. The smaller bags are made of clear plastic; the larger ones are made of white plastic, with fabric woven through it to make the bags sturdier. I buy the 20-pound bags and store them in a cool cupboard; each one usually lasts me (a big rice eater) about 3 months. Another good brand, also imported from Thailand and widely available in Chinese and Southeast Asian markets, is Elephant, identifiable by the charging elephant depicted on the bag. Any jasmine rice will do, though. As with canned coconut milk, which to choose is a matter of personal preference. Experience has taught me that it's best to buy jasmine rice from Chinese or Southeast Asian markets, where the selection is the greatest and the turnover is high. But I also fancy the very good organic jasmine rice grown in California that's available in self-service bins at Whole Foods markets and many health-food stores. I avoid the small boxes of jasmine rice available at select supermarkets, however. They tend to be exorbitantly priced and not particularly fresh. There are no hard rules when selecting rice except one: check expiration dates whenever possible. Fresher rice yields fluffier results; stale, old rice—that is, rice more than a year old—cooks up stiff and occasionally has an "off" fragrance and taste. Not every bag of rice comes with an expiration date, however, which is another reason why you want to buy rice from stores with a rapid turnover.

Store all rice tightly sealed in the bag that it came in or in an airtight plastic or metal container in a cool, dark place, such as a cupboard. Replace what you haven't eaten after a year.

SALT

Garam (INDONESIA, MALAYSIA, AND SINGAPORE)

The most commonly used salt in Indonesia, Malaysia, and Singapore is pure, unrefined sea salt harvested from the thousands of miles of coastline that surround those countries' shores. Good cooks there know that salt is a critical ingredient—the unspoken backbone of nearly every savory dish. There are at least five distinct grades of unrefined sea salt popularly used in kitchens for different culinary purposes. Robust-tasting *garam bata*, for instance, which comes in small bricks, is excellent for use in pickles, while *garam meja*, or table salt, is best for the final seasoning of a dish. Familiarize yourself with the many wonderful, nuanced varieties of salt available in your favorite market. Don't just settle for iodized table salt, which, to my mind, makes foods taste tinny and aggressively salty. I primarily use two varieties in my own kitchen: kosher salt and finely ground sea salt. I tested all of the recipes in this book using kosher salt, a light, coarse-grained salt that lends dishes a clean, delicate saltiness. My favorite brand is Diamond Crystal, widely available in supermarkets. It has a wonderfully fluffy texture that causes the grains to melt into foods almost instantaneously.

South Korean sea salt, a pure, mineral-rich salt that enlivens dishes with its subtle taste, is my second choice. It is widely available in Asian markets (though obviously you're going to find the largest selection in markets that cater to a South Korean clientele). The brand I've used most often is Haitai, which comes in 3-pound (1.4-kilogram) clear-plastic bags and is good for everything from seasoning curries to making pickles. Because it contains no anticaking agents, it tends to clump up, especially in humid environments. You can easily break up the clumps with your fingers before adding the salt to any dish. All South Korean sea salts—and indeed all sea salts—are denser than kosher and table salts. A tablespoon of Haitai sea salt, for instance, is roughly equivalent by weight to 4 teaspoons Diamond Crystal kosher salt, so you'll need to use less.

SHALLOTS

Allium ascolonicum; bawang merah (INDONESIA, MALAYSIA, AND SINGAPORE)

Shallots, not onions, figure prominently in Indonesian, Malaysian, and Singaporean dishes (onions are generally thought to be too harsh, though they do show up in a few Malaysian and Singaporean dishes, even some in this book). They grow especially well in the region's cool volcanic highlands, such as the ring of mountains that surround Bandung, one of West Java's main cities. Cooks use shallots in flavoring pastes, thinly slice them into salads, and deep-fry them for sprinkling over stir-fries, soups, and curries. The shallots in the Malay Archipelago include any number of oval-shaped varieties roughly 1 1/2 inches (4 centimeters) long. They have pink, coppery skin and usually come in clusters of 2 or 3 bulbs attached to a single root. Their flesh is pink and white.

Here, we have two choices of shallots: small Asian types that are nearly identical to those in Southeast Asia, and the larger, commonly available European variety, which have roughly the same appearance but are more elongated. The small Asian types are milder, more aromatic, and sweeter than the European varieties, which are often forcefully oniony. Both, though, will work fine for the recipes in this book. (You'll probably find, however, that the Asian variety deep-fries slightly better because its flesh contains less moisture.)

To peel shallots, start by trimming off the top and base with a sharp knife, as you would an onion. Next, make a shallow, narrow cut down the length of the shallot through its papery skin. Finally, peel away and discard the skin and first layer or two of the shallot.

An important note: When measuring both Asian and European shallots for a recipe, each shallot should be roughly 1 1/3 inches (3.5 centimeters) long by 1 inch (2.5 centimeters) wide, or about the size of a large garlic clove, and weigh 1/2 to 3/4 ounce (15 to 20 grams). If the shallot you are using is larger, cut it to approximate this size. In my recipes, I have included both the number of shallots and their total weight, as weight is the most reliable measuring method.

BUYING AND STORING: Asian shallots, widely available from Chinatown produce vendors and Chinese and Southeast Asian supermarkets, are usually sold in 8-ounce (225-gram) plastic-mesh bags. They're available year-round, but are best when freshly harvested, from midsummer to early fall. Look for bright, shiny bulbs with no signs of rot, mold, or sprouting tops (indicators of spoilage and age). Squeeze them: they should be quite firm and have no soft spots. European shallots are usually sold in bulk. The best come from farmers' markets in the late summer and early fall. Store both varieties inside a paper bag in a cool, dark place, such as a cupboard or a metal-lined onion-storage drawer. Asian shallots tend to spoil more rapidly than European ones. You'll probably have to replace them after 2 weeks.

CRISP-FRIED SHALLOTS

These crisp shallots garnish all manner of savory dishes. Though they do lend subtle texture, their main role is as a flavor enhancer. Cooks sprinkle them on soups, curries, and stir-fries, where they impart a smoky note. A key to making them perfectly is to remove them from the cooking oil the moment they turn uniformly golden. If you leave them in even for a moment longer, they'll overcook and taste bitter. Keep in mind that they continue to darken and crisp for up to 30 seconds after you take them out. Another key is to cut the shallots as thinly as possible. For best results, they should be paper-thin. Also, use a small saucepan. You'll need less oil than if you use a larger pan, and small batches are easier to monitor. You may need to try this recipe a few times before you master it. Store any unused fried shallots in a tightly sealed jar in the refrigerator for up to 1 week.

You can thinly slice garlic cloves lengthwise and fry them in the same way. Garlic slices will take slightly less time to turn golden.

MAKES ABOUT 1 CUP (1 1/2 OUNCES/40 GRAMS)

Peanut oil for frying

7 shallots (about 6 ounces/170 grams), cut lengthwise into paper-thin slices

1. Pour oil to a depth of 1 inch (2.5 centimeters) into a 1 1/2-quart (1.5-liter) saucepan. Don't be tempted to add more oil, or it might bubble up over the edge of the saucepan when the shallots are added. Heat the oil over medium to medium-high heat until hot but not smoking (about 365°F/185°C). To test if the temperature is right, drop in a shallot slice. If it begins to froth and fry immediately, the oil is ready.

2. Add as many of the shallot slices as will fit comfortably in the pan, making sure that they have plenty of room to fry. Using a slotted spoon, move the shallots around in the

oil constantly with a gently undulating motion just until they begin to turn a uniform light gold, 2 to 3 minutes; the timing will depend on how thin the slices are and how hot the oil is. (The oil will be quite frothy at first because of the moisture in the shallots, and then less so as the shallots cook.) You may need to adjust the heat periodically: you don't want the shallots to sit limply in the oil (a sign that the oil is too cool) or fry so aggressively that they pick up burned spots (a sign that the oil is too hot).

3. The moment the shallots are ready, remove them from the oil with the slotted spoon and drain them on paper towels. At first they'll appear slightly soggy and limp, but they'll crisp up after a minute or two. Repeat with the remaining shallots.

SHRIMP

Udang (INDONESIA, MALAYSIA, AND SINGAPORE)

Shrimp are the most popular shellfish in Indonesia, Malaysia, and Singapore, where they are fantastically fresh and sweet tasting. Cooks celebrate this sweetness in curries, stir-fries, and grilled dishes. Shrimp are almost invariably left unpeeled for cooking, as the heads and shells are thought to impart rich flavor to dishes. Unpeeled shrimp also hold their shape better when stir-fried. Don't use the large, gray-shelled farm-raised tiger shrimp for most of the recipes in this book (the exception is Shrimp Satay, page 150). Instead, use sea-harvested pink or white varieties from the Gulf of Mexico (usually called Gulf shrimp by North American fish vendors), which are more tender and flavorful.

BUYING: Although vendors usually advertise their shrimp as fresh, most shrimp available in North America—even wild Gulf shrimp—have been frozen and thawed. Luckily, frozen shrimp are nearly identical to unfrozen in taste and texture. Seek medium-sized unpeeled shrimp, preferably with their heads intact, no more than 3 inches (7.5 centimeters) long. Purchase your shrimp from high-quality fish vendors; Chinatown fish markets are my favorite. (See the Fish entry in this chapter, page 67, for more information about shopping at Chinatown fish markets.) Other good sources for shrimp are upscale supermarkets and online vendors. Always select bright, glistening specimens with no "fishy" odor. Avoid Gulf shrimp with black spots on their shells, a sign of spoilage. (Do not worry about black spots on tiger shrimp; they are often part of their natural shell pattern.) Also avoid shrimp with dry spots, which can indicate freezer burn. Ideally, cook the shrimp you buy as soon as you bring them home. If that isn't possible, use them within a day of purchase. Thawed shrimp don't store well.

SHRIMP CHIPS

Krupuk udang (INDONESIA, MALAYSIA, AND SINGAPORE)

Shrimp chips in Indonesia are not the multicolored novelty food they are in the West, and they're never served as an appetizer. Instead, they are used as a crunchy topping for such savory dishes as Gado-Gado (page 154) and Javanese Fried Rice (page 183), and they're eaten whenever a diner wants to add a crunchy note to the meal. Made of dried shrimp, tapioca flour, eggs, sugar, and salt, shrimp chips are thin, flat, hard disks when unfried. When deep-fried, they puff up to three times their original size, becoming curvy and fantastically crunchy. (The Indonesian name *krupuk* is onomatopoeic for the sound they make when eaten.) The first time I watched Inam, the Alwi family's Jakarta cook, fry up a batch of shrimp chips, I felt like I was observing something magical as the chips puffed from their dry state to swollen crispness in the hot oil.

BUYING AND STORING: The best shrimp chips are imported from Indonesia. They're pale pink, with occasional darker striations of dried shrimp, and you'll find them in plastic bags labeled *krupuk udang,* or a similar spelling, in the Indonesian section of Chinese and Southeast Asian supermarkets. My favorite shrimp chips are made by Nyonya Siok, based in Java. They are pure and subtle tasting. (Also look for fish chips and garlic chips, delightful Indonesian relatives of shrimp chips that are cooked in the same fashion.) Avoid artificially colored, multihued chips from Vietnam or China (the kind often served with Peking duck in Chinese restaurants). Though fun to look at, they possess none of the sophisticated, pure taste of the Indonesian version.

Store unfried shrimp chips tightly wrapped in plastic (or the bag they came in) and they'll keep indefinitely. There's one caveat, however: the drier the shrimp chip, the more readily it will puff up. If shrimp chips have been stored in a humid environment, they'll have likely absorbed moisture and not puff to their full glory. To remedy this, place them on a baking sheet in an oven heated to 200°F (120°C) for 2 to 3 minutes to dry them out before deep-frying them.

FRIED SHRIMP CHIPS

Deep-frying shrimp chips at home is easy. Although you can use a wok or a skillet, I find that a 1 1/2-quart (1.5-liter) saucepan works best. Its small interior means that you'll need less oil, and because you should fry only a few chips at a time, a small pan is perfect. Be careful not to overcook the chips. They should be uniformly pale beige, not golden or singed with brown edges, and have no unpuffed, undercooked portions. Once shrimp chips start expanding, they do so simultaneously and within seconds. For this reason, cook no more than 2 chips at a time. Cooking more will be difficult if not impossible to manage and some will undercook, while others will burn. Remove them from the cooking oil the instant they have completely swelled to prevent them from overcooking. Shrimp chips are best if eaten within a few hours of being fried, as they go stale quickly. Store any that you don't eat right away in an airtight container at room temperature for up to 3 days.

Peanut oil for frying　　　　　　　　　　　**Shrimp chips**

1. Pour oil to a depth of 1 inch (2.5 centimeters) into a 1 1/2-quart (1.5-liter) saucepan and place over medium to medium-high heat until hot but not smoking. To test if the oil is the right temperature (it should be about 365°F/185°C), drop in a shrimp chip; it should begin to twist and expand within a few seconds.

2. Using a pair of tongs or 2 forks, add 2 shrimp chips to the oil. Using the tongs or forks, continuously turn the chips until they contort and puff up completely and no hard portions remain, 15 to 30 seconds. The timing will depend on the heat of the oil and the size and dryness of the chips. If the chips begin to scorch, your oil is too hot. Either remove the pan from the heat or reduce the heat for a few moments until the oil has returned to a good frying temperature.

3. When the chips are ready, immediately transfer them to paper towels to drain. Repeat with the remaining shrimp chips.

SOY SAUCE

Kecap (INDONESIA, MALAYSIA, AND SINGAPORE)

Soy sauce, invented in China thousands of years ago and used for centuries in the cuisines of Indonesia, Malaysia, and Singapore, is made from fermented roasted soybean meal and ground wheat. I call for two kinds of soy sauce in this book. The first is referred to simply as soy sauce. Not to be confused with "lite" soy sauce (which is usually reduced-salt soy sauce), it's primarily used in stir-fries and, occasionally, as a component in dressings. The second is double-black soy sauce, which has been aged longer and mixed with a small quantity of molasses. It's black-brown, has a deeper, more robust flavor than regular soy sauce, and imparts an appetizing light brown tint and a subtly caramelized taste to dishes. (Black soy sauce is a lighter grade than double-black; I prefer the latter.)

BUYING AND STORING: Buy your soy sauce from Asian vendors—you'll have more to choose from—and look for brands containing a minimum of additives. The best are imported from China. My preference for regular soy sauce is the additive-free Pearl River Bridge Superior Soy Sauce, which has a lush full-bodied aroma and taste. It comes in tall glass bottles. Other brands, such as Ho Ho, also imported from China, mimic the labeling of Pearl River Bridge brand but tend to contain preservatives. Kikkoman, a Japanese-style soy sauce (meaning that it's made with more wheat and fewer soybeans), is available in virtually every supermarket. While the quality of Kikkoman's soy sauce is high, it contains the preservative sodium benzoate and is a bit too salty for my taste.

My favorite brand of double-black soy sauce is Koon Chun, a rich, dense product from Hong Kong with a wonderfully pure taste. It comes in squat glass bottles.

Though soy sauce will keep indefinitely in a cool, dark cupboard, it should be replaced after 2 years.

STAR ANISE

Illicium verum; *bunga lawang* (INDONESIA, MALAYSIA, AND SINGAPORE); *baht gook* (CANTONESE)

Star anise, the dried flower of an evergreen tree originally from China, resembles an eight-pointed star, with hard, brown, canoe-shaped sections that contain a shiny tan seed. The aroma and flavor of star anise are pungent and sweet, with intense licorice notes. Though it contains anethole, the same essential oil as that found in aniseeds, the two are not related. Ground star anise is a key ingredient in five-spice powder, the celebrated spice mixture of southern China, but in Indonesia, Malaysia, and Singapore the whole spice is usually used. It is added to meat and poultry dishes, soups, and curries and removed before the dish is served.

BUYING AND STORING: Most of the whole star anise available in North America comes from China. It's sold in plastic bags in Bangladeshi, Indian, and Pakistani spice markets; specialty supermarkets; and in the spice sections of Chinese markets. Purchase star anise with a strong fragrance. You should be able to smell it slightly through the wrapper. Store it tightly sealed in a plastic container in the refrigerator or freezer, where it will remain flavorful for up to 1 year.

SWEET SOYBEAN PASTE

Tauco (tauw-CHO; INDONESIA, MALAYSIA, AND SINGAPORE)

Sweet soybean paste, known as *tauco* or *taucheo* (a Hokkien word), is a thick, golden brown, misolike condiment made of fermented soybeans, rice flour, sugar, and salt, with halved or semiground soybeans floating through it. It was introduced to the Malay Archipelago by

Chinese traders and is used in the region (Vietnam, Taiwan, and Thailand, too) to add saltiness, sweetness, and earthy depth. It's a vital ingredient in making many authentic Indonesian, Malaysian, and Singaporean foods, including Stir-fried Chinese Egg Noodles with Shrimp and Asian Greens (page 191) and Nyonya Chicken and Potato Stew (page 281). Miso can't be substituted. Before adding sweet soybean paste to your cooking, always taste a pinch. Some brands are aggressively salty, and you may need to reduce the amount of salt you add to the dish.

BUYING AND STORING: Sweet soybean paste, not to be confused with Chinese products called brown bean sauce or bean sauce (these are darker and have a different flavor, though these too are made from fermented soybeans), is widely available in jars and bottles in the condiment section of Chinese and Southeast Asian markets. The labels vary: soybean paste, whole soybean sauce, yellow soybeans, salted soybeans, or, less frequently, *tauco* or *taucheo* are but a few of the names you'll encounter. Sweet soybean paste is also a common ingredient in Thai cuisine, so you'll find it in Thai markets as well. My favorite Thai brand is P. Pra Teep Thong. Labeled soybean paste, it's pure and sweet, never overly salty, and comes in 16-fluid-ounce (250-milliliter) glass jars. Another nice Thai brand is Kwong Hung Seng Sauce, sold in 24-fluid-ounce (750-milliliter) bottles. Kokita brand, from Indonesia, is yet another good choice. As always, avoid brands that contain artificial flavorings and preservatives if possible (note that Kokita does contain some preservatives). Sweet soybean paste will keep in the refrigerator for up to 6 months.

TAMARIND

Tamarindus indica; *asam jawa* (INDONESIA, MALAYSIA, AND SINGAPORE)

The tamarind tree, native to East Africa and about the size of a tall maple, is commonly cultivated in Indonesia and Malaysia. The origin of the name is the Arabic *tamr hindi*, or "date of India," though tamarinds are unrelated to dates. The tamarind fruit is a curved, tannish brown 4-inch (10-centimeter) pod with a thin, hard, brittle outer shell that conceals a sticky, coffee brown edible pulp. The taste is a tantalizing mix of sweet and sour, with a nice hint of caramel. The pulp is mixed with very warm water and strained to form tamarind extract, a smooth, light brown, thickish liquid that adds a touch of fruity sourness to curries, stews, soups, and even a few stir-fries, such as Stir-fried Water Spinach, Nyonya Style (page 213). It's especially good in fish dishes, as the tartness neutralizes fishy flavors. I've provided instructions for making the extract in individual recipes.

BUYING, USING, AND STORING: Look for easy-to-find 8-ounce (225-gram) or 1-pound (455-gram) sticky, semihard blocks of tamarind pulp wrapped in plastic at Asian and South Asian markets. Most tamarind pulp in the United States is imported from either Thailand or

India. Along with the pulp, these blocks contain tamarind seeds, bits of pod, and sinew. To measure tamarind pulp, cut into the block with a spoon or small knife. Remove a lump and press it into a measuring spoon or cup, depending on the amount you need. Avoid the bland, already strained tamarind extracts sold in Asian and South Asian markets. Although convenient, they lack the pure taste of fresh tamarind extract. Also, don't use the whole tamarind pods sold in the produce sections of many Asian markets to make tamarind extract. They've been bred for their sweetness, not sourness, and are meant to be eaten like a fruit.

The acidity of tamarind pulp makes it easy to store. Tightly wrapped, it'll keep for up to a year in a cool, dark place. If kept longer, it can become too dry to use.

TEMPEH

Soybeans were introduced to Java by the Chinese. The protein-rich beans grew prolifically in the island's fertile volcanic soil, and over time residents developed tempeh, one of Indonesia's great gifts to the culinary world. Tempeh is made from half-cooked, peeled, and dried soybeans that have been infused with a starter yeast called *ragi tempe*. The beans are then wrapped in a banana leaf and allowed to develop in a warm, dark place over the course of a couple of days. During that time, the yeast forms a velvety, whitish bloom that encases the soybeans, resulting in a pillowy, nutty-tasting cake about 1 1/2 inches (4 centimeters) thick. In Indonesia, tempeh is sold in attractive banana-leaf parcels stacked in vendors' stalls. Here, the cakes are usually 1/2 to 1 inch (12 millimeters to 2.5 centimeters) thick and sold shrink wrapped.

Because it's highly nutritious and inexpensive, tempeh is widely eaten in Indonesia, Malaysia, and Singapore. It is always deep-fried before being added to dishes (it's never eaten uncooked), and appears in a range of preparations, including sambals and curries, and, perhaps most satisfyingly, crisply fried on its own (see Garlic-Marinated Tempeh, page 322). For more information about tempeh, see pages 319 to 327.

BUYING AND STORING: In the 1960s and 1970s, tempeh, discovered by Western travelers to Indonesia, became a staple of meatless cooking in the West. As a result, it's easy to find in health-food stores and some Asian markets. My favorite brand is Turtle Islands Foods, which uses organic soybeans and sells its product in square, plastic-wrapped 8-ounce (225-gram) packages. It's 1 inch (2.5 centimeters) thick and has a clean taste and an appealingly spongy texture. Visit www.tofurky.com for a list of stores that carry it.

Select only plain tempeh for the recipes in this book. Never buy tempeh that contains added flavors (such as barbecue sauce) or added ingredients (such as wild rice or millet). Look for tempeh in the refrigerated section near tofu products or in the freezer section. (Freezing doesn't adversely affect its taste or texture). Black mold spots on the surface and in the interior are nothing to worry about—they're signs that the bacteria are still active—nor do the spots need to be trimmed away before the tempeh is cooked. Spoilage is indicated by sliminess, patches of red or yellow mold, and an ammonia-like odor. Fresh tempeh will keep in the refrigerator for up to 1 week in the package that it came in or wrapped in plastic; frozen tempeh will keep for up to 6 months.

TOFU

Tahu (INDONESIA, MALAYSIA, AND SINGAPORE)

Tofu, also known as bean curd and as *dofu* and *dau foo*, its Japanese and Cantonese names, respectively, is made by coagulating fresh soy milk with a calcium compound until it curdles. The resulting curds are pressed with weights in cloth-lined wooden trays. Custardlike silken tofu, which contains the most moisture, has been pressed the shortest amount of time, while firm tofu, which has a denser, mozzarella-like texture and contains less moisture, has been pressed the longest.

Although originally from China, tofu has long been a staple in the cooking of the Malay Archipelago. Local cooks typically sauté or deep-fry firm tofu, which heightens its taste and gives it a wonderful porous crispness and golden surface, before adding it to a dish. Tofu that hasn't been fried is considered characterless and thought to not properly absorb and mingle with saucy curries. Silken or soft tofu can't be deep-fried, as it can react dangerously with hot oil, causing it to bubble over or even catch fire. Before deep-frying firm tofu, always pat it dry, or it will splatter aggressively when added to the hot oil. Also, be certain to fry it only to the point that its surface is just golden; overfried tofu is dry, tough, and bitter tasting. For more information about tofu, including detailed instructions on how to deep-fry it, see pages 319 to 332.

BUYING AND STORING: For the recipes in this book, you'll only need firm or extra-firm tofu. It is sold in water-filled sealed plastic containers (the water keeps the tofu from drying out) holding either a single large rectangular block or 4 smaller square blocks. Tofu is also occasionally available in open containers and buckets in Asian markets or greengrocers. Even though it's cheaper than tofu in sealed containers, avoid it, as it's highly prone to bacterial contamination. I purchase all my tofu from Chinese and Southeast Asian markets near my New York home. They carry a broad selection of excellent-tasting tofus manufactured by small local companies. Roam through the tofu section of your nearest Asian market to familiarize yourself with the brands made in your area. I avoid tofu from Japanese companies (such as Azumaya), as well as tofu sold in health-food stores (such as Nasoya). Even though the packages are labeled firm or extra-firm, the tofu usually has a higher than desirable moisture content, which means it won't fry well.

Tofu is quite perishable and, like fish or chicken, must be kept refrigerated. When selecting tofu, check the expiration date on the label. Most brands manufactured by Chinese companies allow you to see the tofu inside the container through a see-through portion of the label. Choose tofu that looks bright white with no signs of yellowing. The water should be clear, not cloudy (a sign of spoilage). Store sealed containers toward the rear of your refrigerator (the coolest part) for up to 4 days, depending on the tofu's freshness. Once you open the container, smell the water. It should give off a clean, nondescript aroma, not a swampy or sour odor. Also, test a sliver of tofu. It should taste bland and vaguely sweet, not remotely sour or fermented.

Transfer any tofu that you do not use to a nonreactive bowl filled with fresh water, cover with plastic wrap, and refrigerate for 2 to 3 days. Wrap any tofu that you have deep-fried and have not used in a recipe in plastic wrap and store in the refrigerator for up to 4 days.

TURMERIC
Curcuma domestica; *kunyit* (INDONESIA, MALAYSIA, AND SINGAPORE)

Turmeric, a member of the ginger family, is a rhizome (underground stem) native to the Malay Archipelago. The fresh rhizome, which has a vaguely gingery taste that ground dried turmeric lacks, is a cornerstone aromatic in the region and is often used in flavoring pastes. It not only gives curries and stews an appealing golden color, but also imparts a musky, peppery taste. Each nubby finger is roughly 1 1/2 to 3 inches (4 to 7.5 centimeters) long. It has thin, golden tan skin that resembles the skin of mature ginger, with brown, narrow concentric rings running down its length.

You need to peel fresh turmeric (use a vegetable peeler or sharp paring knife) before using it. The flesh is a vivid carrot orange and has a sharp, pleasantly acrid smell. Chop the rhizome coarsely to facilitate grinding for flavoring pastes. The shiny, deep green, gladiola-like leaves of the turmeric plant, which are called *daun kunyit*, are widely used to season curries and salads with their woodsy taste. Alas, turmeric leaves are not commercially available in North America—not yet, anyway.

A few recipes in this book, such as Celebration Yellow Rice (page 178), call for ground turmeric, the intensely gold, powdered form of the dried rhizome. Though it tastes faintly like fresh turmeric, it lacks its intensity and is used mainly for its ability to tint dishes a lovely shade of yellow.

BUYING AND STORING: Although uncommon in North America, fresh turmeric can sometimes be found in the vegetable sections of South and Southeast Asian markets. Patel Brothers, a Chicago-based chain of Indian markets with outlets all over the United States, carries it most of the time, sold either in bins for shoppers to pick through or in small plastic bags containing a few fingers. (See Sources, page 363, for more information on where to find fresh turmeric.) Look for firm, bright-skinned fingers with no wrinkling, sliminess, or rot; pay particularly close attention to the condition of both ends of each finger. The fingers should smell clean and earthy, not mildewy.

Store fresh turmeric in a paper bag in the vegetable bin of the refrigerator for up to 6 weeks, depending on their freshness. Since fresh turmeric can be difficult to locate, buy at least 20 fingers when you find it, so you'll have a supply on hand the next time you need it. Fresh turmeric will keep, either peeled or unpeeled, in the freezer in a tightly sealed plastic container for up to 1 year; thaw individual fingers at room temperature for about 10 minutes, or until they become soft enough to peel and cut.

Small packages of frozen turmeric imported from Thailand (each package holds about 5 fingers) can be found at many Chinese and Southeast Asian markets, usually tucked away in the freezer section that also contains galangal and *daun pandan* leaves. Store-bought frozen turmeric will keep tightly sealed in the package in which it came or in a plastic container for up to 1 year.

If you can't find fresh or frozen turmeric, use ground turmeric. Look for it in small plastic packages or small glass or plastic bottles in Asian, Bangladeshi, Indian, Pakistani, and most Western supermarkets. Seek ground turmeric that is a pure deep yellow or gold; turmeric that is darker has likely been adulterated with dye. Don't buy dried whole turmeric rhizomes, sometimes available in Indian spice shops, as they're difficult to grind. Store ground turmeric in an airtight container in the refrigerator or freezer for up to 1 year.

ABOVE LEFT: *A home cook stir-fries long beans in her outdoor kitchen in Indonesia's Banda Islands.*

ABOVE CENTER: *Cinnamon (cassia) being ground in a mortar and pestle in Aceh, Indonesia.*

ABOVE RIGHT: *A cook in Georgetown, Malaysia, sorts through dried shrimp, an ingredient popular for its earthy taste.*

4. IN THE KITCHEN: TECHNIQUES AND EQUIPMENT

MAKING FLAVORING PASTES

Called *bumbu-bumbu* in Indonesia and *rempah-rempah* in Malaysia and Singapore, flavoring pastes are the moist, finely ground seasoning mixtures at the heart of nearly every curry and stew and many stir-fries in the region. Made by home cooks in stone mortars with pestles, flavoring pastes are the soul of a dish, the palette from which the cook determines how pungent, aromatic, earthy, or sour it will be. Flavoring pastes are not static. They change and transform as they cook, becoming deeper and more compelling. An uncooked, harsh-smelling flavoring paste, for example, turns deliciously mellow when it's sautéed and its hidden sugars emerge. But while most flavoring pastes are cooked before they're incorporated into dishes—a process that both amplifies and rounds out their flavors—some are not. For example, raw pastes used in certain *rendang* dishes are sautéed after all the liquid in the dish has cooked away, rather than before it's added.

The ingredients of flavoring pastes vary from region to region, dish to dish, cook to cook—even day to day, depending on the mood of the cook or the ingredients available. The most popular are shallots, garlic, dried shrimp paste, ginger, galangal, lemongrass, fresh and dried chiles, tamarind pulp, and dried spices such as coriander seeds, cloves, nutmeg, pepper, and cumin seeds. In Indonesia, Malaysia, and Singapore, there is no widespread tradition of preparing flavoring pastes in advance (cooks believe that flavoring pastes made ahead of time lose their vibrancy). Nonetheless, ready-made imported Indonesian and Malaysian flavoring pastes from such companies as Indofood, Bamboe, and Royco are increasingly available in Asian supermarkets in North America. You should avoid them. They're packed with preservatives and artificial and "natural" flavorings and taste only faintly like a homemade flavoring paste.

GRINDING FLAVORING PASTES

As you gather ingredients to make your own flavoring pastes, make sure that they are as fresh and vivid as they can be. Look, for instance, for young, sweet garlic and plump, fresh chiles. Don't settle for harsh shallots that are past their prime or cumin seeds that have lost their aroma. As with everything you make, your flavoring pastes are only as good as what you put into them. Since all the ingredients will be ground, you don't need to bother chopping them well before grinding. A coarse, casual cut—say, chunks no larger than 1/4 inch (6 millimeters) square—is perfectly fine. The only exceptions are lemongrass, ginger, and galangal. Fibrous sinew runs through these ingredients, so you must slice them thinly against the grain to avoid long, stringy pieces in the final paste.

Flavoring pastes have different consistencies depending on the kind of dish in which they'll be used. Most pastes, especially those intended for curries and stews, are ground to the texture of cooked oatmeal or creamy mashed potatoes, or sometimes to a point in between. A few are slightly coarser. No flavoring paste should be gritty. Hard, sinewy bits of improperly ground dried spices, ginger, or lemongrass can mar the texture of an otherwise silky curry. Also, a properly ground flavoring paste will season a liquid-based dish more effectively than a gritty one. Think about what happens if you stir ground pepper into a liquid: if it's coarse, it sinks slowly to the bottom, while if it's finely ground, it becomes suspended in the liquid.

Most home cooks in Indonesia, Malaysia, and Singapore pound their flavoring pastes and sambals (chile-based condiments similar to salsas) by hand in a stone mortar with a pestle, an arduous task that can take considerable time. Cooks claim that using a mortar and pestle massages ingredients rather than pulverizes them, resulting in a more cohesive (and some say better-tasting) paste. This is one of the main reasons that local kitchens are usually the domain of multiple cooks: it's usually the sole job of one of these cooks, often the youngest and strongest, to grind flavoring pastes, while her elders look over her shoulder and supervise.

As much as I like to follow traditional methods, I now use a small food processor instead of a mortar and pestle to make all of my flavoring pastes. Though the Malay Archipelago's stone mortars are beautiful to behold and the pastes they produce are rustic and flavorful, after preparing many dishes with the one I once picked up years ago in a West Sumatran market, I have ultimately found my food processor to be preferable. Making flavoring pastes by hand can take more than 30 muscle-tiring minutes, especially when the paste contains recalcitrant ingredients such as whole cloves and lemongrass. With a small food processor, I can grind ingredients in no more than 3 minutes. And the

STIR-FRIED CHINESE EGG NOODLES WITH SHRIMP AND ASIAN GREENS (PAGE 191)

STIR-FRIED WATER SPINACH, NYONYA STYLE (PAGE 213)

THE SOTO KING'S CHICKEN SOUP (PAGE 271)

BLACK PEPPER CRAB (PAGE 264)

TOFU AND SUMMER VEGETABLES IN COCONUT MILK (PAGE 327)

BEEF RENDANG (PAGE 304), WITH CELEBRATION YELLOW RICE (PAGE 178) AND
SHREDDED KAFFIR LIME LEAVES (PAGE 73)

results are just as satisfying: gorgeous pastes whose textures and tastes are virtually indistinguishable from those that have been ground the traditional way.

However, if you own a large mortar and pestle—one that can comfortably accommodate at least 1 1/2 cups (15 ounces/425 grams) of ingredients—and have the desire and fortitude to make your own flavoring paste by hand, by all means do so. Start with hard, tenacious ingredients such as whole spices and lemongrass. Once they've been pounded to either a dry or moist powder—depending on whether a moist ingredient has been introduced or not—add progressively softer ingredients, starting with ginger and chiles and ending with shallots and garlic. A drizzle of water can help get a reluctant paste moving, as can a pinch of salt, which causes moist ingredients such as chiles and shallots to soften.

Here are a few simple rules you need to follow for making flavoring pastes in a food processor:

· Use a small food processor with a maximum bowl capacity of 3 or 4 cups (24 or 32 fluid ounces/750 milliliters or 1 liter). (See page 107 for brand recommendations.) If you use a larger model, the ingredients will splatter up the sides and not process properly. The same holds true for blenders, whose beakerlike bowls are great for puréeing milk shakes but not for making small quantities of flavoring pastes. (Conversely, the bowls of spice and coffee grinders are too small to make most of the flavoring pastes in this book.)

· Think of your food processor as a mortar and pestle. Instead of blindly pushing down the pulse or grind button and allowing the ingredients to purée into a generic mush, stop every few seconds or so to gauge the paste's transformation before continuing. Ask yourself questions as you go. Have the shallots melded with the rest of the paste, or can I still see shards? Pinch a bit of the mixture and smush it between your fingers. Is it smooth or gritty? Are the coriander seeds finely ground, or are they still in scrappy pieces? If the answers are yes, keep processing.

· Using a small spatuala or spoon, occasionally scrape down the paste that splatters on the sides and top of the work bowl near the blade. The greater the mass the blade encounters, the more effectively it can do its job. You may need to repeat this step several times until your paste reaches the correct consistency.

· Add a thin drizzle of water, a tablespoon at a time, if the paste is not turning over properly because it's too dry or too hard—this nearly always gets a stubborn paste moving. (My processor has two small, convenient holes in the lid that allow me to add water without stopping the grinding.) Be careful not to add too much water, however. Any more than 2 tablespoons, depending on the quantity of the paste, is too much. Flavoring pastes should never be watery, or they won't sauté properly. And never use cooking oil instead of water to thin a paste, or it will come out too greasy.

· A general note: While most pastes should be smooth, there are a few, such as the sambal-like paste for Rohati's Crisp-Fried Potatoes with Chile and Shallot Sambal (page 221), that should be coarse and splotchy. I've indicated the desired texture of each paste in the recipes.

COOKING FLAVORING PASTES

After you prepare a flavoring paste, the next step is usually sautéing it in oil, a process that helps develop its flavors. (A few pastes are added directly to a dish as it cooks, such as the ones for Potato Rendang, page 223, and Beef Rendang, page 304.) The goal is to achieve a limp, silky, fragrant paste, rather than a caramelized or crusty golden brown one. Pastes that have been sautéed until they are golden taste too deep and sweet; burned ones must be tossed out. Because of their nascent sugars, flavoring pastes burn and scorch easily. Always work with medium-low or low heat to ensure the best results and always keep a close watch over them as they cook, stirring frequently to prevent sticking.

Start by adding the oil called for in the recipe to the pan and allow it to heat. The best way to see if the oil is the correct temperature is to drop a smidgen of paste into it. It should sizzle and sputter around gently, not violently fry or sit motionless. Once you've found the proper temperature, you may need to raise and lower the heat a few times as you cook to compensate for variables, such as a thick pan or a cool ambient room temperature. If the paste shows any signs of scorching or burning, remove the pan from the heat at once and let it cool for a few moments before continuing. Keep in mind that volatile oils naturally present in the chiles and spices in flavoring pastes can cause you to sneeze and make your eyes tear. Indonesian cooks believe that the louder the sneeze, the better the dish will taste! Fear not: the chile-flecked cloud will pass in a few minutes.

Once the flavoring paste is in the pan, use a spatula to move the mixture around gently, usually about every minute or so, to allow it to cook evenly and prevent it from sticking and scorching. If you notice that the paste has absorbed all of the oil and is beginning to scorch, add more oil, 1 teaspoon at a time, until the paste begins to sauté again easily. How will you know when it's done? The technique that cooks in Indonesia, Malaysia, and Singapore follow is called *keluar aromanya* (aroma exiting). Take a good whiff of the paste you're sautéing. It should smell warm and appealing, not harsh or unsavory. All trace of raw garlic and shallots should be gone. The fragrance of the aromatic ingredients in the paste, such as lemongrass, ginger, or cloves, should rise above the pan in a pleasing rush.

Two visual cues will let you know when a flavoring paste is done. First, the paste will have darkened a shade or two from its raw state. Second, the ingredients will partially evaporate and separate from the cooking oil as they cook, leaving behind sizzling oil. The paste will be ready to receive the other ingredients of the dish at this point. All told, sautéing a flavoring paste can take anywhere from 4 to 15 minutes, depending on the temperature of the oil and on how dry or moist the paste is. Keep in mind that whole spices and aromatics such as lime leaves and lemongrass that's been tied into a knot are often added to the paste after it has sautéed (and occasionally before).

MAKING CURRIES AND STEWS

The term *curry* comes from a word meaning "sauce" in Tamil (a southern Indian language). In this book, it refers to any complexly flavored, coconut milk–based dish with beef, poultry, pork, fish, shellfish, vegetables, eggs, tempeh, or tofu as its main ingredient. In Indonesia, a curry is called a *gulai* (pronounced GOO-lie), a word of Sumatran origin, or an *opor* (oh-POUR), a Javanese term; in Malaysia and Singapore, such dishes are usually known as *kare* or *kari* (kah-REE). I refer to curries made with a water base as stews, to differentiate them from those containing coconut milk. But curries and stews share more similarities than differences: they are both boldly seasoned, soul-satisfying, saucy foods designed to complement rice, and they are both cooked using the same basic techniques.

The first thing you need to do to make a curry or stew is to choose the correct pot. Although woks are often used in the Malay Archipelago, I have found that a deep pot, such as a soup pot or stockpot, or a 3- to 4-quart (3- to 4-liter) saucepan, is ideal. The reason is simple: A curry or stew cooked in a shallow pot will evaporate more quickly, which can produce a sauce that's too thick. Also, a large pot offers enough room for you to stir the ingredients comfortably without spilling any liquid over the sides, and gives ingredients space to cook more evenly without being crowded. (Conversely, never choose a pot that's so large that it dwarfs the curry or stew; the liquid should be no more than 6 inches/15 centimeters from the rim.) Because the liquid in curries and stews can be dense, sticking can result. Pots and pans with nonstick surfaces, including those coated with Teflon, are great choices to prevent this from happening. My favorite pot—the workhorse that I've been using for the last 20 years—is the copper-bottomed 7-quart (7-liter) Dutch oven that I inherited from my mom when I moved away from home. It's sturdy, distributes heat beautifully, and its well-seasoned stainless-steel interior surface means that my curries and stews rarely stick to the bottom. I advise against using cast-iron pots, as their thickness makes quickly regulating heat a bit difficult.

Next, sauté the flavoring paste (see page 98 for directions). Once it's ready, it's time to add the curry's or stew's main ingredient. Sometimes you sauté the main ingredient briefly in the flavoring paste before adding the coconut milk or the water (such as with Javanese Chicken Curry, page 275), but usually you add it at about the same time as the liquid. Browning meats and fish is uncommon. Next, stir in the liquid. As you do, scrape up the sautéed flavoring paste from the bottom of the pot, making sure to combine it thoroughly with the liquid. Most curries and stews cook slowly—the longer they simmer, the deeper their flavor becomes—in uncovered pots, though a few recipes call for lids placed ajar, which means less moisture will escape and the final dish will be slightly more soupy.

The most important thing to remember in preparing any curry or stew is to keep the liquid at a steady, sleepy simmer and not let it reach an aggressive boil. As my Malaysian friend Josephine Chua once explained to me, it should be like a "soft breeze, not a harsh wind." To follow Josephine's advice, you'll need to monitor the pot periodically—say, every 15 minutes or so once the liquid has reached the proper simmer—to see if the heat level needs adjustment and to give the ingredients a stir. There are two important reasons why you shouldn't let the liquid boil. First, if you're making a curry or stew containing chicken, beef, or pork, the meat may toughen. Second, if the liquid is coconut milk, it will likely curdle if it boils for longer than a minute or two.

The final step is to determine when the curry or stew is done. Sample a piece of the main ingredient. Meats and poultry should be cooked through and tender but never falling apart or coming away from the bone. Fish should be firm, moist, flaky, and opaque, not raw, soft, saturated with liquid, or separating from the bone. Shrimp should be tender, moist, and just cooked through, not raw or overly firm or chewy; shrimp shells should be smooth and clear, not wrinkly. Vegetables should be well cooked and soft (but not mushy) and only faintly crunchy; undercooked vegetables don't absorb the rich succulence of a curry or stew sauce as effectively as fully cooked ones do.

Another sign that a curry or stew is done is when its oils and fats have risen to the surface in a swirl or pool. This phenomenon is called *berminyak*, a verb that means "to release oil." It's particularly noticeable in curries, because coconut milk, with its high fat content, lets go of its oil as it cooks. But it's also apparent in water-based stews, as both the cooking oil and the fats in the main ingredient (especially meat) also react in this fashion. Be aware, however, that not all curries and stews part with their oils, nor do they always part with them at the precise moment of doneness. The best method for testing whether the main ingredient is sufficiently cooked is to taste it.

STIR-FRYING

Stir-frying (*tumis*), as it has been practiced for nearly two millennia by home cooks in Indonesia, Malaysia, and Singapore, is a cooking process more akin to sautéing than it is to the fast-moving, pyrotechnic display we see in Chinese restaurants. The main difference between stir-frying in this part of the world and in classic Chinese cooking is that the fire tends to be less intense. Aside from that, the equipment and techniques are identical.

All successful stir-fries, regardless of the temperature of the fire, are dependent in large measure on the wok or pot you're using. If you have a wok and are comfortable with it, use it. But if you don't you can still stir-fry effectively. After over a decade of using woks, I discovered several years ago that a variety of pots, including skillets, sauté pans, Dutch ovens, and stockpots, work just as well, if not better. Because Western stoves aren't designed (or allowed) to produce the fiercely high heat that a round-bottomed wok requires, woks usually don't reach the optimum temperature necessary for speedy stir-frying. Recently, flat-bottomed woks, which conduct heat more effectively on our stoves, have come into vogue. Although I've been impressed with them on the occasions that I've used them, I'm faithful to the same Dutch oven that I use for curries and stews. With its truly flat bottom and roomy interior, it conducts heat evenly and accommodates large and small amounts of food equally well. Plus, I love using a pot that I know intimately: Its curves and dimensions as familiar to me as the back of my hand. (A note about stir-frying noodles: Use a pot or wok with a nonstick surface for frying noodles, or you'll need to use an exorbitant amount of oil to keep them from sticking. I always use a large nonstick skillet, not my Dutch oven, though a nonstick regular or flat-bottomed wok works equally well.)

Before beginning any stir-fry, cut all your ingredients into uniform pieces, according to what is called for in the recipe. This helps ensure that they'll cook evenly. Also, dry them thoroughly, or your stir-fry may come out soggy. Arrange all the cut and dried ingredients so that they're within easy reach. It's also a good idea to double check the recipe to make sure you have everything you need close at hand. Searching for a missing ingredient at the last minute can disrupt your flow when stir-frying and compromise the final dish.

Rather than heating your wok or pot over high heat, start with medium-high heat and raise it only if you need to, as most Indonesian, Malaysian, and Singaporean home cooks do. (A few recipes in this book will ask you to start a stir-fry by sautéing a flavoring paste, so you'll need to begin with low or medium-low heat.) Add the oil and gently swirl it around by moving the pan back and forth to coat the bottom evenly. Wait for about 20 seconds—the timing depends on the thickness of the pan and the ambient room temperature—to see if the oil is hot enough to introduce other ingredients. I test the heat by placing the palm of my hand about 3/4 inch (2 centimeters) above the surface of the oil. If I can hold my hand in place for longer than a few seconds, the oil is not yet the right temperature; if I can leave my hand in place for only for a second or two before feeling uncomfortable, the oil is hot enough. Another way I decide whether or not the oil is the correct temperature is by appearance. It should have a runny, shimmery quality (rather than a syrupy and dull one) when I tilt the pan back and forth a few times. Yet another way I judge the oil temperature is to toss in a small piece of the first ingredient I'm going to add, usually garlic. It should sizzle in the pan happily. If it fries aggressively, then I know the oil is too hot; if it sits motionless, I know it's not hot enough.

When the oil is ready, add the ingredients one by one, taking care that you don't crowd them. A crowded wok will lead to unevenly cooked ingredients. You may find it easier to control the stir-fry if you add the ingredients gradually, in small handfuls, instead of all at once. This will give each portion a few seconds to cook down slightly, making more room for those that follow—this is especially practical when stir-frying Asian greens, which tend to be bulky when raw but cook down significantly.

As you stir-fry, use a large heatproof rubber or metal spatula to keep your ingredients moving about the wok or pot so that they don't burn or scorch. You want to stir constantly as you cook, moving the ingredients up and over one another and making sure that all of them are evenly touched by the hot oil and the heat of the pot or wok. Allow the ingredients—especially Asian greens and mung bean sprouts—to remain on the fire only until they have just wilted or, in the case of the two stir-fried shrimp recipes in this book (Stir-fried Tamarind Shrimp, page 255, and Stir-fried Shrimp Sambal, page 262), are just cooked through.

Ingredients continue to cook for a few minutes after you take them off the fire, so it's important to transfer the finished dish to a serving platter the moment it's done. Select a platter large enough to display the dish in more or less a single layer; if the stir-fry is served in a heavy clump, the ingredients on the bottom will continue to cook too long because of the heat of the ingredients on top and may turn mushy. Stir-fries usually taste best when eaten immediately; a few, however, will mellow and improve as they sit.

MAKING RENDANG DISHES

Rendang (pronounced REN-dahng) is an unusual but easy slow-cooking method that results in an extravagantly rich dish. It originated in West Sumatra, though it's now widely known throughout Indonesia, Malaysia, and Singapore. It calls for cooking a main ingredient in intensely spiced coconut milk for hours until the liquid evaporates and the main ingredient is left to panfry in the rendered fats and coconut oil remaining in the pot—the opposite of Western-style braising, in which the main ingredient is first browned and then simmered in liquid. At the point at which the coconut milk has reduced by half, *rendang* dishes are called *kalio* (from the Minang language of West Sumatra), a vibrantly flavored dish with a thick sauce. (Adobo, a cooking method found in the Philippines in which a main ingredient is simmered in vinegar until the liquid reduces, is a not-too-distant relative of *rendang*.)

The *rendang* method serves three purposes. First, it deeply flavors the main ingredient; the longer a *rendang* dish cooks, the more fully the main ingredient will be infused by the aromatic seasonings and the succulent fats in the coconut milk. Second, it tenderizes chewy cuts of meat, making them supple. Third, it extends the life of the main ingredient by removing much of its moisture and replacing it with fats, seasonings, and salt, in much the same way that drying or salting foods does. Stored in tightly wrapped banana leaves, *rendang* dishes were originally intended to be eaten on journeys away from home, and even today West Sumatran cooks believe that they will remain safely edible for 2 or 3 days without refrigeration. Though I've eaten many *rendang* dishes in Southeast Asia that have been kept at room temperature for that period, in my own home I keep them for no more than 3 days in the refrigerator.

Cooks are imaginative in choosing the main ingredient for a *rendang*. In West Sumatra, where the repertory is the most extensive, beef, water buffalo, goat, unpeeled tiny new potatoes, young wild ferns, cassava, small shrimp in their shell, and chunks of tuna are just some of the possibilities. Cooks in Malaysia and Singapore tend to favor *rendang* made with chicken or beef, while those in parts of Indonesia outside of West Sumatra prefer beef or water buffalo. The flavoring pastes that season all *rendang* dishes are similar. Aromatics such as ginger, chiles, galangal, lemongrass, garlic, shallots, kaffir lime leaves, and turmeric are always big players. Spices such as nutmeg, cloves, cinnamon, and cardamom also figure prominently, as do herbs such as lemon basil and *daun salam* leaves.

Though *rendang* dishes are complex tasting, they aren't difficult to make. There are, however, a few tips and techniques you can follow that will make the process go more easily:

- *Rendang* dishes cook best in shallow pans that allow the coconut milk to evaporate more efficiently than a deep pot would. Choose a 12-inch (30-centimeter) skillet or a 4-quart (4-liter) sauté pan. I strongly recommend a pan with a nonstick surface because *rendang* dishes have a tendency to stick, especially during the last 20 minutes or so of cooking when most of the liquid is gone.

- Once a *rendang* dish has begun to cook at a gentle simmer, the liquid will gradually begin to reduce, transforming the thin sauce into a progressively thicker one. This process—

the heart of the method—can take up to 3 hours, depending on the main ingredient, the fat content of the coconut milk, the pan, the cooking temperature, and the ambient temperature and humidity in your kitchen. Be patient and eventually you'll achieve a fabulous *rendang* dish. It's important to maintain a steady, slow simmer during this time. If the liquid boils aggressively for longer than a minute or two, the coconut milk will likely curdle and the main ingredient (if it's beef) may toughen. If the fire is too low and the liquid produces only an occasional bubble, the dish will take more time than necessary to cook and the main ingredient may overcook.

· During the final stage of cooking, when all the coconut milk has evaporated, the main ingredient is prone to sticking to the bottom of the pot. To prevent this, carefully stir it (along with the deliciously crusty flavoring paste that remains) continuously with a spatula. If you stir too roughly, the main ingredient, which has been cooking for a long time and is now "fragile," will likely break apart. Also, reduce the heat slightly. I find that a faint flame is sufficient to achieve the gentle browning required in the final minutes of making *rendang*.

TWICE-COOKING

Cooking chicken, beef, tofu, and tempeh sometimes involves twice-cooking, an Indonesian and Malaysian technique in which the main ingredient is simmered in a seasoned stock before it's grilled or fried. Three recipes in this book call for twice-cooking: Javanese Grilled Chicken (page 289), Grilled Coconut Chicken with Lemon Basil (page 292), and Twice-Cooked Tofu with Coriander (page 330). Verifying the origins of this technique is difficult. An example of it can be seen in the Chinese practice of twice-cooking meats, in which a meat, usually pork, is boiled, then deep-fried. But the primary goal of the Chinese technique seems to be to add texture, while Indonesian, Malaysian, and Singaporean cooks are more concerned about building flavor.

Cooks usually choose from two kinds of liquids for the simmering stage. In Java, the most popular liquid is clear and infused with whole coriander seeds, smashed garlic, salt, and, sometimes, galangal and *daun salam* leaves. After it has simmered, the main ingredient (frequently chicken) is sometimes marinated, often in Indonesian sweet soy sauce, before it's deep-fried or grilled. The other kind of liquid, popular in Sumatra, Sulawesi, and West Malaysia and used only for grilled foods, consists of coconut milk seasoned with an aromatic flavoring paste. The main ingredient (again, frequently chicken, though sometimes fish) simmers in this currylike liquid until it's nearly cooked through. The liquid is then reduced until thick and used later to baste the main ingredient on the grill.

There's one rule of thumb that applies to all twice-cooked dishes: be careful not to overcook the main ingredient during the simmering stage. Generally speaking, it should be roughly 75 percent cooked (unless it's tofu, in which case doneness isn't an issue). Keep in mind that it will have a second round of cooking to ensure it's fully cooked.

USING YOUR SENSES

Follow the example of the best cooks in Indonesia, Malaysia, and Singapore: use all of your senses when you prepare a meal. Don't merely place your ingredients in a pot and expect an amazing dish an hour later. Be cheerfully vigilant, always. Smell raw flavoring pastes, even the ones that cause your eyes to fill with tears. Taste the coconut milk before you add it to the curry so you know how rich it is. Become familiar with the visual clues of every dish as it cooks, such as the moment when a particular flavoring paste darkens a shade, indicating—along with its mellow fragrance—that it's done. Listen for the soft, burbling sound of a *rendang* simmering at the perfect temperature. Most important, taste dishes often, especially when you're first learning them. Tasting connects you to the process of creating a dish, leading you to discover how salty or unsalty it is, for example, and how it progresses from one stage to the next. Each dish tells a story, with a beginning, a middle, and an end—plus a number of fascinating plot twists along the way. Pay attention to these moments and you'll begin to understand what is occurring, the subtle alchemy involved in every change. If you do this, I guarantee you'll soon be concocting a *gulai* (coconut-milk curry) that's as tasty as the dish prepared by a Javanese *ibu* (mother) who's been making it her whole life.

RESTING FOOD

Cooks in Indonesia, Malaysia, and Singapore allow most finished dishes to rest at room temperature for at least 20 minutes before they're eaten. Allowing a dish to rest is a subtle extension of the cooking process, giving flavors an opportunity to meld, balance, and intensify (and it's why most stews and soups taste better the next day). It also gives the dish time to cool down. Piping hot foods lack the subtle layering of flavors of room-temperature foods and therefore don't taste as good. Salads, steamed rice, satays, and most stir-fried dishes are the exceptions to the resting rule. They're usually served right after they're cooked or assembled.

RELAXING

Maintaining a state of relaxation (*bersantai-santai*) in your kitchen may not seem like a technique, but it *is*—perhaps the most important one. Master it, and all the other techniques discussed in this chapter (and indeed in this book) will fall into place more easily. For Indonesians, Malaysians, and Singaporeans, cooking is a joyous act that flows from the heart. They know that when a dish is prepared in a stressful atmosphere, obvious errors will occur, such as a burned flavoring paste or a curdled coconut-milk broth. They also believe that tension can go into a dish and cause it to suffer in ways that are more elusive. In Southeast Asia, serenity and fun are revered. Home kitchens are calm places where jokes are encouraged. Sharp words and raised voices are taboo. Rushing is forbidden. A relaxed cook is considered to be the secret ingredient that enables dishes to come out perfectly. Try applying this subtle technique in your own kitchen. I guarantee that the food you prepare will come out better. And even if something does go awry, handle it the way a home cook in the Malay Archipelago would: laugh it off and hopefully you'll get it right the next time. As my West Sumatran friend Rohati always says with a smile when the rice scorches (yes, it even happens to an expert cook like her) or a dish is oversalted, "Tenang-lah—tidak apa-apa!" (Relax—there's no problem!)

EQUIPMENT

KNIVES AND KITCHEN SHEARS

The following knives, all of which are common in Indonesian, Malaysian, and Singaporean kitchens, should satisfy all your needs: a classic stainless-steel or carbon-steel 8-inch (20-centimeter) chef's knife with a tapering, triangular blade (for, among other things, cutting vegetables, meats, tofu, and tempeh; the handle is also useful for bruising lemongrass stalks); a boning knife (for cutting up chickens); and a small paring knife (for peeling, chopping, and slicing aromatics and for peeling vegetables). Always keep your knives as sharp as possible. Nyonya cooks in Malaysia and Singapore use Chinese-style cleavers to hack chickens and ducks into small pieces, but the use of cleavers is not widespread outside of that community. If you own a Chinese cleaver, by all means use it for such heavy-duty tasks. Otherwise, a good, sharp chef's knife or a sturdy pair of kitchen or poultry shears should do the trick. If you're interested in learning more about knives, go online to www.knifeforums.com. The information there is mind-bogglingly thorough.

POTS, PANS, AND WOKS

The pots and pans in Malay Archipelago kitchens are similar to those found in the West. To make curries and stews, you'll need a good-sized pot, such as a Dutch oven, soup pot, stockpot, or large saucepan (see page 99 for more information on choosing a pot for curries and stews). A 12-inch (30-centimeter) nonstick skillet is handy for making *rendang* dishes, fried rice and noodles, fried chicken, omelets, and fried eggs; a 4-quart (4-liter) sauté pan is also good for *rendang* dishes. A 1 1/2-quart (1.5-liter) saucepan is great for steaming rice and deep-frying shallots, garlic, tofu, tempeh, and shrimp chips. Although small metal woks (called *wajon* or *kwali*) are a fixture of kitchens in Southeast Asia, I find that a Dutch oven or a soup pot or stockpot works just as well for stir-frying. If you do use a wok, a flat-bottomed one will work best on North American stoves. (See page 101 for more information on choosing a pan for stir-frying.)

SMALL TOOLS

I have found that a few small kitchen tools are invaluable when cooking the dishes of the Malay Archipelago:

· A sharp vegetable peeler is essential for peeling carrots, potatoes, and fresh galangal, ginger, and turmeric.

· I like wide, slotted, nylon-headed heatproof spatulas for stir-frying Asian greens. They are also good for flipping fried eggs and omelets.

· I use a stainless-steel slotted spoon to scoop up ingredients from hot oil when I'm deep-frying.

· A sturdy grater, such as a professional-quality four-sided box grater or a Microplane grater, is excellent for achieving lacy freshly grated coconut or for grating whole nutmeg.

- A pair of metal tongs is great for turning ingredients when grilling or frying and makes toasting shrimp paste easy.

MISCELLANEOUS ITEMS

Two pieces of kitchen equipment that you probably already have on hand are remarkably useful when preparing the dishes in this book:

- A half-sheet pan with 1/2-inch (12-millimeter) sides comes in handy when broiling satay or pieces of chicken. The sides prevent juicy marinades from causing messy spills in the broiler.

- When I am cleaning Asian greens, my salad spinner is indispensable. Not only does its slotted basin allow me to wash and drain greens thoroughly, but it also makes drying them quick and easy.

SMALL FOOD PROCESSORS

A small food processor with a capacity of 3 or 4 cups (24 to 32 fluid ounces/750 milliliters to 1 liter) is invaluable for preparing flavoring pastes, dressings, and marinades. My model of choice is Cuisinart's Mini-Prep Plus Processor, a small, sturdy machine with two speeds: chop and grind. The one I currently own has gone through 3 years of intensive use, and its reliability amazes me. Another good small processor is KitchenAid's Chef Series Food Chopper. (Note that some recipes call for a large food processor.)

RICE COOKERS

An electric rice cooker is a wonderful kitchen tool for anyone who cooks rice more than once or twice a week. It will consistently produce fluffy, airy rice, which lets you focus on tasks more important than keeping your eye on the rice pot. You'll find a selection of rice cookers in every Asian supermarket. I recommend that you buy a 1 1/2- to 2 1/2-quart (1.5- to 2.5-liter) model (rather than a smaller one) in case you need to make rice for a large gathering. National and Zojirushi, both Japanese made, are two good brands. Basic models come with two settings, "cook" and "warm," so once the rice is cooked, the machine will keep it warm and fluffy until it's ready to be eaten. Keep in mind that rice cookers shouldn't be used for making Lemongrass-Scented Coconut Rice (page 176) or Celebration Yellow Rice (page 178). The coconut milk used in these recipes tends to make the rice stick to the bottom of the cooker.

ABOVE LEFT: *Warm Spiced Limeade (page 355) sweetened with palm sugar is a favorite beverage in Indonesia.*

ABOVE CENTER: *Lunchtime spreads in Indonesia's Banda Islands almost always include more than five dishes.*

ABOVE RIGHT: *Spoons are sometimes laid out for people who don't want to eat with their hands.*

5. SERVING THE MEAL

Whether a grand banquet or a humble supper is being served, there are never separate courses in traditional Indonesian, Malaysian, or Singaporean meals. Instead, all dishes appear on the table in a colorful mosaic at the same time. The single constant is a large bowl of fragrant, steaming rice. When a cook plans a menu, thought is always given to how the curries, stews, grilled and fried dishes, salads, and stir-fries will balance one another, as well as how they will play off the rice—the foundation on which the other dishes rest.

Even everyday family meals may at first seem elaborate compared with those we know in the West. It's not unusual for five to eight separate dishes, not including rice, to be set out for four guests. Called *lauk pauk*, this style of eating is the origin of the rijsttafel, the Dutch interpretation of Indonesian meals. Diners fill their plates (usually shallow bowls) with rice and then place small servings of the other dishes either on top of the rice or next to it. The elements of the meal will vary according to the ingredients the cook finds at the morning market. But beyond that, she can be as creative as her imagination and skill allow. She will strive to entertain guests with a carefully thought-out range of tastes, textures, aromas, and colors. She will serve, perhaps, a vegetable stir-fry, a fish curry, a grilled fish, an omelet, some spiced fried chicken, a plate containing fresh aromatic herbs to nibble on, and a sambal—a chile-hot side dish that helps tie everything together. Serving fish, chicken, and beef or pork dishes together is common. The portions of all of these dishes, however, will be small. Even a dish like curry—what we in the West would likely regard as the highlight of the meal—is served in a relatively small portion and guests serve themselves only a little bit at a time. When planning her menu, the cook will also consider how her dishes complement and contrast one another. She'll be sure to maintain a balance of rich, hot, spicy, sweet, salty, sour, and savory tastes. Dishes that are too similarly flavored can upset the harmony of a meal. A cook will never, for example, serve more than one dish that is heavily seasoned with nutmeg or generously sweetened with palm sugar. There will almost always be a few soupy dishes on the table—usually a coconut-milk curry and a water-based stew—but usually never more than three, or they could drown the rice. There might be one or two dryish fried dishes, such as fish, tofu, or tempeh. And no meal would be complete without a stir-fried vegetable or some sort of salad or pickle to lend a refreshing accent. Because steamed rice doesn't keep well, it's one of the few items the cook will prepare just before serving the meal—and the only one eaten hot. Most other dishes, with the exception of some stir-fries and salads, will be prepared in the hours leading up to the meal and then be allowed to rest before they are served. Though they're often at room temperature by the time they are eaten, the hot rice on the plate will help warm them up.

PLANNING MEALS IN YOUR OWN HOME

The best approach to serving Indonesian, Malaysian, and Singaporean meals in your own home is to follow tradition. When you're creating menus, consider how the curries, stews, grilled and fried dishes, salads, sambals, and stir-fries will complement one another. Remember to strive for balance, too. Try pairing spicy-hot dishes, such as Rohati's Crisp-Fried Potatoes with Chile and Shallot Sambal (page 221), with mild ones, such as Javanese Spiced Oxtail Stew (page 312); sweet dishes, such as Caramelized Tempeh with Chiles (page 325), with sourish ones, such as Fragrant Fish Stew with Lime and Lemon Basil (page 240); dishes that have a lot of liquid, such as Asiah's Eggplant Curry (page 229), with those that are dry, such as Nyonya-Style Spiced Fried Chicken (page 285). The main difference between you and a traditional Malay Archipelago home cook is that you'll probably make fewer dishes. (For more specific guidance, see the Menu Suggestions that follow almost every recipe.)

It's acceptable to part with tradition in planning menus. Sometimes, for example, I put together meals of my favorite snacks and street foods. Such a menu might be served without rice and feature Shrimp Satay (page 150), Chicken Satay (page 147), Chopped Vegetable Salad with Coconut and Lime Leaf Dressing (page 156), and Bean Sprout and Potato Fritters (page 164). I also sometimes break with tradition by serving one-dish meals, rather than a group of dishes. Javanese Fried Rice (page 183) or Stir-fried Chinese Egg Noodles with Shrimp and Asian Greens (page 191) can satisfy three or four guests; each would be complemented by a light pickle such as Javanese Cucumber and Carrot Pickle (page 132).

EATING WITH ALLAH'S SILVERWARE

Perhaps the biggest culinary surprise I encountered on my first trip to Jakarta wasn't how delicious the food was, but rather how it was eaten. In Indonesia, Malaysia, and Singapore (and nearly all of Southeast Asia, from the Philippines to Myanmar), food is usually eaten with the fingers of your right hand, without the help of utensils. Though spoons and forks are popular with younger generations (the spoon is held in the right hand and used for eating, while the fork, held in the left, is used to guide the food into the spoon), eating with your hand is traditional. The only community who generally do not follow the practice are the region's ethnic Chinese, who reach for a pair of chopsticks instead. The exception is noodle dishes, which are consumed with chopsticks by nearly everyone.

I made my first foray into eating with my fingers while staying with the Alwi family, my friends in Jakarta, Indonesia. I would watch, mesmerized, as the whole family gathered around the table and began to eat from their plates in exactly the fashion that mothers all over the Western world train their young children not to do. But the Alwis did it with such grace that it hardly seemed the act of a messy toddler. "Fingers are Allah's silverware," Ramon, Tanya's younger brother, said to me at one meal. I felt left out. From the day I had arrived, I had been eating with a spoon and fork placed on the table for my benefit. One day, I finally worked up the courage to try eating the traditional way. Hoping that no one was paying close attention, I plunged into a mound of rice and curry with my right hand (the only acceptable hand for eating) and, though the rice felt squishy and I probably turned beet red from embarassment, I persevered.

Over the years I've come to appreciate the pleasure of eating with my fingers. I find it to be a more direct, sensual process, like tossing a salad with my hands rather than using tongs. And I've learned a few general tips for doing it. First, when I serve myself, I try not to drown the rice on my plate with the sauce of a curry or the gravy of a stew. Saturated rice slips away from fingers; rice that's only moist with sauce clings together, making it much easier to grasp. I also pick up the food on my plate in smallish bite-sized clumps, rather than ungainly handfuls, and I employ only my fingertips, as though I were gently squeezing a large strawberry, rather than my whole hand. Finally, I use my thumb to slide the food away from my fingertips and into my mouth, relishing the textures and flavors of each bite.

ABOVE LEFT: *An incense holder at Cheng Hoon Teng Taoist-Buddhist temple in Malacca, Malaysia.*

ABOVE CENTER: *Josephine Chua (pictured here with her eight-year-old son Daniel) is a Nyonya from Malacca, Malaysia. She provided the recipe for Nyonya Sambal (page 120).*

ABOVE RIGHT: *Antique bronze bowls in Malacca, Malaysia.*

6. CONDIMENTS: SAMBALS, DIPPING SAUCES, DRESSINGS, AND PICKLES

One October, as the bright morning sun was fading into a cloudy afternoon, my friend Josephine Chua, an architecture preservationist in her forties, and I were working our way through the *pasar besar*, the old central market in Malacca, Malaysia. Treading cautiously through a thick layer of mud—the result of a downpour the night before—we squeezed past Portuguese Malay housewives sharing cooking secrets with Chinese spice vendors, and Malay women, their hair covered by brightly colored scarves, bargaining good-naturedly with Indian vegetable merchants in crisp, white dhotis (the cloth wraparounds worn instead of pants by Indian men). It wasn't my first visit to Malacca, which had ascended to fame in the sixteenth century under spice traders from Portugal. I'd fallen under the spell of its zigzagging streets and old shophouses in 1982, and had made more than ten trips to the city since then.

Business, Josephine explained, was being conducted in the market in a dizzying array of languages, including Bahasa Malaysia, English, Hokkien, Mandarin, Cantonese, Tamil, Hindi, and Cristang, an archaic Portuguese Malay hybrid spoken only in Malacca. Josephine, a Nyonya (Chinese Malay) who had inherited her passion for cooking from her late father, Charlie, seemed to know at least a little bit of each. But food was the market's lingua franca. Seductive aromas of cumin and just-grilled fish, of sweet, ripe mangoes and freshly grated coconut—delicious smells that required no translation whatsoever—filled my nose.

Josephine prowled the slippery aisles like a cat seeking prey. She poked heaps of green and red chiles that glistened like emeralds and rubies ("too mild") and sniffed rose-colored rounds of dried shrimp paste ("*ayo*—too strong"). Finally, she scooped up some thumb-sized, purple-black eggplants and, as a gift for her favorite aunt, a bag of dark green baby *kai lan* (Chinese broccoli) so recently picked that it still smelled of rich soil. "My late father and I visited this market often when I was a child," Josephine said, as she paid the vendor for the greens. "We would ask merchants about unfamiliar ingredients and then exchange recipes. It was how I came to really know cooking, and how I came to really understand Malacca."

Josephine's need to know her Malaccan heritage, which includes the food and customs of her Nyonya ancestors, is deeply important to her. Her family's lineage in the city dates back to 1765, with the arrival of one of her forebears from China—a long history that she regards as a comforting source of continuity in a time of rapid social change.

Back at her house, and with the market mud rinsed off our shoes, Josephine invited me to watch as she made a traditional Nyonya dinner. The first task was to prepare *sambal belacan* (Nyonya Sambal, page 120), a fiery condiment of raw chiles, garlic, shallots, and grilled dried shrimp paste. I knew sambals well, having tasted hundreds of variations of them during my travels in Indonesia, Malaysia, and Singapore. Cooks use them throughout the region in much the same way that salsas are used in Mexico: to add the heat and extra dimension of chiles to the dishes they accompany.

"*Sambal belacan* is the queen of all Nyonya condiments," Josephine said. "A meal would be unthinkable without it. It is meant to enhance every single dish, from rice to curries." As she pulled a large granite mortar and pestle off a shelf, their surfaces smooth from years of use, she continued, "And this is the queen of all Nyonya kitchen tools." Josephine placed a handful of red Holland chiles in the mortar. She creased her brow thoughtfully for a moment, then added a few more. "You only live once," she said, winking.

To the slow, sweet rhythm of an old Chinese love song playing on the radio, she went about pummeling the chiles. "Come here," she said after a few minutes. "I want you to see what our cooking tradition looks like." I peered into the mortar. The mashed chiles smelled as sharp and delicious as a good vinegar. But, I asked, wouldn't she get the same results with a food processor or blender? Josephine looked at me darkly.

"Using a blender to make sambal is a crime," she said. "A blender just rips the chiles into pieces. A mortar and pestle gently coaxes the best flavor out of them."

Josephine's modesty would prevent her from proclaiming herself the excellent cook that she is, but she moved through the kitchen with the ease and grace that come only from experience and confidence. After she finished making the *sambal belacan*, she moved on to the meal's other dishes, including *acar kuning* (Sweet-Sour Cucumber and Carrot Pickle with Turmeric, page 130); and *ayam pong teh* (Nyonya Chicken and Potato Stew, page 281), a delicate sweet-salty chicken dish seasoned with sweet soybean paste.

Cooking is not the only way that Josephine honors the memory of her father and her ancestors. As a member of the Malacca Historical Research Society, she has been instrumental in the efforts to preserve the sixteenth- and seventeenth-century architecture of Malacca's development-threatened Chinatown. Along with her husband she has also overseen the restoration of Malaysia's oldest place of worship, Cheng Hoon Teng, a Taoist-

Buddhist temple constructed in the early seventeenth century. She has taken me there many times to see its ornate facade and prayer rooms, hazy from the smoke of hundreds of burning joss sticks.

Still, it's cooking that offers Josephine her most immediate connection to the past. "It allows me to communicate directly with my ancestors—to see what they were thinking, to know what they were about," she said as she heated a *kwali* (a small wok) on the stove. "My family wrote down only a few recipes, so I must preserve our cooking for tomorrow, before McDonald's wins the war and my son, Daniel, has no idea what our food tastes like."

When dinner was ready, Josephine's husband, Keong, Daniel, and I gathered around a small dining table just off the kitchen. Josephine placed the food in front of us and smiled. She squeezed some lime juice into the sambal. "Always add lime just before serving the sambal, never before," she explained. "It tastes much fresher this way." She mixed it carefully, as though it was a precious offering to the gods, and then gave me a taste on the tip of a spoon. It was potent and delicious, a testament to the Nyonya past and a prayer for its future.

⌒

The word *sambal* is derived from the south Indian *sambar*, a fiery-hot version of dal, or spiced lentil curry. But sambals in Indonesia, Malaysia, and Singapore are not curries. They are puréed or finely chopped chile-based pastes served in small bowls or dishes for guests to spoon onto their plates when they want extra heat and flavor. Though sambals nearly always use chiles as their foundation, they can contain a variety of other ingredients, including shallots, garlic, palm sugar, dried shrimp paste, lemongrass, and green mangoes. The regional variations are seemingly endless. The sambals of West Malaysia, for instance, tend to have a fine, liquidy consistency, while those of West Sumatra, Indonesia, are more coarsely textured. Throughout the region sambals are served at virtually every meal and eaten in combination with virtually every dish, from coconut milk–based curries to vegetable stir-fries. The most important dish they are served with, however, is rice. Diners combine fluffy, warm rice with sambals for a spare but incomparable balance of flavors and textures.

Sambals fall into two broad categories: raw and cooked. Raw sambals are a favorite in Malaysia, Singapore, and the Spice Islands of eastern Indonesia. Often made of pounded garlic, shallots, chiles, and toasted dried shrimp paste, they are brash and pungent and usually finished with a squeeze of fresh lime juice just before serving. Nyonya Sambal (page 120) is a fiery raw sambal from Malaysia that is made with both short green chiles (hot and grassy tasting) and long red ones (mild and sweet). Its piquant tartness makes it a perfect partner to naturally sweet dishes such as Kevin's Spiced Roast Chicken with Potatoes, Penang Style (page 287). Another raw sambal I've included here, Lemongrass and Shallot Sambal (page 122), is an unusual recipe from Bali. Rather than being ground in a mortar (or a small food processor), the ingredients are very finely chopped, resulting in a pleasantly coarse mixture with a sunny taste.

Cooked sambals, which are gently sautéed in oil until they are mellow and fragrant, are a specialty of Indonesia, though they're also widely eaten in Malaysia and Singapore. They have more subtlety and nuance than their raw counterparts, as cooking not only tames their heat but also draws flavors from the ingredients. Javanese Sambal (page 199), or *sambal bajak* (also called *sambal ulek*), a lustrously red, earthy sambal made of Holland chiles, shallots, dried shrimp paste, and a pinch of palm sugar (which adds a subtle caramel note), is the most popular sambal in Indonesia, turning up throughout the archipelago, not just in Java. It pairs exceptionally well with Tofu and Summer Vegetables in Coconut Milk (page 327) and Lemongrass-Scented Coconut Rice (page 176), though I've found that it can accompany just about every savory dish in the book. Please don't be tempted to buy ready-made *sambal bajak* in a jar, an additive-laden shadow of the freshly made version.

In Indonesia, Malaysia, and Singapore, there's no tradition of making sauces as we know them in the West. Instead, cooks offer varied dipping sauces to accompany dishes. All of these are called *sos* or *saus*, derived from the word *sauce*. The most widely known there (and in North America) is Javanese Peanut Sauce (page 128), a robust but sophisticated condiment that can be served as a dipping sauce with any of the satay recipes in this book (see pages 144 to 150) or slathered as a dressing over Gado-Gado (page 154), a composed vegetable salad of Indonesia. Other dipping sauces are less rich. Usually made with thinly sliced fresh green or red chiles, soy sauce, and, for a tart note, either lime juice or vinegar, they can be joltingly spicy or teasingly sweet and sour. They are served much like sambals: in a small bowl at the center of the table or in smaller bowls at each place setting. Guests dip foods directly into the sauce or spoon some of it judiciously onto their plates. Though dipping sauces complement nearly every savory dish, they have a particularly strong affinity for noodle dishes. Some sauces I've included here pair with specific recipes, though you may find that they go well with many other dishes, too.

In the Malay Archipelago, pickles, or *acar* (pronounced ah-CHAR, a word of Hindi origin), are lightly cured or cooked, intensely seasoned vegetable dishes that are eaten an hour or two after they are made, rather than stored away in jars to be consumed later. Their role at Indonesian, Malaysian, and Singaporean tables is almost identical to that of sambals: They give freshness and zing to meals, balancing the other flavors with their tantalizing blend of sweet and sour and hot. Among the *acar* recipes here are Sweet-Sour Cucumber and Carrot Pickle with Turmeric (page 130), a crunchy classic from Malaysia; Javanese Cucumber and Carrot Pickle (page 132), a simple but delicious dish with fiery slices of fresh green chile; South Indian–Style Eggplant Pickle (page 133), an earthy favorite seasoned with spices and black mustard seeds; and Malaysian Spiced Pineapple Pickle (page 136), a triumph of flavor, with fresh pineapple and a king's ransom of whole spices.

JAVANESE SAMBAL
Sambal Bajak or *Sambal Ulek*
(JAVA, INDONESIA)

—

This is the most popular sambal in Indonesia. It has a mellow, rather than fiery, taste because it's slowly sautéed over a low fire, which brings out the sweetness of the chiles rather than their heat. Although the palm sugar distinguishes this sambal as Javanese, sautéed sambals like this one turn up throughout Indonesia, Malaysia, and Singapore. Tasting neither too hot nor too complex, it's a perfect accompaniment to nearly every savory dish in this book.

MAKES 3/4 TO 1 CUP (ABOUT 7 OUNCES/200 GRAMS)

4 tablespoons peanut oil

1 teaspoon dried shrimp paste (page 65), pressed into a disk about 1/4 inch (6 millimeters) thick

5 shallots (about 3 3/4 ounces/110 grams total), coarsely chopped

3 cloves garlic, coarsely chopped

12 fresh red Holland chiles or other fresh long, red chiles such as Fresno or cayenne, stemmed and coarsely chopped

1 teaspoon palm sugar (page 79), thinly sliced, or dark brown sugar (for a slightly sweeter sambal, increase the sugar by 1 teaspoon)

1/2 teaspoon kosher salt

1. Heat the oil in a 12-inch (30-centimeter) skillet (nonstick will work best) over medium heat. Add the shrimp paste disk and sauté it, turning it over a few times with a spatula, until both sides have golden brown spots around the edges, 2 to 4 minutes. Don't worry if the shrimp paste crumbles as you are sautéing it. If it does break apart, just continue sautéing until all the pieces are edged with golden brown. Using a slotted spoon, remove the shrimp paste from the skillet and allow it to cool for 1 minute. Set the skillet aside with the oil in it.

2. Place the sautéed shrimp paste, shallots, garlic, chiles, palm sugar, and salt in a small food processor. Pulse until you have a chunky-smooth paste the consistency of cooked oatmeal.

3. Reheat the oil in the skillet over medium-low heat. Test to see if the oil is the right temperature by adding a pinch of the ground paste. The paste should sizzle slightly around the edges, not fry aggressively or sit motionless. When the oil is ready, add all the paste and sauté, stirring as needed to prevent sticking, until most of the liquid from the chiles and shallots has evaporated and the paste begins to separate from the oil, 9 to 14 minutes. The aroma should be subtly sweet, not harsh and oniony, and the color should be a few shades darker than when the paste was raw. Taste for salt, and add a pinch more if needed.

4. Transfer the sambal to a small bowl and allow it to cool completely before eating. Leave it in the small bowl for guests to spoon from directly, or place in small individual bowls. Leftover sambal can be refrigerated for up to 1 week, but let it come to room temperature before serving to enjoy its full flavor.

MENU SUGGESTIONS

Try *sambal bajak* with Stir-fried Asian Greens with Garlic and Chiles (page 205), Mien's Garlic Fried Chicken (page 283), Javanese Chicken Curry (page 275), and Javanese Spiced Oxtail Stew (page 312). It's also wonderful with Lemongrass-Scented Coconut Rice (page 176). If you want to break with tradition, serve it alongside a plain omelet with crusty French or Italian bread.

NYONYA SAMBAL
Sambal Belacan
(MALAYSIA)

⌐

This fiery uncooked sambal has a clean quality that offsets the rich sweetness of Nyonya foods beautifully. Increase the amount of dried shrimp paste if you want a saltier, deeper-flavored sambal. It's traditionally served in small individual dipping bowls, each garnished with a few halved *kasturi* limes that are squeezed into the sambal at the start of the meal so the tartness of the juice remains assertive. If you prefer, serve the sambal in a small communal bowl at the center of the table. Leftover Nyonya Sambal will keep in the refrigerator for up to 3 days and can be freshened with a squeeze of lime juice. Be sure to let it reach room temperature before serving—it will taste dull cold.

MAKES ABOUT 1/2 CUP (5 1/4 OUNCES/150 GRAMS)

1 1/2 to 2 1/4 teaspoons dried shrimp paste
  (page 65)

5 to 7 fresh red Holland chiles or other fresh
  long, red chiles such as Fresno or cayenne,
  stemmed and coarsely chopped

12 to 15 fresh green Thai chiles, stemmed

1 shallot (about 3/4 ounce/20 grams), coarsely
  chopped

1 clove garlic, coarsely chopped

3 *kasturi* limes (page 76), halved and seeded,
  or 1 medium-sized Persian lime (no more
  than 2 1/2 inches/6 centimeters long),
  quartered and seeded

1. Place the shrimp paste (use the larger amount for a saltier, more pronounced sambal) in the center of a 5-inch (13-centimeter) square of aluminum foil. Fold the edges of the foil over to form a small parcel, and press down with the heel of your hand to flatten the shrimp paste into a disk 1/4 inch (6 millimeters) thick. Heat a gas burner to medium-low or an electric burner to medium-high. Using a pair of tongs or 2 forks, place the sealed parcel directly on the heat source. Toast until the paste begins to smoke and release a burning, shrimpy smell, about 1 1/2 minutes. With the tongs or forks, turn the parcel over and toast the other side for another 1 1/2 minutes, then turn off the burner. Again using the tongs or forks, remove the parcel and let cool for 30 seconds to 1 minute. Carefully unwrap the foil; the edges of the disk should be black-brown and toasty and the center should be golden with some black-brown patches. Using a spoon, scrape the toasted shrimp paste into a small bowl and allow it to cool for another 30 seconds. Discard the foil.

2. Place the toasted shrimp paste, red and green chiles, shallot, and garlic in a small food processor. Pulse until you have a chunky-smooth paste the consistency of cooked oatmeal. The garlic and shallot should be well ground, but a few small pieces of chile no longer than 1/8 inch (3 millimeters) are fine. (This sambal won't need salt, as the dried shrimp paste will provide enough.)

3. Transfer the sambal to a small bowl for guests to spoon from directly, or place in small individual bowls. Just before eating, squeeze the lime into the sambal and stir well to combine.

MENU SUGGESTIONS

This bold, beautiful sambal is a great counterpoint to rich, sweet Nyonya dishes. A strong combination would be rice (to eat this fiery sambal without it would be, well, like playing with fire), Nyonya Shrimp Curry with Fresh Pineapple and Tomatoes (page 260), Nyonya Chicken and Potato Stew (page 281), Pan-Seared Tamarind Tuna (page 254, and the shrimp variation that follows on page 255), and Spiced Braised Nyonya Pork (page 307). It also goes exceptionally well with Stir-fried Chinese Egg Noodles with Shrimp and Asian Greens (page 191).

LEMONGRASS AND SHALLOT SAMBAL
Sambal Serai
(BALI, INDONESIA)

—

This delicious, easy-to-make uncooked sambal originated in Bali. Try to find the freshest, most flavorful lemongrass you can when making it. Your best bet may be in deep summer at a farmers' market that serves a large Asian community. M'Bok Wayan, a cook in the Sanur, Bali, home of my friend Mira Alwi (Tanya's older sister), makes this sambal to accompany grilled meats and fish.

MAKES ABOUT 1/3 CUP (2 3/4 OUNCES/75 GRAMS)

1 thick stalk fresh lemongrass

**2 fresh red or green Thai chiles, stemmed and
    very finely chopped**

**2 shallots (about 1 1/2 ounces/40 grams total),
    very finely chopped**

1 tablespoon peanut oil

1 tablespoon fresh lime juice

1/4 teaspoon kosher salt

1. Cut off the hard, brown bottom end and the bristly, greenish top of the lemongrass stalk, which will leave you with a pale white-and-lilac piece about 5 inches (13 centimeters) long. Discard the 2 or 3 tough outer layers. Slice the lemongrass very thinly crosswise, then chop the slices as finely as you can—it should be the consistency of sand. Using a very sharp knife will help you enormously. Transfer the lemongrass to a bowl. Make sure that the chiles and shallots are chopped just as finely. Add the chiles, shallots, oil, lime juice, and salt to the bowl. Stir well to combine. Taste for salt, and add a pinch more if needed.

2. Transfer the sambal to a small bowl for guests to spoon from directly, or place in small individual bowls. Let rest for 10 minutes before eating to allow the flavors to meld.

MENU SUGGESTIONS

Pair this citrusy sambal with dishes that will harmonize with the sunny-tasting lemongrass in it, such as Green Beans with Coconut Milk (page 216), Pan-Seared Tamarind Tuna (page 254), Mien's Garlic Fried Chicken (page 283), Kevin's Spiced Roast Chicken with Potatoes, Penang Style (page 287), and Tofu and Summer Vegetables in Coconut Milk (page 327). It also makes a great marinade for roasted or broiled fish.

GREEN MANGO SAMBAL
Sambal Mangga Muda
(SPICE ISLANDS, INDONESIA)

—

Some evenings, Karma Alwi, my friend Tanya's older brother, and I would forgo our usual treks around Jakarta in search of the best street foods, and his wife, Tuti, would cook for us. Tuti, a living Gaugin painting, was born on Ternate, a tiny Indonesian island once known as a major center for clove trading. Although she now lives in the Indonesian capital, Tuti usually wears the bright, floral-print batik dresses of her native island. Her cooking also reflects her origins. Among her favorite condiments is this Ternate classic, a hot-sour sambal with pale golden strips of green, unripe mango studding it.

MAKES ABOUT 1 CUP (ABOUT 9 OUNCES/255 GRAMS)

2 teaspoons dried shrimp paste (page 65)

8 fresh red Holland chiles or other fresh long, red chiles such as Fresno or cayenne, stemmed and coarsely chopped

1 tablespoon fresh lime juice

1/4 small green (unripe) mango, peeled and cut into fine matchsticks no more than 1/2 inch (12 millimeters) long and 1/4 inch (6 millimeters) wide (you should have about 1/2 cup/ 5 1/4 ounces/150 grams; see Cook's Note, page 124)

1. Place the shrimp paste in the center of a 5-inch (13-centimeter) square of aluminum foil. Fold the edges of the foil over to form a small parcel, and press down with the heel of your hand to flatten the shrimp paste into a disk 1/4 inch (6 millimeters) thick. Heat a gas burner to medium-low or an electric burner to medium-high. Using a pair of tongs or 2 forks, place the sealed parcel directly on the heat source. Toast until the paste

begins to smoke and release a burning, shrimpy smell, about 1 1/2 minutes. With the tongs or forks, turn the parcel over and toast the other side for another 1 1/2 minutes, then turn off the burner. Again using the tongs or forks, remove the parcel and let cool for 30 seconds to 1 minute. Carefully unwrap the foil; the edges of the disk should be black-brown and toasty and the center should be golden with some black-brown patches. Using a spoon, scrape the toasted shrimp paste into a small bowl and allow it to cool for another 30 seconds. Discard the foil.

2. Place the toasted shrimp paste, chiles, and lime juice in a small food processor. Pulse until you have a coarse paste; the chiles don't need to be completely ground for this sambal. If the paste won't purée properly and repeatedly creeps up the side of the processor instead of grinding, add up to 1 tablespoon water, a little bit at a time, periodically turning the processor off and scraping the unground portions down toward the blade. Transfer to a bowl.

3. Add the mango to the ground paste and stir well to combine. (You don't have to add salt to this sambal; the dried shrimp paste will provide enough.)

4. Transfer the sambal to a small bowl for guests to spoon from directly, or place in small individual bowls. Let rest for 10 minutes before eating to allow the flavors to meld.

COOK'S NOTE

Seek unripe mangoes (*mangga muda*), sometimes called green mangoes, in Asian and South Asian markets. Their aromatic, sweet-sour taste—somewhere between a fruit and a vegetable—is immensely appealing. Look for small (no more than 4 to 5 inches/10 to 13 centimeters long), firm green fruits (though their skin may have a few reddish flares) with no signs of softness or mushiness and with a faint mango aroma. The skin around the stem should be taut, not wrinkly. Store unripe mangoes in a cool, dark place, but not in the refrigerator, which will cause their flesh to become watery. They should keep for up to 3 days before beginning to soften (unripe mangoes will not ripen and turn sweet, however; they've been picked too soon for that to happen). Leftover unripe mango can be used in Crisp Jicama and Pineapple Salad (page 159) or cut into thick, meaty slices and eaten with salt and a little ground dried chile.

MENU SUGGESTIONS

This piquant and sour sambal goes well with rice, Pan-Seared Tamarind Tuna (page 254), Spice-Braised Tuna (page 242), Nyonya-Style Spiced Fried Chicken (page 285), and Garlic-Marinated Tempeh (page 322).

SWEET SOY SAUCE AND LIME DIPPING SAUCE

Sos Kecap Rawit

(INDONESIA)

❧

This irresistible condiment, which has a natural affinity for fried or grilled foods, is made with Indonesian sweet soy sauce (*kecap manis*). Lime juice and thinly sliced chiles are a lovely foil against the sweetness of the soy sauce.

MAKES ABOUT 1/3 CUP (2 1/2 FLUID OUNCES/75 MILLILITERS)

3 fresh red Holland chiles or other fresh long or short, red chiles such as Fresno or Thai, stemmed and thinly sliced on the diagonal

4 tablespoons Indonesian sweet soy sauce (page 72)

1 tablespoon fresh lime juice

Combine the chiles, soy sauce, and lime juice in a small bowl and mix well. Transfer the sauce to a small serving bowl for guests to spoon from directly, or place in small individual bowls. Try to use all of this sauce in one sitting, as the chiles become limp if they sit for longer than an hour in the soy sauce.

MENU SUGGESTIONS

This sauce goes well with Javanese Fried Rice (page 183), Beef Satay (page 144), or Chicken Satay (page 147)—I think it's even better with satay than peanut sauce. Also try it with rice, Stir-fried Asian Greens with Garlic and Chiles (page 205), and Javanese Spiced Oxtail Stew (page 312).

NYONYA DIPPING SAUCE

(MALAYSIA)

❧

Worcestershire sauce, a holdover from the British colonial days in Malaysia and Singapore, has never tasted as pleasing as it does in this addictive dipping sauce, the traditional accompaniment to *inche kabin* (Nyonya-Style Spiced Fried Chicken).

MAKES ABOUT 4 TABLESPOONS

2 tablespoons Worcestershire sauce

1 1/2 teaspoons fresh lime juice

1 teaspoon soy sauce

2 teaspoons sugar

1 fresh red Holland chile or other fresh long or
   short, red or green chile such as Fresno or
   Thai, stemmed and thinly sliced on the
   diagonal

Combine the Worcestershire sauce, lime juice, soy sauce, sugar, and chile in a small bowl and mix well. Transfer the sauce to a small serving bowl for guests to spoon from directly, or place in small individual bowls. Try to use all of this sauce in one sitting, as the chiles become limp if they sit for longer than an hour in the liquid.

MENU SUGGESTIONS

This sauce is traditionally paired with Nyonya-Style Spiced Fried Chicken (page 285), but it would go equally well with Stir-fried Asian Greens with Garlic and Chiles (page 205) or with most roasted or grilled meats, Asian style or otherwise.

SOY SAUCE, CHILE, AND LIME DIPPING SAUCE
Sos Cili Padi
(MALAYSIA AND SINGAPORE)

This everyday dipping sauce usually accompanies fried noodles or noodle soups. The Chinese in Malaysia and Singapore dip chopsticks full of noodles into it for a salty-hot kick and then often nibble on the chile slices for an extra jolt of heat.

MAKES ABOUT 1/3 CUP (2 1/2 FLUID OUNCES/75 MILLILITERS)

5 to 10 fresh small, red and/or green chiles
   such as Thai, stemmed and very thinly sliced

3 tablespoons soy sauce

1 1/2 tablespoons fresh lime juice

Combine the chiles, soy sauce, and lime juice in a small bowl and mix well. Transfer to a small serving bowl for guests to spoon from directly, or place in small individual bowls.

Try to use all of this sauce in one sitting, as the chiles become limp if they sit for longer than an hour in the soy sauce.

MENU SUGGESTIONS

This sauce is wonderful with Stir-fried Chinese Egg Noodles with Shrimp and Asian Greens (page 191) and Penang-Style Stir-fried Kuey Teow Noodles (page 193), but don't stop there. It complements everything from Bean Sprout and Potato Fritters (page 164) to plain steamed rice and Stir-fried Asian Greens with Garlic and Chiles (page 205).

SWEET-AND-SOUR CHILE DIPPING SAUCE

Saus Lado

(INDONESIA, MALAYSIA, AND SINGAPORE)

This is the traditional accompaniment to Bean Sprout and Potato Fritters (page 164), but it also goes well with virtually any savory Asian or non-Asian fried food, even French fries.

MAKES ABOUT 1/3 CUP (2 1/2 FLUID OUNCES/75 MILLILITERS)

4 fresh red Holland chiles or other fresh long, red chiles such as Fresno or cayenne, stemmed and thinly sliced

1 tablespoon sugar

1/4 teaspoon kosher salt

1 teaspoon palm, cider, or rice vinegar

4 tablespoons warm water

1 clove garlic, very thinly sliced lengthwise

1. Place the chiles, sugar, salt, vinegar, and water in a small food processor. Pulse until you have a smooth liquid. Transfer to a bowl.

2. Add the garlic and then taste for salt and add a pinch more if needed. Transfer to a small serving bowl for guests to spoon from directly, or place in small individual dipping bowls. Let the sauce rest for 10 minutes before serving, to give the garlic time to meld with the other ingredients. Guests can eat the garlic if they like, or they can merely allow it to infuse the sauce.

JAVANESE PEANUT SAUCE

Saus Kacang Tanah

(JAVA, INDONESIA)

—

Here is both the classic dressing for Gado-Gado (page 154) and the traditional dipping sauce for Beef Satay (page 144) and Chicken Satay (page 147). This recipe is a reconstruction of the peanut sauce made by Inam, the cook in the Jakarta home of my friend Tanya Alwi. It has none of the overbearing sweetness of most Asian peanut sauces found in North America. Instead, it's rustic and spare, with just a hint of sweetness. Look for the best-quality unsalted roasted peanuts you can find; this sauce will only be as good as the peanuts you use. Tasteless nuts or old nuts verging on rancidity will yield unappealing results. Briefly roasting the peanuts in a dry skillet on the stove top before grinding them—a technique Inam insisted on—deepens their flavor, in much the same way that pan roasting enhances the flavor of spices. Be careful not to roast the peanuts to the point where they pick up dark brown spots, or the sauce will taste bitter.

This sauce stores well in the refrigerator for up to a week. Reheat it briefly on top of the stove or in a microwave, and then allow it to return to room temperature before serving. If the sauce has become too thick, stir in a little warm water, 1 tablespoon at a time, until it's the consistency of a thick milk shake.

MAKES ABOUT 3 1/2 CUPS (28 FLUID OUNCES/875 MILLILITERS)

1 1/2 cups (about 9 ounces/255 grams)
  unsalted skinned roasted peanuts
1 1/2 teaspoons dried shrimp paste (page 65)
1 fresh red Holland or green Thai chile or other
  fresh long or short, red or green chile such
  as Fresno, cayenne, or serrano, stemmed
  and coarsely chopped, or 2 small dried red
  chiles such as árbol, stemmed and coarsely
  chopped

2 cloves garlic, coarsely chopped
3 to 4 tablespoons palm sugar (page 79), thinly
  sliced, or dark brown sugar
3/4 cup (6 fluid ounces/175 milliliters)
  unsweetened coconut milk
1 tablespoon palm, cider, or rice vinegar
3/4 teaspoon kosher salt
3/4 cup (6 fluid ounces/175 milliliters) water

1. Heat a 12-inch (30-centimeter) skillet over medium heat. (A nonstick pan works best for this sauce, which has a tendency to stick once you start cooking it.) When it's hot, add the peanuts. Rotate the pan gently over the heat, turning the peanuts every 15

seconds or so with a spatula, until they've picked up golden spots, 3 to 6 minutes. Remove the pan from the heat the moment you see signs of the spots becoming darker than golden, as the peanuts can turn brown rapidly. Transfer the peanuts to a bowl and allow them to cool completely. Set the skillet aside (you'll use it again later).

2. Place the peanuts in a large food processor (you need a large processor to accommodate the ingredients in this recipe) and pulse until they are well ground. They should be the consistency of sand. Be careful that you don't pulse too much and end up with peanut butter. Leave the ground peanuts in the processor.

3. Place the shrimp paste in the center of a 5-inch (13-centimeter) square of aluminum foil. Fold the edges of the foil over to form a small parcel, and press down with the heel of your hand to flatten the shrimp paste into a disk 1/4 inch (6 millimeters) thick. Heat a gas burner to medium-low or an electric burner to medium-high. Using a pair of tongs or 2 forks, place the sealed parcel directly on the heat source. Toast until the paste begins to smoke and release a burning, shrimpy smell, about 1 1/2 minutes. With the tongs or forks, turn the parcel over and toast the other side for another 1 1/2 minutes, then turn off the burner. Again using the tongs or forks, remove the parcel and let cool for 30 seconds to 1 minute. Carefully unwrap the foil; the edges of the disk should be black-brown and toasty and the center should be golden with some black-brown patches. Using a spoon, scrape the toasted shrimp paste into a small bowl and allow it to cool for another 30 seconds. Discard the foil.

4. Add the toasted shrimp paste, chile, garlic, and palm sugar to the peanuts in the food processor. Pulse until you have a well-ground mixture. Don't overgrind the mixture—it shouldn't be creamy like smooth peanut butter.

5. Transfer the ground ingredients to the same skillet you used to roast the peanuts. Add the coconut milk and stir well to combine. The mixture will be quite thick. Bring it to a gentle simmer over medium-low to medium heat. Continue to cook at a gentle simmer, stirring constantly, until a few droplets of oil released from the coconut milk appear on the surface, 5 to 7 minutes. (If the oil doesn't do this, don't worry. Just proceed after 7 minutes anyway.) Add the vinegar and salt and stir well to combine. Add the water and stir well to combine. The sauce should be the consistency of pea soup. If it's thicker than that, add warm water, 1 tablespoon at a time, until it's the right consistency. If it's too thin, let it slowly bubble away for 3 to 5 minutes until it thickens.

6. Taste for salt, and add a pinch more if needed. Transfer to a bowl and set aside to cool before using.

SWEET-SOUR CUCUMBER AND CARROT PICKLE WITH TURMERIC
Acar Kuning
(MALAYSIA)

⌒

Made of colorful strips of carrot, cucumber, and chiles that have been lightly cured in salt and seasoned with a gingery flavoring paste, this addictive Malaysian pickle is usually served with the Malaysian version of coconut rice, *nasi lemak*. Black mustard seeds, an ingredient introduced by south Indian spice traders (and the British indentured servants who followed them), have been adopted by Malaysian cooks as their own. Here, they provide the pickle with a hint of earthiness.

MAKES 4 SERVINGS

4 or 5 small Kirby (pickling) cucumbers (about 14 ounces/400 grams total), unpeeled, stemmed, and cut into matchsticks about 2 inches (5 centimeters) long and 1/4 inch (6 millimeters) wide

2 medium-sized carrots (about 7 ounces/200 grams total), peeled and cut into matchsticks about 2 inches (5 centimeters) long and 1/4 inch (6 millimeters) wide

3 shallots (about 2 1/2 ounces/70 grams total), thinly sliced lengthwise

1 or 2 fresh red Holland chiles or other fresh long, red chiles such as Fresno or cayenne, stemmed and sliced on the diagonal about 1/4 inch (6 millimeters) thick

2 1/2 teaspoons kosher salt

FOR THE FLAVORING PASTE

4 shallots (about 3 ounces/85 grams total), coarsely chopped

2 cloves garlic, coarsely chopped

3 candlenuts (page 48) or unsalted macadamia nuts

1 piece fresh ginger, 2 inches (5 centimeters) long, peeled and thinly sliced against the grain (about 2 tablespoons)

1 piece fresh or thawed, frozen turmeric (page 92), 2 inches (5 centimeters) long, peeled and coarsely chopped (about 2 teaspoons), or 2 teaspoons ground turmeric

2 to 8 small dried red chiles such as árbol, stemmed and coarsely chopped

5 tablespoons (2 1/2 fluid ounces/75 milliliters) peanut oil

1/4 teaspoon black mustard seeds (page 47)

4 tablespoons palm, cider, or rice vinegar

4 tablespoons sugar

1. Place the cucumbers, carrots, shallots, and chiles into a nonreactive bowl and sprinkle the salt over them. Massage the salt into the vegetables, then cover the bowl with plastic wrap or aluminum foil and set it aside at room temperature for 1 1/2 to 2 hours, stirring the vegetables every 30 minutes to distribute the salt evenly. The vegetables will lightly cure during this time, softening yet retaining a pleasing, gentle crunchiness.

2. Meanwhile, make the flavoring paste. Place the shallots, garlic, candlenuts, ginger, turmeric, and chiles in a small food processor. Pulse until you have a smooth paste the consistency of creamy mashed potatoes. If the paste won't purée properly and repeatedly creeps up the side of the processor instead of grinding, add up to 2 tablespoons water, 1 tablespoon at a time, periodically turning the processor off and scraping the unground portions down toward the blade.

3. Heat the oil in a 12-inch (30-centimeter) skillet (nonstick will work best) over medium-high heat. When it's hot but not smoking—it should appear shimmery—add the mustard seeds. As soon as they begin to pop and sputter (about 30 seconds), take the pan off the burner and wait a moment for the oil to cool down. Reduce the heat to medium-low, return the pan to the stove top, and let it heat for a minute. Test to see if the oil is the right temperature by adding a pinch of the ground paste. The paste should sizzle slightly around the edges, not fry aggressively or sit motionless. When the oil is ready, add all the paste and sauté, stirring as needed to prevent scorching, until the smell of raw shallots subsides and the aroma of the ginger takes over, 5 to 7 minutes. Add the vinegar and sugar and stir to combine. Raise the heat slightly and bring the liquid to a lively simmer. Stir constantly until the sugar dissolves and the vinegar is well amalgamated with the flavoring paste, about 2 minutes (maybe fewer). Remove the skillet from the heat and set it aside.

4. After the vegetables have been sitting for at least 1 1/2 hours, taste a slice of cucumber. Like a good dill pickle, it should be pleasantly salty but not aggressively so. If the cucumber slice has just the right amount of saltiness, drain the vegetables in a colander, gently pressing down on them with your hands to remove as much brine as possible. Place the vegetables on paper towels to dry for about 15 minutes. If the cucumber slice is too salty (which will likely be the case), you'll need to rinse away some of the salt. Immerse the vegetables in cold water and, with your hands, massage them around in the water to rinse off the brine. Drain the vegetables in a colander, gently pressing down on them with your hands to remove as much brine as possible. Taste another slice of cucumber. If it is still very salty, repeat the rinsing process up to 4 times, or until the saltiness is corrected. Keep in mind, however, that this is a pickle dish, so the vegetables shouldn't be bland. Place the vegetables on paper towels to dry for about 15 minutes. They don't need to be bone-dry, but they shouldn't be soggy.

5. Add the vegetables to the now-cooled flavoring paste in the skillet and stir well with a spoon or spatula to combine.

6. Transfer the pickle to a serving dish and allow to rest for at least 30 minutes before serving. Alternatively, store in a jar with a tight-fitting lid in the refrigerator and eat within 5 days. Bring to room temperature before eating. The taste will be bolder.

MENU SUGGESTIONS

These sunny pickles will spruce up almost any meal, but they're particularly good with Lemongrass-Scented Coconut Rice (page 176), Chile Omelet (page 334), Tofu and Summer Vegetables in Coconut Milk (page 327), and Padang Fish Curry (page 244).

JAVANESE CUCUMBER AND CARROT PICKLE
Acar Timun
(JAVA, INDONESIA)

⸺

Here's an easier-to-make version of Sweet-Sour Cucumber and Carrot Pickle with Turmeric (page 130) Since it contains no flavoring paste, its taste is not as complex, but it's no less tasty. A winning combination of cucumbers, carrots, shallots, and a few slivered green chiles in a sweet-sour brine, *acar timun* is one of the first pickles I fell in love with in Indonesia, where it's commonplace at meals. Some cooks cure the vegetables in salt in the same way they're cured for Sweet-Sour Cucumber and Carrot Pickle with Turmeric. This recipe offers a shortcut, steeping the vegetables in hot salted water for 15 minutes, rather than in salt for 2 hours. The result is a cure that's not as deeply flavorful but just as satisfying.

MAKES 4 SERVINGS

3 small Kirby (pickling) cucumbers (about 10 ounces/285 grams total), unpeeled, stemmed, and sliced into matchsticks about 2 inches (5 centimeters) long and 1/4 inch (6 millimeters) wide

1 large carrot (about 5 ounces/140 grams), peeled and cut into matchsticks about 2 inches (5 centimeters) long and 1/4 inch (6 millimeters) wide

3 shallots (about 2 1/2 ounces/70 grams total), thinly sliced lengthwise

1 1/2 tablespoons kosher salt

**2 cups (16 fluid ounces/500 milliliters) boiling
water**

2 heaping tablespoons sugar

2 tablespoons palm, cider, or rice vinegar

**2 fresh green Thai chiles, stemmed and cut on
the diagonal into slices 1/4 inch (6 millimeters) thick**

1. Combine the cucumbers, carrot, shallots, and salt in a heatproof nonreactive bowl. Pour the boiling water over the vegetables and stir well. Cover the bowl with plastic wrap or aluminum foil and let the vegetables rest for 15 minutes.

2. Drain the vegetables in a colander, gently squeezing out excess water with your hands. They should be fairly dry, but they need not be bone-dry.

3. Transfer the vegetables to a nonreactive bowl. Add the sugar, vinegar, and chiles and stir well to combine. Taste a cucumber. It should have a balance of saltiness, sourness, and sweetness. Keep in mind that this is a condiment and should be fairly strongly flavored. Adjust the seasonings, including the salt, accordingly.

4. Allow the dish to rest for at least 15 minutes, to give the flavors time to settle. Serve the pickle at room temperature, never cold, which will mute the flavor. This pickle should be eaten within 2 hours of making it. If left for longer, it will lose its perkiness and robustly sweet-tart flavor.

MENU SUGGESTIONS

Serve this crunchy condiment with Lemongrass-Scented Coconut Rice (page 176), Beef Satay (page 144), Chicken Satay (page 147), or virtually any savory dish in this book. Its balance of sweet and sour is a perfect complement to countless foods.

SOUTH INDIAN–STYLE EGGPLANT PICKLE

Acar Terung

(MALAYSIA)

⌐

This south Indian–style pickle is popular in Malaysian kitchens, although the sugar in it is a decidedly Malaysian addition. Similar to caponata, the Sicilian eggplant relish, it's made of chunks of Japanese eggplants in a lavishly spiced sweet-sour pickling base. Coriander, fennel, cumin, chiles, ginger, and cinnamon all vie for dominance, creating a lush layering of flavors. The eggplants are fried and then put in the pickling base, rather than cooked in it. Japanese eggplants, which are commonly used in Malaysian cuisine, cook quickly, so frying them first gives you more control, ensuring that they won't come out mushy.

MAKES 4 SERVINGS

FOR THE FLAVORING PASTE

2 tablespoons coriander seeds

1/2 teaspoon fennel seeds

1 teaspoon cumin seeds

3 to 5 small dried red chiles such as árbol, stemmed and coarsely chopped

2 cloves garlic, coarsely chopped

1 piece fresh ginger, 2 inches (5 centimeters) long, peeled and thinly sliced against the grain (about 2 tablespoons)

1 pound (455 grams) small Japanese eggplants (about 4 eggplants), stemmed, unpeeled, halved lengthwise, and cut crosswise into pieces 3 inches (7.5 centimeters) long

1 teaspoon ground turmeric

Peanut oil for frying

1/4 teaspoon black mustard seeds (page 47)

15 fresh curry leaves (page 63; optional)

1 piece cinnamon stick, 2 inches (5 centimeters) long

2 fresh red Holland chiles or other fresh long, red chiles such as Fresno or cayenne, stemmed, halved lengthwise, and cut crosswise into pieces 3 inches (7.5 centimeters) long (optional)

1/3 cup (2 1/2 fluid ounces/75 milliliters) palm, cider, or rice vinegar

1 tablespoon sugar

3/4 teaspoon kosher salt

1. To make the flavoring paste, place the coriander, fennel, cumin, and dried chiles in a small food processor. Pulse until ground to a dusty powder, about 2 minutes.

2. Add the garlic and ginger to the ground spices and pulse until you have a smooth paste the consistency of creamy mashed potatoes. If the paste won't purée properly and repeatedly creeps up the side of the processor instead of grinding, add up to 2 tablespoons water, 1 tablespoon at a time, periodically turning the processor off and scraping the unground portions down toward the blade. Set the flavoring paste aside.

3. Place the eggplant pieces in a large bowl and dust the turmeric over them. With your hands, massage the turmeric into the eggplant until it fairly evenly coats the fleshy side (not the skin side) of each piece.

4. Pour oil to a depth of 1 inch (2.5 centimeters) into a 12-inch (30-centimeter) skillet and heat over medium to medium-high heat until hot but not smoking. To test if the oil is the right temperature (it should be about 365°F/185°C), spear a piece of eggplant onto a fork and dip the edge of the piece into the hot oil. If it begins to fry and a froth of oil immediately bubbles up around it, the oil is ready. Fry the eggplant in batches of no more than a few pieces at a time (you don't want to crowd the skillet) until the fleshy side of each piece just begins to turn golden and you can barely prick it with a fork, about 1 1/2 minutes. The eggplant should be just cooked and not at all soft or mushy. Using a slotted spoon, transfer the eggplant to paper towels to drain.

5. Pour off all but about 2 tablespoons of the oil and raise the heat to medium-high. Toss in the mustard seeds. As soon as they begin to pop and sputter (about 30 seconds), add the curry leaves (if using) and cinnamon and stir them in the oil with a spatula. Sauté the curry leaves until they have translucent patches, 10 to 45 seconds. Remove the pan from the heat and wait a moment for the oil to cool down.

6. Return the pan to medium-low heat. When the oil is hot, add the fresh chiles (if using) and the flavoring paste. Sauté, stirring as needed to prevent scorching, until the aroma of the spices overtakes the garlic and the chiles have wilted significantly, 5 to 7 minutes. Add the vinegar, sugar, and salt and stir to combine. Raise the heat slightly and bring the liquid to a gentle simmer. Stir constantly until the sugar dissolves and the vinegar is well combined with the flavoring paste, about 2 minutes. Remove the pan from the heat.

7. Add the fried eggplant pieces and stir, making sure each piece is well coated with the flavoring paste. Taste a piece of eggplant for salt, and add a pinch more if needed.

8. Transfer the pickle to a serving bowl and set aside for 1 to 2 hours, to allow the flavors to meld and intensify. Eat at room temperature. This pickle is even more delicious the next day.

MENU SUGGESTIONS

Serve this complex-tasting pickle with rice and Pan-Seared Tamarind Tuna (page 254) or Grilled Coconut Chicken with Lemon Basil (page 292). It also works well tucked inside a Western-style roast-meat sandwich or as a delicious component on an antipasto plate in place of caponata.

MALAYSIAN SPICED PINEAPPLE PICKLE
Paceri Nenas
(MALAYSIA)

‏

Pineapples often find their way into sweet-savory dishes in Malaysia. This dish, with large wedges of pineapple in a sumptuously spiced pickling broth, has a spicy, sweet taste that may remind you of Anglo-Indian–style mango chutney. Although usually served as part of a rice meal, it also makes an excellent accompaniment to Western-style roasted meats and poultry, including duck and goose. This recipe was given to me by Asiah Abdul Kadir, an excellent cook in Kelantan, Malaysia, who occasionally adds golden raisins to it. Her best advice: use the sweetest, freshest pineapples you can get your hands on, and don't cook them to the point of mushiness.

MAKES 4 SERVINGS

2 tablespoons peanut oil

1 piece cinnamon stick, 1 inch (2.5 centimeters) long

8 whole cloves

1 teaspoon fennel seeds

3 green cardamom pods, cracked open with the flat side of a knife (page 49)

1 whole star anise

3 cloves garlic, thinly sliced lengthwise

1 piece fresh ginger, 3 inches (7.5 centimeters) long, peeled, thinly sliced with the grain, and cut into narrow matchsticks about 1 inch (2.5 centimeters) long

3 shallots (about 2 1/2 ounces/70 grams total), thinly sliced

2 to 4 tablespoons palm sugar (page 79), thinly sliced, or dark brown sugar

4 tablespoons water

1 small pineapple, about 3 pounds (1.4 kilograms), peeled, cored, and cut into chunky wedges about 2 by 2 by 1 1/4 inches (5 by 5 by 3 centimeters; about 4 cups/2 1/2 pounds/1.1 kilograms; for more information about pineapples, see Cook's Note, page 137)

3 fresh red Holland chiles or other fresh long, red chiles such as Fresno or cayenne, stemmed and halved lengthwise (optional, but they add splendid color and heat)

3/4 teaspoon kosher salt

1. Heat the oil in a 12-inch (30-centimeter) skillet over medium-low heat. When it is hot, add the cinnamon, cloves, fennel, cracked cardamom pods, and star anise and stir well to combine. Sauté, stirring constantly, until the combined aroma of the spices wafts up, about 2 minutes. Add the garlic, ginger, and shallots and continue sautéing, stirring

often, until the garlic and shallots have just wilted, about 3 minutes. Don't let them change color.

2. Add 2 tablespoons palm sugar and the water and stir well. Continue stirring until the palm sugar has dissolved into the water, about 1 minute. Add the pineapple, chiles (if using), and salt and stir well to combine. Raise the heat slightly to bring the liquid to a simmer. Cover and cook, stirring occasionally, until the pineapple is no longer raw and can be easily pierced with a fork, about 5 minutes.

3. Remove the lid and cook at a lively simmer, stirring occasionally, until the liquid has reduced by one-fourth, 6 to 10 minutes. Taste a bit of pineapple for salt, and add a pinch more if needed. Also taste for sweetness. If the pineapple is very sour (or if you merely prefer a pickle that's more sweet than tart), add up to 2 tablespoons more palm sugar and stir until the sugar has dissolved. This pickle shouldn't be too soupy; the liquid should be somewhat syrupy. If it's too soupy, let it continue to cook, with the lid off, until it thickens to the correct consistency.

4. Transfer the pickle to a serving dish and allow it to cool to room temperature before eating.

COOK'S NOTE

Choosing the sweetest, ripest pineapple can be tricky. Keep in mind that pineapples don't sweeten after they are picked. Bringing home the ripest one you can get your hands on is always the best policy. The first thing I do is feel the pineapple. I favor small fruits with heft, knowing that the heavier the pineapple, the juicier it will be. Next, I feel the surface. It should be firm to the touch all over, with absolutely no soft or bruised spots (a sign of rot). The skin should have a nice sheen and a greenish or yellowish tint, depending on the variety of pineapple. I investigate to make sure there is no mold at the base, then give a good sniff. The fragrance should be sweet and fresh, not sour or fermented. Finally, I investigate the leaves. They shouldn't show too much wear and tear, and the innermost leaves should pop off easily when pulled.

MENU SUGGESTIONS

This pickle is perfect with rice, Asiah's Eggplant Curry (page 229), and Acehnese Goat Curry (page 314). It's also wonderful alongside simple roasted meats, much as you would serve a sweet-sour Anglo-Indian fruit chutney.

  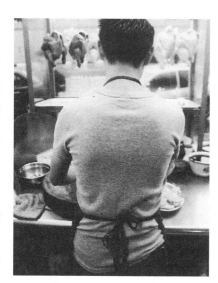

ABOVE LEFT: *The proprietor of a street-food stall in Jakarta, Indonesia.*

ABOVE CENTER: *Nyonya dishes aren't found only in homes—in Georgetown, Malaysia, they're a popular street food.*

ABOVE RIGHT: *Vendor serving chicken rice, a succulent street treat, in Kuala Lumpur's Chinatown.*

7. STREET FOODS: SATAYS, SALADS, AND SNACKS

Before I met Karma, the older brother of my friend Tanya Alwi, Tanya gave me some advice. "Karma has the biggest heart in the world. But let me warn you: he's *very* cerebral," she said. "He's what you in America call an eccentric." It was 1982, during my first trip to Indonesia, and we were stuck in Jakarta traffic in Tanya's mint green Land Cruiser. I stared out the window into the steamy afternoon. It started to pour, with raindrops the size of quarters. A sarong-clad *jamu* (traditional medicine) vendor, her back weighted down with a rattan basket full of gnarled medicinal roots, ran for cover.

We turned off the main road onto a smaller, bumpier one that wound its way toward Karma's home. A few minutes later we reached a one-story cement house tucked away in a grove of old eucalyptus trees. We parked in the driveway and walked to the front porch. The rain had stopped. The chirping of crickets filled the air. Karma sat on the porch in half darkness, his head buried in a small paperback book. He was in his late thirties and had skin the color of milky tea. He wore a pale yellow tunic and, despite the intense heat of that afternoon, a *beci*, an oblong black-velvet hat that marks a devoutly Muslim man in Indonesia. As we approached, Karma remained focused on his book, unmoved by our presence. Tanya sat down in a nearby chair and indicated, with a subtle arching of her eyebrows, that I should do the same. Karma continued to read his book. It was called *Dukun!* and sported a garish grinning skull on the cover. I knew that *dukun* means "witch doctor." After a few more minutes of silence, Karma cleared his throat.

"Indonesia is a riddle that will never be solved," he whispered in English. Then he turned to me and said, "My name is Karma. They say it's no accident that my parents named me that." He lit a clove cigarette. Its fragrant smoke curled around his head like a halo.

In the next few months, Karma and I got together regularly. I would stop by his home in the afternoon, eager to hear him talk about the world. In the dark quiet of his study, I'd listen to him discourse on topics as varied as the origins of language and U.S. imperialism.

But a lot of our time together centered on another activity: eating. Every day at sunset, after we'd worked up an appetite talking, we'd jump into his car and drive around Jakarta in search of the best street-food stalls, or *warung-warung* (the plural form of *warung*). "Jakarta is a melting pot, so there are cooks here from all over the country selling their favorite dishes," Karma explained. "If you want to know what Indonesia tastes like, all you have to do is drive around this city and eat."

On one of these snack expeditions we stopped at a small, tent-covered streetside *warung* specializing in *gado-gado*, the Indonesian vegetable salad topped with peanut dressing. It was a comforting dish, with leafy green lettuce, mung bean sprouts, and thick slices of cooked carrots and fried potatoes in a dressing made of coconut milk and ground peanuts. On another night a few days later, Karma and I decided to forgo a sit-down dinner and stopped instead at a street vendor near his home for a sweet snack of *pisang goreng* (bananas dipped in a tempura-like batter and deep-fried). They were crunchy and warm, a perfect light meal in the Jakarta moonlight.

Another evening, just after *magrib*, the late-afternoon Islamic prayer, Karma told me he had a special treat planned for dinner. "Tonight we're going to try satay," he said. I looked at him in surprise. We had ended our snacking tour the night before with satay. "It's not just any satay," Karma clarified. "We're trying satay in the style of Surabaya, the capital of East Java. It's made of goat, usually. They say that a Surabayan cook who can make a good satay is like a magician, and her *bumbu-bumbu* (flavoring paste) is her incantation."

We soon arrived at the satay place, a small tin hut next to a tangle of tall, green banana plants. In the dim afterglow of sunset, it looked like an exotic jungle ruin. Karma approached the cook, a short woman with muscular arms, and placed our order. She picked up a bowl full of meat already threaded onto bamboo skewers and marched outside without saying a word. "Maybe something bad just happened to her?" I asked.

"No," Karma said. "She's always like this. She focuses on cooking, not friendliness."

I peered through a small window that had been cut in the side of the stall and watched as the cook approached a small hibachi-like grill just a few feet away. The meat hit the grill with a sizzle, and she began to fan the fire vigorously, as though she were calling the flames to life. Plumes of sweet-smelling smoke rose in the air.

"The aroma is incredible. What kind of coals is she using?" I asked.

"Coconut shells," said Karma. "They flavor the meat with the tropics."

After a few minutes, the cook removed the skewers from the grill and laid them atop a leaf she'd just torn from a nearby banana plant. She placed the skewers in front of us. I inhaled deeply. They smelled lush and smoky. "Now," Karma said in the low tone he reserved for very important topics, "I want you to really taste this satay. I want you to experience all its different levels of flavor."

He offered me a skewer. I slid a piece of meat off with my teeth. It gave new meaning to the word *tender*. I closed my eyes and could taste smoke, fresh turmeric, tamarind, and galangal—flavorings I was just beginning to recognize. The goat was intensely complex, as though it had taken in the essence of an entire spice market. "Don't dip the meat in the sauces," Karma said, referring to the *sos kecap rawit* (a mixture of sweet soy sauce and chiles) and the *saus kacang* (peanut sauce) on the side. "They will camouflage its true taste."

As we continued eating, I fell under the cook's spell, each bite tasting more delicious than the one before. In the distance, a gamelan orchestra was tuning up, its chords rising up over the sound of nearby traffic. Karma smiled. It was the kind of only-in-Indonesia soundtrack that he loved. But it was the satay that really stirred my senses.

—

Indonesia, Malaysia, and Singapore are a snacker's paradise. Everywhere you look, from the jammed city boulevards to the smallest rice-farming villages, you see stalls and pushcarts brimming with tempting street foods. After years of visiting, I plan my days around what I'm going to snack on. For breakfast I crave sweet treats like fried plantains. For lunch I can't live without a hearty plate of *gado-gado* at my favorite roadside stall. And later, when the sun sets and I'm *really* starving, I must have my nightly fix of the king of street foods, satay. I'm not particular about the variety. Beef, chicken, goat, and shrimp all suit me just fine.

Street foods in all three countries have been raised to an art form. In Indonesian cities and towns, vendors spill into the streets by the thousands in stalls made of wood or scrap metal, inches away from speeding traffic. They also roam the streets twenty-four hours a day, pushing colorful *kaki lima*, "five-footed" pushcarts (five footed refers to the three wheels of the pushcart—one front, two back—plus the two feet of the person pushing it). In Singapore and Malaysia, where order-obsessed local officials frown on food stalls and pushcarts clogging the streets and sidewalks, vendors (or hawkers, as they're called in those countries) are usually confined to permanent hawker centers or independently owned *kopi tiam* (small, open-air coffee shops), with up to three hundred merchants offering their specialties from tiny stalls under constantly whirring ceiling fans. Vendors promote their foods through tempting displays and in colorful hand-painted signs, with each one boasting the most authentic or best-tasting version of a particular dish, such as the most delicious *popiah*, a fresh spring roll filled with raw and cooked vegetables, or the crispiest *rojak* (page 159), a savory fruit salad. Their kitchens are humble—usually no more than a few burners (often just a single coal-fueled fire) and a sink—but the foods created in them are as sophisticated and delicious as anything I've ever eaten.

Although most of the recipes in this book are for dishes served in homes, almost all those in this chapter are for foods made most famously by street vendors. They are snacks and tidbits, noshes and nibbles—foods designed to intrigue (or gently satisfy) the palate, not fill the belly. I've chosen recipes that are relatively fuss free. You don't need a hawker's deft hand to make them, nor do they require special tools, save bamboo skewers, or ingredients that you won't already have in your Indonesian-Malaysian-Singaporean larder. And though they were originally intended as snacks, I've found that most make wonderful main courses when served with rice.

Satay (spelled *sate* in Indonesia, Malaysia, and Singapore, but pronounced the same way we pronounce it) is the most famous dish in this chapter, and for good reason: nibbling on a satay stick, when it's warm and infused with the primal aroma of the fire it was cooked over, is one of the world's great eating pleasures. Because Thai restaurateurs in the United States regularly serve satay, many people mistakenly believe that satay is from Thailand. Although it is historically eaten in southern Thailand, its actual origins are thought to be the kebabs that Arab spice merchants introduced to Java, Indonesia, by the eighth century. The Javanese embraced the Arab kebabs as if they were their own, developing marinades with their favorite aromatics, including coriander, ginger, galangal, lemongrass, garlic, and shallots.

Countless regional variations exist. Some satays are made of goat, pork, or beef, others of chicken, shrimp, or fish—or even turtle. Most, however, have two things in common: they are marinated in bright-tasting seasonings, and the food is threaded onto thin, short, pointed skewers made of bamboo or the center rib of a coconut palm. (Some regional satays, such as *sate lilit* of Bali, Indonesia, call for ground meat, which is pressed onto the skewer in a small oblong paddy.) The three satay recipes here, Beef Satay (page 144), Chicken Satay (page 147), and Shrimp Satay (page 150), are from Indonesia, Malaysia, and Singapore, respectively. I predict that once you make them, they'll quickly become part of your permanent repertoire.

Though satay is the most recognizable street food, its popularity is nearly eclipsed by salads. Indonesian, Malaysian, and Singaporean salads are not salads in the usual Western sense. Instead, they're robust one-dish meals with contrasting raw and cooked ingredients designed to appeal to the eye as much as the palate. The best known of these is Indonesia's *gado-gado* (page 154). A not-too-distant relation of *gado-gado* is *rojak*, a celebrated street dish with Indonesian origins. My favorite *rojak* (and the recipe I've included here, Crisp Jicama and Pineapple Salad, page 159) is from the Malaysian city of Malacca. It's made of coarsely chopped tropical fruits and topped with a sweet-savory dressing that harmonizes beautifully with the crunchy fruits.

Crisp, deep-fried savory snacks, the final category of street dishes in this chapter, are usually served as breakfast or midday treats. Although you may not regard yourself as a fan of deep-fried foods, I encourage you to try Fried Sweet Plantains (page 161) and Bean Sprout and Potato Fritters (page 164). As long as the cooking oil is intensely hot, they'll come out practically greaseless, like a fine Japanese tempura, with crunchy outer shells concealing warm, moist centers. Though I love these snacks in the morning, they're just as appealing late at night, purchased from a roving *kaki lima* or made in your own kitchen. Serve both with their natural accompaniment, glasses of sweetened hot orange pekoe tea.

COOKING SATAY

Be sure to cut satay meat according to the directions given in each recipe in this chapter. With the exception of shrimp, which are cooked whole, satay meat should be cut thinly, not thick and kebablike. Thin slices absorb aromatic marinades more effectively, resulting in tender, more flavorful satay. Thick-cut satay produces an inferior-tasting, chewy version.

Whether you're cooking satay on a grill or broiling it in the oven, it's important to use the hottest fire possible. Perfect satay, cooked over a forceful live fire, is delicately charred on the outside and just done and juicy on the inside. Cooking time will vary according to the kind of meat you're using, but it should always be a speedy process. (No satay takes longer than 12 minutes to cook.) Beef takes the longest; shrimp, with its delicate flesh and high moisture content, the shortest. Never overcook any satay, or it will be dry and grainy. Conversely, don't undercook it. Rare meat will throw off the balance of flavors.

If you're grilling satay, build your fire as high as you can, stacking the coals evenly so that the food will be quite near to them. You ideally want the coals to be no farther than 2 to 3 inches (5 to 7.5 centimeters) from the grill rack. A hibachi, with its shallow fire bed, works best. You may need to adjust the coals between satay batches to ensure that the heat remains as high, robust, and evenly distributed as possible. A gas grill works fine, but will, of course, provide little of the elemental taste of a charcoal-fueled fire.

If you're broiling satay, preheat the oven for at least 10 minutes so it gets intensely hot. You want the meat to begin to sear the moment it nears the heat source, as it would if it were being cooked on a grill. Adjust the oven rack according to the instructions in the individual recipes. Shrimp satay broils best when only 1 to 2 inches (2.5 to 5 centimeters) from the heat source; beef and chicken are best at a distance of about 3 inches (7.5 centimeters). I use a half-sheet pan with 1/2-inch (12-millimeter) sides (to help prevent spills) to move my satay skewers in and out of the broiler. I don't recommend stove-top grill pans for cooking satay. They do give meat attractive "grill" marks, but rather than searing the meat, they sauté it, which does nothing for its taste or texture.

If you broil satay, the exposed portions of the bamboo skewers will likely scorch or burn. You can try to prevent this by soaking the skewers in water for at least 30 minutes before using them (a good idea even if you're using a grill, since skewers can also burn when exposed to its heat). Make sure to shake off any excess soaking water before threading the meat. A more reliable way to prevent skewers from burning is to place aluminum-foil collars over the exposed portions before sliding the skewers into the oven, though this can be a bit cumbersome if your oven is small.

Satay is one of the few dishes in this book that tastes best when served immediately. Calculate ahead how to get it from the grill or oven to your guests' mouths in as short a time as possible.

BEEF SATAY
Sate Sapi
(JAVA, INDONESIA)

There are few more dependable sounds in Indonesia than the rhythmic rat-a-tat-tat-tat of satay vendors who roam the streets and alleys of every town and village announcing their presence with a wooden stick rapped against their portable grills. When a customer approaches, the satay man sets up his makeshift kitchen—a tiny grill, a basket containing the already skewered meat, a fan to give life to the fire—on the spot and grills skewers to order. The smoky-sweet aroma is irresistible, and soon neighbors can't help but gather to order some for themselves.

This recipe is from Jimi, a West Javanese street vendor with a languid smile. Over the course of three hot nights in the 1980s, on an extended stay in Bogor, West Java, I watched him grill petite skewers of this delicious satay as he made his rounds. Eventually I worked up the courage to ask him for his recipe, which he gladly shared. Ginger, coriander, and palm sugar are the keynote tastes. The tamarind in the marinade acts as a powerful tenderizer, making even very chewy meat tender, so it's important to use a somewhat toothsome piece of beef, such as flank steak or skirt steak. Sirloin steak, while less chewy, will also work well. If you start with tender meat, the marinade is likely to make it mushy.

For a skewerless satay, try using this marinade for a whole piece of flank steak, then broil the meat as you would for London broil.

MAKES ABOUT 20 SKEWERS

FOR THE MARINADE

2 teaspoons tamarind pulp, plus 3 tablespoons
very warm water to make extract

1 tablespoon coriander seeds

3 shallots (about 2 1/2 ounces/70 grams total),
coarsely chopped

2 cloves garlic, coarsely chopped

1 piece fresh or thawed, frozen turmeric (page
92), 1/2 inch (12 millimeters) long, peeled

and coarsely chopped (scant 1 teaspoon),
or 1 teaspoon ground turmeric

1 piece fresh ginger, 1/2 inch (12 millimeters)
long, peeled and thinly sliced against the
grain (about 1 1/2 teaspoons)

2 teaspoons palm sugar (page 79), thinly
sliced, or dark brown sugar

1 teaspoon peanut oil

1/2 to 3/4 teaspoon kosher salt

FOR THE SATAY

1 pound (455 grams) well-marbled, somewhat
chewy beef such as flank steak or skirt steak,
at least 3/4 inch (2 centimeters) thick

About 20 sharp, thin 10-inch (25-centimeter)
bamboo skewers, soaked in water for at
least 30 minutes and drained

Peanut oil for the grill

1. To make the marinade, place the tamarind pulp in a small nonreactive bowl and mix it with the warm water. Let the pulp rest until it softens, 10 to 15 minutes. Squeeze and massage the softened pulp through your fingers, loosening the fruit's auburn pulp from the shiny black seeds, brittle brown skin shards, and sinewy bits of string. With your fingers, remove all the solid pieces from the liquid and discard them. All that will remain is a thick caramel-colored extract. Set the tamarind extract aside.

2. Place the coriander seeds in a small food processor. Pulse until ground to a dusty powder, about 2 minutes.

3. Add the tamarind extract, shallots, garlic, turmeric, ginger, palm sugar, oil, and salt to the ground coriander and pulse until you have a smooth paste the consistency of creamy mashed potatoes. If the paste doesn't purée properly and repeatedly creeps up the side of the food processor instead of grinding, add up to 2 tablespoons water, 1 tablespoon at a time, periodically turning the processor off and scraping the unground portions down toward the blade. Transfer the marinade into a nonreactive bowl large enough to hold the beef.

4. Slice the beef against the grain (as you would if carving a cooked piece of London broil) into long strips 1/4 inch (6 millimeters) thick. The pieces should be no wider than 1 inch (2.5 centimeters).

5. Add the sliced beef to the bowl and combine it well with the marinade, making sure that every piece is evenly coated. Allow the beef to marinate at room temperature for 1 to 2 hours.

6. Thread the beef strips onto the presoaked bamboo skewers, weaving the point of each skewer through the center of the beef about every 1/3 inch (9 millimeters) to make sure it holds tight and remains secure while it cooks. Use 1 to 4 pieces of beef per skewer, depending on how long the pieces are, making sure that the beef extends from the tip to the middle of the skewer. Leave plenty of room at the bottom of the skewer uncovered so that you can grab it easily.

7. **To cook the beef on a grill,** first prepare a medium-hot charcoal fire and oil the grill rack liberally. When the fire is ready (it may take up to 20 minutes), place each skewer on the grill, making sure that the beef, not the skewer, is directly over the heat. Grill the beef until it's cooked through and has begun to pick up a few crispy brown-black spots, 2 to 5 minutes; the timing will depend on how hot the fire is. Turn the skewers over carefully and continue grilling until the other side is browned, another 2 to 5 minutes. Don't overcook the meat, or it will dry out. Test a piece by touching it with your finger. It should be firm, not squishy. Another way to test it is by cutting into the thickest point: it should be faintly pink, neither blood red nor gray.

   To cook the beef in a broiler, position a rack so that the satay skewers will be 3 inches (7.5 centimeters) from the heat source and preheat the broiler for at least 10 minutes. Line a half-sheet pan with aluminum foil. Place the skewers on the pan, arranging them so that the meat is in the center of the pan and the ends of the skewers hang slightly over the side, and then slide the pan into the broiler. (To prevent the exposed portions of the skewers from scorching or burning, you can place aluminum-foil collars over them.) Broil until the meat begins to turn golden brown and develops a few char spots, 5 to 6 minutes. Turn each skewer over to brown the other side, an additional 5 to 6 minutes. Test a piece by touching it with your finger. It should be firm, not squishy. Another way to test it is by cutting into the thickest point: it should be only faintly pink, neither blood red nor gray. Don't overcook the meat, or it will be unpleasantly dry. If the surface doesn't char (your broiler or the distance from the heat source may not allow it to), don't worry. As long as the meat is cooked through, the satay will taste wonderful.

8. Transfer the satay to a serving dish and let the skewers rest until they're cool enough to handle, about 1 minute. Serve immediately.

MENU SUGGESTIONS

I think that serving satay with a dipping sauce is gilding the lily. I prefer to eat it on its own, allowing its aroma and deep flavors to come through loud and clear. But if you like, you can serve this (and all the satays in this chapter) with its traditional accompaniment, the peanut sauce on page 128. Another good dipping sauce is Sweet Soy Sauce and Lime Dipping Sauce (page 125). I prefer it to peanut sauce—it's not as overpowering and blends better, I think, with the complex flavors of satay.

Satay is traditionally served with a sweet-and-sour pickle, such as Javanese Cucumber and Carrot Pickle (page 132), and small cubes of *ketupat*, a boiled jasmine-rice cake. Although satay is meant to be eaten as a snack, it makes an excellent appetizer or main course. Serve it with rice—a flavored-rice dish, such as Lemongrass-Scented Coconut Rice (page 176), complements it especially well—for a complete dinner. If you're serving satay as part of a meal, Stir-fried Bean Sprouts with Chinese Chives (page 208); Stir-fried Water Spinach, Nyonya Style (page 213); and a soupy, rich curry, such as Padang Fish Curry (page 244), are other nice partners.

CHICKEN SATAY

Sate Ayam

(TERENGGANU, MALAYSIA)

❧

This juicy, beautifully flavored chicken satay is from Ibu Maimunah, a cook in Terengganu, a lush, verdant state on the east coast of West Malaysia. It's a classic Malaysian-style satay—a bit sweeter than the satay in Indonesia—and has a glossy, lacquered surface, thanks to the generous amount of palm sugar in the marinade. Though the recipe comes from Terengganu, satays such as this one are popular all over Malaysia, especially at night markets, a popular after-dark form of market going where vendors sell everything from vegetables to takeaway meals. You can also use this delicious marinade for a whole chicken or chicken legs, and roast them. The results will be amazing. Ibu Maimunah showed me a nifty trick the first time I watched her make this satay. She used the thick end of a smashed lemongrass stalk as a basting brush for the chicken. This created an environmentally friendly brush that also imparted the clean taste of fresh lemongrass to the basting oil—a beautiful accent.

I strongly urge you to use chicken thighs. Breasts have too little fat for grilling, resulting in a dry, unappealing satay. Thighs will yield a moister, more delectable dish. I promise.

MAKES ABOUT 30 SKEWERS

FOR THE MARINADE

1 tablespoon coriander seeds

1 tablespoon fennel seeds

2 thick stalks fresh lemongrass

5 shallots (about 3 3/4 ounces/110 grams total), coarsely chopped

3 cloves garlic, coarsely chopped

1 piece fresh or thawed, frozen galangal, 1 inch (2.5 centimeters) long, peeled and thinly sliced against the grain (about 1 tablespoon; optional)

1 piece fresh ginger, 2 inches (5 centimeters) long, peeled and thinly sliced against the grain (about 2 tablespoons)

Scant 1 tablespoon ground turmeric

4 tablespoons palm sugar (page 79), thinly sliced, or dark brown sugar

2 tablespoons peanut oil

1 1/2 teaspoons kosher salt

FOR THE SATAY

3 1/4 pounds (1.5 kilograms) bone-in chicken thighs

1 thick stalk fresh lemongrass

4 tablespoons peanut oil

About 30 sharp, thin 10-inch (25-centimeter) bamboo skewers, soaked in water for at least 30 minutes and drained

1. To make the marinade, place the coriander and fennel seeds in a small food processor. Pulse until ground to a dusty powder, about 2 minutes. Don't remove the ground spices from the food processor at this point. You're going to grind them again along with the other marinade ingredients.

2. Cut off the hard, brown bottom end and the bristly, greenish top of each lemongrass stalk, which should leave you with pale white-and-lilac pieces about 5 inches (13 centimeters) long. Discard the tough outer layers and thinly slice the lemongrass pieces crosswise; they should be no thicker than 1/16 inch (2 millimeters).

3. Add the lemongrass, shallots, garlic, galangal (if using), ginger, turmeric, palm sugar, peanut oil, and salt to the ground spices in the food processor. Pulse until you have a smooth paste the consistency of creamy mashed potatoes. Make sure that the lemongrass is well pulverized. Coarsely ground pieces will be unpleasant in the final dish. If the paste doesn't purée properly and repeatedly creeps up the side of the food processor instead of grinding, add up to 2 tablespoons water, 1 tablespoon at a time, periodically

turning the processor off and scraping the unground portions down toward the blade as you go. Transfer the marinade to a bowl large enough to hold all of the chicken.

4. Remove the skin from each chicken thigh by holding the chicken firmly with one hand and, with the other, slashing and tearing the skin from the flesh with a sharp knife. Cut the meat away from the bone, keeping the meat as whole as possible.

5. Cut the chicken meat into pieces each about 1 inch (2.5 centimeters) wide and 1/4 to 1/3 inch (6 to 9 millimeters) thick. Each piece should ideally be 2 to 3 inches (5 to 7.5 centimeters) long. If any piece is more than 1/2 inch (12 millimeters) thick, slice it in half crosswise.

6. Add the sliced chicken to the bowl and combine it well with the marinade, making sure that every piece is coated. Allow the chicken to marinate at room temperature for 1 to 2 hours. Toss the chicken several times to make sure the marinade is evenly dispersed.

7. Prepare the lemongrass stalk to use as a basting brush by cutting off the hard, brown bottom end and its bristly, greenish top; this should leave you with a piece about 10 inches (25 centimeters) long. Discard the 2 or 3 tough outer layers, then bruise the thick end of the stalk with a heavy, blunt object, such as the wooden handle of a knife or the bottom of a glass measuring cup, until it is bristly and brushlike. Place the bruised end of the lemongrass in a small bowl along with the peanut oil. Let this more flavorful end of the stalk rest for at least 10 minutes in the oil, so that the lemongrass flavor permeates the oil. Reserve the lemongrass and the oil for basting.

8. Thread the chicken strips onto the presoaked bamboo skewers, weaving the point of each skewer through the center of each piece of chicken about every 1/2 inch (12 millimeters) to make sure it holds tight and remains secure as it cooks. Use 1 to 4 pieces of chicken per skewer, depending on how long the pieces are, making sure that the chicken extends from the tip to the middle of the skewer. Leave plenty of room at the bottom of the skewer uncovered so that you can grab it easily.

9. **To cook the chicken on a grill,** first prepare a medium-hot charcoal fire and oil the grill rack liberally. When the fire is ready (it may take up to 15 minutes), place each skewer on the grill, making sure that the chicken, not the skewer, is directly over the heat. Using the bruised end of the lemongrass, lightly baste the chicken with the lemongrass oil. Grill the chicken until it is cooked through and has begun to pick up a few crispy brown-black spots, 3 to 7 minutes; the timing will depend on how hot the fire is. Lightly baste each piece with the lemongrass oil again. Turn the skewers over. Baste them with the lemongrass oil and continue grilling until the other side is similarly browned,

another 3 to 6 minutes. Though you shouldn't overcook the chicken—it will dry out quickly—it's equally important that you not undercook it. Test a piece by touching it with your finger. The chicken should be firm, not squishy. Alternatively, nick off a small piece from the thickest point to see if it's cooked through.

To cook the chicken in a broiler, position a rack so that the satay skewers will be 3 inches (7.5 centimeters) from the heat source and preheat the broiler for at least 10 minutes. Line a half-sheet pan with aluminum foil. Place the skewers on the pan, arranging them so that the meat is in the center of the pan and the ends of the skewers hang slightly over the side. (To prevent the exposed portions of the skewers from scorching or burning, you can place aluminum-foil collars over them.) Using the bruised lemongrass, baste each skewer generously with the lemongrass oil. Slide the pan into the broiler. Broil until the chicken begins to turn golden brown and develops a few char spots, 5 to 7 minutes. Turn each skewer over, baste again, and broil until the other side is browned, an additional 5 to 7 minutes. Test a piece by touching it with your finger. The chicken should be firm, not squishy. Alternatively, nick off a small piece from the thickest point to see if it's cooked through. Though you shouldn't overcook the chicken—it will dry out quickly—it's equally important that you not undercook it. And if it doesn't char (your broiler or the distance from the heat source may not allow it to), don't worry. As long as the chicken is cooked through, the satay will taste delicious.

10. Transfer the satay to a serving dish and let the skewers rest until they're cool enough to handle, about 1 minute. Serve immediately.

MENU SUGGESTIONS

Follow the recommendations for Beef Satay (page 144).

SHRIMP SATAY

(SINGAPORE)

⌒

This excellent recipe from Singapore, a beautiful balance of kaffir lime leaves and coconut milk, can easily be doubled (or tripled or quadrupled) to feed a large group of people. Just remember to figure out in advance how to serve the satay so that it is piping hot. Black tiger shrimp, the most commonly available variety in supermarkets in the United States, will work best. Their thick, moist flesh holds up to grilling better than smaller Gulf shrimp, which have a tendency to dry out when grilled. Always buy unpeeled shrimp and peel them yourself. Already-peeled shrimp have lost much of their flavor. Bamboo skewers 7 inches (18 centimeters) long are ideal, but longer ones can be used.

MAKES ABOUT 20 SKEWERS

FOR THE SATAY

1 1/2 pounds (680 grams) medium-sized head-less black tiger shrimp in the shell, no larger than 3 inches (7.5 centimeters) in diameter

1 tablespoon fresh lime juice

FOR THE MARINADE

4 whole fresh or thawed, frozen kaffir lime leaves

1/2 teaspoon dried shrimp paste (page 65)

5 shallots (about 3 3/4 ounces/155 grams total), coarsely chopped

2 cloves garlic, coarsely chopped

1 to 4 fresh red Holland chiles or other fresh long, red chiles such as Fresno or cayenne, stemmed and coarsely chopped

1 piece fresh ginger, 1 inch (2.5 centimeters)

long, peeled and thinly sliced against the grain (about 1 tablespoon)

5 candlenuts (page 48) or unsalted macadamia nuts

1 tablespoon palm sugar (page 79), thinly sliced, or dark brown sugar

1 teaspoon kosher salt

3 tablespoons peanut oil

1/3 cup (2 1/2 fluid ounces/75 milliliters) plus 2 tablespoons unsweetened coconut milk

About 20 sharp, thin 7-inch (18-centimeter) bamboo skewers, soaked in water for at least 30 minutes and drained

1. First, peel the shrimp. Leave the tail segments intact, if you like, which will make the satay prettier. Devein each shrimp by making a shallow cut along the back and pulling out the thin, veinlike intestinal tract with your fingers.

2. Place the shrimp in a nonreactive bowl. Pour in the lime juice and combine it well with the shrimp. Allow the shrimp to sit, uncovered and unrefrigerated, while you prepare the marinade. (The lime juice helps freshen the shrimp and rid them of any "fishy" taste.)

3. Now, make the marinade. Use a sharp paring knife to remove the thick center stem of each kaffir lime leaf. Stack the leaves on top of one another and cut them lengthwise into the thinnest possible strips.

4. Place the shrimp paste in the center of a 5-inch (13-centimeter) square of aluminum foil. Fold the edges of the foil over to form a small parcel, and press down with the heel of your hand to flatten the shrimp paste into a disk 1/4 inch (6 millimeters) thick. Heat a gas burner to medium-low or an electric burner to medium-high. Using a pair of tongs or 2 forks, place the sealed parcel directly on the heat source. Toast until the paste begins to smoke and release a burning, shrimpy smell, about 1 1/2 minutes. With the tongs or forks, turn the parcel over and toast the other side for another 1 1/2 minutes, then turn off the burner. Again using the tongs or forks, remove the parcel and let cool for 30 seconds to 1 minute. Carefully unwrap the foil; the edges of the disk should be black-brown and toasty and the center should be golden with some black-brown patches. Using a spoon, scrape the toasted shrimp paste into a small bowl and allow it to cool for another 30 seconds. Discard the foil.

5. Place the lime leaves, toasted shrimp paste, shallots, garlic, chiles, ginger, candlenuts, palm sugar, and salt in a small food processor. Pulse until you have a smooth paste the consistency of creamy mashed potatoes.

6. Heat the oil in a 12-inch (30-centimeter) skillet (nonstick will work best) over medium-low heat. Test to see if the oil is the right temperature by adding a pinch of the ground marinade. It should sizzle slightly around the edges, not fry aggressively or sit motionless. When the oil is ready, add the ground marinade and sauté, stirring as needed to prevent scorching (a real possibility because of the palm sugar), until the mixture smells mellow and deeply aromatic, about 5 minutes. The paste should be beginning to separate from the oil but don't worry if it doesn't. Let its aroma be the indicator of its doneness.

7. Add the coconut milk to the skillet and stir well to combine with the sautéed paste. Stirring constantly, bring the coconut milk to a gentle boil. As soon as it begins to bubble, remove the pan from the heat. Test it for salt. Remember, this is a marinade for quite a lot of shrimp, so don't undersalt. Transfer the marinade to a bowl to cool completely. (You can place it in the refrigerator to speed up the process.)

8. When the marinade has cooled to room temperature, pour it over the shrimp and mix well. (Don't drain the lime juice from the shrimp. It will make the satay even more flavorful.) Let the shrimp marinate, uncovered, at room temperature for 1 to 3 hours—the longer you marinate, the more flavorful the shrimp will be. (It's my opinion—and the opinion of many Southeast Asian cooks—that cool temperatures inhibit the marinade process, resulting in a less flavorful dish. But if you're uncomfortable with leaving the shrimp at room temperature for this length of time, by all means refrigerate them.)

9. Thread the shrimp onto the presoaked bamboo skewers, sticking the point straight through the flesh of each shrimp twice: the first time, 1/3 to 1/2 inch (9 to 12 millimeters) from the tip of the tail; the second, into the fleshiest, thickest part of the shrimp, about 1/4 inch (6 millimeters) from the end. Thread 2 shrimp onto each skewer. Discard the extra marinade. Don't be tempted to use it to baste the shrimp, as it will make them too watery.

10. **To cook the shrimp on a grill,** first prepare a very hot charcoal fire and oil the grill rack liberally. When the fire is ready (it may take up to 20 minutes), arrange the charcoal in a high pile. You want the shrimp to be as close to the fire as possible, so they sear quickly. Place each skewer on the grill, making sure that the shrimp, not the skewer, is directly over the heat. Grill the shrimp until they are cooked through and have begun to pick up a few crispy brown-black spots, 2 to 3 minutes; the timing will depend on how hot the fire is. Turn the skewers over carefully and continue grilling until the other side has also picked up crispy brown-black spots, another 2 to 3 minutes. Don't overcook the shrimp. They dry out quickly, and you want them to be as plump and juicy as possible.

    To cook the shrimp in a broiler, position a rack so that the satay skewers will be 1 to 2 inches (2.5 to 5 centimeters) from the heat source and preheat the broiler for at least 10 minutes. You want the oven to be as hot as possible for this satay because the delicate flesh of shrimp cooks best quickly. Line a half-sheet pan with 1/2-inch (12-millimeter) sides with aluminum foil. Place the skewers on the pan, arranging them so that the shrimp is in the center of the pan and the ends of the skewers hang slightly over the side. (To prevent the exposed portions of the skewers from scorching or burning, you can place aluminum-foil collars over them.) Slide the pan into the broiler. Broil until the shrimp begin to develop a few char spots, about 3 minutes. Turn each skewer over to cook the other side, an additional 2 minutes. Test a shrimp for doneness by pressing it with your finger. It should be firm, not squishy. If the shrimp don't char (your broiler or the distance from the heat may not allow them to), don't worry. As long as the shrimp are cooked through, the satay will taste wonderful.

11. Transfer the satay to a serving dish and let the skewers rest until they're cool enough to handle, about 1 minute. Serve immediately.

MENU SUGGESTIONS

Follow the recommendations for Beef Satay (page 144).

GADO-GADO

(JAVA, INDONESIA)

⟶

G*ado-gado* means "potpourri," and this dish is truly that: a mix of raw and cooked vegetables served with a roasted-peanut dressing and topped with crunchy shrimp chips. Salads dressed with peanut sauce and served as appetizers in Thai restaurants in the United States take their inspiration from this dish, but they pale in comparison with the real thing. Rather than assembling the salad with the dressing, as called for in this recipe (and as is traditionally done), you can serve the dressing on the side, allowing your guests to ladle as much (or as little) as they want on top of their salads. Serve the salad with steaming-hot rice on the side, or enjoy it as a one-dish meal without rice.

This recipe is inspired by one I was given many years ago during my second trip to Indonesia. I'd been staying in the Jakarta home of my good friends, the Alwi family, for months. One evening, I heard the hypnotic sound of a small gamelan ensemble coming from an alley behind the house. Curiosity got the better of me, so I went out to see what was going on. There, under the stark light of a streetlamp, an itinerant troupe of transvestites was performing a slow classical West Javanese dance for a small audience of curious neighborhood people. (Known as *banci*, these small ragtag groups of transvestites, widely known for their skill as dancers, travel throughout the country, but especially Java.) After they finished, I told the dancers how beautiful I thought their performance was, and they invited me to share a meal that they had made in their small nearby camp. One of the dishes was this elegant *gado-gado*, which had been prepared by Dewi, a member of the troupe. Dewi was not only a gifted dancer, but a great cook as well.

MAKES 2 OR 3 SERVINGS (OR 4 OR 5, IF SERVING WITH RICE AND OTHER DISHES)

1 1/2 cups (12 fluid ounces/375 milliliters) Javanese Peanut Sauce (page 128), or more to taste

10 to 15 Fried Shrimp Chips (page 86)

4 medium-sized waxy potatoes such as Maine or Yukon Gold, peeled and cut into slices 1/3 inch (9 millimeters) thick (about 2 1/2 cups/13 ounces/370 grams)

Peanut oil for frying

2 cups mung bean sprouts (about 5 ounces/170 grams)

1 large carrot, peeled and cut on the diagonal into slices 1/4 inch (6 millimeters) thick (about 1 1/2 cups/5 ounces/140 grams)

40 green beans or 20 long beans, stemmed and cut into 2-inch (5-centimeter) lengths (about 2 cups/12 ounces/340 grams)

1/2 head leafy green lettuce, torn into fairly large bite-sized pieces

1 Kirby (pickling) cucumber, unpeeled, stemmed, and cut on the diagonal into 1/2-inch (12-millimeter) chunks (about 1 cup/4 ounces/115 grams)

Kosher salt (optional)

1. Prepare the peanut sauce and the fried shrimp chips and set aside.

2. To fry the potatoes, pour oil to a depth of 1/2 inch (12 millimeters) into a 1 1/2-quart (1.5-liter) saucepan (you can use the same pan you used for frying the shrimp chips) and heat over medium to medium-high heat. When the oil is hot but not smoking (about 365°F/185°C), drop in a potato slice. If the slice begins to fry immediately, start frying the rest of the potato slices. If the potato slice sinks to the bottom with nary a sizzle, remove it and wait for the oil to become hotter. With a slotted metal spoon, carefully add the potatoes in small, manageable batches of no more than 5 or 6 slices at a time. Turn the potato slices frequently with the spoon to prevent them from sticking together as they fry. When the slices are evenly light golden on all sides, 4 to 7 minutes total, test to see if they are cooked through by piercing a slice with a fork. It should puncture with only a slight amount of resistance. Don't allow the potatoes to become too brown. The longer they fry, the hotter the oil will become, and the thinner pieces may get too brown before they are fully cooked. Take care to lower and raise the heat occasionally if you see that the potatoes are either sitting limply in the oil or are frying too violently. They'll come out too greasy or darkly colored otherwise. Using the slotted spoon, transfer the potatoes to paper towels to drain. Allow the potatoes to cool while you prepare the other vegetables.

3. Fill a 3-quart (3-liter) saucepan with water and bring to a boil over high heat. Add the bean sprouts and blanch just until they begin to wilt, about 10 seconds. Using the slotted spoon, transfer the beans sprouts to a colander (leave the boiling water in the pan), and run cold water over them until they're cool. Drain the sprouts well, transfer them to a good-sized bowl, and set aside.

4. Add the carrot slices to the same boiling water and boil until they're just fork-tender, about 2 1/2 minutes. Using the slotted spoon, transfer the carrots to the colander (again, leave the boiling water in the pan) and run cold water over them until they're cool. Drain the carrots well, transfer them to the bowl holding the bean sprouts, and set aside.

5. Add the green beans to the same boiling water and boil until they're just crunchy tender, about 1 1/2 minutes. Drain into the colander and run cold water over them until they're cool. Add them to the bowl holding the bean sprouts and carrots. Pat the boiled vegetables dry with a few paper towels. (Don't squeeze them dry, or you'll break them open.) They should have as little water clinging to their surface as possible.

6. Add the cooled fried potatoes, the lettuce, and the cucumber to the boiled vegetables. With your hands or a large spoon, combine them thoroughly. Add the peanut sauce and stir gently to combine thoroughly, being careful not to break up the vegetables. Taste for salt and add some if needed. You may add more sauce, too, but be careful not to overwhelm the vegetables with it. The salad should be neither soggy nor dry but somewhere in between, with the sauce lightly coating every vegetable.

7. Serve the salad on 2 or 3 dinner plates, and garnish each plate with the shrimp chips, dividing them evenly. You can also serve the salad from a large bowl at the center of the table as part of a meal with rice; garnish the bowl with the shrimp chips. But however you serve it, be sure to eat it promptly, as the dressed vegetables (especially the lettuce) will wilt quickly and the shrimp chips will lose their crunch.

MENU SUGGESTIONS

Gado-gado, with its crazy quilt of ingredients, makes an excellent main course. Local cooks sometimes make it more substantial by adding squares of crisp-fried tofu, a handful of Chinese egg noodles, or a few thick slices of *lontong* (rice steamed inside bamboo cylinders and cut into wedges for serving). If you decide to include it as part of a larger meal built around rice, good accompaniments are dry, spicy dishes, such as Pan-Seared Mackerel with Chiles and Garlic (page 252), Nyonya-Style Spiced Fried Chicken (page 285), and Stir-fried Shrimp Sambal (page 262). It's also an excellent party or buffet dish. You can serve the vegetables and peanut sauce separately (as described in the headnote), so that the vegetables retain their crispness.

CHOPPED VEGETABLE SALAD WITH COCONUT AND LIME LEAF DRESSING
Urap
(JAVA, INDONESIA)

This dish is among the foods mentioned in the *Serat Centhini*, a celebrated ancient Javanese poetic text. It's classic court food (though it's also prepared for everyday sustenance) and is an essential part of ritual meals at birthdays or harvest celebrations. The ingredients vary according to what is available at the market but usually include cucumbers, cabbage, long beans, and bean sprouts, while fragrant fresh lemon basil leaves, known in Java as *kemangi*, always appear. The vegetables are really just costars. Instead, the spotlight is trained on the intensely aromatic sweet-sour dressing, which is made of grated coconut, chiles, garlic, lime juice, turmeric, palm sugar, and kaffir lime leaves. Although this dish is traditionally quite sweet—a testament to the Central Javanese affection for palm sugar—you can adjust the seasonings to your liking. Freshly grated coconut is essential. Grated dried coconut not only throws off the flavor profile of the dish, but also the texture.

MAKES 4 SERVINGS

FOR THE DRESSING

5 whole fresh or thawed, frozen kaffir lime leaves

2 cloves garlic, coarsely chopped

2 to 4 fresh red Holland chiles or other fresh long, red chiles such as Fresno or cayenne, stemmed and coarsely chopped

1 piece fresh or thawed, frozen turmeric (page 92), 1 1/2 inches (4 centimeters) long, peeled and coarsely chopped (about 1 1/2 teaspoons), or 1 teaspoon ground turmeric

1 piece fresh ginger, 1 1/2 inches (4 centimeters) long, peeled and thinly sliced against the grain (about 1 1/2 tablespoons)

3 to 4 tablespoons palm sugar (page 79), thinly sliced, or dark brown sugar

3 tablespoons fresh lime juice

1 cup (scant 3 ounces/85 grams) finely grated fresh coconut (page 58)

1 1/2 teaspoons kosher salt

FOR THE SALAD

1 1/2 cups (about 4 ounces/115 grams) mung bean sprouts

20 green beans or 10 long beans, stemmed and cut into 1/2-inch (12-millimeter) pieces (about 1 cup/6 ounces/170 grams)

1 1/2 cups (about 5 ounces/140 grams) finely shredded green cabbage

2 small Kirby (pickling) cucumbers (about 7 ounces/200 grams), stemmed and thinly sliced (about 2 cups/7 ounces, 200 grams)

1 cup (scant 1 ounce/30 grams) loosely packed fresh lemon basil (page 74), Thai basil, or Italian basil leaves

1. First, make the dressing. Use a sharp paring knife to remove the thick center stem of each kaffir lime leaf. Stack the leaves on top of one another and cut them lengthwise into thin strips.

2. Place the lime leaves, garlic, chiles, turmeric, ginger, palm sugar, and lime juice in a small food processor. Pulse until you have a chunky-smooth paste the consistency of cooked oatmeal (the lime juice should keep the mixture turning easily in the processor). Make

sure that the garlic and ginger are completely pulverized. Transfer the paste to a bowl. Add the coconut and salt and stir well to combine, making sure that the coconut is evenly combined with the ground ingredients.

3. Fill a 3-quart (3-liter) saucepan with water and bring to a boil over high heat. Add the bean sprouts and blanch until they just begin to wilt, about 10 seconds. Using a slotted spoon, transfer the bean sprouts to a colander (leave the boiling water in the pan) and run cold water over them until they're cool. Drain the sprouts well, transfer them to a good-sized bowl, and set aside.

4. Add the green beans to the same boiling water and boil until they're just crunchy tender, about 1 1/2 minutes. Using the slotted spoon, transfer the beans to the colander (again, leave the boiling water in the pan) and run cold water over them until they're cool. Drain the beans well, transfer them to the bowl holding the bean sprouts, and set aside.

5. Add the cabbage to the same boiling water and boil the cabbage until it has just wilted but is still crisp, about 30 seconds. Drain the cabbage into the colander and run cold water over it until it's cool. Transfer it to the bowl holding the bean sprouts and green beans. Pat all the boiled vegetables dry with a few paper towels. (Don't squeeze them dry, or you will break them open.) They should have as little water clinging to their surface as possible.

6. Add the cucumbers and basil leaves and, using your hands or a large spoon, gently mix them together thoroughly. Add the coconut dressing to the vegetables and stir gently to combine thoroughly. Taste for salt and sourness, and add a pinch more salt and/or a squeeze more lime juice if needed. Serve promptly, while the basil is still perky and the cucumbers are crisp.

MENU SUGGESTIONS

This sweet yet tart Central Javanese salad can be served as a main course along with steamed rice or crusty bread. Or you can pair it with dishes that contrast with its sweetness: some possibilities include Mien's Garlic Fried Chicken (page 283), Pan-Seared Tamarind Tuna (page 254), and Kevin's Spiced Roast Chicken with Potatoes, Penang Style (page 287). Also consider other Central Javanese dishes, such as Javanese Grilled Chicken (page 289) and Caramelized Tempeh with Chiles (page 325), both natural companions.

CRISP JICAMA AND PINEAPPLE SALAD
Rojak
(MALACCA, MALAYSIA)

⤙

This tantalizing Nyonya fruit and vegetable salad, known as *rojak* (which means "mixed up"), consists of jicama (widely available in Asian and Latin markets and many supermarkets), green (i.e., unripe) mango, fresh pineapple, unripe guava (you can substitute a tart green apple), and unripe papaya with a savory-spicy dressing and a topping of coarsely ground peanuts. Its origins are humble: *rojak* is a classic market snack, meant to be eaten while prowling the aisles in search of the freshest fish or the hottest chiles. Thousands of versions exist in Indonesia, Malaysia, and Singapore. In Indonesia it's known as *rujak* and is sometimes bolstered with sliced boiled beef.

This Nyonya recipe was inspired by Bee Bee Ong, who works in one of Malacca's night markets. Her stall, illuminated by a hissing oil lamp, is packed with customers who line up for their nightly takeaway fix. One key she taught me to making good *rojak* is to select peak-of-the-season ingredients. Another is a miserly hand with the dressing: add it gradually, tasting with each addition so you don't overpower the fruits and vegetables.

Raw, unripe papaya, an optional ingredient in this recipe, has a clean, subtly bitter taste. It's the main ingredient in Thailand's famous *som tom* (shredded papaya salad with chiles) and is widely available in Chinese and Southeast Asian markets. Before using it, peel it as you would an apple. Then halve it and remove its small, white, pearl-like seeds. Leftover unripe papaya can be cooked as you would chayote squash.

MAKES 2 OR 3 SERVINGS

FOR THE TOPPING
1/2 cup (3 ounces/85 grams) unsalted
   skinned roasted peanuts

FOR THE DRESSING
1 tablespoon dried shrimp paste (page 65)
1 tablespoon tamarind pulp, plus 5 tablespoons
   (2 1/2 fluid ounces/75 milliliters) very warm
   water to make extract

1 to 4 fresh red Holland chiles or other fresh
   long, red chiles such as Fresno or cayenne,
   stemmed and coarsely chopped

3 tablespoons palm sugar (page 79), thinly
sliced, or dark brown sugar

3 tablespoons Indonesian sweet soy sauce
(page 72)

FOR THE SALAD

1 small jicama (about 10 ounces/285 grams),
peeled

1/2 medium-sized green (unripe) mango (about
10 ounces/285 grams), peeled and seeded
(see Cook's Note, page 124)

1/4 small unripe papaya (about 7 ounces/200
grams), peeled and seeded (optional)

2 small Kirby (pickling) cucumbers (about
7 ounces/200 grams total), stemmed

1/3 pineapple (about 15 ounces/425 grams),
peeled

1 firm unripe guava (about 4 ounces/115
grams), peeled and seeded, or medium-
sized Granny Smith apple, peeled and cored

Kosher salt (optional)

1. To make the topping, place the peanuts in a small food processor. Pulse until the peanuts are ground to the consistency of coarse bread crumbs. Set aside.

2. To make the dressing, place the shrimp paste in the center of a 5-inch (13-centimeter) square of aluminum foil. Fold the edges of the foil over to form a small parcel, and press down with the heel of your hand to flatten the shrimp paste into a disk 1/4 inch (6 millimeters) thick. Heat a gas burner to medium-low or an electric burner to medium-high. Using a pair of tongs or 2 forks, place the sealed parcel directly on the heat source. Toast until the paste begins to smoke and release a burning, shrimpy smell, about 1 1/2 minutes. With the tongs or forks, turn the parcel over and toast the other side for another 1 1/2 minutes, then turn off the burner. Again using the tongs or forks, remove the parcel and let cool for 30 seconds to 1 minute. Carefully unwrap the foil; the edges of the disk should be black-brown and toasty and the center should be golden with some black-brown patches. Using a spoon, scrape the toasted shrimp paste into a small bowl and allow it to cool for another 30 seconds. Discard the foil.

3. Place the tamarind pulp in a small nonreactive bowl and mix it with the warm water. Let the pulp rest until it softens, 10 to 15 minutes. Squeeze and massage the softened pulp through your fingers, loosening the fruit's auburn pulp from the shiny black seeds, brittle brown skin shards, and sinewy bits of string. With your fingers, remove all the solid pieces from the liquid and discard them. All that will remain is a thick caramel-colored extract.

4. Place the toasted shrimp paste, tamarind extract, chiles, palm sugar, and sweet soy sauce in a small food processor. Pulse until you have a smooth paste; the chiles should be fairly finely ground.

5. Cut the jicama, mango, and the papaya, if using, into thick irregular matchsticks about 3 inches (7.5 centimeters) long by 1/2 inch (12 millimeters) wide. You should have about 1 1/2 cups (9 ounces/255 grams) jicama and 1 cup each of the mango (10 ounces/285 grams) and papaya (6 ounces/170 grams).

6. Cut the cucumbers into irregular pieces about 2 inches (5 centimeters) long by 1/2 inch (12 millimeters) wide. You should have about 2 cups (6 ounces/170 grams).

7. Cut the pineapple into pieces 2 inches (5 centimeters) long by 1/2 inch (12 millimeters) wide. You should have about 2 cups (10 ounces/285 grams).

8. Cut the guava (or the apple) into 8 wedges.

9. Place all the fruits and vegetables in a large bowl. Pour three-fourths of the dressing over the top and toss well with your hands or a large spoon to make sure each piece is evenly coated. Taste a piece of fruit or vegetable. It should be enhanced by the dressing, not overwhelmed by it. Add the rest of the dressing, if needed, along with a pinch of salt, also if needed.

10. Transfer the dressed salad to a serving dish. Evenly sprinkle the ground peanuts over the top. Eat the salad immediately. It becomes limp if allowed to sit for longer than 20 minutes.

MENU SUGGESTIONS

Rojak should not be served with anything else, including rice, which doesn't complement its assertively crisp texture and sharp taste. Its light, appetite-arousing characteristics make it a good choice as a Western-style first course.

FRIED SWEET PLANTAINS
Pisang Goreng
(INDONESIA, MALAYSIA, AND SINGAPORE)

First-time visitors to Indonesia, Malaysia, and Singapore are amazed by the different types of bananas (*pisang*) available in markets—more than thirty varieties are grown in Indonesia alone. (Indeed, some botantists believe that the fruit is native to the Malay Archipelago.) Although bananas are generally eaten plain and ripe as a dessert after a meal, local cooks also like to batter and fry them as a morning or afternoon snack known as *pisang goreng*. To make this recipe, use the ripest plantains (called *pisang raja*, or "king banana") you can find. They should have uniformly deep yellow to gold skin that is amply streaked with black and yields easily to the touch (it shouldn't be mushy or soft, however, signs of a bruised or overripe fruit). Don't use firm, green (or even fully yellow) unripe plantains, which have a starchy, astringent taste and are used as a vegetable in Latin American cuisines. Avoid Cavendish bananas, the West's most popular eating variety, because they fall apart when fried.

This recipe comes from Isa, a street vendor in Penang, Malaysia. He sometimes bolsters this batter with rice flour, which results in a more toothsome coating.

MAKES 18 TO 24 PIECES

1 cup (5 ounces/140 grams) all-purpose flour

1/2 teaspoon baking powder

1/4 teaspoon kosher salt

3/4 cup (6 fluid ounces/175 milliliters) plus 1 tablespoon very cold water

2 drops yellow food coloring (optional)

1 1/2 pounds (680 grams) very ripe, deep yellow to black plantains (3 or 4 medium sized; see Cook's Note, page 163), peeled, halved crosswise, and each half cut lengthwise into thirds

Peanut oil for frying

Powdered sugar for garnish (optional)

1. Sift together the flour, baking powder, and salt into a bowl. Add the water and stir well, making sure to get out all the lumps. If you like, add the food coloring, which will make the final dish an appealing light gold. You should have a smooth batter resembling pancake batter that easily coats the back of a spoon. If it's too thick, add more water, 1 teaspoon at a time; if it's too thin, add more all-purpose flour, 1 teaspoon at a time.

2. Pour oil to a depth of 1 inch (2.5 centimeters) into a 12-inch (30-centimeter) skillet and place over medium to medium-high heat until hot but not smoking. Test the oil to see if it's hot enough (it should be about 365°F/185°C) by adding a drop of batter. If the batter sinks and then rises immediately, the oil is ready; if it drops to the bottom like a sad blob and stays there, heat the oil for a minute or two longer and test again.

3. To make the deep-frying go more easily, fry no more than 2 to 3 plantain pieces at a time. With your fingers, dip each piece into the batter to coat thoroughly. The coating should be about 1/16 inch (2 millimeters) thick; gently shake off any excess. Using a slotted metal spoon, carefully lower the coated pieces into the hot oil and fry, turning

them 2 or 3 times with the spoon, until they are uniformly light tan and crisp. They'll continue to darken slightly after they are removed from the oil. Each piece should fry for a total of 2 to 2 1/2 minutes. If you notice signs of scorching, reduce the heat or remove the pan from the heat altogether and let it cool for a few moments. If the plantains are not frying vigorously enough, increase the heat slightly. They'll be greasy if the heat is too low and scorched if it's too high. If pieces of the batter separate from the plantains and float to the surface of the oil, use the spoon to scoop them out and discard them. When the plantain pieces are ready, use the spoon to transfer them to paper towels to drain.

4. Transfer all the fried pieces to a plate and dust them, if you like, with powdered sugar. Fried plantains are best eaten right away. They lose their crispness if they sit.

COOK'S NOTE

In the West, plantains are thought of as different from bananas. They aren't—they're merely a large, thick-skinned variety of banana. Look for them in Chinese and Latin markets. Remember, the plantains for this recipe (and for Plantains with Coconut Milk and Palm Sugar, page 347) should appear considerably riper than ripened Cavendish bananas, and they should have a sweet, banana-y aroma. Even if they have turned completely black, they're acceptable. If you can find only green or yellow unripe plantains, ripen them at room temperature for up to 5 days in the same way you would conventional bananas (enclosing them in a paper bag will hasten the process). Once they're ripe, continue to store them at room temperature, where they'll keep for another 3 to 4 days. Ripe plantains can also be eaten uncooked, as you would Cavendish bananas. They have a perfumy taste and meaty texture that I prefer.

MENU SUGGESTIONS

For an excellent midday high tea, serve fried plantains with Bean Sprout and Potato Fritters (page 164) and milky, sweet hot tea. They go particularly well with chile-hot dipping sauces such as Sweet-and-Sour Chile Dipping Sauce (page 127) or Sriracha chile sauce, a Thai-style bottled sauce widely available in Asian markets. Believe it or not, they also have an affinity for tomato ketchup. (You might, however, prefer these as a crunchy dessert, perhaps arranged on top of vanilla ice cream, though I find them too rich to top off a meal.)

BEAN SPROUT AND POTATO FRITTERS
Bakwan
(INDONESIA)

⁓

Fritters are a beloved street snack in Indonesia, usually eaten in the late afternoon to tame appetites in the hours before the evening meal. The Dutch introduced fritters to the region, but Indonesian cooks took to them like old friends, intensifying their mild taste with favorite ingredients like garlic and Chinese celery greens. This recipe, which comes from Ibu Djulinas of Padang, West Sumatra, is an Indonesian classic, usually prepared by hawkers who plunge the batter into woks full of hot oil. The fritters are flavored with grated shallots and garlic, Chinese chives, and, most important, Chinese celery greens, which lend a lovely herbal flavor. The addition of potatoes, cut as for hash browns, recalls latkes, or potato pancakes.

To create smooth, round-bottomed fritters, Ibu Djulinas heats the fritter ladle in hot oil for a few minutes before dipping it in the batter, reducing the likelihood that the batter will stick to the ladle. While this makes for more attractive, evenly shaped fritters, I've found the technique tricky to master. Instead, I use a large metal spoon rather than a ladle, scraping a small amount of the batter directly into the oil with the aid of a second spoon.

MAKE ABOUT 25 FRITTERS

2 cups (10 ounces/285 grams) all-purpose flour

2 teaspoons kosher salt

1 1/2 cups (12 fluid ounces/375 milliliters) plus 2 tablespoons water

1 cup (2 1/2 ounces/70 grams) mung bean sprouts

3 Chinese chives (page 55) or scallions (both white and green parts), very thinly sliced on the diagonal

1 tablespoon finely chopped Chinese celery greens (page 55) or regular celery leaves

3 green cabbage leaves, very finely shredded into strips 1 inch (2.5 centimeters) long

1 small waxy potato such as Yukon Gold, peeled and cut into very fine matchsticks (as for hash browns; about 1 cup/3 ounces/85 grams total)

1 clove garlic, grated

2 shallots (about 1 1/2 ounces/40 grams total), grated

Peanut oil for frying

Sweet-and-Sour Chile Dipping Sauce (page 127)

12 fresh green Thai chiles (optional)

1. Sift together the flour and salt into a bowl. Add the water and stir well, making sure to get out all the lumps. You should have a smooth batter resembling slightly thick pancake batter that easily coats the back of a spoon. If it's too thick, add more water, 1 teaspoon at a time; if it's too thin, add more all-purpose flour, 1 teaspoon at a time.

2. Add the bean sprouts, Chinese chives, celery greens, cabbage, potato, garlic, and shallots to the batter and stir gently to combine.

3. Pour oil to a depth of 1 inch (2.5 centimeters) into a 12-inch (30-centimeter) skillet and place over medium to medium-high heat until hot but not smoking. Test the oil to see if it is hot enough (it should be about 365°F/185°C) by adding a drop of batter. If the batter sizzles immediately, the oil is ready; if it sinks to the bottom without sizzling, heat the oil for a minute or two longer and test again.

4. For each fritter, ladle about 1 1/2 tablespoons batter into the hot oil with a large metal spoon, using a smaller metal spoon to scrape off any batter clinging to the larger spoon. Each fritter should be about 2 inches (5 centimeters) long and 1 inch (2.5 centimeters) thick. Cook no more than 3 or 4 fritters at a time to avoid crowding them in the skillet. (Crowding will reduce the temperature of the oil and make the fritters greasy.) Fry the fritters, turning them occasionally with the spoon, until they're uniformly golden and crisp, about 2 minutes total on each side. Using a slotted spoon, transfer the fritters to paper towels to drain.

5. Transfer all the fritters to a platter and serve at once with the dipping sauce and with the whole chiles (if using) for guests to nibble between bites. Eat the fritters promptly after they're fried, as they quickly lose their pleasingly crisp crust.

MENU SUGGESTIONS

Serve the fritters as a party snack with the dipping sauce and whole chiles. You can also serve them as an appetizer, though I find them to be too rich to start a meal.

ABOVE LEFT: *A farmer in Air Hangat, West Sumatra, where rice farming is a way of life.*

ABOVE CENTER: *Green rice paddies are a ubiquitous fixture of West Sumatran landscapes.*

ABOVE RIGHT: *My friend Nas, a rice farmer (far right), and his friends in Air Hangat.*

8. RICE AND NOODLES

It was late 1999, and I was on a rickety Indonesian bus traveling from Padang, West Sumatra, to Dumai, a small port town where I'd be catching a ferry to Malaysia in a couple of days. From my seat, I could hear a tape of traditional flute music, high pitched and entrancing, playing in an endless loop on two tinny speakers above the driver's bald head. I stared out the window at the passing Sumatran jungle in the late-afternoon sun. Prickly rattan vines snaked up huge trees whose heights I could only imagine. I thought about my travels over the last few weeks. Indonesia was in the middle of an economic depression (local newspapers called it the *krises*), the result in large part of the 1998 overthrow of Suharto, the country's long-time president. Gas rationing had become routine, banks were going out of business, and the unemployment rate hovered around 40 percent. Despite all the bad news, everyone I'd met on my travels was as cheerful as ever. "What to do?" my friend Hasan in Padang asked, shrugging his shoulders. "The economy goes up, the economy goes down. But Indonesia goes on."

Around ten o'clock that night, the bus pulled into a dusty, nondescript town on the edge of the jungle. Packs of motorcycles streamed through streets crammed with stalls selling an endless array of the kind of plastic household wares I knew from ninety-nine-cent stores back home. It was an uninviting place, but hunger had gotten the better of me. I walked around for a few minutes and found a vendor who made take-out food. I ordered a plate of egg noodles stir-fried with chile paste and bitter Asian greens. As I ate at a nearby folding table, I looked up to see a group of off-duty bus drivers at the next table observing me.

"It's delicious?" one of them asked.

"It's delicious," I confirmed, meaning it.

When I reboarded the bus fifteen minutes later, I was surprised to find a new passenger occupying my seat, a twenty-something man with catlike eyes and a military haircut. He sat as though he had permanently moved in, his luggage spilling over into the aisle. I squeezed in next to him. As the bus rumbled back to life, I peered over to see what he was up to. It wasn't what I was expecting. He was loading a stubby pistol, admiring each bullet in a display worthy of Dirty Harry. I knew things were bad in Indonesia, but not quite this bad. I shifted in my seat, determined to stay calm.

"Oh, the gun," he said, noticing me. He spoke Indonesian mixed with bits of English. "I suppose you want to know why I have it." I gave a mute nod.

"I'm a policeman," he said. He pulled a badge from his jacket pocket. "My name is Arifin. Where are you headed?" I told him as he placed the gun back into its holster.

"Oh, Dumai is so far. You won't reach there until late tomorrow," he said. "I'm going to my parents' house for the weekend. Why don't you sleep there tonight? Tomorrow you can continue on to Dumai. I'll even take you there." I considered the offer. More than being concerned for my safety, I was worried that the ferry might be sold out when I reached Dumai.

"Maybe I should just go on to Dumai," I said. "What if I can't get a ferry ticket?"

"Don't worry," Arifin replied, smiling. "I'll get you on board. That's what policemen are for."

We arrived at Arifin's family home long after midnight. Attached to the cinderblock structure was a kiosk that housed the family's VCD rental business. Arifin introduced me to his parents, a friendly, sleepy-eyed couple in their sixties who studied me with open curiosity.

They made a bed for me on the sofa in the living room. I collapsed onto it and drifted off to sleep. It was bliss finally to be horizontal. After a short time, though—it must've been around four-thirty—I woke up to the musky smell of stir-frying garlic. I forgot about sleeping, got up from the sofa, and followed the aroma. Arifin's mother, Siti, was making breakfast in the kitchen. A few candles flickered in a corner, providing the only source of light. I asked if I could watch her. With a shy nod, she gave consent.

Soon, her meal was ready, laid out in a maze of plates on a small dining table just off the kitchen. Siti had made lemongrass-marinated fried chicken; a sweet-and-sour pickle; and garlicky Indonesian-style fried rice. There were four steaming plates of rice, one for each of us, each portion topped with a fried egg, thick cucumber wedges, and a few crunchy shrimp chips.

"You want me to make pancakes for you instead?" asked Siti, obviously teasing me.

"Pancakes?" I exclaimed. "Ibu, I haven't come to Sumatra to eat American food."

She laughed. It was exactly what she wanted to hear.

Arifin and his father joined us around the table. The meal was robust and satisfying, especially the fried rice. As we were finishing up, Arifin watched me, amazed. "I have never seen a foreigner who liked Indonesian food so much," he said, a smile appearing in the corners of his lips. I told him about where I was from and about my extensive travels in Indonesia, Malaysia, and Singapore. I also told him that I was interested in the foods of the region. He stood up and began clearing the plates from the table. "I have a cousin named Nas who owns a rice paddy. Would you like to see his village, Air Hangat? I have to go there this morning to deliver something to him."

"You're sure I'll be able to get a ferry ticket?" I asked. I was still concerned about getting to Malaysia.

"Don't worry," he answered, lighting up a clove cigarette. "You're in good hands."

As it turned out, it took us five hours by motorcycle, back in the same direction we had traveled from the night before, to get to Nas's village. But I had no objections. I'd resigned myself to let go and enjoy whatever happened, a skill, learned years earlier, that was invaluable when traveling in Indonesia. I was also happy to see the landscape of rolling green hills and small clusters of wooden houses that I'd missed in the darkness on the bus ride the night before.

We arrived midday at Air Hangat, a compact village with dirt roads, the Barisan Mountains that run nearly the entire length of Sumatra rising in the distance. The air was sweet with the smell of cooking fires and with cinnamon bark, which was drying in the sun on rattan mats in front of houses everywhere I looked. I followed Arifin as we approached his cousin's home. The door was wide open. Arifin called out the traditional Islamic greeting, *assalaam alaikum* (peace be with you). Nas, a short, muscular man in his forties, appeared and shyly held out his hand to greet us. As we walked inside, Arifin whispered to me, "I think this is the first time Nas has met a *bule* [white man]."

We sat down in a small, simple living room. A few minutes later, Nas's wife, a reserved woman in a faded purple sarong, brought us jasmine tea and sticky-rice sweets. Talking as we ate, I learned that Nas had overseen his family's rice paddy (called *padi* in Indonesia, the same word as ours) his entire life, as had his father and his father's father before him. Virtually every family in the vicinity owned rice paddies. It was an ancient way of life here, with innumerable traditions associated with it. I asked if they would tell me about some of them.

"Community is the law of the rice paddy," Nas offered quietly. "In Air Hangat each family helps the others tend and harvest their paddies. There is no competition." He spoke in a local dialect that I could barely understand, so Arifin translated. "If a family has a bad harvest, the other families in the village contribute to make up for its loss. We are like one big family," Nas continued.

I also learned that here in the warm heart of Sumatra, just a few degrees south of the equator, there are no distinct seasons, save two monsoonal periods when the daily rains become noticeably heavier. The region's generous climate guarantees excellent rice-growing conditions year-round. At any given time the rice in one family's paddies will be nearing maturity, while in another's it will just be beginning to take root.

It was a twenty-minute walk from the house to the green rice fields just outside the village. These weren't the dramatic terraced paddies of Java and Bali seen in Asian photography coffee-table books. Instead, the paddies were laid out in a neat, flat grid of rectangles and squares, and joined together by low mud retaining walls that doubled as footpaths. Nas and Arifin strolled along at a steady, rhythmic clip, navigating the narrow walkways like old pros. I lacked their expertise. As I tried to keep up with them, I lost my footing and took a dive, feet first, into the paddy's green-gray muck.

"You must walk like this in the paddy," Arifin said, laughing, as I scraped the mud off my wet pants. He demonstrated a splayed-out, penguinlike gait. "If you try to walk straight, you will fall over and the paddy will eat you up."

Nas grew a rice variety known as IR8, a hearty, fast-growing hybrid developed in the Philippines in the 1960s. Although for decades Nas's father had grown ancient local varieties, Nas and the other farmers of Air Hangat had started planting IR8 fifteen years earlier to increase their yield. The results were spectacular: each farmer was averaging three crops per year. (It takes this particular rice roughly four months from seed to harvest.) Still, getting by financially for Nas and his family had become difficult since the *krises*, Nas told me, as it had for all the other families in this tight-knit village. The troubled Indonesian economy had caused prices of everyday necessities to inflate beyond the reach of almost everyone.

We reached Nas's paddy. Bisected by a number of crisscrossing retaining walls and about the size of an Olympic swimming pool, it extended in front of us in gorgeous shades of gold and dusty green. The crop, Nas told me, had been growing for just over three months. I reached out my arm and brushed my fingers over the nearby stalks. The narrow, grain-covered tips were dry and husky. I pulled a stalk from its base and studied it. It curved gracefully from the weight of its grains, like a tree branch loaded with fruit. Nas plucked another stalk and rubbed a few grains between his fingers to remove their hulls. It made a smooth, crisp sound, like paper being crumpled. Inside the hulls were perfectly formed, light amber grains of rice. They were vaguely translucent, like small pieces of butterscotch candy. Nas assessed the size of the grains and then inhaled them deeply. His smile revealed satisfaction. "It will be two weeks before we harvest," he said. In the distance I could see the silhouettes of a group of farmers working in a nearby paddy. Nas waved to the group, but they were too lost in their work to notice.

"They're my second cousins," he said. "They live a few houses away."

As we approached, I could see that they were harvesting a small paddy that had been drained to facilitate the work. While the three men in the group moved through muddy earth gathering bunches of rice stalks and snipping them with small scythes, three women in conical bamboo hats—"Their wives," Arifin whispered—threshed bunches of the stalks into two wooden boxes. The rice grains pattered like rain as they landed on the wood.

"This small paddy will take only a few hours to harvest," Arifin said. "It's a fast process." I wanted to know what would happen next. Within a few hours, he told me, the unhulled grains would be laid out on rattan mats to dry in the sun. Over the course of a few days, the rice would begin to pull away from the hard, inedible hulls that encased it. The dried grains would then be put in a bucket-sized wooden mortar and gently pounded with a long wooden pestle to crack open the hulls. The hulls would be discarded, and the rice would be stored in a cool, dark place. Some of the rice would be eaten by the family who had harvested it, some would be given to other families in need, and some would be sold at a nearby market.

Nas exchanged greetings with his cousins, explaining to them who I was. "*Selamat siang* [good afternoon]," I said to them. One of the women handed me the tip of a rice stalk and smiled. I thanked her and tucked the souvenir in my backpack.

Connected to one of the footpaths of an adjacent paddy was an elevated bamboo hut used for meals or naps or both. Called *pondok*, these structures dot virtually every rice paddy in Southeast Asia, though they're known by different names in different countries. Arifin, Nas, and I climbed up an old wooden ladder onto the *pondok*. Nas opened up his army green backpack and placed on the floor a simple lunch that his wife had prepared for us. Inside three small stainless-steel food containers were chile sambal, golden deep-fried hard-cooked eggs, and steamed rice that had come from Nas's paddy.

"I'm sorry we have nothing fancier to offer," Nas said as he unpacked three torn banana leaves—our plates—and placed them in front of us. We quietly began to eat. The meal was pure and delicious. The sharp heat of the sambal blended perfectly with the egg and the rice, which tasted of the Sumatran sun.

"That was one of the best lunches I've ever eaten," I said to Nas as I folded over my empty banana leaf. The three of us sat silently listening to wind rustle the surrounding paddy. I rested my head on my arms and looked out. Puffy cumulus clouds were gathering on the horizon, their bases' etched with ominous gray streaks. It would probably rain soon. After about twenty minutes, Arifin broke the silence. It was time to head back home, he said. It would be getting dark within an hour.

The next day at dawn, Arifin and I set out on his motorcycle on the long journey to the ferry office in Dumai. As he'd promised, I was able to get a ticket. "See?" he said with a satisfied smile. "I told you there would be no problem." We said good-bye to each other with a handshake and I boarded the boat, a low-slung vessel that looked more like an oversized speedboat than a ferry. I made my way through the crowded deck toward the edge. As the shore of Sumatra made a hazy retreat on the horizon, my mind ran through the last few weeks I had spent in Indonesia. I reached into my backpack and found my souvenir rice stalk. I removed a few grains, rolled them between my fingertips, and then tossed them overboard, wishing to myself that things would start to go better for this country that I loved so much.

—

Rice, known as *beras* (buh-RAHS) when raw and *nasi* (NAH-see) when cooked, is not only an important pantry staple in Indonesia, Malaysia, and Singapore, but also the foundation of nearly every meal. The grain has ancient roots in the region. It's believed that rice was carried to the Malay Archipelago by spice seekers from India about three thousand years ago. The ancient Javanese in particular took to it fervently, becoming exceptional rice farmers who developed means of growing and harvesting that have yet to be improved.

Throughout the region, rituals similar to those in West Sumatra surround the cultivation of rice. Perhaps these rituals are at their most intricate and complex in Bali, where the grain symbolizes life in all its guises. Dewi Sri, the Balinese Hindu goddess who guides rice growing, is prayed to with sober reverence. (Interestingly, Dewi Sri is also honored throughout Muslim Indonesia, an echo of the country's ancient Hindu past and an example of the way its religions are mixed.) Before a seed is even planted in Bali, Hindu seers and priests are consulted to see which day will be the most auspicious, and evil spirits who may cause a crop to fail are placated by strewing the empty paddy with rice that has been soaked in palm wine. The *kliang subak*, the villager who is appointed by the local rice-field council to determine when water should be released to irrigate Bali's paddies, is accorded almost as much respect as Dewi Sri.

In the West, rice is usually a side dish, meant to provide the starch accompaniment to the more important meat and vegetable dishes on the plate. In Indonesia, Malaysia, and Singapore, the order is reversed: rice is the main dish, while all other dishes, from curries to stir-fries, are designed to complement it. Rice and savory foods (except for noodles, which are always eaten solo) are inevitably linked—without one, there's usually not the other. Serving most dishes without rice is akin to eating a pasta sauce without the pasta.

Because rice is viewed as a canvas onto which the flavors of a meal will be layered, locals favor varieties that have a simple, slightly aromatic taste, rather than a nutty, robustly flavored grain, such as India's basmati. The chosen rice is always long grain, which has a drier, springier consistency than short-grain varieties. With its light, fluffy texture, long-grain rice interacts better with soupy sauces, absorbing them more readily. To approximate the many varieties eaten in Indonesia, Malaysia, and Singapore, the best choice in North America is jasmine rice imported from Thailand, which is readily available in Asian markets and in most Western supermarkets. Its clean, mildly perfumed taste complements strongly flavored and subtle dishes alike. (See page 81 for more information about jasmine rice.) The easiest way to cook rice in your own home is to steam it in a pot, an easy technique that ensures grains that won't clump together. (See below for my favorite recipe for steaming rice on the stove, plus advice about using rice cookers.) Neither salt nor oil is added to plain steamed rice, though cooks in the Malay Archipelago—especially in Java—often place a few knotted or torn *daun pandan* leaves (see Cook's Notes, page 175) in the pot for their delicious vanilla-like aroma.

Cooks have also devised other ways to boost the appealing flavor of steamed rice, with perhaps the most delicious examples being the coconut rice dishes of the region, including *nasi uduk* (Lemongrass-Scented Coconut Rice, page 176) and *nasi kuning* (Celebration Yellow Rice, page 178). Both are steamed with thinned coconut milk, instead of water, and seasoned with such citrusy aromatics as kaffir lime leaves and lemongrass. Another intensely seasoned rice dish is Spiced Nyonya Rice (page 180), a Malaysian specialty made with basmati rice steamed in a chicken stock flavored with nine spices, including fennel, star anise, and cinnamon. This is the only recipe in this chapter that calls for basmati rice, whose nutty flavor complements the spicy stock better than jasmine rice does.

Many rice dishes stand on their own as robust one-dish meals. Inam, the Alwi family's cook, prepared fried rice every morning for breakfast with the rice left over from the previous day's dinner. She sautéed it with a vibrant flavoring paste, transforming it into a nuanced dish worthy of a royal banquet. Javanese Fried Rice (page 183), seasoned with shallots, red chiles, and Indonesian sweet soy sauce, is a re-creation of Inam's breakfast specialty. Another excellent dish based on leftover rice is Herbal Rice Salad (page 186), a refreshing classic from northern Malaysia made with minced lemongrass and a bouquet of tropical herbs.

STEAMED RICE
Nasi Putih
(INDONESIA, MALAYSIA, AND SINGAPORE)

—

Fluffy, pillowy, just-steamed rice is the cornerstone of almost every meal in Indonesia, Malaysia, and Singapore. It's traditionally cooked two ways. The first is to boil it in a large amount of water until the rice is half cooked; the water that remains in the pot is then drained off and the rice is allowed to steam, partially covered, until tender. The other method is quicker and, to my mind, more reliable: boiling the rice in a smaller amount of water. Soon after the rice comes to a full boil, you cover the pot, skip the draining-off step, and allow the rice to steam until it's fluffy. This recipe calls for the second technique. Always use Thai or North American jasmine rice. Its clean, aromatic taste and springy texture are the perfect counterpoint to the dishes in this book.

Some people are hearty rice eaters, while others, of course, aren't. When I plan a meal, I allow 1/2 cup (3 1/2 ounces/100 grams) uncooked jasmine rice per person, which yields about 1 1/2 cups (7 1/2 ounces/215 grams) cooked rice. This amount is generally enough to satisfy all my guests without running out. If there's leftover rice, I store it covered in the refrigerator and then wrap it in aluminum foil and reheat it in a warming oven for lunch or dinner the next day. If there's enough, I use it to make other rice dishes, such as Javanese Fried Rice (page 183). The best water-to-rice ratio for making steamed jasmine rice on the stove is roughly 1 part rice to 1 1/4 parts water. Keep in mind that each bag of rice you buy will require a slightly different ratio. For example, the older (and thus, drier) the rice, the more water it will require to come out tender. Whenever you buy a new bag of rice (even a brand you've bought before), pay close attention to your measurements and how the rice comes out the first time you make it. Adjust the water-to-rice ratio based on the results. If the rice is too hard, increase the water by 2 or 3 tablespoons; if it's too soft or gummy, decrease the water by 2 or 3 tablespoons. You may need to continue to adjust the ratio a few more times until you find the right proportions for a particular bag of rice.

For the fluffiest, best-tasting rice, you must rinse the rice thoroughly in cold water at least 4 times before cooking it (instructions are in the recipe). Rinsing serves two purposes. First, it removes debris such as tiny twigs and rice hulls and any dust clinging to the rice grains. Second, it breaks down the surface starch on the grains, which can make rice come out sticky.

Always serve rice steaming hot—the best showcase for its taste and texture—never lukewarm or cold. To make sure that I serve my guests steaming-hot rice, I usually prepare it last, starting it about a half hour before I serve the meal, and it's the final dish I bring to the table. Serve it in a high mound in a deep bowl, which helps keep it warm as the meal progresses. If it's spread out on a platter, it cools and dries out rapidly.

This recipe can be used for any dish in this chapter that calls for cooked rice. Follow the same instructions for both quantities.

MAKES 2 GENEROUS SERVINGS, OR 4 SMALL SERVINGS
1 cup (7 ounces/200 grams) jasmine rice
1 1/4 cups (10 fluid ounces/310 milliliters) water

MAKES 4 GENEROUS SERVINGS, OR 6 SMALL SERVINGS
2 cups (14 ounces/400 grams) jasmine rice
2 1/2 cups (20 fluid ounces/625 milliliters)
   water

1. Place the rice in a 1 1/2- or 2-quart (1.5- or 2-liter) saucepan. Fill the pot halfway with cold water. If any rice hulls or small twigs float to the surface, scoop them aside with your hand and discard them. Gently swirl your fingers through the rice until the water becomes cloudy from the surface starch on the rice grains, about 20 seconds. Be careful not to massage the rice aggressively. You don't want to crack or break the grains. Allow the rice to settle for a few seconds. Tilt the pot over a sink and drain out all the water, cupping the rice with your hand to prevent it from spilling out of the pot. Repeat this process with 3 more changes of water. The water after the first 2 rinses will be quite cloudy; by the fourth rinse, it will be much less so. The water need not run completely clear by the final rinse. Slightly cloudy water is fine. Leave the rinsed rice in the pot.

2. Add the cooking water to the rinsed rice. Gently shift the pot back and forth a few times, letting the rice settle in a flat, even layer at the bottom.

3. Place the pot over high heat and bring the water to a rolling, noisy boil. Allow the rice to boil vigorously for 15 seconds. Immediately reduce the heat to the lowest possible setting and cover the pot tightly with the lid. Continue cooking for 15 minutes. Don't be tempted to lift or remove the lid during this time. You'll lose essential cooking steam if you do.

4. Remove the pot from the heat and allow the rice to continue to steam, covered, away from the heat for an additional 10 minutes. This period ensures that the rice will be fully tender and makes it less prone to sticking to the bottom of the pot. Open the pot and fluff the rice gently with a fork, being careful to break as few grains as possible.

5. Transfer the rice to a deep serving bowl, and fluff it again well with a fork, lifting it into a peaked mound. Serve the rice piping hot.

COOK'S NOTES

To make their rice taste more fragrant, Indonesian cooks add 2 or 3 *daun pandan* leaves (page 64) to the pot, first tying them into a knot or tearing them in half so they'll release their essence. This dark green herb infuses the rice with a subtle vanilla-like aroma. I urge you to try it.

Many home cooks in Malaysia and Singapore have eschewed the stove-top method of steaming rice in favor of an electric rice cooker (page 107). I, too, like the ease with which rice cookers turn out perfect rice nearly every time without having to be monitored. If you make rice often, a rice cooker is a worthwhile purchase. Follow the individual manufacturer's instructions on how to operate your particular appliance. When you make rice in a rice cooker, the rice-to-water ratio suggested in the above recipe may need to be modified—you'll likely need a tablespoon or two less water for the rice to come out neither too hard nor too soft. Experiment until you find a good ratio. Note that using a rice cooker won't preclude you from rinsing the rice before you cook it; refer to step 1 for instructions on how to rinse rice properly.

LEMONGRASS-SCENTED COCONUT RICE
Nasi Uduk
(JAVA, INDONESIA)

R ice that has been cooked in coconut milk and seasoned with aromatics is a velvety-rich, alluring dish. It turns up in countless incarnations all over the Malay Archipelago (see page 178 for the Malaysian and Singaporean version, *nasi lemak*). This is the Javanese version, which is flavored with lemongrass and *daun salam* leaves, the woodsy-tasting Indonesian herb. The aromatics are submerged in the rice as it cooks, infusing the cooking liquid—and, in turn, the rice—with their essences. The hint of lemongrass is appealing, while the topping of crisply fried shallots adds smoky succulence. Friends for whom I have cooked this rice tell me it's the best rice they've ever eaten. It pairs well with just about anything that plain rice is served with, including curries and stir-fries, though it's also wonderful on its own, perhaps with a Malaysian pickle or a salad of baby lettuces. I prefer to eat *nasi uduk* warm rather than hot, as its flavors are even more delicious.

Don't try to halve this recipe—that would result in the aromatics sitting on top of the rice, rather than being submerged in it, yielding a poorly flavored dish. It's also not a good idea to make this dish in a rice cooker, as the fats and proteins in the coconut milk and the cooker's high, continuous heat can easily lead to the bottom layer of rice sticking and burning.

MAKES 4 TO 6 SERVINGS

2 cups (14 ounces/400 grams) jasmine rice

3 thick stalks fresh lemongrass, tied into a knot (page 76)

1 1/2 cups (12 fluid ounces/375 milliliters) water

1 cup (8 fluid ounces/250 milliliters) unsweet-ened coconut milk

1 teaspoon kosher salt

10 whole *daun salam* leaves (page 64; optional)

2 tablespoons Crisp-Fried Shallots (page 84; optional)

1. Place the rice in a 1 1/2- or 2-quart (1.5- or 2-liter) saucepan. Fill the pot halfway with cold water. If any rice hulls or small twigs float to the surface, scoop them aside with your hand and discard them. Gently swirl your fingers through the rice until the water becomes cloudy from the surface starch on the rice grains, about 20 seconds. Be careful not to mas-sage the rice aggressively. You don't want to crack or break the grains. Allow the rice to settle for a few seconds. Tilt the pot over a sink and drain out all the water, cupping the rice with your hand to prevent it from spilling out of the pot. Repeat this process with 3 more changes of water. The water after the first 2 rinses will be quite cloudy; by the fourth rinse, it will be much less so. The water need not run completely clear by the final rinse. Slightly cloudy water is fine. Leave the rinsed rice in the pot.

2. Add the lemongrass, cooking water, coconut milk, salt, and *daun salam* leaves (if using) to the rinsed rice. Stir well to combine, making sure that the lemongrass stalks and *daun salam* leaves are as fully submerged in the rice as possible.

3. Place the pot over high heat and bring the liquid to a boil, stirring with a large spoon to prevent the rice at the bottom of the pot from scorching or burning. Don't worry if the liquid thickens considerably as it comes to a boil, a result, in part, of the fats in the coconut milk combining with the starch in the rice. Also don't worry if the lemongrass knots become unraveled from the stirring. The finished rice will still be fine. Allow the rice to boil for 15 seconds, continuing to stir to prevent the rice at the bottom of the pot from scorching or burning. Immediately reduce the heat to the lowest possible setting and cover the pot tightly with the lid. Continue cooking for 15 minutes. Don't be tempted to lift or remove the lid during this time. You'll lose essential cooking steam if you do.

4. Meanwhile, if you'll be using the fried shallots, make them now and set aside.

5. Remove the pot from the heat and allow the rice to continue to steam, covered, away from the heat for an additional 10 minutes.

6. Open the pot and discard the lemongrass and *daun salam* leaves (if used). Gently fold the rice over with a spoon, evenly distributing the aromatic flavors that may be

concentrated in pockets in the rice. Transfer the rice to a deep serving bowl and fluff it well with a fork, lifting it into a peaked mound. Top with fried shallots (if using). Serve hot or warm. (If serving the rice warm, keep it covered with aluminum foil until then.)

VARIATION: GINGER-SCENTED COCONUT RICE (*NASI LEMAK*)

To make this gingery Malaysian and Singaporean version of Lemongrass-Scented Coconut Rice, known as *nasi lemak* (fatty rice), substitute a piece of ginger 2 inches (5 centimeters) long, peeled and bruised until juicy with a heavy, blunt object, for the *daun salam* leaves. *Nasi lemak* is traditionally served as a breakfast dish with a halved hard-cooked egg, a wedge of cucumber, a tablespoon or so of fried peanuts, and small portions of a sambal and a pickle, such as Javanese Sambal (page 119) and Sweet-Sour Cucumber and Carrot Pickle with Turmeric (page 130). Do not garnish *nasi lemak* with fried shallots.

MENU SUGGESTIONS

This lush and aromatic dish goes well with nearly every dish I can think of, though it has a particular affinity for Tofu and Summer Vegetables in Coconut Milk (page 327) and all egg dishes. For a traditional Jakarta-style *nasi uduk* meal, serve it with Mien's Garlic Fried Chicken (page 283), Garlic-Marinated Tempeh (page 322), Javanese Sambal (page 119), and *lalap*, a side dish composed of a few peeled and halved Kirby cucumbers, a few halved Roma tomatoes, and a few sprigs of fresh lemon basil (page 74), Thai basil, or Italian basil, all of which guests can nibble between bites of rice.

CELEBRATION YELLOW RICE
Nasi Kuning
(INDONESIA, MALAYSIA, AND SINGAPORE)

—

This variation on coconut rice gets its vivid golden color from turmeric and its abundant flavor from lemongrass and kaffir lime, *daun pandan*, and *daun salam* leaves. *Nasi kuning*, literally "yellow rice," is usually reserved for birthdays, weddings, anniversaries, or the celebration surrounding a baby's first taste of solid food. It originated in Java and is now eaten all over Indonesia, Malaysia, and Singapore. Although grated fresh turmeric is traditionally used to achieve the yellow color, I have found that using ground turmeric from the spice cupboard is easier and doesn't noticeably affect the taste of the dish.

Yellow rice is often served molded into an inverted cone shape, a dish known as *tumpeng*. The cone's peak is crowned with a splayed-open red chile, while its sides are garnished with symmetrical rows of peanuts and omelet strips. *Tumpeng* is said to represent a holy volcano worshipped by the Javanese in pre-Muslim times. Served humbly and unshaped in a bowl, however, *nasi kuning* makes an excellent alternative to steamed white rice.

As with Lemongrass-Scented Coconut Rice (page 176), it's best not to halve this recipe, since the aromatics would be sitting on top of the rice as it cooks, rather than being submerged in it. Also, I don't recommend making this dish in a rice cooker, which can lead to the bottom layer of rice sticking and burning.

MAKES 4 TO 6 SERVINGS

2 cups (14 ounces/400 grams) jasmine rice

1 1/2 cups (12 fluid ounces/375 milliliters) water

1 1/2 teaspoons ground turmeric

1 cup (8 fluid ounces/250 milliliters) unsweetened coconut milk

1 teaspoon kosher salt

2 thick stalks fresh lemongrass, each tied into a knot (page 76)

3 whole fresh or thawed, frozen kaffir lime leaves, gently crumpled with your hands to release their essence

4 fresh or thawed, frozen *daun pandan* leaves (page 64), each tied into a knot or torn in half (optional)

4 whole *daun salam* leaves (page 64; optional)

1. Place the rice in a 1 1/2- or 2-quart (1.5- or 2-liter) saucepan. Fill the pot halfway with cold water. If any rice hulls or small twigs float to the surface, scoop them aside with your hand and discard them. Gently swirl your fingers through the rice until the water becomes cloudy from the surface starch on the rice grains, about 20 seconds. Be careful not to massage the rice aggressively. You don't want to crack or break the grains. Allow the rice to settle for a few seconds. Tilt the pot over a sink and drain out all the water, cupping the rice with your hand to prevent it from spilling out of the pot. Repeat this process with 3 more changes of water. The water after the first 2 rinses will be quite cloudy; by the fourth rinse, it will be much less so. The water need not run completely clear by the final rinse—slightly cloudy is fine. Leave the rinsed rice in the pot.

2. In a bowl, combine the cooking water and the turmeric, and stir well to combine.

3. Add the turmeric-water mixture, coconut milk, salt, lemongrass, kaffir lime leaves, and the *daun pandan* and *daun salam* leaves (if using) to the rinsed rice. Stir well to combine,

making sure that the lemongrass stalks and all the leaves are as fully submerged in the rice as possible.

4. Place the pot over high heat and bring the liquid to a boil, stirring with a large spoon to prevent the rice at the bottom of the pot from scorching or burning. Don't worry if the liquid thickens considerably as it comes to a boil. This is a result of the fats in the coconut milk combining with the starch in the rice. Also don't worry if the lemongrass knots become unraveled from the stirring. The finished rice will still be fine. Allow the rice to boil for 15 seconds, continuing to stir to prevent the rice from scorching or burning. Immediately reduce the heat to the lowest possible setting and cover the pot tightly with the lid. Continue cooking for 15 minutes. Don't be tempted to lift or remove the lid during this time. You'll lose essential cooking steam if you do.

5. Remove the pot from the heat and allow the rice to continue to steam, covered, away from the heat for an additional 10 minutes.

6. Open the pot and discard the lemongrass, kaffir lime leaves, and the *daun pandan* and *daun salam* leaves (if used). Gently fold the rice over with a spoon, evenly distributing the aromatic flavors that may be concentrated in pockets in the rice. Transfer the rice to a deep serving bowl and fluff it well with a fork, lifting it into a peaked mound. Serve hot or warm. (If serving the rice warm, keep it covered with aluminum foil until then.)

MENU SUGGESTIONS

The gently aromatic taste of this dish complements virtually any curry, stew, salad, or stir-fry. I like to make a light meal of *nasi kuning* and accompany it only with Javanese Cucumber and Carrot Pickle (page 132). Other excellent (and more substantial) companions would be Chicken Satay (page 147), Potato Rendang (page 223), Stir-fried Shrimp Sambal (page 262), and Javanese Spiced Oxtail Stew (page 312).

SPICED NYONYA RICE
Nasi Kemuli
(MALAYSIA)

My Nyonya friend Josephine Chua has logged many hours researching the origins of this sublimely spiced rice main dish (also known as *nasi kebuli*), a favorite of her family in Malacca, Malaysia. She believes it's a Javanese dish taken to the Malay Archipelago by

Arab traders. (Datin Amy Hamidon, also a Nyonya from Malacca, explained to me that *kebuli* is a reference to Kabul, Afghanistan, another apparent source of the dish.) Indeed, it closely resembles the rice pilafs and *biriyani* (intensely seasoned Indian rice dishes that often include goat or chicken), minus the meat, of the Middle East and South Asia. Most of the important spices—nutmeg, clove, star anise, poppy seed, coriander, cumin, fennel, cinnamon, cardamom—of the old spice-trading routes are represented in the stock used to cook the rice.

Josephine uses basmati rice for this recipe, believing that the floral fragrance of jasmine rice counteracts the perfume of the spices. Basmati, from northern India, has long, thin grains characterized by a nutty taste. It's available in South Asian markets and many specialty markets. The chicken pieces are used only to flavor the stock and not eaten with the rice, though the meat could go to an aromatic chicken salad. Unlike the recipes for coconut rice (pages 176 and 178), this rice can be effectively steamed on the stove top or in a rice cooker. (Note that the grains of basmati are thinner than those of jasmine rice and thus require slightly less water to cook.)

MAKES 4 TO 6 SERVINGS

FOR THE STOCK

1 1/2 pounds (680 grams) bone-in chicken pieces, preferably thighs or drumsticks (dark meat is more flavorful)

3 whole star anise

1 teaspoon whole cloves

3 tablespoons coriander seeds

1 tablespoon fennel seeds

1 tablespoon cumin seeds

1 tablespoon white or black poppy seeds

1 whole nutmeg, cracked open with a nut-cracker or a heavy, blunt object

1 tablespoon green cardamom pods, cracked open with the flat side of a knife (page 49)

1 piece cinnamon stick, 2 inches (5 centimeters) long

4 cups (32 fluid ounces/1 liter) water

2 tablespoons Crisp-Fried Shallots (page 84)

2 tablespoons crisp-fried garlic slices (see Crisp-Fried Shallots, page 84)

2 cups (14 ounces/400 grams) basmati rice

1 tablespoon double-black soy sauce (page 87)

1 tablespoon soy sauce

1 tablespoon sugar

Kosher salt (optional)

3 tablespoons ghee or clarified butter (see Cook's Note, page 183; optional)

1. To make the stock, combine the chicken pieces, all the spices, and the water in a 4-quart (4-liter) saucepan and bring to a rolling boil over high heat. Reduce the heat to low, cover, and simmer until the stock is intensely aromatic, about 2 hours. (This dish will

taste better if you don't skim the chicken fat off the top.) Remove from the heat, let cool, and strain through a fine-mesh sieve into a large measuring cup; you should have about 2 1/2 cups (20 fluid ounces/625 milliliters). Reserve the chicken pieces for another use or discard them. (You can double the stock recipe and save the balance to use whenever you need a flavorful chicken stock. It will keep in an airtight container in the refrigerator for 5 days or in the freezer for 1 month.)

2. While the stock is simmering, fry the shallots and garlic and set them aside.

3. Place the rice in a 1 1/2- or 2-quart (1.5- or 2-liter) saucepan. Basmati rice imported from India sometimes contains tiny stones, so carefully pick through it with your fingers, discarding any that you find. Fill the pot halfway with cold water. If any rice hulls or small twigs float to the surface, scoop them aside with your hand and discard them. Gently swirl your fingers through the rice until the water becomes cloudy from the surface starch of the rice grains, about 20 seconds. Be careful not to massage the rice aggressively. You don't want to crack or break the grains. Allow the rice to settle for a few seconds. Tilt the pot over a sink and drain out all the water, cupping the rice with your hand to prevent it from spilling out of the pot. Repeat this process with 3 more changes of water. The water after the first 2 rinses will be quite cloudy; by the fourth rinse, it will be much less so. The water need not run completely clear by the final rinse—slightly cloudy is fine. Leave the rinsed rice in the pot.

4. Add 2 1/3 cups (18 1/2 fluid ounces/575 milliliters) of the stock, the double-black soy sauce, soy sauce, and sugar to the rinsed rice. Stir well to combine, then gently shift the pot back and forth a few times, letting the rice settle in a flat, even layer at the bottom.

5. Place the pot over high heat and bring the water to a rolling boil. Allow the rice to boil vigorously for 15 seconds. Immediately reduce the heat to the lowest possible setting and cover the pot tightly with the lid. Continue cooking for 15 minutes. Don't be tempted to lift or remove the lid during this time. You'll lose essential cooking steam if you do.

6. Remove the pot from the heat and allow the rice to continue to steam, covered, away from the heat for an additional 10 minutes. This period ensures that the rice will be fully tender and makes it less prone to sticking to the bottom of the pot. Open the pot and fluff the rice gently with a fork, being careful to break as few grains as possible. Check for salt, and add a pinch if needed. Add the ghee (if using) and, using a large spoon, gently fold the rice over to combine. (I hope you use the ghee or clarified butter; either one adds a lovely richness to this dish.) With the spoon, gently fold 5 teaspoons each of the fried shallots and garlic into the rice, making sure they are evenly distributed. Reserve the remaining 1 teaspoon of each for garnish.

7. Transfer the rice to a deep serving bowl and fluff it again well with a fork, lifting it into a peaked mound. Garnish with the reserved fried shallots and garlic. The complex flavors of this dish are more fully enjoyed when the rice is served warm, not piping hot. (If you do decide to serve the rice warm, keep it covered with aluminum foil until then.)

COOK'S NOTE

Ghee, a classic Indian ingredient, is clarified butter that has been sautéed until it's golden and nutty tasting. It's widely available in jars at Indian, Pakistani, and Bangladeshi markets. Ordinary clarified butter may be substituted. To make your own clarified butter, melt 1/2 cup (4 ounces/115 grams) unsalted butter over low heat in a 1 1/2- or 2-quart (1.5- or 2-liter) saucepan. When the butter is fully melted, tilt the pan toward you and remove the milky foam from the surface with a spoon. Gently simmer the remaining clear liquid for about 30 seconds, which allows the taste to intensify. Remove from the heat and slowly pour off the clear liquid into a bowl, leaving any milk solids behind in the bottom of the pan. Store leftover clarified butter in a tightly sealed jar in the refrigerator for up to a week.

MENU SUGGESTIONS

This dish is traditionally eaten on its own, though Josephine sometimes pairs it with Stir-fried Tamarind Shrimp (page 255), Nyonya-Style Spiced Fried Chicken (page 285), Asiah's Eggplant Curry (page 229), and Javanese Cucumber and Carrot Pickle (page 132). Alternatively, serve it alongside a salad of baby lettuces dressed with olive oil and lime juice for a light meal.

JAVANESE FRIED RICE

Nasi Goreng

(JAVA, INDONESIA)

⌁

Fried rice, or *nasi goreng*, is the favorite breakfast of Indonesia. There are as many versions as there are cooks, but the most common—and the most delicious—are simple, usually consisting of little more than leftover rice stir-fried with a zingy flavoring paste. Additional ingredients, such as vegetables or meat, are rarely, if ever, added to true Indonesian-style fried rice. This recipe, based on the fried rice that Inam, the Alwi family's cook, made when I stayed with the family in the 1980s, is the classic Javanese version. The seasonings—chiles, palm sugar, dried shrimp paste—gently accentuate the rice without overpowering it. Topped with a fried egg (eggs are rarely mixed into fried rice, as they are in Chinese cooking), and eaten with crunchy shrimp chips and quartered or sliced cucumbers, it is earthy and satisfying.

Two pointers that will ensure success: Use chilled cooked rice, which clumps less than warm or room-temperature cooked rice. And, because rice has a tendency to stick aggressively to the pan when it's sautéed, you'll have an easier time if you use a nonstick pan.

MAKES 4 SERVINGS AS A MAIN COURSE

8 Fried Shrimp Chips (page 86; optional)

FOR THE FLAVORING PASTE

1 teaspoon dried shrimp paste (page 65)

2 shallots (about 1 1/2 ounces/40 grams total), coarsely chopped

1 clove garlic, coarsely chopped

1 to 2 fresh red Holland chiles or other fresh long, red chiles such as Fresno or cayenne, stemmed and coarsely chopped

1 tablespoon palm sugar (page 79), thinly sliced, or dark brown sugar

4 tablespoons peanut oil, or as needed

4 eggs

Kosher salt

5 cups (25 ounces/710 grams) cooked jasmine rice, made from about 2 cups (14 ounces/400 grams) uncooked rice (see Steamed Rice, page 173), chilled in the refrigerator for at least 1 hour

1 1/2 tablespoons Indonesian sweet soy sauce (page 72)

4 Kirby (pickling) cucumbers or 2 small-seeded conventional cucumbers, stemmed, peeled, and quartered or sliced into thick pieces on the diagonal (optional)

1. If you are using the shrimp chips, fry them now and set aside to use as a garnish.

2. To make the flavoring paste, place the shrimp paste in the center of a 5-inch (13-centimeter) square of aluminum foil. Fold the edges of the foil over to form a small parcel, and press down with the heel of your hand to flatten the shrimp paste into a disk 1/4 inch (6 millimeters) thick. Heat a gas burner to medium-low or an electric burner to medium-high. Using a pair of tongs or 2 forks, place the sealed parcel directly on the heat source. Toast until the paste begins to smoke and release a burning, shrimpy smell, about 1 1/2 minutes. With the tongs or forks, turn the parcel over and toast the other side for another 1 1/2 minutes, then turn off the burner. Again using the tongs or forks,

remove the parcel and let cool for 30 seconds to 1 minute. Carefully unwrap the foil; the edges of the disk should be black-brown and toasty and the center should be golden with some black-brown patches. Using a spoon, scrape the toasted shrimp paste into a small bowl and allow it to cool for another 30 seconds. Discard the foil.

3. Place the toasted shrimp paste, shallots, garlic, chiles, and palm sugar in a small food processor. Pulse until you have a smooth paste the consistency of creamy mashed potatoes. If the paste won't purée properly and repeatedly creeps up the side of the processor instead of grinding, add up to 2 tablespoons water, 1 tablespoon at a time, periodically turning the processor off and scraping the unground portions down toward the blade. Set the flavoring paste aside.

4. Heat the 4 tablespoons oil in a 12-inch (30-centimeter) skillet (nonstick will work best) over medium heat. When the oil is hot—it should appear slightly shimmery—crack an egg into it. Season the egg with a pinch of salt. When the white is just beginning to turn brown and crispy around the edges, carefully turn the egg over with a spatula. Sauté until the yolk is set, about 1 minute. You want the surface of the egg to be golden and the yolk to be fairly firm. Runny, undercooked eggs are not appealing in this dish. Transfer the egg to a plate and set aside. Fry the remaining eggs in the same manner, setting them all aside. Leave the oil behind in the pan (there should be about 3 tablespoons oil; add more if necessary). Allow the pan to cool for a few minutes before proceeding to the next step.

5. Reheat the oil left in the pan over medium-low heat. When it's hot, add the flavoring paste and sauté, stirring often to prevent scorching, until the shallots and garlic no longer smell raw and the paste begins to separate from the oil, about 5 minutes. If the paste doesn't separate, don't worry. Just remove the pan from the heat after 5 minutes anyway. Don't let the paste brown; it should be only gently cooked.

6. Using your fingers, not a spoon, add the cooked rice to the skillet, breaking up as many large clumps as you can as it goes into the pan. Raise the heat to high and cook, stirring constantly, until every grain of rice is hot and coated in the oil and the flavoring paste, about 5 minutes. Use the spatula to break up any clumps that remain in the rice. The best way to accomplish this, I find, is to cut into the clumps with the edge of the spatula, pressing down and wiggling the spatula a bit until they break up. If you continue stirring constantly, the rice shouldn't brown or scorch. If you notice signs of browning, reduce the heat slightly.

7. Add the sweet soy sauce and stir well to combine. Continue to cook, stirring constantly, for another 30 seconds. Taste for salt, and add a pinch if needed. If you're not using a

nonstick skillet and the rice begins to stick, add more oil—up to 1 tablespoon—and reduce the heat slightly. This may help the situation.

8. Spoon the rice onto 4 dinner plates, dividing it evenly and arranging it into a neat mound on each plate. Top each mound with a fried egg. Place the shrimp chips and cucumbers (if using) alongside the rice, not on top of the eggs. Serve immediately.

MENU SUGGESTIONS

Although usually eaten in the morning to kick off the day, fried rice also can be eaten for lunch or dinner, especially when accompanied by a light salad or a simple dish like Mien's Garlic Fried Chicken (page 283). Sweet Soy Sauce and Lime Dipping Sauce (page 125) is the perfect condiment for the rice.

HERBAL RICE SALAD
Nasi Ulam
(MALAYSIA)

I first encountered this extraordinary main-dish rice salad known as *nasi ulam* (or sometimes *nasi kerabu*) in Terengganu, on the northeast coast of peninsular Malaysia. I had gone into a small tea shop that was getting ready to close for the night and it was the only food available.

"It's an old Malay dish," explained the cook, a friendly Chinese woman who began to assemble it for me. I watched as she placed handfuls of toasted coconut and tropical herbs so finely chopped that they resembled green lace atop a small mound of rice. She deftly mixed everything together, offering me a taste so that she could adjust the seasonings to suit my palate. It was amazingly aromatic, like no other rice salad I'd ever had. I was an immediate convert.

The flavors of this salad aren't set in stone. Some cooks prefer to emphasize citrusy herbs, such as lemon basil and kaffir lime leaves, while others favor herbs that have more bite, such as Vietnamese basil. Many cooks in Malaysia buy *nasi ulam* herb bundles at their local markets. These bundles often include torch-ginger flower (*bunga kantan*), a bright pink gladiola-like bud with a musky taste, and *daun kaduk*, peppery-tasting glossy green leaves that grow alongside rice paddies. But whatever herbs you use, the best way to chop them is to stack them, roll them up lengthwise into a tight bundle, and then slice them crosswise as thinly as possible with the sharpest knife you own (what French cooks call a chiffonade). Be sure to use the freshest, sweetest shallots you can find. Old, harsh-tasting shallots will overpower the dish. (To make a Westernized version of this rice salad, try substituting fresh dill, chervil, and a little marjoram or oregano—not too much, or the dish will taste bitter—for the Asian herbs.)

For best results, use rice that's at room temperature; warm rice will cook the delicate herbs, while cold rice will result in a hard-textured, unpalatable dish.

MAKES 4 SERVINGS AS A MAIN COURSE, 6 SERVINGS AS A SIDE DISH

4 heaping tablespoons Toasted Grated Coconut (page 59)

About 50 fresh lemon basil (page 74), Thai basil, or Italian basil leaves (about 1 small bunch)

About 35 fresh mint leaves (about 1/2 small bunch)

About 60 fresh Vietnamese basil leaves (see Cook's Note, page 188) or cilantro leaves (about 1 small bunch)

1 thick stalk fresh lemongrass

3 whole fresh or thawed, frozen kaffir lime leaves

3 to 4 tablespoons small dried shrimp (page 65)

3 shallots (about 2 1/2 ounces/70 grams total), very thinly sliced lengthwise

5 cups (25 ounces/710 grams) cooked jasmine rice, at room temperature, made from about 2 cups (14 ounces/400 grams) uncooked rice (see Steamed Rice, page 173)

2 tablespoons fresh lime juice

About 1 teaspoon kosher salt

1/2 teaspoon freshly ground black pepper

1. Prepare the Toasted Grated Coconut and set aside.

2. Working in batches, stack the lemon basil leaves, roll up lengthwise into a tight bundle, and slice crosswise as thinly as possible with a very sharp knife. You should have about 5 loosely packed, heaping tablespoons of the sliced herb. Cut the mint leaves in the same manner; you should have about 3 loosely packed, heaping tablespoons of the sliced herb. Finally, cut the Vietnamese basil leaves in the same manner; you should have about 5 loosely packed, heaping tablespoons of the sliced herb. Set all the herbs aside.

3. Cut off the hard, brown bottom and the bristly, greenish top of the lemongrass, which should leave you with a pale white-and-lilac piece about 5 inches (13 centimeters) long. Discard the 2 or 3 tough outer layers. With the same sharp knife, cut the lemongrass on the diagonal into the thinnest possible slices, making them as close to paper-thin as you

can. (The lemongrass slices will be difficult to chew if they're too thick.) Set the lemongrass aside.

4. Again with the sharp knife, remove the tough center vein and hard stem of each kaffir lime leaf. Cut the leaves lengthwise into the narrowest possible strips—as narrow as a strand of hair if your knife will allow it. (The lime leaves will be difficult to chew if they are sliced too thickly.) Set the sliced lime leaves aside.

5. Place the dried shrimp in a small food processor and pulse until you have a fine powder resembling sawdust. Set the powdered shrimp aside.

6. In a large bowl, combine the sliced herbs, lemongrass, and lime leaves; the powdered shrimp; the shallots; and the rice. With a large spoon (or, better yet, your hands, which will allow you to distribute the ingredients more evenly), combine the ingredients until the herbs and the rice are well mixed and the rice is free of clumps. Add the lime juice and mix once more.

7. Add the salt and pepper and taste for seasoning. Because the herbs and shallots are intensely flavored, you may need to add less than 1 teaspoon salt. This dish should be neither salty nor acidic. It should be subtle and intensely fragrant, with the clean taste of each herb clearly coming through. Add a squeeze of lime juice if needed.

8. Transfer to a serving bowl and eat at once. The herbs in this dish will wilt and lose their zing if allowed to sit for longer than 30 minutes.

COOK'S NOTE

Widely available in stores specializing in Southeast Asian and Vietnamese foods, Vietnamese basil, which is also known as *daun laksa*, *daun kesum*, *polyganum* (its Latin name), and *rau ram* (its true Vietnamese name), looks like thick, dark green blades of grass. It has an appealingly peppery taste and is used as a flavoring in many Malaysian soups, in particular the aromatic Georgetown noodle soup known as *asam laska* (page 195). Though cilantro tastes nothing like Vietnamese basil, its fresh, clean taste makes it a good substitute.

MENU SUGGESTIONS

This rice salad is traditionally eaten as a one-dish meal, though you might want to serve it as a side dish and pair it with mild, sauce-free dishes, such as Mien's Garlic Fried Chicken (page 283), Pan-Seared Tamarind Tuna (page 254), or Garlic-Marinated Tempeh (page 322).

Curries and other saucy dishes may throw this salad's delicate flavors off balance. Served in small portions, this dish makes an interesting Western-style appetizer.

NOODLES

Noodles were probably introduced to Indonesia, Malaysia, and Singapore by Chinese spice traders in about the third century. Over time, Malay Archipelago cooks adapted traditional Chinese noodle recipes to suit the local taste for heightened flavors by incorporating dried shrimp paste, fresh herbs, and aromatic spices. Today, most home cooks excel at making these flavorful dishes (and the noodle recipes in this chapter all come from home cooks), but street hawkers are the region's true noodle specialists. On nearly every street in every city there's at least one vendor who is adept at making a particular noodle dish. The favorites include *char kuey teow* (rice noodles stir-fried with eggs and a robust mix of chiles and other seasonings), *mee jawa* (Chinese egg noodles in a piquant sweet potato–based gravy), *wantan mee* (thin Chinese egg noodles and sliced roast pork served with pickled green chiles), and any number of *laksa* dishes (rice or egg noodles immersed in a variety of vibrantly seasoned soups and curries). But whether noodle dishes are served at home or eaten at a street stall, most Indonesians, Malaysians, and Singaporeans regard them as a light repast or snack rather than a full-fledged meal, and they're rarely—if ever—served with rice.

Noodles are used primarily two ways in Indonesian, Malaysian, and Singaporean dishes: stir-fried or in soups and curries. The most popular dishes in the first category showcase ingredients designed to enhance the subtle taste of noodles. An example is Stir-fried Chinese Egg Noodles with Shrimp and Asian Greens (page 191), a soulful mix of thick, spaghetti-like Chinese egg noodles, shrimp, *choy sum*, and sweet soybean paste. Penang-Style Stir-fried Kuey Teow Noodles (page 193) is a classic Malaysian dish from the food-obsessed city of Georgetown. It's made of fresh flat rice noodles (called *kuey teow*) stir-fried over blazing heat with a fiery blend of dried chiles, shrimp paste, and garlic.

On the other end of the noodle-dish spectrum are spicy noodle soups. The best known are the various types of *laksa* of Malaysia and Singapore. Chicken Curry Noodle Soup, Kuala Lumpur Style (page 195) is a version of *laksa* with Chinese egg noodles and a sensational spice-infused coconut broth. Garnished with bean sprouts and thinly sliced Holland chiles, it's one of the world's great noodle dishes.

To make the noodle recipes in this book, you'll need two types of noodles. The first are fresh Chinese egg noodles. Made of wheat flour and eggs, these thick, delicately flavored noodles, the most popular in the region, are prized for their ability to absorb flavors. Fresh, precooked Chinese egg noodles are widely available in packages in the refrigerated noodle or pasta sections of Asian markets and select supermarkets. Be sure to buy noodles that are the thickness and shape of spaghetti and are an appealing pale gold, not an intense yellow, which indicates color additives. Avoid both thin, vermicelli-like and flat, fettuccine-like fresh Chinese egg noodles. Although both are wonderful, they're not appropriate for these recipes. Also avoid dried Chinese egg noodles, which have a dull taste.

Labeling can be erratic on packages of fresh Chinese egg noodles: some will be called lo mein (which means "stir-fried noodles" in Cantonese); others, regular mein. The only sure way to identify the noodles you'll need for these recipes is by how they look. If you can't find fresh Chinese egg noodles, fresh Italian fettuccine, cooked until tender, drained, and immediately tossed with a few teaspoons of peanut oil to prevent the noodles from sticking together, makes an acceptable substitute.

Check expiration dates carefully when buying egg noodles. If there's no expiration date, choose noodles that are springy and brightly colored, not hard and stiff. According to my Chinese Malay friend Helen, who owns a New York Malaysian restaurant called Taste Good, many commercial fresh Chinese egg noodles aren't what they used to be. Some manufacturers load the dough with preservatives that make them appear fresh, when in fact they're a few weeks old. Look for brands that have a minimum of chemical additives. Barring that, practice what Helen calls mindful ignorance and purchase the noodles that instinct tells you are the freshest and purest, and always cook them within a day or two of purchase. I always give fresh noodles a good sniff before I cook with them. They should smell sweet and doughy, not sour or fermented.

Some fresh Chinese egg noodles have been precooked, and their packages are clearly labeled "ready to eat." To use them, you need only rinse them under cold running water to rid them of the oil that was added after cooking to prevent them from sticking together. Chinese egg noodles that are uncooked will be dusted in flour. To precook them, bring a large pot full of unsalted water to a rolling boil, add the noodles, and cook until tender, 3 to 5 minutes; the timing will depend on their thickness and freshness. Drain into a colander and rinse under cold water until cool. Toss the noodles immediately with a few teaspoons of peanut oil to prevent them from clumping together.

The other noodles that you'll need for the recipes here are fresh *kuey teow* (pronounced kway TEE-ow). These thin, bright white, flat rice-flour noodles are 1/4 to 1/2 inch (6 to 12 millimeters) wide. Their soft, velvety texture and bland taste are a perfect backdrop for intense seasonings. Look for them in the refrigerated noodle section of Chinese markets; they're not available dry. Don't confuse them with the wide, flat, much thicker noodles called *sha he fen* that are sold in 1-pound (455-gram) sheets and are used for dim sum, not stir-frying. *Kuey teow* dry out quickly, so use them within a day or two of purchase. Also, because they're often covered in not-very-delicious cottonseed oil to keep them from sticking together, always rinse them well under cold running water before cooking with them.

If you can't find fresh *kuey teow*, dried rice-flour fettuccine-like noodles called *hor fun* in Cantonese (the variety used to make pad Thai) can be substituted. They're available in the dried-noodle section of Asian markets and select Western supermarkets. To cook them, add them to plenty of unsalted boiling water and cook until tender, 30 seconds to 2 minutes; the timing will depend on the thickness of the noodle. Drain into a colander and rinse under cold water until cool. Toss the noodles immediately with a few teaspoons of peanut oil to prevent them from clumping together.

STIR-FRIED CHINESE EGG NOODLES WITH SHRIMP AND ASIAN GREENS

Mee Goreng Tauceo

(MALAYSIA AND SINGAPORE)

——

Fresh Chinese egg noodles, the shape and thickness of spaghetti and called *mee* or "yellow noodles," are a core ingredient in Malaysian and Singaporean cooking. They're a perfect foil for assertive, sweet ingredients, such as the sweet soybean paste (*tauco*) in this recipe. Although cooks in Malaysia and Singapore have devised many ingenious ways to stir-fry egg noodles, this recipe stands out for its lightness and freshness. It's traditionally eaten on its own; enjoy it as a light lunch or supper along with fiery Nyonya Sambal (page 120) or any chile-based sauce. If possible, use a nonstick wok or skillet to make this dish, as fresh Chinese egg noodles have a tendency to stick to the pan. Also, because this dish requires rapid stir-frying, clean, cut, and measure all your ingredients before you begin cooking.

MAKES 3 OR 4 SERVINGS AS A MAIN COURSE

1 pound (455 grams) precooked fresh Chinese egg noodles (pages 189 to 190), rinsed, drained, and cut in half, or uncooked fresh Chinese egg noodles (pages 189 to 190)

10 stalks *choy sum* or 5 whole small heads baby bok choy or Shanghai choy, about 7 ounces (200 grams) total

4 tablespoons peanut oil

2 cloves garlic, coarsely chopped

2 tablespoons sweet soybean paste (page 88)

7 ounces (200 grams) medium-sized shrimp (10 to 15 shrimp), peeled, heads removed, and deveined (you can leave the tails on, if you like)

1 1/2 cups (about 4 ounces/115 grams) mung bean sprouts (optional; if not using, increase the amount of *choy sum* by 3 stalks or baby bok choy or Shanghai choy by 2 heads)

4 tablespoons warm water

2 teaspoons double-black soy sauce (page 87)

1/4 teaspoon kosher salt

Freshly ground black pepper (optional)

1. If you're using fresh Chinese egg noodles that are not precooked, cook them first (see page 190 for directions), cut them in half, and set aside.

2. To prepare the *choy sum*, inspect it carefully, discarding or trimming any spoiled stems or leaves. Cut 1 inch (2.5 centimeters) off the base of each stalk and rinse the greens in several changes of the coldest possible water. If you're using baby bok choy or baby Shanghai choy, inspect the heads carefully, discarding or trimming any spoiled stems or leaves. Cut 1/8 inch (3 millimeters) off the base of each head and rinse the greens in several changes of the coldest possible water. (Take care to clean baby bok choy or Shanghai choy carefully, as it tends to have hidden pockets of sand where the leaves meet the center stem). Cut the cleaned *choy sum* into pieces 2 1/2 to 3 inches (6 to 7.5 centimeters) long; if you're using baby bok choy or Shanghai choy, leave the heads whole or cut them in halves or quarters lengthwise, depending on size. Dry the greens in a salad spinner or set them aside to dry on a kitchen towel or on paper towels. They don't need to be bone-dry; a little dampness is fine.

3. Heat the oil in a wok or 12-inch (30-centimeter) skillet (nonstick will work best) over medium heat. When it's hot—it should appear slightly shimmery—add the garlic and the sweet soybean paste (be mindful that the soybean paste may splatter a bit when it's added to the hot oil) and sauté, stirring constantly with a large spatula, until the garlic is no longer raw but has not yet begun to change color, 1 to 2 minutes. If the garlic starts to turn golden, take the pan off the heat to cool for a few moments before continuing.

4. Add the shrimp to the skillet and stir-fry just until they begin to turn pink, about 2 minutes. Add the greens and raise the heat to high. Stir-fry vigorously until the greens just begin to wilt, 1 to 2 minutes. Add the bean sprouts (if using) and continue to stir-fry vigorously for another 15 seconds.

5. Reduce the heat slightly and quickly add the noodles, using your hands and detangling them as you drop them into the skillet. Stir the noodles well to combine them with the greens, bean sprouts, and shrimp. Add the warm water, soy sauce, and salt and stir well to combine. Cook, stirring constantly, until the noodles are hot and have soaked

up all the liquid, about 2 minutes. (Note that the noodles will have increased slightly in size once they have soaked up the liquid.) Taste a noodle for salt, and add a pinch more if needed.

6. Transfer the noodles to a large platter or bowl and serve immediately. Although inauthentic, I like to top these noodles with freshly ground black pepper, which provides a nice layer of flavor.

PENANG-STYLE STIR-FRIED KUEY TEOW NOODLES
Char Kuey Teow
(MALAYSIA AND SINGAPORE)

⟶

Char kuey teow is arguably Malaysia's most celebrated noodle dish. It embodies the tradition of the stir-fried noodle dishes of southern China, but is given a distinctly Malaysian jolt with chiles and dried shrimp paste. Its flat, thin, wide fresh rice noodles (*kuey teow*), egg, shrimp, bean sprouts, and Chinese chives all come together in a sultry whole. This recipe is from my friend Mai Loon, a home cook in Penang, Malaysia, who got her inspiration from sisters Jook Kee and Mee Heng, owners and operators of the popular Sisters' Char Kuey Teow stall in Penang for more than forty years.

Prep all the ingredients first and put them within easy reach of the stove, as you'll have no time to search for ingredients between steps. If you want to double the recipe, cook it in two batches, which makes it much easier to control. A nonstick skillet or wok will also make things easier for you, as the noodles can sometimes stick. When made by members of the Chinese community in Malaysia and Singapore, *char kuey teow* is usually stir-fried in rendered pork lard, which provides a rich, succulent taste. I've substituted just-as-delicious peanut oil here. This dish should be eaten on its own as a light meal. Soy Sauce, Chile, and Lime Dipping Sauce (page 126) is the ideal condiment.

MAKES 2 SERVINGS AS A MAIN COURSE

8 ounces (225 grams) fresh flat rice noodles
   (page 190), rinsed and drained, or dried
   ***hor fun* noodles (page 191)**

FOR THE FLAVORING PASTE

3 small dried red chiles such as árbol, stemmed and broken in half

3 tablespoons peanut oil

2 tablespoons double-black soy sauce (page 87) or Indonesian sweet soy sauce (page 72)

1 teaspoon sugar, if not using sweet soy sauce

1 teaspoon water

2 cloves garlic, coarsely chopped

7 ounces (200 grams) medium-sized shrimp (10 to 15 shrimp), peeled, heads removed, and deveined

1 teaspoon dried shrimp paste (page 65)

1 large egg, cracked (but not beaten) into a cup or small bowl

1 1/2 cups (about 4 ounces/115 grams) mung bean sprouts

7 Chinese chives or 5 scallions (both white and green parts), tops and roots removed and cut into 2-inch (5-centimeter) lengths

Kosher salt (optional)

1. If you were unable to find fresh rice noodles and purchased dried *hor fun* noodles in their place, cook them first (see page 191 for directions) and set aside.

2. To make the flavoring paste, place the chiles in a bowl, add warm water to cover, and let soak for 20 minutes to soften. Meanwhile, place the shrimp paste in the center of a 5-inch (13-centimeter) square of aluminum foil. Fold the edges of the foil over to form a small parcel, and press down with the heel of your hand to flatten the shrimp paste into a disk 1/4 inch (6 millimeters) thick. Heat a gas burner to medium-low or an electric burner to medium-high. Using a pair of tongs or 2 forks, place the sealed parcel directly on the heat source. Toast until the paste begins to smoke and release a burning, shrimpy smell, about 1 1/2 minutes. With the tongs or forks, turn the parcel over and toast the other side for another 1 1/2 minutes, then turn off the burner. Again using the tongs or forks, remove the parcel and let cool for 30 seconds to 1 minute. Carefully unwrap the foil; the edges of the disk should be black-brown and toasty and the center should be golden with some black-brown patches. Using a spoon, scrape the toasted shrimp paste into a small bowl and allow it to cool for another 30 seconds. Discard the foil.

3. Remove the softened chiles from the water and discard the water. Place the chiles and toasted shrimp paste in a small food processor and pulse until you have a smooth paste the consistency of creamy mashed potatoes. If the paste won't purée properly (this is, after all, a very small quantity of ingredients) and repeatedly creeps up the side of the processor instead of grinding, add up to 2 tablespoons water, 1 tablespoon at a time, periodically turning the processor off and scraping the unground portions down toward the blade.

4. Heat 1 tablespoon of the oil in a wok or 12-inch (30-centimeter) skillet (nonstick will work best) over medium-low heat. Test to see if the oil is the right temperature by adding a pinch of the ground paste. The paste should sizzle slightly around the edges, not fry aggressively or sit motionless. When the oil is ready, add all the paste and sauté, stirring as needed to prevent scorching, until the paste begins to separate from the oil, 4 to 6 minutes. Transfer the flavoring paste to a bowl and set it aside. Keep the pan handy; you'll be using it again shortly.

5. In a cup or small bowl, combine the soy sauce; sugar, if using double-black soy sauce; and water and set aside.

6. In the pan you used to sauté the flavoring paste, heat the remaining 2 tablespoons of oil over medium-high heat. When the oil is hot but not smoking—it should appear shimmery—add the garlic and sauté, stirring constantly, until it just begins to turn golden, about 2 minutes. Add the sautéed flavoring paste and stir well to combine. Add the shrimp and raise the heat to high. Stir-fry vigorously just until the shrimp turn pink, about 2 minutes.

7. Add the rice noodles and the soy sauce mixture. Stir-fry, moving all the ingredients about constantly, until the noodles are heated through and have soaked up most of the liquid, about 2 minutes.

8. With the spatula, make a well in the center of the noodles and pour the egg into it. Using the spatula, scramble the egg briskly in the well; let it rest until it begins to set, about 30 seconds. Mix the noodles and the scrambled egg together. Add the bean sprouts and Chinese chives. Vigorously stir-fry the ingredients until the chives and bean sprouts just begin to wilt, about 30 seconds. Taste a noodle, and add a pinch of salt if needed.

9. Divide the noodles between 2 plates and serve at once.

CHICKEN CURRY NOODLE SOUP, KUALA LUMPUR STYLE
Kare Laksa
(MALAYSIA)

⌣

Laksa, or curry noodle soup, is the unofficial national dish of Malaysia. There are countless versions. Some, especially those from the southern part of West Malaysia, use coconut milk as their base, while those from the north, including the celebrated *asam laksa* of Penang, call for stewing small local sardines (*ikan cerut*) for hours until the flesh of the fish deeply permeates a tamarind-based stock. *Laksa* is a chameleon, radically changing its ingredients and flavors from one town to the next. I particularly like the spice-rich version eaten in the Malaysian capital of Kuala Lumpur. In this dish, known by locals as *kare laksa*, curry *laksa*, or curry *mee*, fresh Chinese egg noodles are bathed in a spice-infused coconut-milk curry that contains chicken and tofu. It makes a superb one-dish meal, perfect for an intimate dinner party. An appetizer of Shrimp Satay (page 150) would start things off beautifully.

Bone-in chicken will yield a more flavorful curry, as will chicken with its skin intact, though you may remove the skin if you prefer. Use sharp kitchen shears, a chef's knife, or a heavy cleaver to cut the bone-in chicken. An excellent substitute for the mung bean sprouts are 10 to 15 *choy sum* stalks. Trim the bases, cut into pieces 2 inches (5 centimeters) long, and immerse in boiling water for 1 minute, or until just tender, before adding them to the serving bowl.

MAKES 4 SERVINGS AS A MAIN COURSE

FOR THE FLAVORING PASTE

1 teaspoon dried shrimp paste (page 65)

3 tablespoons coriander seeds

1 teaspoon cumin seeds

1/2 teaspoon fennel seeds

2 whole cloves

10 black peppercorns

1/4 teaspoon ground turmeric

2 to 5 small dried red chiles such as árbol, stemmed and broken in half

5 shallots (about 3 3/4 ounces/110 grams total), coarsely chopped

1/2 cup (4 fluid ounces/125 milliliters) water

4 tablespoons peanut oil, plus more for frying

1 piece cinnamon stick, 1/2 inch (12 millimeters) long

2 thick stalks fresh lemongrass, each tied into a knot (page 76)

2 medium-sized bone-in or boneless chicken thighs, cut in half crosswise

3 cups (24 fluid ounces/750 milliliters) water

1 1/2 cups (12 fluid ounces/375 milliliters) unsweetened coconut milk

2 teaspoons sugar

1 3/4 teaspoons kosher salt

8 ounces (225 grams) firm fresh tofu (2 small squares)

4 cups (10 ounces/285 grams) mung bean sprouts

1 pound (455 grams) precooked Chinese egg noodles (pages 189 to 190), rinsed and drained, or uncooked fresh Chinese egg noodles (pages 189 to 190)

FOR THE GARNISH

1 fresh red Holland chile or other fresh long, red chile such as Fresno or cayenne (page 53), stemmed and very thinly sliced on the diagonal

4 fresh mint sprigs (optional)

8 *kasturi* limes (page 76), halved and seeded, or 1 Persian lime, quartered and seeded

Javanese Sambal (page 119; optional)

1. To make the flavoring paste, place the shrimp paste in the center of a 5-inch (13-centimeter) square of aluminum foil. Fold the edges of the foil over to form a small parcel, and press down with the heel of your hand to flatten the shrimp paste into a disk 1/4 inch (6 millimeters) thick. Heat a gas burner to medium-low or an electric burner to medium-high. Using a pair of tongs or 2 forks, place the sealed parcel directly on the heat source. Toast until the paste begins to smoke and release a burning, shrimpy smell, about 1 1/2 minutes. With the tongs or forks, turn the parcel over and toast the other side for another 1 1/2 minutes, then turn off the burner. Again using the tongs or forks, remove the parcel and let cool for 30 seconds to 1 minute. Carefully unwrap the foil; the edges of the disk should be black-brown and toasty and the center should be golden with some black-brown patches. Using a spoon, scrape the toasted shrimp paste into a small bowl and allow it to cool for another 30 seconds. Discard the foil.

2. Place the coriander, cumin, fennel, cloves, peppercorns, turmeric, and dried chiles in a small food processor. Pulse until the spices are ground to a dusty powder, about 2 minutes. There should be no large pieces of whole spices.

3. Add the toasted shrimp paste, shallots, and water to the ground spices. Pulse until you have a smooth paste the consistency of a very thick cream soup. Set the flavoring paste aside.

4. Heat the 4 tablespoons oil in a 4-quart (4-liter) saucepan, Dutch oven, or soup pot over medium-low heat. Test to see if the oil is the right temperature by adding a pinch of the ground paste. The paste should sizzle slightly around the edges, not fry aggressively or sit motionless. When the oil is ready, add the cinnamon stick, stirring it around until its fragrance rises up from the pan, about 30 seconds. Add all the ground paste and sauté at a lively, steady simmer, reducing the heat as necessary to prevent scorching and stirring every minute or so, until the shallots no longer smell raw and the paste begins to separate from the oil, 5 to 7 minutes. Be careful not to let the flavoring paste cook for too long. It should be limp and silken, not golden and crusty.

Add the lemongrass and chicken and stir well to combine with the flavoring paste. Raise the heat to medium and sauté, stirring often, until the chicken is golden on all sides, about 5 minutes.

5. Add the water, coconut milk, sugar, and salt and stir well to combine. Raise the heat slightly and bring to a gentle simmer. Immediately reduce the heat and, with the pot uncovered, cook the liquid at a very gentle simmer, stirring occasionally, until the chicken is tender and cooked through, 30 to 40 minutes. Taste the liquid for salt, and add a pinch more if needed.

6. While the chicken cooks, rinse the tofu under cold running water for 30 seconds. Dry it thoroughly with paper towels, then cut it into 1- to 1 1/2-inch (2.5- to 4-centimeter) cubes.

7. Pour oil to a depth of 1 inch (2.5 centimeters) into a 1 1/2- to 2-quart (1.5- to 2-liter) saucepan and place over medium to medium-high heat until hot but not smoking. To test if the oil is the right temperature (it should be about 365°F/185°C), spear a cube of tofu onto a fork and slip a corner of the cube into the oil. If the oil is ready, it will immediately bubble vigorously around the tofu.

8. Working in small batches, add the tofu cubes to the hot oil with tongs or a pair of forks (crowding will cool down the oil and make the tofu greasy). Fry the cubes, turning them often, until they are just golden and crisp on all sides, 3 to 5 minutes total. Be sure not to fry the tofu beyond the point it is just golden, or its exterior will be tough and the tofu will taste slightly bitter. Using the tongs or a slotted spoon, transfer the tofu to paper towels to drain. Add all the fried tofu to the simmering liquid once you've drained it.

9. About 15 minutes before serving the dish, fill a 4-quart (4-liter) saucepan with water and bring to a boil over high heat. Add the bean sprouts and blanch until they just begin to wilt, about 10 seconds. Using a slotted spoon, transfer the beans sprouts to a colander (leave the boiling water in the pan), and run cold water over them until they're cool. Drain the sprouts well, transfer them to a bowl, and set aside.

10. If you're using precooked fresh Chinese egg noodles, you'll need to warm them. Add them to the boiling water you used to blanch the bean sprouts and cook at a rolling boil until warmed through, about 30 seconds. Drain the noodles into the colander and set them aside in a warm place until you are ready to serve the dish. If you're using fresh uncooked Chinese egg noodles, cook them in the boiling water until tender, 3 to 5 minutes (the timing will depend on their thickness and freshness) and drain.

11. To serve, divide the bean sprouts evenly among 4 large, shallow soup bowls. Divide the noodles evenly among the bowls, placing each portion in a small mound over the bean sprouts. Evenly ladle the chicken-and-tofu curry into the bowls. Garnish with the chile slices and the mint sprigs (if using). Eat promptly, with lime juice squeezed over the top to heighten the flavor. If desired, serve the sambal on the side for guests to add extra fire to the broth.

ABOVE LEFT: *Cucumbers and an Indonesian variety of lime called* jeruk nipis.

ABOVE CENTER: *Rohati, a native of Pandang, West Sumatra.*

ABOVE RIGHT: *Kabocha-like squash called* labu *are used in both sweet and savory dishes.*

9. VEGETABLES

It was barely six o'clock in the morning, but Rohati and I were already on the move. "Luck shines on those who keep on schedule!" she said cheerfully as we walked down a dark side street near her home in Padang, in West Sumatra, Indonesia. Palm trees shivered in the breeze. A rooster crowed in the distance. But we had good reason for being awake so early. Rohati had agreed to give me a tour of the *pasar*, the sprawling public market that serves the large city and the many towns and villages that surround it.

"Without the freshest vegetables, there is no cooking," Rohati said, checking inside her purse to make sure that she hadn't forgotten her shopping list. With that, she raised her right arm to hail a *bendi*, one of the horse-drawn carriage taxis common throughout Indonesia, and we clip-clopped into the morning light.

I'd been introduced to Rohati a few years earlier by her cousin Arzein, who also lives in Padang. "You haven't eaten Minang food until you've eaten at Rohati's," he'd raved. Minang is the term for the devoutly Muslim West Sumatran ethnic group, the Minangkabau, of which Arzein and Rohati are part. The Minang are known throughout Indonesia, Malaysia, and Singapore for their powerfully spiced cuisine.

I remember the afternoon when I first met Rohati. Arzein and I were in her neighborhood and decided to stop by. Even though our visit was unannounced, Rohati put aside her paperwork (she oversees the bookkeeping for the small furniture-repair business of her husband, Syofyan) and invited us in for lunch. I was immediately struck by her grace and beauty. In her red blouse and chic leather mules, she was the picture of elegance.

"*Silakan* [Welcome]," she said, gesturing us into a dimly lit sitting room.

As soon as we sat down, Rohati's twenty-three-year-old daughter, Dewi, placed steaming glasses of tea before us. I watched as the tea leaves drifted lazily to the bottom of my glass. After about twenty minutes, Rohati called us into the next room. The lunch, most of which she had prepared earlier for her family, was laid out on a small dining table in ceramic serving bowls. It included an earthy curry of fiddlehead ferns called *gulai paku* (page 226); *kentang balado*, deep-fried potatoes in a red chile and shallot paste (page 221); and *tumis sayur*, a simple stir-fry of greens with garlic and chiles (page 205). "I'm sorry there isn't more," she apologized. "Please, come again tomorrow. I'll prepare something more special."

I'd heard that Minang cooks have unwritten rules about serving only lavish meat dishes to first-time guests. To offer everyday fare, such as the vegetarian food we savored, is considered poor manners. But Rohati's meal was amazing, a testament to the Minangkabau skill at balancing chile and spice with the freshest vegetables. She leaned over the pad on which I was scribbling cooking notes and whispered something to me. "There is no secret here," she said. "Only love." I put my notepad down and continued to eat.

When Rohati and I reached the outskirts of the market, the reason that she liked to arrive early was instantly clear. Even at seven o'clock, the place was already jam-packed with customers. After making our way through a maze of crates and untethered goats, we entered the main hall and climbed the stairs to the second floor. From this vantage point, the huge market extended like a vast tapestry. It was the most radiant display of vegetables that I'd ever seen. Mounds of chiles four feet high lay next to equally high piles of water spinach. Hundreds of vendors called out their offerings in an overlapping singsong that rose above the hall in what sounded like a single chant. Rohati grabbed my arm and escorted me back downstairs toward an area devoted to spices and aromatics. "I have a regular route when I come to the *pasar*," she said. "First, I look for garlic." We stopped at a stall specializing in shallots and garlic. She picked up a head of the small, lilac-skinned garlic that local cooks covet.

"Smell it," she said, her eyes widening. I popped open a tiny clove no larger than a cardamom pod from its skin and inhaled. It was sweet and fresh. Next on Rohati's shopping list were shallots. West Sumatra's shallots, *bawang merah* (literally "red onion"), grow in small clumps containing two or three bulbs and have shimmery, coppery skins and purple-pink flesh. Rohati bought a pound, along with a bunch of bright green Chinese chives (*daun bawang*), before we went on to a neighboring stall. There, the display looked like a still life painted by a Dutch master. Baskets of spices spilled over onto bunches of kaffir lime leaves and fresh turmeric rhizomes just pulled from the ground. But Rohati didn't linger. Her pantry was already well stocked with these ingredients, and she required only a day's worth of fresh turmeric leaves (*daun kunyit*), an herb used for seasoning curries. She picked up a bunch to check them for freshness.

"Hey, you leaving your husband for the white man?" the merchant, a big-haired woman in her forties, joked with Rohati on seeing me. "No, he's just my American servant!" Rohati shot back.

We left that section of the market and headed for another that spilled onto the streets outside. There, under a canopy of umbrellas made from old movie posters painted on fabric—"*Terminator II*—Arnold Aktion Man!" said one—is where Rohati buys her long beans, cucumbers, eggplants, potatoes, and greens. Farmers from the surrounding villages unload their vegetables from oxcarts, tumbling them onto the ground in multicolored heaps and selling them right on the spot.

Rohati and I stopped in front of a merchant who was offering big bunches of water spinach. I leaned over and smelled the grassy aroma. Known throughout Indonesia, Malaysia, and Singapore as *kangkung*, this bright green vegetable has a long, hollow, pencil-thin stem that holds up well to stir-frying over high heat. Its deliciousness makes it the most popular green in the region. After rejecting five bunches, she homed in on an especially nice bunch hidden in the back. "Ahh, this is the one," she said, holding it like a bouquet of flowers.

By nine-thirty, Rohati and I had finished shopping. We loaded our bags filled with groceries onto a *bendi* and negotiated the price—just thirty-five cents—for the twenty-minute ride back to Rohati's home. Sitting in the back seat, I watched central Padang, the oldest part of the city, drift by. There was an old Chinese Taoist temple, its nail-polish-red pillars gleaming in the sun. I also spotted a quartet of shrimp praus gliding up the port canal. Nearer to Rohati's home I saw rows and rows of cloves spread out to dry on rattan mats on the roadside.

It was hot that morning and it would get even hotter as the day wore on. So as soon as Rohati and I arrived at her house, we got to work in the kitchen. Helping us were Dewi, her daughter, and Rohana, her eighty-year-old mother. Rohati placed the vegetables we had bought on a table. "We'll start with *rendang kentang*—it will take the longest to cook," she said.

Rendang kentang (page 223) is a celebrated dish that calls for dry-braising potatoes in an intensely spiced coconut-milk broth. We had purchased tan-skinned, grape-sized potatoes to make it, which Rohana was now rinsing clean. Rohati selected the ingredients for the flavoring paste: a stalk of lemongrass pared down to its flavorful ivory core; a handful of red Holland chiles, for color and sweet heat; a handful of green Thai chiles, for strong heat; and fresh turmeric, galangal, shallots, garlic, and ginger. Rohati told Dewi to grind them together in a mortar. As Dewi pounded away, the paste loosened and began to spill over the sides of the mortar. Rohati let out a gasp worthy of Sarah Bernhardt. Dewi promptly wiped off the mess she'd made. Dewi then stirred the flavoring paste into a wok brimming with frothy coconut milk that had already been gently simmering for some time. It would need to reduce by half before the potatoes were added, a process that would take about forty-five minutes.

Meanwhile, Rohati cleaned the water spinach. "Since it's now February, the dry season," she said as she snipped off the root end of each stalk, "this *kangkung* will be sweet. I'll cook it quickly, with just a little oil, garlic, and chile. If this was the rainy season, it might have a duller taste, and I would need to add water and perhaps some small dried fish for balance." With a smooth, hand-sized rock, she whacked six cloves of unpeeled garlic on a wooden cutting board until they were bruised and juicy. Next she poured a few spoonfuls of coconut oil into a wok. When it was hot, she tossed in the garlic (which was still unpeeled, since the skin of local garlic is very tender and Rohati believes it adds flavor) and red chiles. They sputtered for just a few seconds before she added the water spinach, which had been washed and cut up. She stir-fried the vegetable with a large, wood-handled spoon, making sure that the hot oil kissed every leaf and stem. When it had just wilted, Rohati transferred the greens to a large serving plate. The dish would sit and mellow there, turning a deep forest green, until the rest of our lunch was ready.

We turned our attention back to the *rendang kentang*. The time had come to add the potatoes, the *daun salam* leaves, and a few stalks of lemon basil to the broth. I peered into the wok. The liquid had reduced to a thick, rich paste. It was the slow but dependable alchemy of *rendang* in action. After awhile, Rohati asked me to sample one of the potatoes, whose skins were just beginning to turn golden brown. I took one out with a spoon, blew on it for a few seconds, and popped it into my mouth. The clean freshness of the lemongrass and chiles melted perfectly into the earthy sweetness of the potatoes. It was another masterpiece.

─

Searching for the finest, freshest vegetables is an essential practice of all home cooks in Indonesia, Malaysia, and Singapore. Cooks are trained from a young age to recognize subtle signs that tell them when the vegetables in their local market are as perfect as they can be. They use all their senses in the selection process—even their sense of hearing. The clean, sharp snap of a particularly tender green bean, for example, is music to their ears. The reason for such careful consideration is simple. Along with rice and fish, vegetables are the most important foods at their table. Nearly every sit-down meal includes at least two or three vegetable dishes, from spicy coconut-milk curries to stir-fries. They are the foods that give poetry and lightness to the meal, that balance a heavy meat dish or a complex fish curry.

The region's vegetable-cooking traditions go back to at least 2500 BC, to when the first Malay tribesmen reached the verdant shores of the Malay Archipelago from the harsher environments of Central Asia. These early migrants found that the islands' rich soils, warm temperatures, and consistent rainfall made for a year-round cycle of planting and harvesting. They adapted to this abundance by making vegetables a staple of their diet. To this day, vegetable farms cover nearly every inch of arable land. Large-scale, mechanized farming is a rarity here. Instead, wherever you are, even in big cities, you'll see people using simple hand tools to till the land. On my first trips to Jakarta, I was amazed by the fields of vegetables that then thrived right next to busy streets. Women in sarongs busily picked red chiles and eggplants as jeeps sped past nearby.

The most popular vegetables in the region are native varieties of greens, eggplants, potatoes, long beans, green beans, carrots, cabbage, and mung bean sprouts. Some of these vegetables, such as long beans, grew in the wild when the first Malays arrived. Others, such as potatoes and carrots, were introduced by outsiders who came to the Malay Archipelago in search of spices. Most are widely available in North America, even in conventional supermarkets. There are two primary approaches for preparing them. In the first, vegetables are treated much the way they are treated in Chinese cooking—which is to say they're only minimally seasoned and are stir-fried. These dishes include Stir-fried Asian Greens with Garlic and Chiles (page 205) and Stir-fried Bean Sprouts with Chinese Chives (page 208), both of which are traditionally cooked in a small wok called a *kwali* or *wajon*. Salt and garlic, not elaborate flavoring pastes, are the core seasonings of these dishes, though the region's appreciation for bold flavors is revealed in the use of chiles and black pepper.

The other approach to preparing vegetables involves assertive spicing and longer cooking times. These robust dishes are more akin to Indian-style vegetable curries than Chinese stir-fries. They call for vibrant, multilayered seasonings, including spices, lemongrass, lemon basil, and dried shrimp paste, rather than just salt and garlic. Frequently cooked in coconut milk, they're thought to have more soul than vegetable stir-fries. Among the recipes here that represent this kind of vegetable cooking are Ching Lee's Braised Lemongrass Long Beans (page 218), a Singaporean favorite, and Fern Curry with Shrimp (page 226), a classic peasant dish from West Sumatra, Indonesia. Although both dishes are intensely seasoned (and also cooked for much longer than a stir-fry), they're not so complex that the flavor of the main ingredient—the vegetable—is masked.

STIR-FRIED ASIAN GREENS WITH GARLIC AND CHILES

Tumis Sayur

(INDONESIA, MALAYSIA, AND SINGAPORE)

Few dishes are more purely satisfying than stir-fried Asian greens. Malay Archipelago cooks agree: meals in Indonesia, Malaysia, and Singapore are almost unthinkable without greens on the table. Greens are so popular that a single market vendor often sells as many as fifteen different kinds, from the tender mustard greens known as *sayur sawi*, similar to bok choy, to pleasingly bitter young papaya leaves (*daun papaya*), which are stir-fried along with their small white flowers.

On our shores, young, tender Asian greens with slender stems, such as water spinach, bok choy, baby bok choy or Shanghai choy, *choy sum*, and baby *kai lan*, work best for stir-frying. Chinese and Southeast Asian markets will likely carry at least two of these varieties at any given time. Farmers' markets stock them in the summer months (and virtually year-round in places with temperate climates such as Southern California and Florida). Always buy unblemished greens that have no signs of yellowing, and cook them as soon as possible. They don't store well.

I learned this particular recipe on a blisteringly hot afternoon many years ago from Sharifah, the wife of a Malaysian fisherman I knew. The greens she served were crisp and flavorful, the essence of good eating. Sharifah told me that the key to making the greens taste their best is to cook them as quickly as possible.

"*Alhamdililah* [Praise God]," Sharifah said, as she watched me polish off the plate all by myself. "Maybe you're half Malaysian and do not know it."

MAKES 4 SERVINGS

1 medium-sized bunch (about 13 ounces/370 grams) tender Asian greens such as bok choy, baby bok choy, baby Shanghai choy, *choy sum*, baby *kai lan*, or water spinach (see headnote and page 43 for more information on Asian greens)
3 tablespoons peanut oil
4 cloves garlic, peeled, bruised until juicy with the flat side of a knife, and coarsely chopped into 3 or 4 chunks
1/4 teaspoon kosher salt
1 to 2 fresh red Holland chiles or other fresh long, red chiles such as Fresno or cayenne, stemmed and thinly sliced on the diagonal (optional, but the chiles add appealing color and gentle heat)

1. Carefully inspect the greens, discarding or trimming off any spoiled stems or leaves. Trim off the bottoms and discard. Gently wash the greens in several changes of the coldest possible water; tepid water will cause them to wilt, and you want them to stay as perky as possible before they're cooked. Take care to clean bok choy or baby bok choy or Shanghai choy carefully, as they tend to have hidden pockets of sand where the leaves meet the center stem.

2. Cut the greens into pieces 2 1/2 to 3 inches (6 to 7.5 centimeters) long. If any of the stems are particularly wide—say, more than 1 inch (2.5 centimeters)—or are tough or sinewy looking, cut them in half lengthwise. If you're using baby bok choy or Shanghai

choy, you can either leave the heads whole or cut them in halves or quarters lengthwise. Dry the greens in a salad spinner or set them aside to dry on a kitchen towel or on paper towels. They don't need to be bone-dry; a little dampness is fine.

3. Heat the oil in a wok, 12-inch (30-centimeter) skillet, Dutch oven, or soup pot (any pot large and wide enough to hold the greens comfortably will do) over medium-high heat. When it's hot but not smoking—it should appear shimmery—add the garlic, salt, and chiles (if using). Stir-fry vigorously until the garlic just begins to lose its rawness, about 1 minute. Don't let the garlic turn golden or golden brown, which would give this dish an inappropriate roasted taste.

4. Add the greens. Raise the heat slightly and immediately begin to stir-fry the greens vigorously around the pan. Continue to stir-fry vigorously until the greens just begin to go limp but the leaves are still spring green and the stems are still crunchy crisp, 2 to 5 minutes; the timing will depend on the type of greens. Taste for salt and add only a pinch more if needed (a little salt goes a long way with greens).

5. Transfer the cooked greens to a large platter and serve promptly. Don't pile them in a small bowl. They'll continue to cook for a minute or two after they're removed from the heat, and a serving bowl that crowds them may cause them to overcook and become mushy.

MENU SUGGESTIONS

Greens are so ubiquitous on the tables of the Malay Archipelago that it's hard to think of them as being a better match with one dish than with another. But if you're still seeking guidance on what to serve them with, try rice; a spicy sambal, such as Javanese Sambal (page 119); a curry, such as Javanese Chicken Curry (page 275); and a deeply spiced dish, such as Beef Rendang (page 304) or Chicken Rendang with Cinnamon and Star Anise (page 278). You may discover that different types of greens are better suited to particular dishes. For example, you may prefer sweetish bok choy with a rich curry, rather than a more bitter green, like baby *kai lan*. For the record, I have no such preferences. As long as I have my greens, I'm happy.

STIR-FRIED BEAN SPROUTS WITH CHINESE CHIVES
Tauge Goreng

(JAVA, INDONESIA)

This lively stir-fry of mung bean sprouts with black pepper, garlic, shallots, chiles, and Chinese chives is a specialty of Bogor, in West Java, Indonesia. I learned a valuable lesson the afternoon that I watched Nanik, the wife of my friend Hasan, make it. Not only do bean sprouts cook rapidly, Nanik told me, but they also shed their internal water like tears and continue doing so until they cool down. "Cook them only until they just begin to wilt. Any longer will result in a sad dish," she said, transferring a wok's worth of still-crunchy sprouts to a serving plate. Buy the cleanest-smelling, most porcelain white mung bean sprouts you can find. Make sure that they're 2 to 3 inches (5 to 7.5 centimeters) long, with small, bright yellow seedpods. Don't mistakenly purchase soybean sprouts, which have larger seedpods and thicker shoots. For the best result, cook the bean sprouts the same day you buy them. Some Javanese cooks replace the Chinese chives with a handful of fresh lemon basil leaves (page 74), which imparts an appealing fruity taste. If you're using scallions instead of Chinese chives and they're very thick, slice them in half lengthwise. As with every stir-fry, have all the ingredients prepped and within easy reach before you begin cooking.

MAKES 3 OR 4 SERVINGS

2 tablespoons peanut oil

1 shallot (about 3/4 ounce/20 grams), very thinly sliced lengthwise

1 clove garlic, very thinly sliced lengthwise

1 fresh red Holland chile or other fresh long, red chile such as Fresno or cayenne, stemmed and very thinly sliced on the diagonal (optional, but the chile adds beautiful color and a touch of fire)

1 pound (455 grams) mung bean sprouts

1 tablespoon soy sauce

4 Chinese chives (page 55) or 3 scallions (both white and green parts), tops and roots removed and cut into 2-inch (5-centimeter) lengths

Scant 1/4 teaspoon freshly ground fine black pepper

1/4 teaspoon kosher salt

1. Heat the oil in a wok or 12-inch (30-centimeter) skillet over medium heat. When it's hot—it should appear slightly shimmery—add the shallot, garlic, and chile and stir-fry vigorously until the shallot and garlic begin to soften and turn translucent, about 1

minute. Don't allow the shallot and garlic to become golden or golden brown. If you notice that they start to change color, temporarily remove the pan from the heat and allow it to cool for a few moments.

2. Add the bean sprouts and soy sauce and increase the heat to medium-high to high. Stir-fry vigorously until all of the sprouts take in an even amount of heat, about 1 minute. Add the chives, pepper, and salt and continue to stir-fry until the chives wilt and the bean sprouts are just barely cooked through but still crisp, 1 to 2 minutes longer. The sprouts will continue to cook on their own for a few minutes after you remove them from the fire. Taste a sprout for salt, and add a pinch more if needed.

3. Transfer to a large serving dish and eat at once. The bean sprouts will become limp and watery if allowed to sit longer than 10 minutes.

MENU SUGGESTIONS

I'm content to eat this dish with nothing more than steaming rice and a just-fried egg—the combination of the crispness of the bean sprouts and the spare luxuriousness of the warm egg is deeply satisfying. But it's also wonderful paired with Lemongrass-Scented Coconut Rice (page 176), Spiced Braised Nyonya Pork (page 307), and a coconut milk–based curry, such as Asiah's Eggplant Curry (page 229).

SAUTÉED CABBAGE WITH GINGER AND CRISPY INDIAN YELLOW LENTILS

Muttakos Poriyal

(SINGAPORE)

Chopped cabbage sautéed with black mustard seeds, ginger, curry leaves, and cumin is at the heart of this irresistible Singaporean Indian dish, which originated in the south Indian state of Tamil Nadu. Raw *thuvar dal* (small, yellow lentils), panfried until golden and slightly translucent, deliver a subtle crunch and earthiness. This dish is a specialty of my friend Lila, a strict vegetarian who was born in Madras but now lives in Singapore with her son who immigrated there. I coaxed it from her one afternoon. "Why would you want such a boring recipe?" she fussed. "I must give you something fancier."

"No," I insisted, "I like how simple the dish is. It makes cabbage into something special."

"Hmm," she said after a moment. "I like that idea. I'll let you watch me make it."

Lila often substitutes chopped water spinach (page 46) or baby bok choy for the cabbage. But whatever vegetable she chooses, she usually serves the dish alongside rice and a soupy curry. I find that it also makes a lovely meal on its own, with rice or an Indian flat bread such as nan or chapati. Go out of your way to use freshly grated coconut. Fresh coconut lends a faint sweetness to the dish that grated dried coconut of unknown age never will. Have everything ready to go before you start cooking, as this dish comes together quickly.

MAKES 4 SERVINGS

3 tablespoons peanut oil

1/4 teaspoon black mustard seeds (page 47)

1/4 teaspoon cumin seeds

1 heaping teaspoon small Indian yellow lentils (see Cook's Note, page 211)

2 small dried red chiles such as árbol, stemmed and broken in half

10 to 20 fresh curry leaves (page 63; optional, but they lend color and a nice peppery green taste)

1/2 medium-sized white onion, finely minced

1 teaspoon ground turmeric

1 pound (455 grams) green cabbage (about 1/2 small head), cored and coarsely chopped into 1/4-inch (6-millimeter) pieces

1 piece fresh ginger, 1 inch (2.5 centimeters) long, peeled, very thinly sliced with the grain, and cut into fine matchsticks (about 1 tablespoon)

1/2 teaspoon kosher salt

4 tablespoons finely grated fresh coconut (page 58) or grated dried coconut

1. Heat the oil in a 3- or 4-quart (3- or 4-liter) saucepan over medium-high heat. When it's hot but not smoking—it should appear shimmery—toss in the mustard seeds and begin sliding the pan back and forth over the heat. The mustard seeds will start to pop and sputter within 30 seconds. When nearly all of the mustard seeds have popped (just a few seconds more), remove the pan from the heat for about 30 seconds to cool slightly.

2. Return the pan to medium heat and add, in quick succession, the cumin, yellow lentils, red chiles, and curry leaves (if using), distributing them evenly in the oil with a spatula or spoon. Sauté until the yellow lentils begin to turn a deep gold and the curry leaves have picked up translucent spots, about 45 seconds. Add the onion and cook, stirring, until it's soft and limp and no longer raw, 2 to 4 minutes, reducing the heat if necessary to make sure that it doesn't change color and become golden. You want the onion to remain white. Add the turmeric and stir well to mix.

3. Add the cabbage, ginger, and salt and vigorously stir everything with the spatula, making sure that the cabbage is tinted an even yellow from the turmeric. Reduce the heat to low and cover the pan. Gently cook the cabbage, stirring occasionally to prevent sticking, until it's cooked through and slightly translucent, about 7 minutes. Taste a few pieces. They should be crunchy tender to the tooth, neither firm nor mushy. Add the coconut, stirring well to combine. Taste for salt, and add a pinch more if needed.

4. Transfer to a serving bowl or plate. You may remove the broken chiles if you prefer, though I like cautiously crunching down on them. Let the cabbage rest for at least 5 minutes before eating; this dish should be served warm or at room temperature, as its flavors are muted by heat. It will make an excellent leftover for the next day.

COOK'S NOTE

Indian yellow lentils, or *thuvar dal*, are small, pale yellow dried legumes that resemble the common yellow split pea in size (though they're slightly smaller) and color but have an earthier and more astringent taste. A staple in the Indian cuisines of Malaysia and Singapore, they are simmered until soft and then mashed to make *sambar*, a richly spiced lentil gravy, or sautéed until golden and used in vegetable dishes to add crunch and contrast, as in this cabbage recipe. Always rinse Indian yellow lentils thoroughly and pick through them for stones and twigs before using. They're widely available in Bangladeshi, Indian, and Pakistani markets, and you can store them for as long as 6 months in a cool, dry cupboard.

MENU SUGGESTIONS

This Indian dish works well in a variety of contexts. It's divine when served with nan or another Indian flat bread and a lentil dal. But it's also good alongside fluffy jasmine rice and such eclectic dishes as Garlic-Marinated Tempeh (page 322) and Javanese Cucumber and Carrot Pickle (page 132).

BRAISED CABBAGE WITH DRIED SHRIMP
Pow Choy Ha Mai
(MALAYSIA)

———

I learned the recipe for this simple but superb dish of cabbage braised with garlic and dried shrimp from Kok Sia, a Malaysian Chinese friend in Petaling Jaya, in Malaysia. Kok Sia looks for the freshest, firmest cabbages she can find to make it. Firm green head cabbage works well, as does Savoy. Napa cabbage, also known as Chinese cabbage, contains more water than other cabbages and results in a watery dish. Kok Sia serves this as the vegetable component of a large family meal, but I often eat it solo, along with crusty bread, as a simple light meal.

MAKES 4 SERVINGS

1 to 1 1/2 tablespoons small dried shrimp (page 65)

1/2 cup (4 fluid ounces/125 milliliters) warm water

1 pound (455 grams) green cabbage (about 1/2 small head), cored and tough outer leaves discarded

2 1/2 tablespoons peanut oil

2 cloves garlic, coarsely chopped

1 teaspoon sugar

1/4 teaspoon kosher salt

Freshly ground black pepper

1. Combine the dried shrimp (use the larger amount for a more pronounced shrimp flavor) and warm water in a small bowl and let the shrimp soak just until they begin to soften, about 10 minutes. Remove the shrimp and set them aside. Don't discard the water; you'll use it to cook the cabbage.

2. Meanwhile, one at a time, peel the leaves from the cabbage. Cut them into 1 1/2-inch (4-centimeter) squares (they don't need to be perfect), and set them aside. You should have about 3 cups (12 ounces/340 grams).

3. Heat the oil in a 3-quart (3-liter) saucepan over medium heat. When it's hot—it should appear slightly shimmery—add the garlic. Sauté, stirring constantly with a spatula, until the garlic just begins to turn golden, 1 to 2 minutes. Be careful not to let the garlic brown, or the dish will have a musky taste.

4. Add the cabbage, sugar, salt, softened shrimp, and 3 tablespoons of the water used for soaking the shrimp. Sauté, stirring constantly, until the cabbage has just begun to pick up translucent spots here and there, about 2 minutes. Reduce the heat to low. Cover the pan and continue to cook, stirring occasionally, until the cabbage is tender and only faintly crunchy (it shouldn't be mushy), 5 to 7 minutes.

5. Remove the lid and add a few grinds of pepper. Stir to combine. Taste for salt, and add a pinch if needed. Raise the heat to high and cook, stirring often to prevent scorching, until most of the water has evaporated. This dish should be nearly free of liquid, though a small amount (up to 3 tablespoons) is okay.

6. Transfer to a serving dish and eat promptly.

MENU SUGGESTIONS

Kok Sia's subtle, easy-on-the-palate dish is good alongside rice and a couple of spicy dishes, such as Pan-Seared Mackerel with Chiles and Garlic (page 252) and Nyonya-Style Spiced Fried Chicken (page 285).

STIR-FRIED WATER SPINACH, NYONYA STYLE
Kangkung Belacan
(MALAYSIA)

Water spinach, a hollow-stemmed green with a rich, almost nutty taste, is called *kangkung* in Malaysia and Indonesia (and the Philippines, too). I urge you to familiarize yourself with it. I have liked its pleasing crispness ever since I first encountered it in a stir-fry like this one, a Nyonya classic. Sautéed with a flavoring paste of chiles, shallots, garlic, and shrimp paste, it personifies the Nyonya way with vegetables. The tart tamarind serves as a counterpoint to the sweetness of the soybean paste, while the salty shrimp paste contrasts with (and ultimately deepens) the taste of the water spinach. The result is an irresistibly lovely tangle of green and red.

Water spinach is ubiquitous in the Malay Archipelago. Many cooks don't even bother to buy it at the market. They just pluck it from the edges of rice paddies and roadside ditches, where it grows wild like the water-loving weed that it is. There are hundreds of varieties, but two are most commonly seen in markets in Asia and North America. The more typical is deep green and has long, narrow leaves that extend from a thin, strawlike center stem that's slightly thinner than a pencil. The other is pale to lime green and has stubby, triangular leaves and slightly thicker (but still hollow) stems. The latter is grown directly in soil, rather than in swampy earth. Both varieties are comparable in texture and taste. Western spinach, which is similar in name only, doesn't make a good substitute.

MAKES 4 SERVINGS

1 teaspoon tamarind pulp, plus 3 tablespoons very warm water to make extract

1 medium-sized bunch water spinach (about 13 ounces/370 grams; see Cook's Note, page 216)

FOR THE FLAVORING PASTE

1/2 teaspoon dried shrimp paste (page 65)

3 shallots (about 2 1/2 ounces/70 grams total), coarsely chopped

1 clove garlic, coarsely chopped

1 to 3 fresh red Holland chiles or other fresh long, red chiles such as Fresno or cayenne, stemmed and coarsely chopped

1 tablespoon sweet soybean paste (page 88)

2 tablespoons peanut oil

2 teaspoons soy sauce

Kosher salt (optional)

1. Place the tamarind pulp in a small nonreactive bowl and mix it with the warm water. Let the pulp rest until it softens, 10 to 15 minutes. Squeeze and massage the softened pulp through your fingers, loosening the fruit's auburn pulp from the shiny black seeds, brittle brown skin shards, and sinewy bits of string. With your fingers, remove all the solid pieces from the liquid and discard them. All that will remain is a thick caramel-colored extract. Set the tamarind extract aside.

2. Inspect the water spinach, discarding any yellowed or spoiled stems or leaves. Trim off the bottom ends (about 1 inch/2.5 centimeters) and discard. Wash the greens in several changes of the coldest possible water; tepid water will cause them to wilt, and you want them to stay as perky as possible before they're cooked. Test the stems for toughness by biting into a few; discard stems that are thicky and woody. Cut the greens into 3-inch (7.5-centimeter) lengths. If any of the stems are thicker than 1/3 inch (9 millimeters), cut them in half lengthwise, or they'll likely be too chewy when cooked. Dry the greens in a salad spinner or set them aside to dry on a kitchen towel or on paper towels. The leaves should be very dry. Damp leaves will result in a watery dish.

3. To make the flavoring paste, place the shrimp paste in the center of a 5-inch (13-centimeter) square of aluminum foil. Fold the edges of the foil over to form a small parcel, and press down with the heel of your hand to flatten the shrimp paste into a disk 1/4 inch (6 millimeters) thick. Heat a gas burner to medium-low or an electric burner to medium-high. Using a pair of tongs or 2 forks, place the sealed parcel directly on the heat source. Toast until the paste begins to smoke and release a burning, shrimpy smell, about 1 1/2 minutes. With the tongs or forks, turn the parcel over and toast the other side for another 1 1/2 minutes, then turn off the burner. Again using the tongs or forks, remove the parcel and let cool for 30 seconds to 1 minute. Carefully unwrap the foil; the edges of the disk should be black-brown and toasty and the center should be golden with some black-brown patches. Using a spoon, scrape the toasted shrimp paste into a small bowl and allow it to cool for another 30 seconds. Discard the foil.

4. Place the toasted shrimp paste, shallots, garlic, chiles, and sweet soybean paste in a small food processor. Pulse until you have a smooth paste the consistency of creamy mashed potatoes. If the paste will not purée properly and repeatedly creeps up the side of the processor instead of grinding, add up to 2 tablespoons water, 1 tablespoon at a time, periodically turning the processor off and scraping the unground portions down toward the blade.

5. Heat the oil in a wok, 12-inch (30-centimeter) skillet, Dutch oven, or soup pot (any pot large and wide enough to hold the greens comfortably will do) over medium-low heat. Test to see if the oil is the right temperature by adding a pinch of the ground paste. The paste should sizzle slightly around the edges, not fry aggressively or sit motionless. When the oil is ready, add all the paste and sauté, reducing the heat as necessary to prevent scorching and stirring often, until the paste begins to separate from the oil, 5 to 7 minutes. The sugar in the sweet soybean paste makes this flavoring paste prone to burning. If you notice signs of overbrowning, remove the pan from the heat immediately, reduce the heat, and resume sautéing only after the pan has cooled down a bit.

6. Add the water spinach, tamarind extract, and soy sauce. With a spatula or large spoon, stir until the water spinach is well combined with the flavoring paste. Raise the heat to medium-high and begin to stir-fry the water spinach vigorously around the pan until the greens just begin to go limp but the leaves are still spring green and the stems are still crunchy crisp, 3 to 4 minutes. Taste for salt, and add a pinch if needed. (The dried shrimp paste, sweet soybean paste, and soy sauce may provide enough saltiness.)

7. Transfer the cooked greens to a large serving plate. Don't put them in a small dish, which will concentrate their heat and may make them mushy. Eat immediately.

COOK'S NOTE

Thanks to modern shipping and the gentle climates of California and Florida, people living in the northern United States can now acquire previously hard-to-find greens with relative ease. In the case of water spinach, also known as Chinese watercress, morning glory, or *ong choy* (the Cantonese name, which translates as "hollow vegetable" and refers to the strawlike stem), this is a mixed blessing. This delicate vegetable is highly perishable and prone to spoilage in ways that most other vegetables are not. Water spinach is at its best when it's cooked and consumed only a few hours after it has been harvested (a trait it shares with baby lettuces).

Suffice it to say, the water spinach available in markets is generally not at the peak of freshness, and keeping it tucked away in the fridge crammed inside a plastic produce bag will do nothing to make it fresher. I recommend, if possible, cooking it the day you purchase it. Although a healthy bunch may keep for up to a few days in the refrigerator, hidden decayed stems may compromise the flavor of the entire bunch. Try to find farmers in your area who grow water spinach during the summer months. Bunches that I've purchased in mid-July from vendors at farmers' markets in California and New York are as good (and as fresh) as any I've eaten in Southeast Asia.

MENU SUGGESTIONS

This slightly tart, slightly pungent stir-fry is excellent alongside rice and with other dishes that won't overwhelm its delicate balance of flavors. Good possibilities are Kevin's Spiced Roast Chicken with Potatoes, Penang Style (page 287), Pan-Seared Tamarind Tuna (page 254), and Chile Omelet (page 334).

GREEN BEANS WITH COCONUT MILK
Sambal Goreng Buncis
(INDONESIA)

This is a simple, comforting dish of green beans cooked with coconut milk, galangal, and *daun salam* leaves. Though green beans aren't native to the Malay Archipelago (and neither, for that matter, are the tomatoes or the chiles in this recipe), they are held in high esteem by Indonesian cooks. I got this recipe many years ago from Inam, the family cook of my friend

Tanya Alwi, but every Indonesian cook is familiar with it or with some variation on it. It's a touchstone in Indonesian cuisine, as common as macaroni and cheese in the United States. Inam sometimes made it with dried shrimp paste, but I think it tastes more appealing without. Be sure to cook the green beans until they're soft and supple. Crisp, lightly cooked beans don't meld as effectively with the coconut milk. I've made this dish with green cabbage leaves cut into 1-inch (2.5-centimeter) squares instead of green beans, and I've also made it without the tomato wedges. But no matter what I've used, the results have always been splendid. Serve it with plenty of hot steamed rice to mop up the rich, delicious sauce.

MAKES 4 SERVINGS

2 tablespoons peanut oil

4 shallots (about 3 ounces/85 grams total), thinly sliced lengthwise

2 cloves garlic, thinly sliced lengthwise

1 to 4 fresh red Holland chiles or other fresh long, red chiles such as Fresno or cayenne, stemmed and thinly sliced on the diagonal

1 piece fresh or thawed, frozen galangal, 1 inch (2.5 centimeters) long, peeled and bruised until juicy with a heavy, blunt object such as the bottom of a glass measuring cup (optional, but adds a hint of woodsy flavor)

2 whole *daun salam* leaves (page 64; optional)

1 pound (455 grams) green beans, stemmed and cut on the diagonal into 1-inch (2.5-centimeter) lengths

1 very ripe medium-sized tomato, cored and cut into 10 wedges

2/3 cup (5 fluid ounces/150 milliliters) unsweetened coconut milk

2/3 cup (5 fluid ounces/150 milliliters) water

1 teaspoon palm sugar (page 79), thinly sliced, or dark brown sugar

1/2 teaspoon kosher salt

1. Heat the oil in a 3- or 4-quart (3- or 4-liter) saucepan over medium-low heat. When it's hot, add the shallots, garlic, chiles, galangal (if using), and *daun salam* leaves (if using). Sauté, stirring often to prevent scorching, until the garlic and shallots are limp and just beginning to turn slightly golden, 5 to 7 minutes. Be careful not to let them become any darker than slightly golden, or they'll throw off the flavor of the dish.

2. Raise the heat to medium, add the green beans and tomatoes, and stir well to combine. Sauté, stirring constantly, until the green beans pick up some shiny spots where they are beginning to cook and soften, about 2 minutes.

3. Add the coconut milk, water, palm sugar, and salt and stir well to combine. Bring the coconut milk to a gentle boil. Immediately reduce the heat to medium-low, cover, and cook the beans at a gentle simmer, stirring occasionally, until they are deep green and

fork-tender (but not mushy), 15 to 20 minutes. (Be careful never to allow the coconut milk to come to a boil, or it may curdle.) The beans should be soft and only slightly crunchy, similar to old-fashioned southern-style green beans. The liquid will not have thickened much since you added it, so there will still be a fair amount. Taste for salt, and add a pinch more if needed.

4. Transfer the beans and sauce to a serving bowl. If you've used galangal and *daun salam* leaves, you can discard them. If you decide to leave them in, tell your guests not to eat them, as they are only seasonings. Allow the dish to rest and cool a bit before eating. It will taste better.

MENU SUGGESTIONS

Serve this easy-to-make soupy dish with Celebration Yellow Rice (page 178), Twice-Cooked Tofu with Coriander (page 330), and Grilled Coconut Chicken with Lemon Basil (page 292). It can also be served as a Western-style vegetable side dish, though you may want to halve the coconut milk and water so that it'll be a bit less liquidy on dinner plates.

CHING LEE'S BRAISED LEMONGRASS LONG BEANS
Kacang Panjang Belacan
(SINGAPORE)

⁓

Here's a splendid Nyonya-style dry braise of long beans that goes equally well with hot steamed rice or crusty bread. The recipe, which includes a combination of Malaysian and Chinese ingredients, was given to me by Ching Lee, a good friend from Singapore. The sunny flavoring paste, made of lemongrass, ginger, candlenuts, and dried shrimp paste, is finished with a splash of double-black soy sauce and complements the long beans perfectly. Be sure to use a thick lemongrass stalk, which will yield a more citrusy flavor. Locating a bunch of long beans outside of Chinatown or an Asian market used to be difficult, but the beans are now increasingly easy to find. They're even making frequent appearances at my local— and non-Asian—New York City supermarket. Unfortunately, regular green beans are not a good substitute, as I've found that they turn mushy when prepared this way.

MAKES 4 SERVINGS

1 pound (455 grams) long beans (about 40 beans)

FOR THE FLAVORING PASTE

1 thick stalk fresh lemongrass

1/2 teaspoon dried shrimp paste (page 65)

3 shallots (about 2 1/2 ounces/70 grams total), coarsely chopped

1 to 3 fresh red Holland chiles or other fresh long, red chiles such as Fresno or cayenne, stemmed and coarsely chopped

3 candlenuts (page 48) or unsalted macadamia nuts

1 piece fresh ginger, 2 inches (5 centimeters) long, peeled and thinly sliced against the grain (about 2 tablespoons)

3 tablespoons peanut oil

4 tablespoons water

1 1/2 teaspoons sugar

2 teaspoons double-black soy sauce (page 87)

Kosher salt (optional)

1. First, discard any shriveled, less-than-fresh beans and then wash the remaining beans and remove their stems and tips. Cut into 1 1/2-inch (4-centimeter) lengths and set aside.

2. Prepare the flavoring paste by cutting off the hard, brown bottom and the bristly, greenish top of the lemongrass, which should leave you with a pale white-and-lilac piece about 5 inches (13 centimeters) long. Discard the 2 or 3 tough outer layers, and then cut the lemongrass crosswise into slices 1/4 inch (6 millimeters) thick and set aside.

3. Place the shrimp paste in the center of a 5-inch (13-centimeter) square of aluminum foil. Fold the edges of the foil over to form a small parcel, and press down with the heel of your hand to flatten the shrimp paste into a disk 1/4 inch (6 millimeters) thick. Heat a gas burner to medium-low or an electric burner to medium-high. Using a pair of tongs or 2 forks, place the sealed parcel directly on the heat source. Toast until the paste begins to smoke and release a burning, shrimpy smell, about 1 1/2 minutes. With the tongs or forks, turn the parcel over and toast the other side for another 1 1/2 minutes, then turn off the burner. Again using the tongs or forks, remove the parcel and let cool for 30 seconds to 1 minute. Carefully unwrap the foil; the edges of the disk should be black-brown and toasty and the center should be golden with some black-brown patches. Using a spoon, scrape the toasted shrimp paste into a small bowl and allow it to cool for another 30 seconds. Discard the foil.

4. Place the toasted shrimp paste, lemongrass, shallots, chiles, candlenuts, and ginger in a small food processor. Pulse until you have a smooth paste the consistency of creamy

mashed potatoes, about 1 minute. Make sure that the lemongrass is well pulverized. Coarsely ground pieces will be unpleasant in the final dish. If the paste won't purée properly and repeatedly creeps up the side of the processor instead of grinding, add up to 2 tablespoons water, 1 tablespoon at a time, periodically turning the processor off and scraping the unground portions down toward the blade.

5. Heat the oil in a 3-quart (3-liter) saucepan over medium-low heat. Test to see if the oil is the right temperature by adding a pinch of the ground paste. The paste should sizzle slightly around the edges, not fry aggressively or sit motionless. When the oil is ready, add all the paste and sauté, stirring as needed to prevent scorching, until the smell of raw shallots subsides, the aroma of lemongrass takes over, and the paste begins to separate from the oil, about 5 minutes. Be sure that the paste remains limp—it shouldn't be dry and crusty. Add the long beans and stir to combine with the paste and the oil.

6. Add the water and stir once more. Raise the heat to medium and allow the liquid to come to a noisy simmer for about 10 seconds. Reduce the heat to medium-low and cover the pan. Simmer the beans, stirring occasionally, until they just begin to lose their rawness and yield slightly to the prick of a fork, about 7 minutes. (The cooking time may vary by as much as 5 minutes, depending on the tenderness and freshness of the beans.)

7. Remove the lid, raise the heat slightly, and continue simmering for another 2 minutes, letting the liquid that remains in the pot cook away. Add the sugar and soy sauce and stir to combine. Allow the flavors to combine for 1 minute, then taste for salt and add a pinch if needed. (The soy sauce will probably add enough salt.) Continue cooking until no sauce remains and the long beans are sautéing solely in oil, another 2 minutes or so. By this point, the long beans should be well cooked and succulent, but they shouldn't be mushy.

8. Transfer the beans to a serving dish and let rest for at least 10 minutes before you eat them, which will allow the tastes to intensify and blend.

MENU SUGGESTIONS

Particularly good partners for this dryish, citrusy dish are rice and soupy dishes such as Nyonya Shrimp Curry with Fresh Pineapple and Tomatoes (page 260), Nyonya Chicken and Potato Stew (page 281), and Acehnese Goat Curry (page 314).

ROHATI'S CRISP-FRIED POTATOES WITH CHILE AND SHALLOT SAMBAL

Kentang Balado

(WEST SUMATRA, INDONESIA)

⌒

This dish of crisp-fried potato wedges blanketed in a vivid chile-shallot paste has no Western counterpart that I know of, yet it's so spare and simple it seems to have come straight from a Midwest farmhouse kitchen—albeit a Midwest farmhouse kitchen with a cook who's insane for chiles. But as Rohati, my friend in Padang, West Sumatra, taught me, the dish is not just about fire. It's also about the deliciousness of forceful flavors. To reduce the number of chiles would compromise its authenticity. West Sumatran cooks often substitute deep-fried 2-inch (5-centimeter) chunks of Japanese eggplant or deep-fried whole hard-cooked eggs for the fried potatoes. The sautéed flavoring paste can also be served on its own, without the fried potatoes, as a West Sumatran sambal condiment known as *sambalado*. It would pair well with crusty bread as a fiery appetizer. Just think of it as the devil's tapenade.

Firm, fleshy chiles at the peak of freshness are essential here. Hothouse-raised red Holland and Fresno chiles are available year-round. If you can't find them, make this dish in late summer, when many varieties of long, fresh red chiles, such as cayenne, are available at farmers' markets. When frying the potatoes, be careful to cook them only until they are golden, or the dish will taste bitter. Serve this dish with plenty of steamed white rice to cushion its considerable heat.

MAKES 4 SERVINGS

FOR THE FLAVORING PASTE

2 shallots (about 1 1/2 ounces/40 grams total), coarsely chopped

1 1/2 pounds (680 grams) medium-sized waxy potatoes (about 7) such as Maine or Yukon Gold, or very small red potatoes (about 10), no more than 2 inches (5 centimeters) in diameter

10 to 13 fresh red Holland chiles or other fresh long, red chiles such as Fresno or cayenne, stemmed and coarsely chopped

Peanut oil for frying

1 teaspoon palm, cider, or rice vinegar

1/2 teaspoon kosher salt

1. Place the shallots in a small food processor and pulse until well pulverized. (It's fine if some of the shallot pieces are not completely ground; they're going to be ground again in a moment.) Add the chiles and continue to pulse just until they begin to break up and tint the shallots ruby red, 10 to 15 seconds more. The result should be a rough paste, not a smooth one, with small bits and pieces of chile skin still intact. Set aside.

2. Peel the potatoes and trim away any green or bruised spots. If using medium-sized potatoes, cut each potato in half lengthwise, and then cut each half lengthwise into thirds, yielding 6 wedges from each potato. If using small red potatoes, just halve them lengthwise.

3. Pour oil to a depth of about 1 inch (2.5 centimeters) into a 3-quart (3-liter) saucepan and place over medium to medium-high heat. When the oil is hot but not smoking (about 365°F/185°C), spear a potato wedge onto a fork and dip a corner of the wedge into the oil. If the potato begins to fry immediately, the oil is ready. With a slotted metal spoon, carefully add the potatoes in small, manageable batches of no more than 5 or 6 wedges at a time. Fry the potatoes, turning the wedges frequently with the spoon to prevent them from sticking together, until they're lightly golden on all sides, 4 to 6 minutes total. To test if they are cooked through, pierce a wedge with a fork. It should puncture the wedge with slight resistance. Using the slotted spoon, transfer the potatoes as they become cooked to paper towels to drain. Don't allow the potatoes to become too brown; the longer they fry, the hotter the oil will become, and some of the wedges may become too brown before becoming fully cooked. Take care to raise and lower the heat occasionally if you see that the potatoes are either sitting limply in the oil or are frying too violently. They will come out too greasy or darkly colored otherwise.

4. Turn off the heat and remove the pan to a cooler place on the stove. Let the oil cool for a few minutes, then pour off all but about 3 tablespoons. Heat the cooled oil in the pan over medium-low heat. Test to see if the oil is the right temperature by adding a pinch of the ground paste. The paste should sizzle slightly around the edges, not fry aggressively or sit motionless. When the oil is ready, add all the paste, the vinegar, and the salt and bring the mixture to a bubbly simmer. Continue cooking, stirring as needed to prevent scorching, until the flesh of the chiles begins to meld with the shallots and the smell of raw shallots dissipates, 4 to 5 minutes. Reduce the heat slightly and cook until the paste begins to separate from the oil and the paste is about 2 shades darker than when it was raw, about 2 minutes longer. It should smell mellow and cooked, not raw and fiery.

5. Return the fried potatoes to the pan, and gently fold them into the paste, covering them evenly but being careful not to break them open as you do so. Taste for salt and add more if needed.

6. Transfer the potatoes to a serving dish or bowl. You should eat this dish warm or cool but not cold or hot. The potatoes will be mealy if served cold, and the dish may be overbearingly spicy if served hot.

MENU SUGGESTIONS

If you can stand the heat, this dish is quite lovely served with a crusty artisanal bread and Stir-fried Asian Greens with Garlic and Chiles (page 205). If you are serving it along with rice, other West Sumatran recipes, such as Beef Rendang (page 304), Padang Fish Curry (page 244), and Fern Curry with Shrimp (page 226), complement it particularly well.

POTATO RENDANG
Rendang Kentang
(WEST SUMATRA, INDONESIA)

I got the recipe for this sweet-fiery dish of slow-braised new potatoes, their jackets coated in crisp flavoring paste, from my West Sumatran friend Rohati. She counts it among her favorites. Rohati views the long time it takes to cook this dish as an asset: the longer it cooks, the more delicious it becomes, with each note—ginger, galangal, lemongrass, lemon basil, *daun salam* leaves, garlic, shallots, chile—deeply penetrating the potatoes. It's important to use potatoes no larger than an inch (2.5 centimeters) in diameter; the dish won't taste nearly as flavorful if you use larger ones. It's also important not to peel the potatoes, as you'll end up with mashed potatoes if you do. Baby Yukon Golds or fingerlings will yield excellent results, as will baby blue-fleshed Peruvian potatoes. Rohati often substitutes *paku*, West Sumatra's version of fiddlehead ferns, for the potatoes, resulting in an equally wonderful dish. And don't forget to serve up the golden scrapings from the bottom of the pan, as they are indescribably delicious. See page 102 for more information about cooking foods using the *rendang* method. Unlike in the recipes for Beef Rendang (page 304) and Chicken Rendang with Cinnamon and Star Anise (page 278), here the coconut milk is allowed to reduce slightly before the flavoring paste and main ingredient are added.

MAKES 4 TO 6 SERVINGS

**2 1/2 cups (20 fluid ounces/625 milliliters)
unsweetened coconut milk**

FOR THE FLAVORING PASTE

1 thick stalk fresh lemongrass

**4 shallots (about 3 ounces/85 grams total),
coarsely chopped**

2 cloves garlic, coarsely chopped

**5 to 10 fresh red Holland chiles or other fresh
long, red chiles such as Fresno or cayenne,
stemmed and coarsely chopped**

**5 to 15 fresh green Thai chiles, stemmed and
coarsely chopped (optional, depending on
how piquant you want the dish to be)**

**1 piece fresh or thawed, frozen turmeric (page
92), 2 inches (5 centimeters) long, peeled
and coarsely chopped (about 2 teaspoons),
or 2 teaspoons ground turmeric**

**1 piece fresh ginger, 2 inches (5 centimeters)
long, peeled and thinly sliced against the
grain (about 2 tablespoons)**

**1 piece fresh or thawed, frozen galangal,
2 inches (5 centimeters) long, peeled
and thinly sliced against the grain
(about 2 tablespoons; optional)**

**3 stems fresh lemon basil (page 74), Thai basil,
or Italian basil**

3 whole *daun salam* leaves (page 64; optional)

**1 1/2 pounds (680 grams) very small potatoes
such as baby Yukon Gold, fingerling, or**

**Peruvian blue, no more than 1 inch
(2.5 centimeters) in diameter**

3/4 teaspoon kosher salt

Peanut oil, if needed

1. First you'll need to reduce the coconut milk slightly. Pour it into a 12-inch (30-centimeter) skillet (nonstick works best) and bring to a low boil over medium heat. As soon as it begins to approach a boil, reduce the heat to medium-low. Continue to cook the coconut milk, uncovered, at a steady simmer until swirls of oil just begin to appear on the surface, about 15 minutes. (If that doesn't happen, don't fret. The coconut milk you're using probably has a low fat content. Just proceed to the next step anyway after 15 minutes.)

2. Meanwhile, make the flavoring paste. Cut off the hard, brown bottom and the bristly, greenish top of the lemongrass, which should leave you with a pale white-and-lilac piece about 5 inches (13 centimeters) long. Discard the 2 or 3 tough outer layers, and then cut the lemongrass crosswise into slices 1/4 inch (6 millimeters) thick and set aside.

3. Place the lemongrass, shallots, garlic, chiles, turmeric, ginger, and galangal in a small food processor. Pulse until you have a smooth paste the consistency of creamy mashed potatoes. If the paste won't purée properly and repeatedly creeps up the side of the processor

instead of grinding, add up to 2 tablespoons water, 1 tablespoon at a time, periodically turning the processor off and scraping the unground portions down toward the blade.

4. Add the flavoring paste, basil, and *daun salam* leaves (if using) to the simmering coconut milk and stir well to combine. Allow the liquid to come to a steady gentle simmer and continue to cook uncovered, stirring occasionally with a spoon or spatula to prevent sticking, until the liquid has reduced by half, about 45 minutes. Be sure to keep the coconut milk at a steady gentle simmer during this time (though a lively simmer is also acceptable). If it boils, it may separate and curdle.

5. While the coconut milk is simmering, scrub the unpeeled potatoes and slit them halfway through with a sharp knife. (Be careful not to cut all the way through.) This will allow the flavors to penetrate the flesh. Set them aside.

6. When the coconut milk has reduced by half, add the slit potatoes to the pan and then the salt, and stir well to combine. Return the coconut milk to a steady gentle simmer. With the pot uncovered, continue simmering, stirring often to prevent sticking, until the liquid has become thick and pastelike and the fats have separated from the remaining solids, 30 to 45 minutes longer. If the coconut milk you're using is low in fat, there may only be a small amount of oil—perhaps less than 1 tablespoon—in the pan at this point. Add the peanut oil until there is roughly 2 tablespoons oil in the pan.

7. Reduce the heat to low and gently sauté the potatoes in the rendered oils and fats, stirring often and scraping up the flavoring paste with a spatula to prevent sticking and scorching but being careful not to break apart the potatoes. Continue to cook until the potatoes and flavoring paste are medium dark brown (the color of a well-roasted chicken), 25 to 30 minutes longer. The dish should be quite dry.

8. Transfer the potatoes and all of the sautéed flavoring paste to a serving dish. Allow the dish to rest for at least 30 minutes before serving, which will intensify its flavors. If you eat it while it's still hot, you won't be able to appreciate its full complexity. The dish should keep tightly covered in the refrigerator for up to 5 days.

MENU SUGGESTIONS

These potatoes are wonderful when partnered with rice, Stir-Fried Asian Greens with Garlic and Chiles (page 205), Stir-fried Shrimp Sambal (page 262), and Acehnese Goat Curry (page 314). The last dish in particular beautifully echoes the flavorings in the potatoes. (Note that although it might seem odd to serve rice with potatoes, potatoes are thought of as a vegetable, not a starch, in Indonesia, Malaysia, and Singapore.) If you want to forgo traditional Indonesian accompaniments, this superflavorful dish goes well with a classic roast beef or a simple roast chicken, or even with plenty of rice or good French bread and a salad of bitter lettuces. It also works as a breakfast side dish, as an Indonesian-style substitute for hash browns or home fries.

FERN CURRY WITH SHRIMP
Gulai Paku
(WEST SUMATRA, INDONESIA)

Tender young ferns are a favorite vegetable in the Malay Archipelago and often end up in salads and coconut-milk curries. I'd often seen bunches of them for sale in markets, but I never knew whether they were grown on farms or harvested in the wild. One afternoon my friend Nas, a Sumatran rice farmer, cleared up the mystery.

"Fern farms? Not possible," he said as we walked down a footpath near his village home. "Fern seeds are too small to plant. The jungle is our fern farm." Ferns, he went on, are not the only produce the jungle provides. Nas's wife, Warisa, an excellent cook, regularly supplements her meals with other wild vegetables, such as *cengkol*, a bitter-tasting seedpod, and young jackfruit, both of them gathered from the dense jungle that encircles their home.

As the sun was setting, we arrived at a river grove overgrown with ferns. Nas inspected a young plant, carefully running his fingers through its fronds. "Look for pale green specimens that have just opened—they're the sweetest and most tender," he said, "and be sure not to disturb the plant, as others from the village also come here to harvest." We soon returned home bearing bundles of just-snipped ferns still warm from the sun. I watched as Warisa went about making this recipe in her outdoor kitchen: a pure, earthy-tasting coconut-milk curry that combined the ferns with shrimp.

Though the young fiddlehead fronds of a North American fern species known as ostrich fern are not endemic to the Malay Archipelago, they make an excellent substitute for the numerous varieties of ferns eaten there. Look for them at farmers' markets in the first warm weeks of spring. Choose bright green, tightly coiled fiddleheads, with no bruising. Cook them within a day or two of purchase, as they spoil rapidly. If you live in an area where fresh fiddleheads are not available or you would like to make this dish out of season, frozen fiddleheads, available year-round from several online companies (see Sources, page 363, for one recommendation), will work fine. You need only blanch frozen fiddleheads for a few seconds to thaw them right before cooking. (A note of caution: Many ferns that grow wild in North America are poisonous, so never harvest them unless you're an expert.)

I don't recommend peeling the shrimp or removing their heads for this dish, as the shells and heads lend significant flavor to the broth. This makes for messy eating as you peel and slurp, but your taste buds won't mind a bit. Omit the shrimp entirely for a satisfying vegetarian version of this dish.

MAKES 4 SERVINGS

2 1/2 cups (about 11 ounces/310 grams)
    fresh or frozen fiddlehead ferns

FOR THE FLAVORING PASTE

3 shallots (about 2 1/2 ounces/70 grams total), coarsely chopped

1 clove garlic, coarsely chopped

1 piece fresh or thawed, frozen turmeric (page 92), 1 inch (2.5 centimeters) long, peeled and coarsely chopped (about 1 teaspoon), or 1 teaspoon ground turmeric

1 piece fresh ginger, 2 inches (5 centimeters) long, peeled and thinly sliced against the grain (about 2 tablespoons)

3 to 15 fresh green or red Thai chiles, stemmed and coarsely chopped

2 tablespoons peanut oil

1 piece *asam gelugor* (page 43; optional, but adds a pleasantly tart flavor)

1 stem fresh lemon basil (page 74), Thai basil, or Italian basil (optional, but adds a delicious herbal hint)

7 ounces (200 grams) medium-sized shrimp in the shell, preferably with heads intact (10 to 15 shrimp)

1 1/2 cups (12 fluid ounces/375 milliliters) unsweetened coconut milk

1/2 cup (4 fluid ounces/125 milliliters) water

1/2 teaspoon kosher salt

1/2 teaspoon sugar

1. To clean fresh fiddleheads, use kitchen shears or a sharp paring knife to snip off the bottom 1/4 inch (6 millimeters) of the stem jutting out from the center coil of each fern. Next, remove as much of the light brown, paper-thin sheath from each fiddlehead as possible. (This papery sheath protects the fiddleheads from insects and cold weather as they unfurl; much of it is naturally discarded by the time they're harvested, but some tenacious bits, which are unpleasant to eat, may remain.)

2. Rinse and drain the fresh fiddleheads in at least 3 changes of cold water. Fill a 3-quart (3-liter) saucepan with water to a depth of 3 inches (7.5 centimeters) and bring it to a

vigorous boil over high heat. Add the fiddleheads and boil for 3 to 4 minutes. Drain the fiddleheads into a colander and run cold water over them to halt the cooking. Drain them once more and set aside. If using frozen fiddleheads, blanch them for a few seconds in vigorously boiling water, drain them into a colander, and rinse with cold running water to halt the cooking. Drain again and set aside.

3. To make the flavoring paste, place the shallots, garlic, turmeric, ginger, and chiles in a small food processor. Pulse until you have a smooth paste the consistency of creamy mashed potatoes, with no visible pieces or chunks of shallot or garlic. If the paste won't purée properly and repeatedly creeps up the side of the processor instead of grinding, add up to 2 tablespoons water, 1 tablespoon at a time, periodically turning the processor off and scraping the unground portions down toward the blade.

4. Rinse and dry the 3-quart saucepan, add the oil, and place over medium-low heat. Test to see if the oil is the right temperature by adding a pinch of the ground paste. The paste should sizzle slightly around the edges, not fry aggressively or sit motionless. When the oil is ready, add all the paste and sauté, stirring as needed to prevent scorching, until the garlic and shallots no longer smell raw and the paste begins to separate from the oil, 5 to 7 minutes. Add the *asam gelugor* and basil, if using, and the shrimp, stirring well to combine. Raise the heat slightly and cook until the shrimp turn pink, about 2 minutes.

5. Add 1/2 cup (4 fluid ounces/125 milliliters) of the coconut milk, all of the water, and the fiddleheads and stir well to combine. Raise the heat slightly and bring the coconut milk to a gentle simmer. Immediately reduce the heat a bit and continue to cook, stirring often, until the fiddleheads are fork-tender but not mushy, about 10 minutes. They should be deep forest green, not spring green, by the time they're finished cooking. Add the salt and sugar and stir to combine.

6. Stir in the remaining 1 cup (8 fluid ounces/250 milliliters) coconut milk and then raise the heat slightly. Bring the mixture to a gentle simmer, stirring constantly, until the coconut milk is heated through, about 2 minutes. Remove the basil stem and *asam gelugor*, if used. Taste once more for salt, and add a pinch if needed.

7. Transfer to a serving dish. Set the curry aside to rest for 10 to 15 minutes or longer before eating, which will allow the flavors to intensify and mingle.

MENU SUGGESTIONS

I like the immediacy of this dish when served with nothing more than rice or a crusty artisanal bread. If you prefer to include it as part of a more comprehensive rice meal, consider making Mien's Garlic Fried Chicken (page 283), Gado-Gado (page 154), or Tempeh Sambal with Lemon Basil (page 324). These are all dry dishes that will enhance this soupy curry particularly well.

ASIAH'S EGGPLANT CURRY
Kari Terung
(MALAYSIA)

This delicately spicy, soupy coconut-milk eggplant curry is an everyday dish in Malaysian homes, usually served with plenty of steamed rice to absorb the rich sauce. If they're available, use pale violet Japanese eggplants. Their subtle, buttery taste pairs better with coconut milk than the flesh of dark purple Japanese eggplants, which can be slightly bitter. The recipe is from Asiah, a woman in her sixties who lives in Kota Baru, a city on West Malaysia's northeast coast overlooking the South China Sea. We ate it without benefit of rice, devouring the eggplant like it was candy, while sitting on a rattan mat on the floor of her home.

MAKES 4 SERVINGS

1 pound (455 grams) small Japanese eggplants (about 4 eggplants), unpeeled, stemmed, halved lengthwise, and cut crosswise into pieces 3 inches (7.5 centimeters) long

1 teaspoon ground turmeric

1 tablespoon tamarind pulp, plus 3 tablespoons very warm water to make extract

Peanut oil for frying

2 cloves garlic, thinly sliced lengthwise

3 shallots (about 2 1/2 ounces/70 grams total), thinly sliced lengthwise

1 to 5 fresh green Thai chiles, stemmed and halved lengthwise (optional, but traditional)

2 teaspoons coriander seeds, finely ground in a small food processor or spice grinder

1/2 teaspoon finely ground pure chile powder

1/2 teaspoon cumin seeds

1/4 teaspoon fennel seeds

1 piece cinnamon stick, 3 inches (7.5 centimeters) long

3/4 cup (4 fluid ounces/125 milliliters) unsweetened coconut milk

3/4 cup (4 fluid ounces/125 milliliters) water

1 teaspoon sugar

1/2 teaspoon kosher salt

1. Place the eggplant pieces in a large bowl and dust the turmeric over them. With your hands, massage the turmeric into the eggplant until it evenly coats the fleshy side (not the skin side) of each piece. Set aside.

2. Place the tamarind pulp in a small nonreactive bowl and mix it with the warm water. Let the pulp rest until it softens, 10 to 15 minutes. Squeeze and massage the softened pulp through your fingers, loosening the fruit's auburn pulp from the shiny black seeds, brittle brown skin shards, and sinewy bits of string. With your fingers, remove all the solid pieces from the liquid and discard them. All that will remain is a thick caramel-colored extract. Set the tamarind extract aside.

3. Pour oil to a depth of 1 inch (2.5 centimeters) into a 3-quart (3-liter) saucepan and place over medium to medium-high heat until hot but not smoking. To test if the oil is the right temperature (it should be about 365°F/185°C), spear a piece of eggplant onto a fork and dip the edge of the piece into the hot oil. If it begins to fry and a froth of oil immediately bubbles up around it, the oil is ready. Fry the eggplant in batches of no more than 3 pieces at a time (you don't want to crowd the pan) until the fleshy side of each piece just begins to turn golden and you can barely prick it with a fork, about 1 1/2 minutes. The eggplant should be just cooked and not at all soft or mushy, as it will cook more later in the coconut milk. Using a slotted spoon, transfer the eggplant to paper towels to drain.

4. Turn off the heat and remove the pan. Let the oil cool for a few minutes, then pour off all but about 2 tablespoons. Place the pan over medium-low heat. Add the garlic and shallots and cook them until they just begin to turn limp and translucent, about 2 minutes; don't let them brown.

5. Add the green chiles (if using), ground coriander, chile powder, cumin, fennel, and cinnamon. Sauté, stirring gently to prevent the spices from scorching, until the spices have thoroughly flavored the oil and a fragrant aroma floats up from the pan, about 3 minutes.

6. Add the coconut milk and water, stir to combine, and raise the heat to medium. Bring the coconut milk to a lively simmer, and immediately reduce the heat until the liquid is at a steady gentle simmer. Stir in the tamarind extract, sugar, and salt. Continue to simmer the coconut milk gently until it has begun to take in all the seasonings, about 15 minutes.

7. Add the fried eggplant pieces and allow the coconut milk to return to a gentle simmer. Cook until the eggplant is fork-tender but *not* mushy, 1 to 2 minutes. It's crucial that the eggplant be just cooked through, not overcooked and falling apart. Taste the liquid for salt, and add a little if needed.

8. Transfer the eggplant and sauce to a bowl and allow the dish to rest for at least 10 minutes. Serve slightly warm or at room temperature, the best showcase for its flavors.

MENU SUGGESTIONS

Asiah served this succulent and spicy dish with steamed rice (page 173), Malaysian Spiced Pineapple Pickle (page 136), and a goat curry (Acehnese Goat Curry, page 314, is similar).

ABOVE LEFT: *Captain Buyung's fishing boat at dusk.*

ABOVE CENTER: *Rowing into Bau-Bau in the early morning after a night at sea; baskets hold fish that will end up in dishes such as Fragrant Fish Stew with Lime and Lemon Basil (page 240)*

ABOVE RIGHT: *Grilled red snapper* (ikan merah) *is caught in the South China Sea.*

10. FISH AND SHELLFISH

It was late October 2002, and the warm sea air felt good on my face. I was on the deck of the *Bukit Siguntang*, an Indonesian passenger liner, on a two-day journey on the Banda Sea from Banda, in Indonesia's Spice Islands, to Makassar, the capital of southern Sulawesi (the large Indonesian island to the east of Borneo). I'd spent two weeks in Banda, the ancestral home of my friend Tanya Alwi, watching the nutmeg harvest there. But now it was time to start heading back to New York. I stared out at the silvery ocean and saw a group of dolphins breaching the surface.

It had been a quiet trip so far, filled with short naps and long meals. But all that changed when the ship docked at Ambon, an old clove- and nutmeg-trading port known in history books by its Dutch name, Amboina. On the pier below more than a thousand passengers were waiting to board, most of them men no older than twenty-five. I leaned over the edge to get a closer look. Many of the men wore flowing gray or brown tunics and wraparound turbans, and they spoke to one another in hushed voices, as though conversing in a private language. I asked Nilam, a fellow passenger, what was going on. "They're from the Laskar Jihad camps on Ambon," she explained, as she looked down at the hubbub, the expression on her face dark.

I knew of the Laskar Jihad from newspaper accounts. It was a fundamentalist Islamic organization whose members' dream was to forge a vast Southeast Asian Muslim nation in all areas in the region where Islam is practiced, from Indonesia and the southern Philippines to Malaysia and southern Thailand. The men began to pile onto the ship, laying out rattan mats and settling onto the decks, the stairways, the hallways—whatever space could be fashioned into a seat or bed for the trip ahead.

"Because of the bomb, their leaders have probably ordered them to disband the camps where they were living," Nilam continued. She was referring to the 2002 terrorist attack in Bali's Kuta Beach, which had occurred just two weeks earlier. "Anyone with ties to fundamentalist Islam is under suspicion now." She paused, sighing, and said, "Indonesia is a strange place, no?"

Nilam had it only partly right. The whole world seemed a strange place to me. I watched the men as they continued to board. Up close, their menace disappeared. In fact, they were no more frightening than an easygoing group of grownup kids. If it weren't for their tunics and turbans, they could've been going to a rock concert. Still, big crowds aren't my style, so I decided to break up my journey at Bau-Bau, the next port of call, where I'd wait out the Jihad exodus for a few days.

The *Bukit Siguntang* docked at Bau-Bau at noon under a blazing sun. I'd been there years earlier. Situated on the small island of Buton, it's a toy box of a town, with brightly painted wooden houses that look like Dr. Seuss drew them. Centuries ago, Bau-Bau was home to a powerful spice-trading sultanate, and clove trees grew in abundance. Now it's not much more than an oversized fishing village. Most of its roads are unpaved, and there's only one hotel you might want to stay in. I grabbed the ship's handrail and inched down the crowded, narrow gangway. When I reached the dock, one of the Laskar Jihad members approached me. "*Selamat jalan*," he said politely. I smiled back and wished him the same: "Happy journey."

I made my way down a path to Bau-Bau's main street. Townseople, stunned to see a foreigner, stared at me as if I'd just dropped down from Mars. There was a traffic jam of pushcart vendors selling food, including grilled grouper, plain except for a lashing of salt, and golden yellow fish curries and stews. But as delicious as everything looked, I wasn't interested in eating. I wanted to let a friend, Muhammad, know I was in town. I walked into a *telepon* kiosk and picked up a phone.

"Surprise!" I said. "It's James, from America. I just arrived in Bau-Bau. I'm fleeing the Laskar Jihad!" Muhammad laughed and invited me to his house for lunch. I flagged down an *ojek*—a motorcycle taxi—and sped through town clutching my suitcase.

Muhammad, whom I'd met on my last visit to Bau-Bau, was a handsome, twenty-eight-year-old professor of oceanography at the local college. He lived in a small house with his parents. When I arrived, a simple meal of grilled tuna—which had been caught earlier that morning in the Flores Sea, Muhammad said—stir-fried water spinach, and rice was waiting on the table, compliments of Muhammad's mother, Sufi. Muhammad and I dug in.

As we ate, Muhammad told me about everything that had been going on in his family in the years since we'd seen each other. The most important news he offered was that his thirty-year-old brother Budi had recently quit his job as a road laborer to become a fisherman, the old family trade, on a boat owned by a friend of his.

"We're going out on the boat tonight," Muhammad said. "Will you join us?"

"Me, pass up a sea trip?" I asked. "Not in this lifetime!"

Later that afternoon, after checking into a hotel room, I met up with Muhammad and Budi at the old pier close to their home. We looked out on the sea as a few seagulls circled lazily overhead. The water's surface appeared flat and motionless, as smooth and reflective as a mirror. "It's so still," I said. "It looks like we'll have an easy trip today."

"Buton fishermen call it *laut minyak*, or 'oil sea,'" Budi said. He was a powerfully built man, more stout than his brother. "*Laut minyak* happens often this time of year, but it does not always mean an easy trip. The weather can change."

"Does *laut minyak* mean a big catch?" I asked.

"With the sea, there's no telling," he replied, shrugging his shoulders.

We walked to the edge of the pier. Budi explained that there was a fish market held there every morning, so local fishermen could sell their day's catch. At this hour, though, the market was a memory and the pier was quiet, save for a handful of crewmen quietly scrubbing down their small trawlers anchored just offshore. I asked which boat we'd be sailing on.

"That one," he said, pointing to a thirty-footer out in the water. It was a humble wooden vessel, probably more than forty years old, but with a new coat of turquoise paint that sparkled in the sun. Upward-curving wooden arms extended from the boat's sides, giving it the appearance of a butterfly frozen in flight. The purpose of the arms, Budi explained, was to hold the cast net in place. A slightly imperfect homemade red-and-white Indonesian flag was tethered to the top of the mast. The boat bobbed to and fro, as if impatient to get going.

Soon, Budi, Muhammad, five crewmates, and I were pushing a dugout rowboat into the waist-high warm water off the shore. (We would leave the rowboat behind once we reached the fishing boat.) As we rowed toward the trawler, Muhammad introduced me to the crew. There was the captain, Buyung, a thin fortyish man with a regal air; Andy, a bright-eyed deckhand; Dayat, a Bau-Bau native who'd been a fisherman for more than thirty years; Syaf, an older man of few words; and Akir, an Ambon native whose deeply tanned body was rippled with muscles.

When we arrived at the fishing boat, the crew's first order of business was lifting the anchor, which Akir had the honor of cranking up. I sat on the wooden deck as Captain Buyung started the engine, a small but loud contraption that coughed up a cloud of blue smoke. Captain Buyung studied the sextant intently.

"We're headed to an area about forty kilometers away," said Budi, yelling over the sound of the engine. "Captain Buyung has had good luck there many times before."

"What happens when we get there?" I asked, yelling back.

"We wait. If he thinks the conditions are good, we drop the net." Budi paused, smiling mysteriously. "But most of all, we wait." He lit a clove cigarette and inhaled deeply. "Once, I had a dream," he continued. "I dreamed I caught a fish so beautiful that I couldn't bear to sell it."

236 • CRADLE OF FLAVOR

Two hours later, Bau-Bau was no longer in sight and we were moving quickly on the open sea. To the west, the sun was setting over a tiny green uninhabited island. To the south, ominous gray clouds appeared on the horizon. Thunder boomed in the distance. At the rear of the boat was a makeshift kitchen consisting of a hotplate and a wooden crate that doubled as a countertop. Dayat began preparing dinner. There was no catch yet, so the meal would be simple: rice, a stir-fry of *sayur sawi* (mustard greens), and a few hard-cooked eggs from the chickens in Dayat's backyard. When dinner was ready, he scooped up generous portions onto tin plates. As we ate, it started to rain, an almost daily occurrence this close to the equator.

After we finished our dinner, Captain Buyung switched on the small circular fluorescent lights that ran along the boat's sides, filling the deck with pearly white light. "They are used to attract fish toward the net," explained Muhammad. Commercial fishermen in the Malay Archipelago typically use artificial light to lure fish and squid, he continued. But I knew that it was a controversial method: Many marine environmentalists back home believe that the practice leads to overfishing. Lights, such as the ones on Captain Buyung's boat, also attract a multitude of sea creatures—including many endangered ones.

"It won't change anytime soon," Muhammad told me. "Fishermen in Bau-Bau were using oil lamps to attract fish long before the invention of electricity." I watched as Captain Buyung walked the length of both sides of the boat to make sure that each light was functioning properly. A few miles away, I could see three other trawlers that had sailed from Bau-Bau. With their fishing lights now switched on, they resembled Cheshire cats grinning in the night. We soon came to a stop. Captain Buyung and Akir peered over the railing to see what was lurking in the water. What had been blackness before was now an illuminated wonderland of sea life. Hundreds of neon-striped mackerel, and nearly as many iridescent squid, were swimming below the boat. A huge, jet black manta ray zoomed by, flapping its heavy wings like a gigantic underwater bird. I asked Captain Buyung if this would be a good place to drop the net. It certainly seemed like it to me.

"*Belum tahu,*" he said, telling me he didn't know yet. There were many things to consider, including the fact that the weather was looking increasingly threatening. We continued to chat. I learned from Captain Buyung that he'd been sailing off Bau-Bau since he was nine years old. He knew the currents and the fish they carried along with them as well as he knew his daughter's smile. Fishing was his religion.

Suddenly, rain began to pound the deck. The thunderstorm squall in the distance earlier had caught up with us. Within minutes, swells rose up on either side of the boat, rocking it forcefully. Lightning cracked overhead. I held on tight.

It was well past midnight when the storm finally subsided. Most of the crew had fallen asleep together in a knot under a tent just beyond the wheelhouse. I was wide awake, however, and was staring up at the sky, transfixed. On the open sea, under all those stars, I could hear nature breathing. At three o'clock, Captain Buyung gave word to drop the net. Muhammad had the thankless task of rousing the crew from their sleep. Then the real work started. First, the anchor was tossed overboard, hitting the water with a terrific splash. Syaf and Akir began unfurling the net. It was sixty or seventy feet long, much larger than it seemed when it lay folded on the deck. Maneuvering like tightrope walkers, Dayat and Andy made their way onto the wooden arms jutting from the sides of the boat and began to tie the net down. Andy threw off his shirt and pants and jumped into the water. He resurfaced a minute later on the other side of the boat, grasping the corner of the net in his hands. Dayat grabbed hold of it and began securing it.

"The net is thirty feet below us," said Budi. "It will take a few hours before the captain gives orders to lift it." As he spoke, I could feel my eyelids growing heavier. Exhaustion had finally gotten the better of me. I excused myself and fell asleep against a crate, dreaming about all that sea life down below.

About two hours later, a ruckus woke me up. I watched as the entire crew busily moved around the boat. The moment had come to lift the net and see what fish had been snared. The men coaxed and gathered the net upward, taking turns cranking a large winch in the center of the deck. They moved with the effortless camaraderie that's achieved only by working together for a long time. The net, its belly filled with a mass of fish, was soon suspended over the boat. Someone pulled a lever, and its contents spilled out in a loud whoomp. The deck's surface was a mosaic of squirming fish. Through all the fluttering I could make out blue tuna, red snappers, silver-green mackerels, and squid.

"The catch is fantastic!" Budi shouted in my direction. "You bring good luck, James!"

All the crew members squatted down, ankle high in flapping fish, and began sorting them by type. They tossed the fish into seven sturdy rattan barrels, one for the mackerel, another for the tuna, and so on. "This is the fun part," said Muhammad as he hurled a chubby gray tuna into a basket six feet away. The sun was beginning to break through the sky. It was time to head back to shore.

Morning light blanketed Bau-Bau when we dropped anchor off the pier that we had departed from the previous afternoon. Handling them as if they held jewels, Akir and Andy placed the baskets of fish in the rowboat that would take us ashore. In a way, the baskets did hold jewels: the size of the catch would determine how much money the crew would take home. We rowed slowly toward the pier, our boat sluggish from all the extra weight it was carrying.

At least twenty other local crews had returned to Bau-Bau before us and the pier was bustling with fishermen selling their catch. Everywhere you looked were three-foot-high mounds of glistening sea creatures piled directly on the dock. Housewives picked through them in search of the healthiest and sweetest specimens, which would, no doubt, end up a few hours later in an array of delicious fish and shellfish curries and stews.

Budi, Muhammad, and the crewmen sat on the pier surrounded by their baskets. They were grinning from ear to ear. It was the best catch they'd had in weeks. They would earn good money, take the night off, and sleep in their own beds. Their wives would kiss them. They would be happy.

Budi pulled me aside. "Look at this," he said, proudly displaying a shiny two-and-a-half-foot red snapper. "We'll take it home and my mother will make lunch. It will be a celebration of our catch." It would be even better than that. It would be a celebration of the sea.

⌒

The oceans, seas, bays, inlets, and straits that encircle the coasts of Indonesia, Malaysia, and Singapore provide its people with their most crucial source of protein. Fish and shellfish rank below only rice and vegetables in their importance in the daily diet, and they appear on tables at almost every meal. Over the centuries, the region's fishermen have perfected the art of catching the great schools of fish, shrimp, and squid that are so abundant in the local warm sea waters. Most of their tools are the same as they have always been. Simple wooden fishing boats are believed to be just as effective as modern radar-equipped trawlers (and they don't lead as easily to overfishing), while handmade nets and cages have proven themselves to be every bit as sturdy as their factory-made counterparts.

Fishermen take their catch to public fish markets called *pasar ikan*, such as the one in Bau-Bau, every morning or afternoon, depending on when they return from the sea. At the markets that dot the coastal villages and towns of the more than fifteen thousand islands in the region, fishermen usually sell their own catch, rather than engage the help of a middleman or wholesaler. They call out their offerings in a seductive singsong—"Ikan basah, ibu!" (Fresh fish for you, ma'am!)—to customers seeking fish with bright, clear eyes and firm, sweet flesh. The most popular varieties are kingfish (*ikan tenggiri*), tuna (an Indonesian word), common mackerel (*ikan kembong*), red snapper (*ikan merah*), grouper (*ikan kerapu*), and shrimp (*udang*). After a round of good-natured bargaining, the fisherman will likely slip the fish or shellfish into a satchel made from a banana leaf for easy transport. Once home, the buyer will probably cook the fish within an hour or two.

Farm-raised freshwater fish, such as tilapia and carp, also find their way into local cooking, especially in inland areas, where sea fish are scarce. Dried fish are a popular subcategory of food from the sea that I don't cover in the recipes in this chapter. Though I adore the many varieties, especially Malaysian and Singaporean *ikan bilis* (whole dried anchovies), it's difficult to find good-tasting dried fish in North American markets.

Because eating fish and shellfish is an ancient tradition in the Malay Archipelago, cooks have an innate understanding of the best ways to cook them. They know, for example, that some varieties, such as pompano, with its light-tasting, fragile flesh, is better suited to steaming, while heartier-tasting varieties, such as tuna or mackerel, should be braised, used in stews, or pan seared. They also know that ginger, lime juice, lemon basil, lemongrass, kaffir lime leaves, and tamarind are the flavorings that both enhance the natural sweetness of all fish and shellfish and counteract fishiness.

Brightly seasoned fish curries and stews, based on coconut milk or on water, respectively, are the most popular of all fish dishes. Cooks begin with a whole fish and cut it crosswise into thick, bone-in pieces, rather than fillet it, since bones—and the collagen they contain—lend flavor and body. Among the region's best-loved fish curries and stews are Fragrant Fish Stew with Lime and Lemon Basil (page 240), a dish from Sulawesi, Indonesia, that resembles bouillabaisse; Padang Fish Curry (page 244), a gingery coconut-milk–based dish from West Sumatra; and Indian-Style Fish Stew with Okra (page 249), an aromatic dish from Malaysia that pairs kingfish with fenugreek, coriander, and tamarind.

Pan searing is another favored way to prepare fish. It calls for sautéing the fish over robust heat until its flesh is cooked through and its surface is golden brown, and then strewing it with sautéed aromatics, as in Pan-Seared Mackerel with Chiles and Garlic (page 252). But for the deepest flavor of all, cooks turn to a grill. Everyday meals often consist of little more than a fish marinated in fresh lime juice and grilled until just blackened over a smoky fire, a stir-fried vegetable, a sambal, and steaming-hot rice. I'm including a less minimal recipe for grilled fish: Grilled Whole Fish with Lemon Basil and Chiles (page 256), a Javanese classic with a flavoring paste made from lemongrass, candlenuts, and chiles.

Shrimp (*udang*), squid (*sotong* in Malaysia and Singapore, *cumi-cumi* in Indonesia), and crab (*ketam*) appear on tables with almost the same frequency as ocean-caught and fresh-water fish, and they're used in similarly seasoned curries and stews. Nyonya Shrimp Curry with Fresh Pineapple and Tomatoes (page 260), a coconut-milk curry from Malaysia that could easily be made with fish, is a delicious combination of sweet, tart, and spicy flavors. But whenever my mind turns to shellfish, I always recall a feast I had at the home of Mad Zan, a Malaysian fisherman. Every dish on the table, all of which were prepared by his wife, Norsiah, included shrimp or crab he'd caught that morning. My favorite was Stir-fried Shrimp Sambal (page 262), a fiery dish of shrimp in a hot chile paste. As I ate it, I felt that I was tasting the true soul of the sea.

FRAGRANT FISH STEW WITH LIME AND LEMON BASIL
Ikan Kuning
(SULAWESI, INDONESIA)

This recipe comes from Sufi, the mother of my friend Muhammad, who lives in Bau-Bau, in southern Sulawesi. By the time Sufi brought the stew to the table, she had tasted it at least eight times, checking for the right balance of sourness, saltiness, pungency, and herbs. "No one flavor should control this dish," she said, as she took a final taste. Although the precise combination of ingredients is particular to Sulawesi, where cooks have a passion for lemon basil and *lots* of lime juice, variations on this sensational dish are cooked everywhere in the Malay Archipelago.

Making this stew is relatively straightforward. A whole medium-firm ocean fish, such as red snapper or rock cod, cut into thick bone-in steaks works best; freshwater tilapia is a good choice, too. The head and tail should be included; they help intensify the broth. If you don't want to cook a whole fish (or if a whole fish isn't available), snapper, rock cod, or tilapia fillets can be substituted, but the overall flavor of the dish won't be as rich.

Be careful not to overcook the fish. The flesh should be firm and tight, not falling away from the bone or separating from the skin. Serve this dish in a wide, shallow bowl to show off the herbs, chunks of fish, and beautiful turmeric-yellow broth.

MAKES 4 SERVINGS

1 whole red snapper, rock cod, or tilapia, with head and tail intact, about 2 pounds (900 grams), cleaned and cut crosswise through the bone into pieces 2 inches (5 centimeters) wide, or 1 3/4 pounds (800 grams) snapper, rock cod, or tilapia fillets or bone-in steaks

4 tablespoons fresh lime juice

FOR THE FLAVORING PASTE

3 shallots (about 2 1/2 ounces/70 grams total), coarsely chopped

1 clove garlic, coarsely chopped

1 to 5 fresh red Holland chiles or other fresh long, red chiles such as Fresno or cayenne, stemmed and coarsely chopped

1 piece fresh ginger, 1 1/2 inches (4 centimeters) long, peeled and thinly sliced against the grain (about 1 1/2 tablespoons)

1 piece fresh or thawed, frozen galangal, 1 inch (2.5 centimeters) long, peeled and thinly sliced against the grain (about 1 tablespoon; optional)

1 piece fresh or thawed, frozen turmeric (page 92), 2 inches (5 centimeters) long, peeled and coarsely chopped (about 2 teaspoons), or 1 teaspoon ground turmeric

3 tablespoons peanut oil

2 fresh or thawed, frozen *daun pandan* leaves (page 64), cut into pieces 3 inches (7.5 centimeters) long (optional)

3 thick stalks fresh lemongrass, each tied into a knot (page 76)

8 whole fresh or thawed, frozen kaffir lime leaves

1 1/2 cups (12 fluid ounces/375 milliliters) water

1/2 teaspoon kosher salt

3 stems fresh lemon basil (page 74), Thai basil, or Italian basil, cut in half, plus about 10 leaves for garnish

1. In a nonreactive bowl roomy enough to hold the fish pieces (including the head and tail, if using a whole fish), combine the fish and lime juice and marinate the fish, unrefrigerated and uncovered, for 15 to 30 minutes. Turn the fish over a few times while it marinates to make sure the juice coats each piece evenly.

2. To make the flavoring paste, combine the shallots, garlic, chiles, ginger, galangal, and turmeric in a small food processor. Pulse until you have a smooth paste the consistency of creamy mashed potatoes. If the paste doesn't purée properly and repeatedly creeps up the side of the food processor instead of grinding, add up to 2 tablespoons water, 1 tablespoon at a time, periodically turning the processor off and scraping the unground portions down toward the blade as you go.

3. Heat the oil in a 3- or 4-quart (3- or 4-liter) saucepan, Dutch oven, or soup pot over medium-low heat. Test to see if the oil is the right temperature by adding a pinch of the ground paste. The paste should sizzle slightly around the edges, not fry aggressively or sit motionless. When the oil is ready, add all the paste, *daun pandan* leaves (if using), lemongrass, and lime leaves. Sauté, stirring as needed to prevent scorching, until you no longer smell raw shallots and garlic and the aroma of the *daun pandan*, lemongrass, and lime leaves takes over, about 5 minutes. Be careful not to let the flavoring paste brown.

4. Add the fish (including the head and tail, if using a whole fish) and the lime-juice marinade. Stir gently to combine the fish with the flavoring paste. Add the water and raise the heat to medium. Bring the liquid to a gentle simmer. Add the salt and stir well to combine. Adjust the heat to allow the liquid to remain at a steady, gentle simmer. Cook the fish pieces, occasionally turning them with a spatula or a large spoon, until

they're just cooked through, about 10 minutes. To test the fish for doneness, pierce a piece at its thickest point; it should be opaque. Be careful not to overcook the fish. You don't want it to be falling apart. Also, be careful not to break the fish pieces when you turn them. Taste the liquid for salt, and add a pinch more if needed.

5. Add the lemon basil stems, then gently transfer the fish, broth, and all the seasonings to a wide serving bowl. Allow the fish to rest in the liquid for at least 10 minutes, to give the flavors time to develop. Just before serving, garnish with the lemon basil leaves. The lemongrass, *daun pandan*, and lime leaves aren't for eating, but I leave them in the serving bowl because they look beautiful and they let your guests see what has contributed to making the dish taste so great. The lemon basil leaves, of course, can be eaten.

MENU SUGGESTIONS

This stew needs rice, as it's too intense to eat on its own. Try pairing it with dry dishes that won't conflict with its herbal flavors. A few good possibilities are Spiced Braised Nyonya Pork (page 307), Chicken Rendang with Cinnamon and Star Anise (page 278), Nyonya-Style Spiced Fried Chicken (page 285), and Stir-fried Water Spinach, Nyonya Style (page 213). A good choice for a sambal would be Green Mango Sambal (page 123).

SPICE-BRAISED TUNA
Ikan Bumbu Rujak
(SPICE ISLANDS, INDONESIA)

I got the recipe for this sumptuous, mahogany brown braise from Aca, a woman in Bandaneira, the capital of the Bandas, the Indonesian islands that Christopher Columbus was looking for when he bumped into the Americas by mistake. Indonesian sweet soy sauce (*kecap manis*) provides sweetness, while tamarind extract and quartered tomatoes, the latter tossed in at the very end and cooked until barely fork-tender, contribute a hint of tartness. Be careful not to overcook the tuna. It's essential that it be moist, not dry and coarse. Using dark maroon Pacific yellowfin or bluefin tuna with fat streaking its flesh will result in a more succulent dish.

MAKES 4 SERVINGS

1 tablespoon tamarind pulp, plus 3/4 cup
(6 fluid ounces/175 milliliters) very
warm water to make extract

FOR THE FLAVORING PASTE

4 shallots (about 3 ounces/85 grams total),
coarsely chopped

3 cloves garlic, coarsely chopped

1 piece fresh ginger, 2 inches (5 centimeters)
long, peeled and thinly sliced against the
grain (about 2 tablespoons)

4 tablespoons peanut oil

2 pieces cinnamon stick, each 4 inches (10
centimeters) long

2 whole nutmegs, cracked open with a nutcracker or a heavy, blunt object such as the
bottom of a glass measuring cup

1 teaspoon whole cloves

2 thick stalks fresh lemongrass, each tied into a
knot (page 76)

1 pound (455 grams) skinless tuna fillet, cut
into chunky pieces about 2 inches (5 centi-

2 to 5 fresh red Holland chiles or other fresh
long, red chiles such as Fresno or cayenne,
stemmed and coarsely chopped

meters) long by 1 inch (2.5 centimeters)
thick

4 tablespoons Indonesian sweet soy sauce
(page 72)

4 tablespoons water

2 firm, ripe small tomatoes such as Roma
(about 6 ounces/170 grams total), cored and
quartered

Kosher salt (optional)

1. Place the tamarind pulp in a small nonreactive bowl and mix it with the warm water. Let the pulp rest until it softens, 10 to 15 minutes. Squeeze and massage the softened pulp through your fingers, loosening the fruit's auburn pulp from the shiny black seeds, brittle brown skin shards, and sinewy bits of string. With your fingers, remove all the solid pieces from the liquid and discard them. All that will remain is a thick caramel-colored extract. Set the tamarind extract aside.

2. To make the flavoring paste, place the shallots, garlic, ginger, and chiles in a small food processor. Pulse until you have a completely smooth paste. Set aside.

3. Heat the oil in a 3- or 4-quart (3- or 4-liter) saucepan, Dutch oven, or soup pot over medium-low heat. Test to see if the oil is the right temperature by adding a pinch of the ground paste. The paste should sizzle slightly around the edges, not fry aggressively or sit motionless. When the oil is ready, add all the paste and sauté, stirring as needed to

prevent scorching, until the shallots and garlic no longer smell raw, about 5 minutes. Be careful not to brown the flavoring paste. Add the cinnamon, nutmegs, cloves, and lemongrass, stirring well to combine. Sauté the spices and lemongrass until their aroma wafts up from the pan, about 2 minutes.

4. Add the tuna and raise the heat slightly. Sauté, stirring often, until the tuna has just begun to pick up golden spots, about 3 minutes. Add the tamarind extract, sweet soy sauce, and water and stir well to combine. Bring the mixture to a gentle simmer, then immediately reduce the heat to low. Allow the liquid to simmer gently until the flavors have intensified and the tuna is cooked, about 4 minutes. Test a piece of tuna by slicing it in half; it should be faintly pink in the center, similar to medium-cooked beef.

5. Add the tomatoes and continue cooking until they can just be pierced with a fork, about 2 minutes; they shouldn't be mushy. Taste for salt, adding a pinch if needed (the sweet soy sauce will probably have added enough salt to the dish).

6. Gently transfer the fish and all the seasonings to a wide serving bowl. Allow the dish to rest for at least 10 minutes, to give the flavors time to develop. Just before serving, you may remove the lemongrass and spices. I prefer to leave them in the dish, however, making sure that my guests know that they're there for their beauty, not to eat.

MENU SUGGESTIONS

So as not to detract from the warm flavors of this dish, serve it with steamed rice (page 173) and a few dryish dishes, such as Javanese Cucumber and Carrot Pickle (page 132), Shrimp Satay (page 150), Mien's Garlic Fried Chicken (page 283), and Tempeh Sambal with Lemon Basil (page 324).

PADANG FISH CURRY
Gulai Ikan Masin
(WEST SUMATRA, INDONESIA)

Here's another recipe from Rohati, my cooking guru in West Sumatra, Indonesia. It's a butter yellow coconut-milk curry seasoned with lemongrass, lime leaves, garlic, ginger, and turmeric. Whole green Thai chiles provide heat without overwhelming the entire dish; guests can remove them if they wish. A note of caution: Don't sauté the flavoring paste over a high flame. It will burn quickly, giving the curry an inappropriately musky flavor. Instead, sauté it gently over medium-low heat until it releases its pleasantly pungent aroma in good time, about 5 minutes.

Gulai ikan masin ("salty fish curry") tastes better if it's not served steaming hot, so allow it to rest for 20 minutes or so before serving. Rohati occasionally adds a few stems of lemon basil to the coconut milk, which adds a subtle perfume. Skin-on red snapper, rock cod, or tilapia fillets work well in this curry (the skin helps to hold the fish together as it cooks, and provides extra flavor), but bone-in steaks work even better. A whole version of any of these fish, including the head and tail, will yield the tastiest results.

MAKES 4 SERVINGS

FOR THE FLAVORING PASTE

5 shallots (about 3 3/4 ounces/110 grams total), coarsely chopped

2 cloves garlic, coarsely chopped

1 piece fresh or thawed, frozen turmeric (page 92), 1 inch (2.5 centimeters) long, peeled and coarsely chopped (about 1 teaspoon), or 1/2 teaspoon ground turmeric

1 piece fresh ginger, 1 1/2 inches (4 centimeters) long, peeled and very thinly sliced against the grain (about 1 1/2 tablespoons)

3 candlenuts (page 48) or unsalted macadamia nuts

3 tablespoons peanut oil

2 thick stalks fresh lemongrass, each tied into a knot (page 76)

3 whole fresh or thawed, frozen kaffir lime leaves

2 whole *daun salam* leaves (page 64; optional)

1 1/4 cups (10 fluid ounces/310 milliliters) unsweetened coconut milk

1 1/4 cups (10 fluid ounces/310 milliliters) water

1 teaspoon sugar

3/4 teaspoon kosher salt

1 whole red snapper, rock cod, or tilapia with head and tail intact, about 2 pounds (900 grams), cleaned and cut crosswise through the bone into pieces 2 inches (5 centimeters) wide, or 1 3/4 pounds (800 grams) snapper, rock cod, or tilapia fillets or bone-in steaks

5 to 15 fresh green Thai chiles, stemmed

1. To make the flavoring paste, place the shallots, garlic, turmeric, ginger, and candlenuts in a small food processor. Pulse until you have a smooth paste the consistency of creamy mashed potatoes. If the paste won't purée properly and repeatedly creeps up the side of the processor instead of grinding, add up to 2 tablespoons water, 1 tablespoon at a time, periodically turning the processor off and scraping the unground portions down toward the blade.

2. Heat the oil in a 3- or 4-quart (3- or 4-liter) saucepan, Dutch oven, or soup pot over medium-low heat. Test to see if the oil is the right temperature by adding a pinch of the ground paste. The paste should sizzle slightly around the edges, not fry aggressively or sit motionless. When the oil is ready, add all the paste, the lemongrass, lime leaves, and *daun salam* leaves (if using) and sauté, stirring as needed to prevent scorching, until the shallots and garlic no longer smell raw and the aroma of lemongrass and lime leaves takes over, 5 to 7 minutes.

3. Add the coconut milk, water, sugar, and salt, stir to combine, and raise the heat to medium. Bring the liquid to a very gentle simmer and immediately reduce the heat to medium-low. Continue to simmer uncovered, stirring often, until the taste of the flavoring paste melds with the coconut milk, 10 to 15 minutes. Taste to see if it has reached this point. The flavors should be balanced and harmonious.

4. Add the fish (including the head and tail, if using a whole fish) and chiles and continue to cook at a very gentle simmer, stirring occasionally, until the fish and chiles are just cooked through, 5 to 10 minutes. To test the fish for doneness, pierce a piece at its thickest point; it should be opaque. Be careful not to overcook the fish. You don't want it to be falling apart. Also, be careful not to break the fish pieces when you turn them. Taste the liquid for salt, and add a pinch more if needed.

5. Carefully transfer the fish and sauce to a wide serving bowl. You can remove the lemongrass and kaffir lime leaves and the *daun salam* leaves, if used, or leave them in the bowl to continue to season the dish. Allow the curry to rest for at least 20 minutes before serving.

MENU SUGGESTIONS

Pair this dish with other West Sumatran dishes, such as Rohati's Crisp-Fried Potatoes with Chile and Shallot Sambal (page 221) and Beef Rendang (page 304), and, of course, with rice. Other good choices are Caramelized Tempeh with Chiles (page 325) and Ching Lee's Braised Lemongrass Long Beans (page 218).

HOT-AND-SOUR FISH STEW WITH BAMBOO SHOOTS

Masam Jing

(ACEH, INDONESIA)

—

This spicy-sour classic from Aceh, the one-time spice-trading sultanate at the northern tip of Sumatra, is an interesting study in how subtle variations in ingredients can radically transform a dish. Here, a few more candlenuts in the flavoring paste turn the broth rich and opaque, as though it contained coconut milk. Pea-sized wild eggplants, which help cool the intensity of this dish, are often substituted for the bamboo shoots. Other substitutions include *ampan*, a kind of Acehnese wild nettle, and fresh-picked marijuana stems, a common seasoning herb in Aceh that imparts an earthy, green taste—and, of course, a narcotic buzz. As with Fragrant Fish Stew with Lime and Lemon Basil (page 240), a whole red snapper or rock cod, cut into thick pieces on the bone, will work best.

This recipe comes from Kois, an Aceh native who left his homeland years ago and now lives in southern Sumatra. Whenever he eats this dish, his village, with its cool mountain breezes and thick jungles, immediately appears in his mind's eye. "I feel like I'm sitting in my childhood home," he said to me as he finished a portion of this soul-nourishing stew.

MAKES 4 SERVINGS

FOR THE FLAVORING PASTE

4 shallots (about 3 ounces/85 grams total), coarsely chopped

1 clove garlic, coarsely chopped

2 to 5 fresh red Holland chiles or other fresh long, red chiles such as Fresno or cayenne, stemmed and coarsely chopped

2 to 5 fresh green Thai chiles, stemmed and coarsely chopped

1 piece fresh or thawed, frozen turmeric (page 92), 1 inch (2.5 centimeters) long, peeled and coarsely chopped (about 1 teaspoon), or 1 teaspoon ground turmeric

4 candlenuts (page 48) or unsalted macadamia nuts

2 tablespoons fresh lime juice

1 whole red snapper, rock cod, or tilapia with head and tail intact, about 2 pounds (900 grams), cleaned and cut crosswise through the bone into pieces 2 inches (5 centi-

meters) wide, or 1 3/4 pounds (800 grams) snapper, rock cod, or tilapia fillets or bone-in steaks

1/2 teaspoon kosher salt

1 stem fresh lemon basil (page 74), Thai basil, or Italian basil (optional)

2 pieces *asam gelugor* (page 43; optional)

1 1/2 cups (12 fluid ounces/375 milliliters) water

2 to 2 1/2 cups (about 8 ounces/225 grams) thin bamboo shoot tips (see Cook's Note, page 249), halved or quartered if they are thicker than 1/2 inch (12 millimeters) at the base

2 tablespoons fresh lime juice

1. To make the flavoring paste, place the shallots, garlic, chiles, turmeric, candlenuts, and lime juice in a small food processor. Pulse until you have a chunky-smooth paste the consistency of cooked oatmeal. If the paste won't purée properly and repeatedly creeps up the side of the processor instead of grinding, add up to 2 tablespoons water, 1 tablespoon at a time, periodically turning the processor off and scraping the unground portions down toward the blade.

2. In a nonreactive bowl roomy enough to hold the fish pieces (including the head and tail, if using a whole fish), combine the fish, salt, basil (if using), and *asam gelugor* (if using). Add the ground flavoring paste and, using your hands or a big spoon, combine it with the fish pieces, making sure the paste evenly coats the pieces. Allow the fish to marinate uncovered at room temperature for 10 to 20 minutes.

3. Transfer the fish mixture (including the basil and *asam gelugor*) to a 3- or 4-quart (3- or 4-liter) saucepan, Dutch oven, or soup pot. Add the water, stir well to combine, and place over high heat. Bring the liquid to a gentle boil. As soon as it boils, immediately reduce the heat to medium-low. Cook the fish pieces at a steady, gentle simmer, occasionally turning them with a spatula or a large spoon, until they're just cooked through, about 10 minutes. To test the fish for doneness, pierce a piece at its thickest point; it should be opaque. Be careful not to overcook the fish. You don't want it to be falling apart. Also, be careful not to break the fish pieces when you turn them.

4. Gently fold the bamboo shoots into the broth, making sure not to break the fish, which will be very fragile. Continue to simmer the broth, stirring occasionally, until the bamboo shoots are warmed through and have begun to absorb the flavors of the broth, about 2 minutes. Add the lime juice and taste for salt, adding a pinch if needed.

5. Remove the *asam gelugor* and discard (you can leave the basil, if you like). Using a large spoon, carefully transfer each piece of fish, one at a time, to a shallow serving bowl or platter. Pour the bamboo shoots and broth over the fish. Allow the dish to rest for at least 10 minutes before eating, which will give its sharp, hot flavors time to temper a bit.

COOK'S NOTE

Look for canned thin bamboo shoot tips, which are thinner than most bamboo shoots because they're younger, in Chinese markets. They're shaped like thin asparagus stalks and are easily identifiable by a drawing of one on the label. Rinse them under cold running water before using. My favorite brand, Slender, is imported from Kiangsi, China, and comes in 28-ounce (800-gram) cans. If you can't find thin bamboo shoots, any brand of canned whole shoots will do. The best is Ma Ling, imported from China in 16-ounce (455-gram) cans. The shoots are quite large in diameter, however (sometimes more than 1 inch/2.5 centimeters at the base, even those that have been halved), so you'll need to halve or quarter them before using.

MENU SUGGESTIONS

Serve this potent dish with steamed rice (page 173) and a few mild dishes, such as Stir-fried Asian Greens with Garlic and Chiles (page 205) and Garlic-Marinated Tempeh (page 322).

INDIAN-STYLE FISH STEW WITH OKRA
Asam Pedas
(MALAYSIA)

Silver-skinned kingfish, also known as Spanish mackerel, is the most popular fish in Malaysia, where it's called *ikan tenggiri*. Prized for its firm, moist flesh and clean taste, it shows up in countless dishes, but to my mind it's best suited to this slightly tart, spicy stew, a Malaysian classic. There are numerous regional variations of this dish, called *asam pedas*, or "sour hot," but this Indian-inspired version, studded with okra, tomatoes, aromatic spices, and lemongrass, is my favorite. It demonstrates the casual way in which flavorings and cooking styles converge in Malaysia. Fenugreek seeds, a classic Indian spice and the dominant seasoning note, are rarely used in Malay cooking but are right at home here, as are okra, curry leaves, and black mustard seeds, all traditional Indian ingredients.

MAKES 4 SERVINGS

1 tablespoon tamarind pulp, plus 2 1/2 cups (20 fluid ounces/ 625 milliliters) very warm water to make extract

FOR THE FLAVORING PASTE

2 tablespoons coriander seeds

1/2 teaspoon fennel seeds

1/2 teaspoon cumin seeds

1/4 teaspoon black peppercorns

2 to 8 small dried red chiles such as árbol, stemmed and coarsely chopped

2 thick stalks fresh lemongrass

3 shallots (about 2 1/2 ounces/70 grams total), coarsely chopped

3 cloves garlic, coarsely chopped

4 tablespoons peanut oil

1 teaspoon black mustard seeds (page 47)

1/4 teaspoon fenugreek seeds (see Cook's Note, page 251)

25 fresh curry leaves (page 63; optional)

1 teaspoon sugar

1 teaspoon kosher salt

1 whole kingfish, common mackerel, tilapia, red snapper, or grouper with head and tail intact, 2 pounds (680 to 900 grams),

cleaned and cut crosswise through the bone into pieces 3 inches (7.5 centimeters) wide, or 1 1/2 to 2 pounds (680 to 900 grams) kingfish, common mackerel, tilapia, red snapper, or grouper fillets or bone-in steaks

10 medium-sized okra pods, stemmed

2 firm, ripe small tomatoes such as Roma (about 6 ounces/170 grams total), cored and quartered

1. Place the tamarind pulp in a nonreactive bowl and mix it with the warm water. Let the pulp rest until it softens, 10 to 15 minutes. Squeeze and massage the softened pulp through your fingers, loosening the fruit's auburn pulp from the shiny black seeds, brittle brown skin shards, and sinewy bits of string. With your fingers, remove all the solid pieces from the liquid and discard them. All that will remain is the caramel-colored extract. This particular tamarind extract will be thinner than most of the others in this book. Set the tamarind extract aside.

2. Next, make the flavoring paste. Place the coriander, fennel, cumin, peppercorns, and chiles in a small food processor. Pulse until ground to a dusty powder, about 2 minutes. Don't remove the ground spices from the food processor at this point. You're going to grind them again along with the other paste ingredients.

3. Cut off the hard, brown bottom and the bristly, greenish top of the lemongrass stalks, which should leave you with pale white-and-lilac pieces about 5 inches (13 centimeters) long. Discard the 2 or 3 tough outer layers, and then cut the lemongrass pieces crosswise into slices 1/4 inch (6 millimeters) thick.

4. Add the lemongrass, shallots, and garlic to the food processor and pulse until you have a smooth paste the consistency of creamy mashed potatoes. Make sure that the

lemongrass is well pulverized. Coarsely ground pieces will be unpleasant in the final dish. If the paste won't purée properly and repeatedly creeps up the side of the processor instead of grinding, add up to 2 tablespoons water, 1 tablespoon at a time, periodically turning the processor off and scraping the unground portions down toward the blade.

5. Heat the oil in a 3- or 4-quart (3- or 4-liter) saucepan, Dutch oven, or soup pot over medium-high heat. When it's hot but not smoking—it should appear shimmery—toss in the mustard seeds. As soon as they begin to pop and sputter (about 30 seconds), add, in quick succession, the fenugreek seeds and curry leaves (if using), distributing them evenly in the oil with a spatula. Sauté until the fenugreek seeds have darkened a shade or two and the curry leaves have picked up translucent spots, about 30 seconds. Remove the pan from the heat and allow it to cool for 1 minute—otherwise, the flavoring paste, which you are about to add, will burn.

6. Return the pan with the fenugreek seeds and curry leaves to medium-low heat. Test to see if the oil is the right temperature by adding a pinch of the ground paste. The paste should sizzle slightly around the edges, not fry aggressively or sit motionless. When the oil is ready, add all the flavoring paste and sauté, stirring as needed to prevent scorching, until the paste begins to separate from the oil and releases its extremely aromatic fragrance, 5 to 7 minutes.

7. Add the tamarind extract and raise the heat to medium-high. Bring the liquid to a vigorous simmer and then immediately reduce the heat to medium-low. Add the sugar and salt and simmer gently, uncovered, for 3 minutes to meld the flavors.

8. Add the fish to the broth and give it a gentle stir. Continue to cook the liquid at a very gentle simmer, uncovered, until the fish is nearly cooked through, about 5 minutes. Never allow the liquid to come to a boil, which may cause the fish to overcook.

9. Add the okra and tomatoes and continue to cook until the okra has just turned fork-tender, 6 to 8 minutes; the timing will depend on its size and tenderness. Taste for salt, and add a pinch more if needed.

10. Transfer the fish, vegetables, and sauce to a shallow serving bowl and let cool for at least 10 minutes before eating.

COOK'S NOTE

Fenugreek seeds, which are native to India, are used in the Malay Archipelago in fish curries and pickles. They are about 1/8 inch (3 millimeters) long and have a taut, tan lentil-like exterior and an aromatic, bitter flavor. Look for the seeds in South Asian and specialty markets, and store them in a tightly sealed airtight container in your refrigerator or freezer for up to a year.

MENU SUGGESTIONS

Good pairings with this vibrant dish are rice and a few others that won't conflict with its pleasing sourness or intense aroma. Try Sautéed Cabbage with Ginger and Crispy Indian Yellow Lentils (page 209), Stir-fried Shrimp Sambal (page 262), Grilled Coconut Chicken with Lemon Basil (page 292), and Chile Omelet (page 334).

PAN-SEARED MACKEREL WITH CHILES AND GARLIC
Chuan-Chuan
(MALAYSIA)

I adore this easy Portuguese Malay classic. In it, wedges of Spanish mackerel, also known as kingfish, are pan seared until golden and crisp. Garlic, ginger, onion, and chiles are added to the pan juices and sautéed until wilted, followed by double-black and regular soy sauce, black pepper, and a splash of vinegar (which complements the assertive taste of the mackerel). The seasonings and juices are then poured over the fish. Malaccan-born Jennifer Kuan, who gave me this recipe, inherited it from her Portuguese Malay husband's auntie. Jennifer prepares it often for the same reason I do: it's a snap to make and it tastes wonderful.

MAKES 4 SERVINGS

5 tablespoons (2 1/2 fluid ounces/75 milliliters) peanut oil

1 whole kingfish or common mackerel, about 1 1/2 pounds/680 grams and 12 to 15 inches (30 to 38 centimeters) long, cleaned with head and tail discarded (or saved to make stock, if you like) and cut crosswise through the bone into pieces 3 inches (7.5 centi-meters) wide, or 1 1/2 pounds (680 grams) bone-in kingfish or common mackerel steaks

2 tablespoons water

1/2 teaspoon double-black soy sauce (see page 87)

1 teaspoon soy sauce

1/2 teaspoon sugar

1/4 teaspoon freshly ground black pepper

6 cloves garlic, thinly sliced lengthwise

1 piece fresh ginger, 3 inches (7.5 centimeters) long, peeled, thinly sliced with the grain, and cut into fine matchsticks (about 3 tablespoons)

1 medium-sized red onion (about 6 ounces/170 grams), halved and thinly sliced lengthwise

1 to 2 fresh red Holland chiles or other fresh long, red chiles such as Fresno or cayenne, stemmed and thinly sliced on the diagonal

1 teaspoon palm, cider, or rice vinegar

1. Heat the oil in a 12-inch (30-centimeter) skillet (nonstick works best) over medium heat. When it's hot—it should be slightly shimmery—add the fish and sauté, turning once, until cooked through and the surface has picked up appealing golden brown, crispy spots, 5 to 6 minutes on each side. To test for doneness, pierce the flesh. It should be just opaque throughout. Transfer the fish to a serving platter. Pour off half of the oil from the skillet and set the skillet aside.

2. Meanwhile, in a small cup or bowl, combine the water, both soy sauces, sugar, and ground pepper. Stir well and set aside.

3. Return the skillet to medium heat and heat the oil. When it's hot—again, it should appear slightly shimmery—add the garlic, ginger, onion, and chiles and sauté, stirring often, until the garlic is lightly golden (but not brown) and the onion slices are wilted and beginning to pick up golden spots, 5 to 7 minutes.

4. Add the soy sauce mixture to the skillet, stir well, and bring to a sputtery bubble. As soon you see bubbles, add the vinegar and allow it to warm through for a few seconds. Remove the pan from the stove. (There's no need to add salt, since the soy sauces provide enough saltiness.)

5. Spoon the sauce and aromatics over the fish, making sure to cover each piece evenly. Serve promptly.

MENU SUGGESTIONS

Good partners for this homey dish are steamed rice (page 173), Stir-fried Asian Greens with Garlic and Chiles (page 205), and Javanese Chicken Curry (page 275). It also pairs well with crusty bread and a salad of bitter lettuces.

PAN-SEARED TAMARIND TUNA

Tuna Goreng

(SPICE ISLANDS, INDONESIA)

—

In this easy dish from Indonesia's Spice Islands, boneless, skinless chunky tuna pieces are marinated in tamarind extract and salt and then seared in a skillet. The tamarind extract becomes teasingly sweet as it cooks, and the result is moist, delicate fish with a lightly caramelized exterior. Look for the darkest, freshest tuna fillet available, preferably one with a fair amount of visible fat. The meat should be glossy, a deep maroon, and give off no fishy smell. Fat-free, light maroon tuna—the kind commonly used for sushi—will yield a dry dish.

MAKES 4 SERVINGS

1/2 cup (5 ounces/140 grams) tamarind pulp, plus 1 cup (8 fluid ounces/250 milliliters) very warm water to make extract

1/2 teaspoon kosher salt, or more to taste

1 pound (455 grams) skinless tuna fillet, cut into 1 1/2-inch (4-centimeter) pieces no more than 1 inch (2.5 centimeters) thick

5 tablespoons (2 1/2 fluid ounces/75 milliliters) peanut oil

1. Place the tamarind pulp in a nonreactive bowl and mix it with the warm water. Let the pulp rest until it softens, 10 to 15 minutes. Squeeze and massage the softened pulp through your fingers, loosening the fruit's auburn pulp from the shiny black seeds, brittle brown skin shards, and sinewy bits of string. With your fingers, remove all the solid pieces from the liquid and discard them. All that will remain is a thick caramel-colored extract.

2. In a nonreactive bowl roomy enough to hold the fish pieces, combine the tamarind extract and salt. Taste it and add more salt as needed. Remember, the mixture is being used as a marinade, so it should be well salted. Add the tuna and mix it well to make sure that every piece of fish is evenly coated with the tamarind extract. Marinate uncovered at room temperature for 30 minutes to 1 hour, turning the tuna pieces once or twice.

3. Heat the oil in a 12-inch (30-centimeter) skillet (nonstick works best) over medium-high heat. While the oil is heating, remove the tuna pieces from the marinade and pat off the excess liquid with a paper towel. The pieces will splatter wildly in the oil if they are too wet, but you want some tamarind extract to remain. Discard the extra tamarind

extract. When the oil is hot but not smoking—it should appear shimmery—add the tuna pieces in batches, making sure not to crowd the pan. Sauté the tuna, turning once, until the outside of each piece is dark caramel and the inside is medium-rare to medium, 2 to 4 minutes on each side; the timing will depend on the thickness of the fish and the heat of the oil.

4. Transfer the tuna to a serving dish and serve warm.

VARIATION: STIR-FRIED TAMARIND SHRIMP (*UDANG ASAM*)

Josephine Chua, my Nyonya friend in Malacca, Malaysia, has an elderly uncle who likes to make this shrimp dish. Like Pan-Seared Tamarind Tuna, it calls for a straightforward marinade of tamarind extract and salt. The shrimp, which must be in the shell, are then stir-fried over very high heat, becoming lightly caramelized. They can be marinated for up to 24 hours before they hit the wok or skillet. The longer they marinate, the more flavorful they'll be. Serve the shrimp with steamed rice (page 173) and Nyonya Sambal (page 120) or Sweet Soy Sauce and Lime Dipping Sauce (page 125).

To make the shrimp variation, substitute 1 pound (455 grams) medium-sized shrimp in the shell with heads intact (this dish won't come out properly with peeled or headless shrimp) for the tuna. Marinate the shrimp in the tamarind extract and 1 teaspoon salt uncovered at room temperature for at least 1 hour or covered for up to overnight in the refrigerator. Transfer the marinated shrimp to a colander to drain well and then squeeze the shrimp dry with a few paper towels. They don't need to be bone-dry, but they also shouldn't be wet with the extract or they won't sear properly.

To cook, heat 3 tablespoons peanut oil in a wok or 12-inch (30-centimeter) skillet over high heat. When the oil begins to smoke—it should be very hot—add the shrimp and stir-fry them, moving them constantly around the wok with a spatula, until they're caramel-pink and have begun to pick up golden brown scorch marks, 3 to 4 minutes. Serve promptly.

MENU SUGGESTIONS

In Banda, where tamarind and fresh-caught tuna are plentiful and inexpensive, this is an everyday dish. It's usually paired with rice and a hot-sour sambal, such as Green Mango Sambal (page 123), which gives the meal zing. Other good choices are Stir-fried Asian Greens with Garlic and Chiles (page 205), Asiah's Eggplant Curry (page 229), and Malaccan Beef and Vegetable Stew (page 309). These same dishes will complement the shrimp variation.

GRILLED WHOLE FISH WITH LEMON BASIL AND CHILES
Pepes Ikan
(JAVA, INDONESIA)

⟶

This Javanese favorite, a whole fish that's steamed in a vivid flavoring paste and then grilled, contains a spectrum of sweet, herby, hot, earthy, and salty tastes—all the elements that Java's cooks enjoy playing off one another. Though it's often served in homes, especially at banquets, this dish is a specialty of street hawkers, who cook it over small charcoal grills in makeshift roadside *warung-warung* (eating stalls). Chicken prepared in the same fashion is known as *pepes ayam*.

A variety of fish can be used. Good choices are snapper, rock cod, and tilapia (my favorite). Don't worry if you don't have a traditional Asian steamer for cooking the fish. I improvise with a large soup pot and a colander. It's almost impossible to overcook the fish when steaming it, so don't panic about nailing the cooking time precisely. Keep in mind that you'll grill the fish after steaming it, which ensures that it will be fully cooked by the time you serve it.

I give instructions for wrapping the fish in banana leaves, but the most important part of the process is to seal the parcel well, even if it requires using more leaves than indicated here. If you can't find banana leaves (they're almost always available frozen in Latin and Chinese markets), you can substitute foil, though foil imparts none of the subtle herbal taste of banana leaves and makes the presentation much less dramatic.

MAKES 4 SERVINGS

1 whole red snapper, rock cod, or tilapia, 1 1/2 to 2 pounds (680 to 900 grams) and 12 to 15 inches (30 to 38 centimeters) long, cleaned with head and tail intact and sharp, pointy fins trimmed off

1 1/2 tablespoons fresh lime juice

1 teaspoon kosher salt

FOR THE FLAVORING PASTE

1 teaspoon tamarind pulp, plus 3 tablespoons very warm water to make extract

1 thick stalk fresh lemongrass

2 shallots (about 1 1/2 ounces/40 grams total), coarsely chopped

1 clove garlic, coarsely chopped

6 to 10 fresh red Holland chiles or other fresh long, red chiles such as Fresno or cayenne, stemmed and coarsely chopped

1 piece fresh or thawed, frozen turmeric (page 92), 1/2 inch (12 millimeters) long, peeled and coarsely chopped (about 1/2 teaspoon), or 1/2 teaspoon ground turmeric

1 piece fresh ginger, 2 inches (5 centimeters) long, peeled and thinly sliced against the grain (about 2 tablespoons)

5 candlenuts (page 48) or unsalted macadamia nuts

3 tablespoons coarsely chopped ripe red tomato (about 1 small Roma)

1 tablespoon palm sugar (page 79), thinly sliced, or dark brown sugar

1/4 teaspoon kosher salt

1 cup (about 1 ounce/30 grams) loosely packed fresh lemon basil (page 74), Thai basil, or Italian basil leaves

2 fresh or thawed, frozen banana leaves (see Cook's Note, page 259), each about 10 by

30 to 35 inches (25 by 75 to 88 centimeters), plus 1 extra leaf for making ties, or aluminum foil

3 fresh or thawed, frozen *daun pandan* leaves (page 64; optional)

1. Using a sharp knife, lightly score the skin of the fish on both sides, cutting on the diagonal at 1-inch (2.5-centimeter) intervals. This will allow the seasonings to penetrate the flesh more effectively. Don't cut more than 1/8 inch (3 millimeters) deep.

2. Place the fish in a nonreactive bowl. Add the lime juice and salt, rubbing it into the cavity as well as the scored skin. Set the fish aside to marinate, uncovered and unrefrigerated, while you prepare the flavoring paste. Turn the fish a few times as it marinates to make sure that it's evenly coated with the juice.

3. Meanwhile, make the flavoring paste. Place the tamarind pulp in a small nonreactive bowl and mix it with the warm water. Let the pulp rest until it softens, 10 to 15 minutes. Squeeze and massage the softened pulp through your fingers, loosening the fruit's auburn pulp from the shiny black seeds, brittle brown skin shards, and sinewy bits of string. With your fingers, remove all the solid pieces from the liquid and discard them. All that will remain is a thick caramel-colored extract. Set the tamarind extract aside.

4. Cut off the hard, brown bottom and the bristly, greenish top of the lemongrass stalks, which should leave you with pale white-and-lilac pieces about 5 inches (13 centimeters) long. Discard the 2 or 3 tough outer layers, and then cut the lemongrass pieces crosswise into slices 1/4 inch (6 millimeters) thick.

5. Place the tamarind extract, lemongrass, shallots, garlic, chiles, turmeric, ginger, candlenuts, tomato, palm sugar, and salt in a small food processor. Pulse until you have a chunky-smooth paste the consistency of cooked oatmeal. Make sure that the lemongrass

is well pulverized. Coarsely ground pieces will be unpleasant in the final dish. Transfer the paste to a nonreactive bowl and fold in the lemon basil leaves. Set aside.

6. Make a banana-leaf parcel for the fish, a process similar to wrapping a rectangular box in gift paper. You want the fish to be securely wrapped so that it doesn't leak while it steams. First, place 2 banana leaves on top of each other so that they overlap by half. Place the fish and the lime-juice marinade on top of the section where the leaves overlap. Smear one-third of the flavoring paste on top of the fish, making sure you rub it into the score marks. Turn the fish over and smear the second side with another one-third of the flavoring paste. Place the remaining one-third of the paste and the *daun pandan* leaves (if using) in the cavity.

7. Carefully bring the top and bottom ends of the banana leaves together so that they meet above the fish. Hold the leaves together as you fold them over and under the bottom of the fish. Gently tuck the side ends completely under the fish to form a large rectangular package that fully encloses the fish. Be careful as you work, as the leaves can tear easily. Cut 3 or 4 ribbonlike strips from the remaining leaf, and use the strips to secure the parcel, tying them around the parcel along its length at regular intervals. It's fine if the parcel seems overwrapped. The steam will still penetrate. Alternatively, you can use aluminum foil. Tear a piece of foil twice the length of the fish. Place the fish lengthwise in the center of the foil. Fold the extra foil at the tail and head ends toward the center of the fish. Fold over the top and bottom sides, making sure that the entire fish is sealed in the foil.

8. Fill a wok or a 4-quart (4-liter) Dutch oven or soup pot about half full with water. Place a steamer, wire rack, or colander into (or on the lip of) the pot, making sure that the bottom of the steamer is at least 1 inch (2.5 centimeters) above the water line. Add more or less water as necessary. Place the banana leaf parcel in the steamer.

9. Place the pot over high heat and bring the water to a rolling boil. Cover and steam the fish for 35 minutes, making sure that the boiling water never touches the bottom of the steamer, which can make the fish soggy. Check the water level every 10 minutes, and if it drops below 1 inch (2.5 centimeters) deep, add more hot water and return the water to a boil. After 35 minutes, carefully remove the wrapped parcel from the steamer.

10. **To cook the banana-leaf parcel on a grill,** first prepare a very hot charcoal fire and oil the grill rack liberally. When the fire is ready (it may take up to 20 minutes), arrange the charcoal in a high, even pile. You want the banana-leaf parcel to be as close to the coals as possible, so it chars relatively quickly. Place the banana-leaf parcel on the rack and grill until it is brown and slightly charred on the first side, about 2 to 5 minutes.

Carefully turn the parcel over and continue grilling until the second side is brown and slightly charred, about 2 to 5 minutes longer. If you've used foil, grill the parcel until the foil develops singe marks, about 2 to 3 minutes on each side.

To cook the banana-leaf parcel in a broiler, position a rack so that the banana-leaf parcel will be 3 to 4 inches (7.5 to 10 centimeters) from the heat source and preheat the broiler for 10 minutes. Line a half-sheet pan with aluminum foil and place the banana-leaf parcel on the foil-lined pan. Slide the pan under the broiler. Broil until the banana leaf begins to develop brown patches (a few black spots are okay), about 4 to 7 minutes. Gently turn the parcel over and broil on the second side until brown patches appear, about 4 to 7 minutes longer. If you've used foil, broil the parcel until the foil develops singe marks, about 3 to 4 minutes on each side.

11. Transfer the parcel to a large serving plate. If you've used banana leaves, do this carefully, as the leaves will be brittle and cracked.

12. Open the parcel and allow the fish to rest for at least 15 minutes before serving. This gives the powerful flavors time to balance.

COOK'S NOTE

Banana leaves (*daun pisang*) are used to wrap foods for steaming or grilling. They're like nature's aluminum foil, easily clipped from banana trees that grow almost everywhere in the Malay Archipelago. They impart a subtle grassy flavor to savory and sweet dishes alike. Banana leaves are also frequently used as dinner plates, serving trays, and, when tied into neat, airtight bundles, as take-out containers. If you don't have fresh banana plants at your disposal, frozen banana leaves work just as well. They're sold at Latin and Chinese or Southeast Asian markets, usually imported from Thailand or the Philippines, and come in 1-pound (455-gram) packages containing about 20 whole or nearly whole leaves, each separated along its central spine. Keep them frozen until ready to use, as they thaw quickly, usually within a few minutes. Once thawed, wipe each leaf clean with a damp cloth to remove dust. Discard unused frozen leaves after a year.

MENU SUGGESTIONS

Serve this spectacular dish along with rice and a coconut milk–based curry, such as Javanese Chicken Curry (page 275, or the West Sumatran variation, page 277); a stir-fry of greens, such as Stir-fried Water Spinach, Nyonya Style (page 213); and a pickle, such as South Indian–Style Eggplant Pickle (page 133). A sambal isn't really necessary, as the flavoring paste in the dish is similar to one.

NYONYA SHRIMP CURRY WITH FRESH PINEAPPLE AND TOMATOES

Udang Masak Nenas

(MALACCA, MALAYSIA)

⁓

A Malaccan acquaintance, Kenneth, gave me this recipe, a rich and spicy Nyonya dish in which shrimp, pineapple, and tomatoes loll in an orange coconut-milk broth. It's a typical Nyonya blend of sweet, tart, spicy tastes. Use shrimp in their shells, preferably with their heads on, if possible, as the shells and heads impart substantial flavor. And don't use canned pineapple in place of the fresh, or the dish will be disappointing. For tips on choosing a ripe, sweet pineapple, see page 137. Serve the dish no longer than an hour after it's cooked. The bromelain (a naturally occurring enzyme) in the pineapple makes the shrimp turn mushy if allowed to sit for longer than that.

MAKES 6 SERVINGS

FOR THE FLAVORING PASTE

2 thick stalks fresh lemongrass

3 shallots (about 2 1/2 ounces/70 grams total), coarsely chopped

1 clove garlic, coarsely chopped

3 to 7 fresh red Holland chiles or other fresh long, red chiles such as Fresno or cayenne, stemmed and coarsely chopped

1 to 4 fresh green Thai chiles, stemmed and coarsely chopped (optional, but traditional for their heat)

1 piece fresh or thawed, frozen turmeric (page 92), 2 inches (5 centimeters) long, peeled and coarsely chopped (about 2 teaspoons), or 1 teaspoon ground turmeric

4 candlenuts (page 48) or unsalted macadamia nuts

3 tablespoons peanut oil

2 cups (about 13 ounces/370 grams) triangular fresh pineapple slices (each about 2 inches/ 5 centimeters long by 1 1/4 inches/3 centimeters thick; don't use skin or core)

2 cups (16 fluid ounces/500 milliliters) water

2 tablespoons sugar

3/4 teaspoon kosher salt

1 pound (455 grams) medium-sized shrimp in the shell, preferably with heads intact

2 firm, ripe small tomatoes such as Roma (about 6 ounces/170 grams total), cored and quartered

1 cup (8 fluid ounces/250 milliliters) unsweetened coconut milk

1. To make the flavoring paste, cut off the hard, brown bottom and the bristly, greenish top of each lemongrass stalk, which should leave you with a pale white-and-lilac piece about 5 inches (13 centimeters) long. Discard the 2 or 3 tough outer layers, and then cut the lemongrass pieces crosswise into slices 1/4 inch (6 millimeters) thick.

2. Place the lemongrass, shallots, garlic, chiles, turmeric, and candlenuts in a small food processor. Pulse until you have a smooth paste the consistency of creamy mashed potatoes. Make sure that the lemongrass is well pulverized. Coarsely ground pieces will be unpleasant in the final dish. If the paste won't purée properly and repeatedly creeps up the side of the processor instead of grinding, add up to 2 tablespoons water, 1 tablespoon at a time, periodically turning the processor off and scraping the unground portions down toward the blade.

3. Heat the oil in a 3- or 4-quart (3- or 4-liter) saucepan, Dutch oven, or soup pot over medium-low heat. Test to see if the oil is the right temperature by adding a pinch of the ground paste. The paste should sizzle slightly around the edges, not fry aggressively or sit motionless. When the oil is ready, add all the paste and sauté, stirring as needed to prevent scorching, until the garlic no longer smells raw and the paste begins to separate from the oil, 5 to 7 minutes.

4. Add the pineapple and stir well to combine. Add the water, sugar, and salt and raise the heat to medium. Bring the liquid to a gentle boil. Immediately reduce the heat to medium-low and simmer, uncovered, until the pineapple begins to lose its rawness and you can just puncture it with a fork without much resistance, about 5 minutes.

5. Add the shrimp and stir to combine. Continue cooking at a gentle simmer until the shrimp is pink and cooked through, about 4 minutes.

6. Add the tomatoes and simmer until they're no longer raw and you can just puncture them with a fork (but they aren't mushy or falling apart), 1 to 2 minutes.

7. Add the coconut milk and stir to combine. Cook, stirring constantly, until the coconut milk is heated through and has just begun to take in the essence of the flavoring paste, about 2 minutes. The dish will now be a beautiful bright orange. Taste for salt, and add a pinch more if needed.

8. Transfer to a wide, shallow serving bowl. Allow the dish to rest and cool for at least 10 minutes before eating. It will taste better.

MENU SUGGESTIONS

The rich, fiery taste of this dish makes it a great companion to milder ones, such as Nyonya Chicken and Potato Stew (page 281), Nyonya-Style Spiced Fried Chicken (page

285), Stir-fried Asian Greens with Garlic and Chiles (page 205), and rice. The traditional sambal accompaniment is Nyonya Sambal (page 120), which balances the sweetness of the pineapple.

STIR-FRIED SHRIMP SAMBAL
Sambal Udang
(MALAYSIA)

This Malaysian dish is my favorite shrimp dish from the region. It's a fiery-hot, ruby red stir-fry that goes well with rice or nothing at all. In Malaysia, small, whole unshelled shrimp are traditionally used for this dish; after cooking, their thin shells and heads become tender enough to eat. Small squid, cleaned and cut into 1 1/2-inch (4-centimeter) pieces, can be substituted for the shrimp, but I find that squid is trickier to cook, as it toughens quickly. I got this recipe from Norsiah, the wife of Mad Zan, a Malaysian fisherman. Norsiah makes it with shrimp that her husband catches, and as the couple eats, they can hear the Strait of Malacca lapping away just steps outside their front door.

MAKES 4 SERVINGS

FOR THE FLAVORING PASTE

1 teaspoon dried shrimp paste (page 65)

3 shallots (about 2 1/2 ounces/70 grams total), peeled and coarsely chopped

2 cloves garlic, coarsely chopped

5 to 10 fresh red Holland chiles or other fresh long, red chiles such as Fresno or cayenne, stemmed and coarsely chopped

3 candlenuts (page 48) or unsalted macadamia nuts

1 teaspoon palm sugar (page 79), thinly sliced, or dark brown sugar

1/2 teaspoon kosher salt

3 tablespoons peanut oil

1 pound (455 grams) medium-sized shrimp in the shell, preferably with heads intact

1. To make the flavoring paste, place the shrimp paste in the center of a 5-inch (13-centimeter) square of aluminum foil. Fold the edges of the foil over to form a small parcel, and press down with the heel of your hand to flatten the shrimp paste into a disk 1/4

inch (6 millimeters) thick. Heat a gas burner to medium-low or an electric burner to medium-high. Using a pair of tongs or 2 forks, place the sealed parcel directly on the heat source. Toast until the paste begins to smoke and release a burning, shrimpy smell, about 1 1/2 minutes. With the tongs or forks, turn the parcel over and toast the other side for another 1 1/2 minutes, then turn off the burner. Again using the tongs or forks, remove the parcel and let cool for 30 seconds to 1 minute. Carefully unwrap the foil; the edges of the disk should be black-brown and toasty and the center should be golden with some black-brown patches. Using a spoon, scrape the toasted shrimp paste into a small bowl and allow it to cool for another 30 seconds. Discard the foil.

2. Place the toasted shrimp paste, shallots, garlic, chiles, candlenuts, palm sugar, and salt in a small food processor. Pulse until you have a chunky-smooth paste the consistency of cooked oatmeal. Make sure not to overprocess this paste. Some bits and pieces of chile skin and slivers of shallot are fine. If the paste doesn't purée properly and repeatedly creeps up the side of the food processor instead of grinding, add up to 2 tablespoons water, 1 tablespoon at a time, periodically turning the processor off and scraping the unground portions down toward the blade as you go.

3. Heat the oil in a wok or 12-inch (30-centimeter) skillet (nonstick works best) over medium-low heat. Test to see if the oil is the right temperature by adding a pinch of the ground paste. The paste should sizzle slightly around the edges, not fry aggressively or sit motionless. When the oil is ready, add all the paste and sauté, stirring as needed to prevent scorching, until the shallots and garlic no longer smell raw and the paste begins to separate from the oil, 5 to 7 minutes. The aroma should be subtly sweet, not harsh and oniony, and the color should be a few shades darker than the raw paste.

4. Add the shrimp, then raise the heat to medium-high. Stir-fry, stirring constantly to combine the shrimp with the flavoring paste and to prevent scorching, until the shrimp are pink and just cooked through, 3 to 5 minutes. Taste a bit of the flavoring paste, and add a pinch more salt if needed.

5. Transfer to a serving plate and serve immediately.

MENU SUGGESTIONS

Try this pungent dish with Lemongrass-Scented Coconut Rice (page 176), Chicken Rendang with Cinnamon and Star Anise (page 278), Asiah's Eggplant Curry (page 229), and Acehnese Goat Curry (page 314).

BLACK PEPPER CRAB
Ketam Lada Hitam
(SINGAPORE)

⁓

Here's a popular, easy-to-make hawker-stall favorite from Singapore: stir-fried crab encrusted with a paste made of crushed peppercorns, garlic, turmeric, and ginger. It's a spicy, rustic dish, best eaten with lots of cold beer or iced tea to cool the piquancy of the peppercorns. Whole live crabs are typically used in Singapore, but I've found that this dish is easier to make with precooked crab in its shell, such as quartered and cleaned Dungeness crabs or king or snow crab legs.

MAKES 4 SERVINGS

FOR THE FLAVORING PASTE

4 tablespoons black peppercorns

8 cloves garlic, coarsely chopped

1 piece fresh or thawed, frozen turmeric (page 92), 3 inches (7.5 centimeters) long, peeled and coarsely chopped (about 1 tablespoon), or 2 teaspoons ground turmeric

1 piece fresh ginger, 3 inches (7.5 centimeters) long, peeled and thinly sliced against the grain (about 3 tablespoons)

3/4 teaspoon kosher salt

3 tablespoons peanut oil

3/4 cup (6 fluid ounces/175 milliliters) water

3 pounds (1.4 kilograms) cooked king crab or snow crab legs and claws, thawed, if frozen, and cracked or halved, or cooked Dungeness crabs, thawed, if frozen, and cleaned and quartered

1. Place the peppercorns in a small food processor and pulse until coarsely ground, about 30 seconds. Add the garlic, turmeric, and ginger and pulse until you have a relatively smooth paste. Don't worry if each peppercorn isn't fully ground; bits and pieces of pepper are fine. If the paste doesn't purée properly and repeatedly creeps up the side of the food processor instead of grinding, add up to 2 tablespoons water, 1 tablespoon at a time, periodically turning the processor off and scraping the unground portions down toward the blade as you go.

2. Heat the oil in a wok, Dutch oven, or 12-inch (30-centimeter) skillet (nonstick works best) over medium-low heat. Test to see if the oil is the right temperature by adding a pinch of the ground paste. The paste should sizzle slightly around the edges, not fry aggressively or sit motionless. When the oil is ready, add all the paste and sauté, stirring as needed to prevent scorching, until the garlic no longer smells raw and the paste begins to separate from the oil, 5 to 7 minutes.

3. Add the water and crab pieces and raise the heat to medium-high. Stir-fry the crab pieces, stirring them constantly with the spatula to combine them with the flavoring paste and to prevent scorching, until the crab pieces are hot and their surface is evenly coated with the flavoring paste, about 5 minutes.

4. Transfer the crab pieces to a large serving platter and serve immediately. Eat this delightfully messy dish with small hammers or nutcrackers and nut picks to remove the meat from the shells.

MENU SUGGESTIONS

You can serve this powerhouse dish with rice and other dishes, but frankly it pairs better with its traditional Singaporean accompaniments: plenty of ice-cold Tiger beer or sweetened iced tea with plenty of lemon.

ABOVE LEFT: *A Muslim schoolgirl in East Java, Indonesia.*

ABOVE CENTER: *People in Java believe that banyan trees are home to powerful spirits.*

ABOVE RIGHT: *Nutmeg fruits in Indonesia's Spice Islands; the fruits split open lengthwise, signaling their ripeness.*

11. POULTRY

Gatot, a forty-five-year-old vegetable vendor from Surabaya, Indonesia, whom I'd met through my friend Tanya Alwi, was at the wheel of his black minivan as we went hurtling through the East Javanese countryside. He zoomed fearlessly through village after village, swerving to avoid goats, chickens, people on bicycles, rice drying on the road, whatever stood in the way. But it was all for a good cause. We were in pursuit of what Gatot had promised me was the world's best *soto ayam*, a boldly spiced Indonesian chicken soup, and we didn't have a minute to spare. "I want to take you to my friend Achson, in the town of Lamongan," Gatot had said to me a few hours earlier in Surabaya. "They call him the Soto King. We must go quickly, though. He usually sells out each day by sunset." I'd fallen in love with the soup on my first trip to Indonesia in 1982. I wasn't going to pass up this opportunity to sample the best.

Soon we were driving into Lamongan, a laid-back city whose streets were filled with shady mango trees and more red-tiled buildings than I could count. We arrived at the main market, where, Gatot told me, the Soto King sold his famous soup from a small pushcart. It was five-thirty, and there wasn't a minute to spare. "Gatot!" Achson, a tall man in his late fifties, with big, thick hands, shouted when he saw us. "How are you? I haven't seen you in so long!" Gatot said hello to Achson and explained who I was.

"I'm so happy you've come," Achson said, turning to me. "But why have you arrived so late? I only have enough *soto* left for one small portion."

My heart sank. Who would be the lucky recipient of the soup? Gatot pulled me aside. "Mr. James," he said, placing an arm around my shoulder, "you take it. Who knows when you'll next come to Lamongan?" I smiled, making a mental note to remember him in my will. Achson ladled the soup into a bowl. I could smell its seductive aroma rising from a few feet away. I took a sip. It was intensely delicious, a warm rush of cumin, citrusy lemongrass, and sweet chicken. "*Enak sekali* [Really tasty]," I said. But I was deeply sad there wasn't more.

Achson studied my downcast expression. "I tell you what," he said. "Tomorrow is our *bumbu-bumbu* [flavoring paste] day. My wife and I make it once a week. Why don't you come to my house? You can watch us and I'll make some *soto* especially for you. It's not every day that I get a customer from America." I beamed from ear to ear.

Gatot and I arrived at Achson's home the next morning promptly at ten. The house was a small, pink stucco building neatly framed on two sides by potted lemongrass plants. We were greeted by Achson's wife, Renny, a smiling woman, also in her fifties and as tall as her husband. She led us through the house to an outdoor kitchen in the back that was shaded with a makeshift blue-tarp roof. Achson was seated on a small, low bench over a large stone mortar and pestle. He was just beginning to concoct his *bumbu-bumbu*. Tiny yellow songbirds occasionally darted down into the kitchen from nearby trees.

"This will be enough *bumbu-bumbu* for the week," Achson said as he began crushing a small mountain of spices in the mortar and pestle. I asked him if he could reveal the proportions he was using. "You'll have to turn to Renny for that information," he said, raising an eyebrow, as though there was more to the story. "She won't let me do the measuring."

Renny blushed. She put the chicken she was plucking on a counter, rinsed her hands, and walked to a small cache of metal canisters sitting on the floor. "My husband," she whispered to me, "has a fantasy that I am the boss. Actually, we are both the boss." She proceeded to dip her hands into the canisters and show me seemingly random amounts of spices: two handfuls of cumin seeds, three times as many coriander seeds, a satchel's worth of fresh turmeric, and so on. Like all of the region's great cooks, Renny measured by *agak-agak* (instinct), not set amounts.

Renny walked back to the counter and resumed plucking the chickens. There were three just-killed brown and red birds, each of which would soon end up in a pot already brimming with a broth seasoned by lemongrass and lime leaves. "The chicken is the most important element of *soto*," said Achson, taking a break from the mortar and pestle and looking up at me. "And good chicken is always *ayam kampong*." He was referring to the Indonesian version of free-range chicken, literally "village chicken," meaning antibiotic-free birds that had been allowed to roam at will in village backyards. "Lamongan cooks believe that a chicken's life essence penetrates the food in which the bird is used," Achson continued. "If a chicken has had a miserable life, it will result in a miserable dish." The chickens, feather free and gutted, were now simmering away in the pot, heads, feet, and all. I wasn't sure if they'd led happy lives, but even if they hadn't, I figured that they'd be grateful to wind up in a dish as delicious as this one promised to be.

Renny stirred the pot, keeping the stock cooking at a drowsy simmer. "Boiling the chickens," she said as she placed her spoon down, "will cause their flesh to toughen." Meanwhile, Achson scraped the now-ground flavoring paste onto a large plate. It was the color of curry powder, but far more aromatic. He poured a steady stream of coconut oil into a jumbo-sized wok and fired it up. As soon as the oil was hot, he added the *bumbu-bumbu* and quickly stirred it all around, careful not to let it scorch. The fragrance of spices immediately filled the air.

About forty minutes later, Renny had removed the chickens from the pot and was shredding the meat into fine strips with her hands. In spite of the speed at which she was working, she passed over nothing, discovering flesh secreted away even in the birds' bony shins. By the time she was finished, there was a pile of meat large enough to fill an enormous bowl. It looked and smelled good enough to eat just as it was. "My biggest customers are people who want to bring the soup home to eat it," Achson said. I told him the American term for this sacred eating tradition. "Takeout," he muttered to himself in English a few times as he spooned some of the sautéed flavoring paste into the stock. A moment later, Renny appeared at the pot and added the shredded chicken. She stuck the edge of a spoon into the stock, placed a drop of it onto the back of her hand, and tasted it. "More salt," she said definitively, then added a handful.

Although sometimes *soto* is garnished with *perkedel* (potato fritters), shrimp chips, halved hard-cooked eggs, and blanched bean sprouts, Achson told me he prefers to serve his without adornment, save for crisply fried shallots and finely chopped Chinese celery greens. "I think if a cook adds too many garnishes to his *soto*, he is hiding something from the customer," he said as he handed Gatot and me each a large bowl just off the stove. Each portion had been ladled over a mound of steamed white rice, forming a luscious chicken-rice soup. I inhaled the bowl deeply. It smelled of lemongrass and kaffir lime leaves. We dug in.

"Is it good?" Achson asked, anticipation flickering in his eyes.

It wasn't good. It was phenomenal, bursting with chicken, cumin, coriander, black pepper, and the grassy taste of celery greens. Achson was right. To embellish this soup with extra garnishes would have been an insult to its integrity. "I'll never eat *soto* again without thinking of this one," I said.

After we finished, Gatot and I stepped into his car, sated and smiling. From the window, we watched as Achson pushed a three-wheeled cart—his wooden *soto* pushcart—onto the driveway, Renny trailing right behind him. They would soon be heading to the market to sell their soup. They seemed a good match, I thought to myself, the King and Queen of Soto.

⟝

Fowl, especially chicken, is treated reverently in the kitchens of Indonesia, Malaysia, and Singapore. Cooks have devised countless colorful ways to prepare it, from Mien's Garlic Fried Chicken (page 283), a judiciously seasoned dish, to Nyonya Chicken and Potato Stew (page 281), with its complex layering of flavors. Cooks in the region can choose from two types of chickens. The first are factory-raised birds, which resemble the white-feathered varieties we know in the West (though theirs are significantly smaller). But the more popular type is *ayam kampong*, the chickens that Achson had raved about. These free-roaming birds are small, lithe, and colorful, with rust and gold plumage. They are prized for their clean, pure taste and firm, succulent texture, and around nearly every village home in the region you'll see an extended family of them pecking about down some well-worn footpath.

People who live in cities, such as Kuala Lumpur and Jakarta, buy live *ayam kampong* brought from the countryside to urban markets. When selecting a chicken, they choose one that's full of vim and vigor. "I look for a chicken that has a lot of fight in it," Rohati, my friend in Padang, Indonesia, told me one time with a slightly wicked laugh. Once selected, chickens are killed and plucked on the spot by the vendor. At home, cooks cut them into small pieces to suit the dish they're going to make (see page 50 to learn how to do this in your own kitchen).

Over the years, I've learned three methods from Indonesian, Malaysian, and Singaporean cooks for cooking chicken. The first, known as twice-cooking, is a two-step technique that probably originated in Java, Indonesia, and imparts a hearty taste and deep fragrance to the meat. (See page 104 for more information about twice-cooking.) The initial step involves gently simmering a cut-up chicken in a clear broth or coconut milk that's been flavored with lemongrass, coriander seeds, and *daun salam*, among other aromatics, until it's just a few beats shy of fully cooked. The chicken is then removed from the stock and grilled over a fire or deep-fried, which intensifies its taste and gives it a deliciously crispy exterior. This method is used for two recipes in this chapter, Javanese Grilled Chicken (page 289), which is tender and scrumptious, its skin crackly from the coating of Indonesian sweet soy sauce used as a marinade, and Grilled Coconut Chicken with Lemon Basil (page 292), a deeply flavorful dish, thanks to generous amounts of ginger and kaffir lime leaves in the simmering liquid.

The second method is slow-cooking a chicken to make a curry. Flavored with such spices and aromatics as cinnamon, cloves, coriander, cardamom, pepper, ginger, chiles, garlic, and shallots, this method draws exquisite flavor from the meat and renders the flesh supple and moist. Among the chicken curry recipes here are Javanese Chicken Curry (page 275) and West Sumatran Chicken Curry (page 277). Chicken Rendang with Cinnamon and Star Anise (page 278) is a dry-braised *rendang* variation in which the chicken is cooked until all the aromatic broth is absorbed into the meat.

The third method involves marinating a chicken and then deep-frying it. Mien's Garlic Fried Chicken (page 283) and Nyonya-Style Spiced Fried Chicken (page 285), both of which are cooked in this fashion, are easy-to-make, delicately seasoned dishes that go as well with Western-style meals as they do with Asian ones.

Soto, Achson's specialty and perhaps the most celebrated chicken dish of Indonesia, Malaysia, and Singapore, isn't associated with any particular cooking method. It's merely the Malay Archipelago's version of that universal favorite, chicken soup, made zesty with local ingredients. There are hundreds of regional variations on *soto*. The *soto* of Bandung, West Java, for instance, has soybeans in the broth, while Malaysian *soto* is often thickened with candlenuts. But of the many that I've sampled, Achson's version, reproduced here as The Soto King's Chicken Soup (below), stands out for its full-bodied flavor.

Duck, though not as popular as chicken, appears often in local dishes, especially in Bali and in the Nyonya cuisine of Malaysia and Singapore. In Bali, flocks of ducks are a common sight. You'll see them waddling up and down the muddy retaining walls that separate the island's signature rice paddies—until, that is, they're roasted over open fires or cooked in spicy curries. A Malaysian and Singaporean Nyonya favorite is Nyonya Duck Soup with Salted Mustard Greens (page 295), a pure and rejuvenating Chinese-style soup that's traditionally sipped between bitefuls of other dishes at meals.

THE SOTO KING'S CHICKEN SOUP

Soto Ayam Lamongan

(JAVA, INDONESIA)

~

Soto is a spiced chicken soup originally from Java. Indonesians often slurp it down next to the street hawker's pushcart where it was sold. But *soto* doesn't require a hawker's skills to prepare, and cooks regularly make it at home, too. Here is Achson's recipe. A quartered chicken is simmered in a stock seasoned with kaffir lime leaves and lemongrass. The chicken is then boned and the meat is returned to the stock along with a sautéed flavoring paste of garlic, shallots, turmeric, ginger, galangal, and candlenuts (which act as a subtle thickening agent). A generous amount of lime juice, squeezed in at the end, unites the flavors, making this vivid-tasting dish even more so. A wide range of garnishes, such as halved hard-cooked eggs, shrimp chips, and potato fritters, also often accompany *soto*, but I prefer mine the way Achson serves his, with nothing more than glass noodles (transparent noodles made of mung-bean starch; see Cook's Notes, page 274) and a sprinkle of Chinese celery greens and fried shallots.

MAKES 4 OR 5 SERVINGS WITHOUT RICE, OR 6 SERVINGS WITH RICE

2 tablespoons Crisp-Fried Shallots (page 84)

1 whole free-range chicken, 3 to 3 1/2 pounds (1.4 to 1.6 kilograms), quartered

2 quarts (2 liters) water (see Cook's Notes, page 274)

2 thick stalks fresh lemongrass, each tied into a knot (page 76)

6 whole fresh or thawed, frozen kaffir lime leaves

1 teaspoon kosher salt

FOR THE FLAVORING PASTE

1 teaspoon black peppercorns

1 1/2 tablespoons coriander seeds

2 teaspoons cumin seeds

5 shallots (about 3 3/4 ounces/110 grams total), coarsely chopped

3 cloves garlic, coarsely chopped

3 candlenuts (page 48) or unsalted macadamia nuts

1 piece fresh or thawed, frozen turmeric (page 92), 2 inches (5 centimeters) long, peeled

and coarsely chopped (about 2 teaspoons), or 1 1/2 teaspoons ground turmeric

1 piece fresh or thawed, frozen galangal, 2 inches (5 centimeters) long, peeled and thinly sliced against the grain (about 2 tablespoons; optional)

1 piece fresh ginger, 2 inches (5 centimeters) long, peeled and thinly sliced against the grain (about 2 tablespoons)

3 tablespoons peanut oil

1 small package (2 ounces/55 grams) glass noodles (see Cook's Notes, page 274)

Boiling water to cover glass noodles

1 tablespoon fresh lime juice

2 tablespoons finely chopped Chinese celery greens (page 55) or regular celery leaves

3 limes, quartered

1. Prepare the fried shallots and set aside.

2. Combine the chicken, 2 quarts (2 liters) of water, lemongrass, lime leaves, and salt in a 4-quart (4-liter) saucepan, Dutch oven, or soup pot. Place over medium-high heat and bring to a rolling boil. Using a large spoon, skim off the foam that rises to the top. Cover, reduce the heat to medium-low, and let the liquid cook at a lively simmer until the chicken is tender, about 45 minutes. Continue to skim off the foam every 10 minutes or so to yield a clear broth.

3. Meanwhile, make the flavoring paste. Place the peppercorns, coriander, and cumin in a small food processor. Pulse until the spices are ground to a dusty powder, about 2 minutes.

4. Add the shallots, garlic, candlenuts, turmeric, galangal (if using), and ginger to the ground spices. Pulse until you have a smooth paste the consistency of creamy mashed potatoes. If the paste won't purée properly and repeatedly creeps up the side of the processor instead of grinding, add up to 2 tablespoons water, 1 tablespoon at a time, periodically turning the processor off and scraping the unground portions down toward the blade.

5. Heat the oil in a 2-quart (2-liter) saucepan over medium-low heat. Test to see if the oil is the right temperature by adding a pinch of the ground paste. The paste should sizzle slightly around the edges, not fry aggressively or sit motionless. When the oil is ready, add all the paste and sauté, stirring as needed to prevent scorching, until the paste begins to separate from the oil and the aroma of coriander and cumin takes over, 5 to 7 minutes.

6. By now the chicken should be cooked through and just beginning to fall away from the bone. If it isn't, allow it to simmer for another 10 minutes or so. Remove and discard the lemongrass and lime leaves from the stock. Set the stock in the pot aside (don't discard it). Transfer the chicken quarters to a bowl and set them aside until they are cool enough to handle. When they are, tear the flesh and skin—discard the bones—into the finest pieces you can manage; this works best if you tear *with* the grain of the flesh, not against it. (You can discard the skin if you like, though it is traditionally used in *soto*.)

7. Add the flavoring paste and the chicken pieces to the stock and stir well to combine. Bring to a gentle boil over medium-high heat. Reduce the heat to medium-low and allow to simmer until the essence of the flavoring paste begins to bind with the stock, about 10 minutes.

8. Meanwhile, place the glass noodles in a bowl and cover them with boiling water. Let the noodles soak until they soften, 10 to 15 minutes. Once they're soft, hold the noodles in a tight bunch and, with a pair of kitchen shears or a knife, snip or cut them into pieces 4 to 5 inches (10 to 13 centimeters) long (longer pieces can be a bit tricky to eat, as the noodles are quite slippery). Drain the softened noodles into a colander and set aside.

9. Taste the simmering soup for salt, and add a pinch more if needed. Remove the pan from the heat, add the lime juice, and stir to combine. Taste once more for salt.

10. To serve the soup, you can divide the glass noodles among shallow, wide soup bowls (there will be enough soup for about 6 bowls), ladle the soup over them, and sprinkle the fried shallots and celery greens on top just before serving. My favorite serving method, however, is to add the noodles to the soup while it's still in the pot, and then transfer the soup to a tureen and garnish with the shallots and celery just before serving. In both cases, put the lime quarters at the center of the table for guests to squeeze into the soup as desired. Serve the *soto* warm, not piping hot, which will allow guests to discern its layered flavors more clearly. It will taste even more delicious reheated the next day.

COOK'S NOTES

When making *soto* (and Nyonya Duck Soup with Salted Mustard Greens, page 295), you'll achieve a tastier stock if you use bottled spring water or filtered tap water. This might sound extreme, but it's a timeworn tip I picked up from Achson, who swears that fresh-drawn well water is one of the key reasons his *soto* tastes so good. Since you've already taken the time and trouble to acquire the proper ingredients, why not consider water an equally important element, especially since it makes up more than half of this dish?

Called *mie sohun* in Malaysia and Indonesia, glass noodles are thin, vermicelli-like noodles made from the starch of the mung bean, the green-skinned pulse that eventually becomes a bean sprout. The noodles are white and opaque when dry, but become soft and translucent after they're soaked in boiling water for a few minutes. If you squint your eyes, the soaked noodles resemble strands of glass, hence their poetic-sounding name. They're virtually taste-less on their own, but they add texture to many soups and curries and are delicious when stir-fried. Glass noodles are sold dry in 2-ounce (55-gram) bags (though sometimes bigger bags are available) in all Asian markets. They're occasionally labeled cellophane noodles or bean threads. You can store them indefinitely in a dry, cool cupboard. Once you rehydrate them, though, use them the same day.

MENU SUGGESTIONS

Soto can be served as a soup course in soup bowls; as a dramatic main course, also in soup bowls; or as part of a meal built around rice (you can offer small bowls for guests if they wish to sip the soup instead of spooning it over their rice). If you serve *soto* as a compo-nent of a larger meal with rice, try Ching Lee's Braised Lemongrass Long Beans (page 218) and Garlic-Marinated Tempeh (page 322) as accompaniments. Since it doesn't have to be eaten the moment you've finished cooking it, *soto* makes an excellent buffet dish. A piping-hot pot of *soto* should remain warm enough to eat for at least 45 minutes. Place the fried shallots, celery greens, and lime quarters on the side for guests to garnish their own bowls.

JAVANESE CHICKEN CURRY
Opor Ayam
(JAVA, INDONESIA)

⁓

A gorgeous coconut-milk curry from Java, Indonesia, perfumed with lemongrass, ginger, cinnamon sticks, and coriander. It's one of the benchmark dishes by which Indonesian home cooks are judged. If a young cook's *opor ayam* is as rich and delicate as it should be, she is well on her way to becoming skilled in the kitchen. The dish is a perfect showcase for a high-quality free-range chicken. A whole bird, cut into small, bone-in serving pieces, will yield the best results, though whole chicken parts can be substituted without really compromising the taste of the dish. If you have the inclination to make them, fried shallots are traditionally strewn on top just before the dish is served.

Daun salam leaves, the seasoning herb prized in Indonesian cooking, helps give this dish its unique aroma. I've often seen bay leaves listed as a substitute for *daun salam* in recipe books on Indonesian cuisine. While bay leaves have an aggressively mentholated taste, *daun salam* leaves are subtle, with a faintly foresty flavor. The only thing the two herbs share in common is that they are both green leaves and grow on trees. If you are unable to find *daun salam* leaves, omit them. The dish will still taste exquisite.

MAKES 4 SERVINGS

2 tablespoons Crisp-Fried Shallots (page 84),
   optional

FOR THE FLAVORING PASTE

1 tablespoon coriander seeds

1 fresh red Holland chile or other fresh long, hot
   red chile such as Fresno or cayenne,
   stemmed and coarsely chopped (optional,
   but provides subtle heat and color)

6 shallots (about 5 ounces/140 grams),
   coarsely chopped

2 cloves garlic, coarsely chopped

1 piece fresh or thawed, frozen galangal,
   1 1/2 inches (4 centimeters) long, peeled
   and thinly sliced against the grain (about
   1 1/2 tablespoons; optional)

1 piece fresh ginger, 2 inches (5 centimeters)
   long, peeled and thinly sliced against the
   grain (about 2 tablespoons)

1 whole free-range chicken, 3 pounds (1.4 kilograms), or 2 1/2 pounds (1.2 kilograms) free-
range chicken breasts, wings, thighs, and/or
drumsticks (dark-meat pieces will result in a
tastier dish)

3 tablespoons peanut oil

2 pieces cinnamon stick, each 4 inches (10
centimeters) long

1 thick stalk fresh lemongrass, tied into a knot
(page 76)

5 whole fresh or thawed, frozen kaffir lime
leaves

4 whole *daun salam* leaves (page 64; optional)

2 cups (16 fluid ounces/500 milliliters)
unsweetened coconut milk

1 1/4 cups (10 fluid ounces/310 milliliters) water

3/4 teaspoon kosher salt

1. If you'll be garnishing this curry with fried shallots, fry them first and set aside.

2. Next, make the flavoring paste. Place the coriander in a small food processor. Pulse until it is ground to a dusty powder, about 2 minutes.

3. Add the chile, shallots, garlic, galangal (if using), and ginger, to the ground coriander. Pulse until you have a smooth paste the consistency of creamy mashed potatoes. If the paste won't purée properly and repeatedly creeps up the side of the processor instead of grinding, add up to 2 tablespoons water, 1 tablespoon at a time, periodically turning the processor off and scraping the unground portions down toward the blade. Set aside.

4. Rinse the chicken under cold running water and pat it dry with paper towels. If using a whole chicken, cut it into 16 pieces. (For instructions on how to do this, see page 50.) If using precut chicken parts, you can leave them whole. Set aside.

5. Heat the oil in a 3- or 4-quart saucepan, Dutch oven, or soup pot over medium-low heat. Test to see if the oil is the right temperature by adding a pinch of the ground paste. The paste should sizzle slightly around the edges, not fry aggressively or sit motionless. When the oil is ready, add all the paste and sauté, stirring as needed to prevent scorching, until the garlic and shallots no longer smell raw and the paste begins to separate from the oil, 5 to 7 minutes. Add the cinnamon, lemongrass, lime leaves, and *daun salam* leaves (if using) and stir to combine them with the flavoring paste. Continue sautéing until you can clearly smell the fragrance of cinnamon, about 1 minute.

6. Add the chicken and raise the heat to medium. Sauté the chicken in the flavoring paste, moving it around often with a large spoon or spatula to prevent sticking or scorching. Turn each piece so that it sautés in the oil and cook the pieces until fairly evenly golden brown, about 10 minutes. (You need not brown the chicken in 2 batches. It's fine if the

chicken is piled in 2 layers, as long as you adjust the pieces in the pot so they all eventually brown.)

7. Add 1 cup (8 fluid ounces/250 milliliters) of the coconut milk, the water, and the salt to the chicken. Stir well to combine, blending the flavoring paste with the liquids and scraping the bottom of the pot to bring up all the bits of flavor stuck to the surface. Bring to a low, steady simmer and let simmer uncovered, stirring occasionally, until the fats from the chicken and coconut milk have risen to the surface and the chicken is tender and cooked through but not falling off the bone, 40 to 50 minutes. You may need to lower and raise the heat occasionally if the simmer becomes too aggressive or too gentle. Don't allow the liquid to boil, however, or the chicken may toughen and the coconut milk may curdle. When the chicken is done, taste for salt and add a pinch more if needed.

8. Add the remaining 1 cup coconut milk and allow it to heat through and begin to take on the flavors of the curry, about 2 minutes. If there's too much oil floating on the surface of the curry for your taste, skim off some of it, but not too much, as it's intensely flavorful. Taste for salt once more.

9. Transfer the chicken and sauce to a shallow serving bowl. You can remove the cinnamon and the kaffir lime and *daun salam* leaves (if used), or you can leave them in the bowl to continue to season the dish. Allow the dish to rest and cool at room temperature for at least 20 minutes before eating, which will give the flavors time to blend and intensify. Just before serving, garnish the curry with the fried shallots (if using).

VARIATION: WEST SUMATRAN CHICKEN CURRY (*GULAI AYAM LADO HIJAU*)

To make a spicy-hot West Sumatran version of Javanese Chicken Curry, all you need to do is make a different flavoring paste. The other ingredients and cooking steps remain the same. An equivalent amount of Long Island duck—the whole bird cut into 16 pieces (follow the instructions for cutting up a chicken on page 50 for how to do this)—is an excellent substitute for the chicken, though you may need to cook it slightly longer until tender. To make the flavoring paste, in a small food processor combine the following spices and pulse until ground to a dusty powder: 2 teaspoons coriander seeds; 1 teaspoon cumin seeds; 1 teaspoon fennel seeds; 1/2 teaspoon whole cloves; 1 whole nutmeg, cracked open with a nutcracker or a heavy, blunt object such as the bottom of a glass measuring cup; 6 green cardamom pods, cracked open with the flat side of a knife (page 49), seeds reserved, and papery hulls discarded.

Add the following ingredients to the processor (do not remove the ground spices): 3 shallots (about 2 1/2 ounces/70 grams total), coarsely chopped; 4 cloves garlic, coarsely chopped; 5 to 25 fresh green Thai chiles, stemmed and coarsely chopped (the more you use, the more authentic the recipe!); 1 piece fresh ginger, 2 inches (5 centimeters) long, peeled and thinly sliced against the grain (about 2 tablespoons); 5 candlenuts (page 48) or unsalted macadamia nuts; and 1 piece fresh or thawed, frozen turmeric (page 92), 2 inches (5 centimeters) long, peeled and coarsely chopped (about 2 teaspoons), or 1 1/2 teaspoons ground turmeric. Pulse until you have a smooth, creamy paste. Proceed with cooking as directed in step 5 for Javanese Chicken Curry. Omit the fried shallots garnish; they'll throw off the balance of flavors.

MENU SUGGESTIONS

A silky-rich curry like this one is best served with plain steamed rice or country-style French or Italian bread for mopping up its sauce. Avoid serving it with another dish containing coconut milk, which would be a conflict of interest. Instead, spare dishes, such as Stir-fried Asian Greens with Garlic and Chiles (page 205), Stir-fried Shrimp Sambal (page 262), or Tempeh Sambal with Lemon Basil (page 324), will work best. Any of the sambals in chapter 6 also make excellent accompaniments. All of these suggestions would also work for the spicy West Sumatran variation.

CHICKEN RENDANG WITH CINNAMON AND STAR ANISE
Rendang Ayam
(MALAYSIA)

Conventional Western kitchen wisdom dictates that the longer you cook chicken, the drier its flesh becomes. The reverse is true with this dish, a Malaysian twist on Sumatra's Beef Rendang (page 304; also see page 102 for more information on *rendang* cooking): the longer the chicken simmers, the more succulent and moist it becomes—even, surprisingly, the breast meat. I got this recipe—crispy-skinned pieces of chicken dry-braised in a powerfully spiced coconut-milk stock—from Yuni, a twenty-four-year-old home cook from Kelantan, Malaysia. "My mother always taught me to be bold with spicing," she told me. "She said it honors our ancestors." Watching the dish cook, from its soupy, coconut-milk-curry-like start to its pan-seared finish, is a study in the alchemy of braising. Use a whole chicken, as opposed to chicken parts. A 3-pound (1.4-kilogram) free-range fryer, its firm, tight flesh cut into 16 bone-in pieces, will withstand long cooking better than a larger bird. Avoid using a previously frozen chicken, as freezing traps water molecules in the bird's flesh, which may cause the meat to become mushy during the slow cooking that this recipe requires. Note that the flavoring paste in this recipe is sautéed before the coconut milk is added, an exception to the usual sequence for a *rendang* dish.

MAKES 4 SERVINGS

FOR THE FLAVORING PASTE

3 thick stalks fresh lemongrass

5 shallots (about 3 3/4 ounces/110 grams total), coarsely chopped

3 cloves garlic, coarsely chopped

1 piece fresh or thawed, frozen turmeric (page 92), 2 inches (4 centimeters) long, peeled and coarsely chopped (about 2 teaspoons), or 1 1/2 teaspoons ground turmeric

1 piece fresh or thawed, frozen galangal, 1 1/2 inches (4 centimeters) long, peeled and thinly sliced (about 1 1/2 tablespoons; optional)

2 to 10 small dried red chiles such as árbol, stemmed

1 whole free-range chicken, 3 to 3 1/2 pounds (1.4 to 1.6 kilograms)

3 tablespoons peanut oil

2 pieces cinnamon sticks, each 4 inches (10 centimeters) long

4 whole star anise

6 green cardamom pods, cracked open with the flat side of a knife (page 49)

2 1/2 cups (20 fluid ounces/625 milliliters) unsweetened coconut milk

1 piece *asam gelugor* (page 43; optional, but provides a subtly sour note to an otherwise sweetish dish)

1 teaspoon sugar

4 whole fresh or thawed, frozen kaffir lime leaves

3/4 teaspoon kosher salt

1. First, make the flavoring paste. Cut off the hard, brown bottom and the bristly, greenish top of each lemongrass stalk, which should leave you with pale white-and-lilac pieces about 5 inches (13 centimeters) long. Discard the 2 or 3 tough outer layers, and then cut the lemongrass pieces crosswise into slices 1/4 inch (6 millimeters) thick and set aside.

2. Place the lemongrass, shallots, garlic, turmeric, galangal, and chiles in a small food processor. Pulse until you have a chunky-smooth paste the consistency of cooked oatmeal. Make sure that the lemongrass is well pulverized. Coarsely ground pieces will be unpleasant in the final dish. If the paste won't purée properly and repeatedly creeps up the side of the processor instead of grinding, add up to 2 tablespoons water,

1 tablespoon at a time, periodically turning the processor off and scraping the unground portions down toward the blade. Set aside.

3. Rinse the chicken under cold running water and pat it dry with paper towels. Cut it into 16 pieces. (For instructions on how to do this, see page 50.) Set aside.

4. Heat the oil in a 12-inch (30-centimeter) skillet (nonstick works best) over medium-low heat. Add the cinnamon, star anise, and cardamom and sauté, stirring often, until you can smell their combined fragrances wafting up from the pan, about 2 minutes. Test to see if the oil is the right temperature for sautéing the flavoring paste by adding a pinch of the paste. It should sizzle slightly around the edges, not fry aggressively or sit motionless. When the oil is ready, add all the paste and sauté, stirring as needed to prevent scorching, until the garlic no longer smells raw and the paste begins to separate from the oil, 5 to 7 minutes.

5. Add the coconut milk, *asam gelugor* (if using), sugar, lime leaves, and salt. Stir well to combine and bring to a gentle boil. Reduce the heat to medium-low and cook at a slow, steady bubble, uncovered and stirring every 5 minutes, until the liquid has reduced by about one-fourth, about 20 minutes. Never allow the coconut milk to boil, or it may curdle. You'll probably need to adjust the heat periodically to maintain an even simmer.

6. Add the chicken to the coconut milk and stir well to combine. Continue to simmer gently, uncovered and stirring every 10 minutes or so to prevent the chicken from sticking to the bottom of the pan, until the liquid has reduced by about 95 percent and is the consistency of thick pea soup. This will take from 1 to 1 1/2 hours, depending on how hot the fire is and the richness of the coconut milk. Taste for salt, and add a pinch more if needed. If there's an excessive amount of oil in the pan at this point—say, more than 1/2 cup (4 fluid ounces/125 milliliters) because either the chicken or the coconut milk was exceptionally high in fat—remove it with a large spoon until only about 1/3 cup (2 1/2 fluid ounces/75 milliliters) remains. Otherwise, the final dish might be too oily for some diners. (Don't discard the removed oil—it's excellent for sautéing boiled, halved small new potatoes.)

7. Reduce the heat to low (the chicken and the remaining sauce are prone to scorching) and allow the chicken to brown slowly in the rendered fat. (The fat may be foamy at this point, but it will settle down when the cooking stops.) Stir every 5 minutes or so to prevent sticking and scorching, being careful not to break the chicken apart. Continue sautéing the chicken until it is a medium golden brown—the color of toffee—about 25 minutes longer. The surface of the chicken should be barely moist and have an appetizing oily sheen.

8. Transfer the chicken to a serving dish and let rest for at least 10 minutes before serving. You can discard the whole spices, *asam gelugor* (if used), and lime leaves, if you like. Don't serve this dish too hot or too cold. Warm room temperature is the best showcase for its intensely aromatic flavors.

MENU SUGGESTIONS

This dish is traditionally served with steamed white rice, a spicy, soupy dish such as Fragrant Fish Stew with Lime and Lemon Basil (page 240), and a sweet-tart pickled dish, such as Sweet-Sour Cucumber and Carrot Pickle with Turmeric (page 130).

NYONYA CHICKEN AND POTATO STEW
Ayam Pong Teh
(MALAYSIA)

Here's a savory-sweet Nyonya classic from Malaysia flavored with double-black soy sauce, palm sugar, and sweet soybean paste. Sugarcane juice forms the stew's liquid base, but the stock is, surprisingly, ultimately only subtly sweet. The recipe comes from my friend Josephine Chua in Malacca. She often fries the potatoes until golden brown before adding them to the stock, giving the dish extra depth. If you decide to do this, add the potatoes just a minute or two before removing the chicken from the fire, as they won't need to cook to become tender. Josephine is a staunch traditionalist when it comes to all things culinary. She even thinks the food processor I use to make this dish is treasonous. My opinion? Not all modernizations are bad.

Look for sugarcane juice in health-food stores or in Asian markets, where it's available in bottles, cans, boxes, or, occasionally, fresh. Seek brands with no added sweeteners or artificial flavorings. Water can be substituted if you can't find sugarcane juice, though the dish won't taste as delicious.

MAKES 4 SERVINGS

5 shallots (about 3 3/4 ounces/110 grams total), coarsely chopped

5 cloves garlic, coarsely chopped

1 whole free-range chicken, 3 to 3 1/2 pounds
(1.4 to 1.6 kilograms), or 3 pounds (1.4 kilograms) free-range chicken thighs and/or
drumsticks

6 tablespoons (3 fluid ounces/90 milliliters)
peanut oil

4 tablespoons sweet soybean paste (page 88)

2 to 3 tablespoons double-black soy sauce
(page 87), depending on how salty you want
the dish

2 tablespoons palm sugar (page 79), thinly
sliced, or dark brown sugar

3 cups (24 fluid ounces/750 milliliters) fresh
or canned sugarcane juice (see headnote)
or water

4 medium-sized waxy potatoes (about
1 pound/455 grams) such as Maine
or Yukon Gold

Kosher salt (optional)

1. Place the shallots and garlic in a small food processor and pulse until you have a smooth paste. If the paste won't purée properly and repeatedly creeps up the side of the processor instead of grinding, add up to 2 tablespoons water, 1 tablespoon at a time, periodically turning the processor off and scraping the unground portions down toward the blade. Set aside.

2. Rinse the chicken under cold running water and pat it dry with paper towels. If using a whole chicken, cut it into 16 pieces. (For instructions on how to do this, see page 50.) If using precut chicken parts, you can leave them whole. Set aside.

3. Heat the oil in a 3- or 4-quart (3- or 4-liter) saucepan, Dutch oven, or soup pot over medium-low heat. Test to see if the oil is the right temperature by adding a pinch of the shallot-garlic paste. The paste should sizzle slightly around the edges, not fry aggressively or sit motionless. When the oil is ready, add all the paste and sauté, stirring as needed to prevent scorching, until the shallots and garlic no longer smell raw and the paste is limp and just beginning to turn golden, 3 to 4 minutes. Take care not to brown or burn the shallot-garlic paste, reducing the heat if necessary. Add the soybean paste, double-black soy sauce, and palm sugar and stir well to combine, mashing the palm sugar with the back of the spatula. Cook until the palm sugar has dissolved and the mixture begins to bubble, 1 to 2 minutes.

4. Add the chicken pieces and the sugarcane juice. Stir well with a large spoon to combine the liquid with the sautéed shallot-garlic paste and the soybean paste. Raise the heat to high and bring the liquid to a boil. Immediately reduce the heat to medium-low so that the liquid soon reaches a gentle simmer. Continue to cook uncovered, at a very slow bubble, stirring occasionally.

5. Meanwhile, peel the potatoes and trim away any green or bruised spots. Slice each potato in half lengthwise and then cut each half lengthwise into thirds, yielding 6

wedges from each potato. If you're using potatoes no larger than 2 inches (5 centimeters) in diameter, just halve them lengthwise. Set aside.

6. After the stew has cooked for 40 minutes, add the cut-up potatoes. Continue to cook at a slow bubble until the chicken is tender and cooked through and the potato wedges are fork-tender but not mushy or falling apart, about 30 to 45 minutes. The longer this dish cooks, the more delicious it will taste. Taste for salt, and add a pinch if needed. (The soy sauce will probably add enough salt to the dish.) If there are more than a few tablespoons of oil on the surface of the stew, you may want to skim some of it off—it's up to you.

7. Transfer the chicken, potatoes, and all the liquid to a wide serving bowl. Allow the dish to rest at room temperature for at least 30 minutes before serving to let the flavors develop. Serve the dish warm, not piping hot, to better show off its flavors.

MENU SUGGESTIONS

Ayam pong teh is traditionally paired with Nyonya Sambal (page 120) and steamed white rice (page 173). Other fine accompaniments are Stir-fried Asian Greens with Garlic and Chiles (page 205) and a dry fish dish such as Pan-Seared Tamarind Tuna (page 254, or the shrimp variation, page 255).

MIEN'S GARLIC FRIED CHICKEN
Ayam Goreng
(SPICE ISLANDS, INDONESIA)

⌒

Of the many versions of fried chicken I've eaten in Indonesia, this is my favorite—crispy and toffee brown on the outside, sweet and succulent on the inside, thanks to its unusual prefrying marinade of garlic and palm vinegar. The first time I tasted it—in a hot Jakarta kitchen in the early 1980s—I was startled. Mien Alwi, the then-fifteen-year-old sister-in-law of my friend Tanya Alwi, had cooked it. "Wow—how did you make this?" I asked. She looked at me with her big doe eyes and retreated shyly to the next room. It took me a few weeks to convince her to give me the recipe. Boy, was I happy when I did.

MAKES 4 OR 5 SERVINGS

1 whole free-range chicken, 3 to 3 1/2 pounds
(1.4 to 1.6 kilograms), or 3 pounds (1.4 kilograms) free-range chicken wings, thighs,
and/or drumsticks

8 cloves garlic, peeled and smashed until juicy
with the flat side of a knife

1 cup (8 fluid ounces/250 milliliters) palm,
cider, or rice vinegar

1 1/2 teaspoons kosher salt

Peanut oil for frying

1. Rinse the chicken under cold running water and pat it dry with paper towels. If using a whole chicken, cut it into 10 pieces. (For instructions on how to do this, see page 50.) If using precut chicken pieces, you can leave them whole. Set the chicken aside.

2. In a large nonreactive bowl, combine the garlic, vinegar, and salt. Add the chicken pieces and combine them well with the mixture. Let the chicken marinate, uncovered, at room temperature for 1 to 2 hours, stirring once or twice to make sure that the marinade coats every piece. (Because the chicken has been cut up, some blood from the meat will be absorbed into the marinade, causing the pieces to appear dull and colorless. Don't worry, however, as they'll still fry up crisp and golden brown.)

3. Remove the chicken pieces from the marinade and pat them thoroughly dry with paper towels, gently squeezing each piece to remove excess liquid. (If the chicken isn't well dried when you place it in the hot oil, it will splatter wildly.) Set aside.

4. Pour oil to a depth of 1 inch (2.5 centimeters) into a 12-inch (30-centimeter) skillet and place over medium to medium-high heat until hot but not smoking (about 365°F/185°C). To test the temperature of the oil, drop in a small cube of bread. The oil should bubble around the cube and the cube should turn golden brown in 15 to 20 seconds. When the oil is ready, stand back from the stove and gently slide as many of the chicken pieces into the hot oil as will fit without touching. (You'll probably need to fry the chicken in 2 batches.) Fry on the first side until deep golden brown and crispy, about 10 minutes; the timing will depend on how hot the oil is. Turn the chicken pieces over with 2 forks or a pair of tongs and continue to fry them. You may need to raise and lower the heat a few times to main-tain the proper frying temperature. The oil should always be bubbling vigorously. If the oil surrounding the chicken is motionless, the oil temperature is too low and the chicken may come out greasy. It should take 20 to 25 minutes total to fry the chicken. If you are not sure if the chicken is cooked through, test it by poking a fork into the thickest portion and then pressing down on it. The juices that are released should run clear, not pink.

5. Remove the chicken pieces with the forks or tongs to a wire rack or paper towels and let drain for a few minutes before transferring them to a serving platter. Serve promptly—the chicken will be at its most scrumptious while still hot.

MENU SUGGESTIONS

This dish goes well with Lemongrass-Scented Coconut Rice (page 176); a brothy vegetable curry, such as Green Beans with Coconut Milk (page 216) or Asiah's Eggplant Curry (page 229); a sambal, such as Nyonya Sambal (page 120) or Javanese Sambal (page 119); and a sweet-sour pickle, such as Javanese Cucumber and Carrot Pickle (page 132).

NYONYA-STYLE SPICED FRIED CHICKEN
Inche Kabin
(MALAYSIA)

Here's a signature Nyonya dish in which a cut-up chicken is marinated in a cupoard's worth of spices and then deep-fried. It is one of the great chicken dishes of the East. After you've made the marinade with this particular ratio of flavorings once or twice, you can experiment and adjust them to your liking. Would you prefer a sweeter dish? Increase the amount of fennel and coriander. Would you like a spicier one? Increase the black pepper and chiles. This dish is traditionally served with a dipping sauce made with Worcestershire sauce and fresh lime juice.

MAKES 4 OR 5 SERVINGS

1 whole free-range chicken, 3 to 3 1/2 pounds (1.4 to 1.6 kilograms), or 3 pounds (1.4 kilograms) free-range chicken wings, thighs, and/or drumsticks

FOR THE MARINADE

1 piece cinnamon stick, 6 inches (15 centimeters) long, broken into 1/2-inch (12-millimeter) pieces

2 to 5 small dried red chiles such as árbol, stemmed

1 tablespoon coriander seeds

1 teaspoon cumin seeds

1 teaspoon fennel seeds

1 teaspoon black peppercorns

2 teaspoons ground turmeric

2 teaspoons sugar

2 teaspoons kosher salt

5 shallots (about 3 3/4 ounces/110 grams total), coarsely chopped

1/2 cup (4 fluid ounces/125 milliliters) unsweetened coconut milk

Peanut oil for frying

Nyonya Dipping Sauce (page 125)

1. Rinse the chicken under cold running water and pat it dry with paper towels. If using a whole chicken, cut it into 16 pieces. (For instructions on how to do this, see page 50.) If using precut chicken parts, you can leave them whole. Set aside.

2. Now make the marinade. Place the cinnamon, chiles, coriander, cumin, fennel, pepper, and turmeric in a small food processor. Pulse until ground to a dusty powder, about 2 to 3 minutes.

3. Add the sugar, salt, and shallots to the ground spices and pulse until you have a smooth paste the consistency of creamy mashed potatoes. If the paste won't purée properly and repeatedly creeps up the side of the processor instead of grinding, add up to 2 tablespoons water, 1 tablespoon at a time, periodically turning the processor off and scraping the unground portions down toward the blade.

4. In a large nonreactive bowl roomy enough to hold all the cut chicken, combine the ground paste with the coconut milk. Stir the mixture well to combine, making sure that there are no lumps of paste. Add the chicken pieces and stir well to cover every piece of chicken with the marinade.

5. Cover the bowl and marinate the chicken in the refrigerator for at least 3 hours, stirring once or twice to make sure that the marinade coats every piece. (If you can spare the time, marinate the chicken overnight. This will yield the tastiest dish.) About 30 minutes before you're ready to deep-fry the chicken, remove it from the refrigerator so it can come to room temperature.

6. Remove the chicken pieces from the marinade and thoroughly pat them dry with paper towels, gently squeezing each piece to remove excess liquid. (If the chicken isn't well dried when you place it in the hot oil, the oil will splatter wildly.) Set aside.

7. Pour oil to a depth of 1 inch (2.5 centimeters) into a 12-inch (30-centimeter) skillet and place over medium to medium-high heat until hot but not smoking (about 365°F/185°C). To test the temperature of the oil, drop in a small cube of bread. The oil should bubble around the cube and the cube should turn golden brown in 15 to 20 seconds. When the oil is ready, stand back from the stove and gently slide as many of the chicken pieces into the hot oil as will fit without touching. (You'll probably need to fry the chicken in 2 batches.) Fry on the first side until deep golden brown and crispy, about 10 minutes; the timing will depend on how hot the oil is. Turn the chicken pieces over

with 2 forks or a pair of tongs and continue to fry them. You may need to raise and lower the heat a few times to maintain the proper frying temperature. The oil should always be bubbling vigorously. If the oil surrounding the chicken is motionless, the oil temperature is too low and the chicken may come out greasy. It should take 20 to 25 minutes total to fry the chicken. If you're not sure if the chicken is cooked through, test it by poking a fork into the thickest portion and then pressing down on it. The juices that are released should run clear, not pink. Be careful not to overcook the chicken to the point that the bits of marinade clinging to the surface start to blacken, or the dish may taste bitter.

8. Remove the chicken pieces with the forks or tongs to a wire rack or paper towels and let drain for a few minutes before transferring them to a serving platter. Serve promptly along with the dipping sauce. The chicken will be at its most delicious while still hot.

MENU SUGGESTIONS

Serve this dish with steamed white rice and dishes that will accentuate its spicing, such as Stir-fried Water Spinach, Nyonya Style (page 213), Padang Fish Curry (page 244), and Sweet-Sour Cucumber and Carrot Pickle with Turmeric (page 130).

KEVIN'S SPICED ROAST CHICKEN WITH POTATOES, PENANG STYLE

(PENANG, MALAYSIA)

An uncommonly documented offshoot of Malaysian and Singaporean cooking is the cooking of the Eurasians, locals whose ancestry is part British (or, occasionally, Dutch, or both). This is a Eurasian classic: chicken marinated in regular and double-black soy sauce, Worcestershire sauce, bay leaves, and Asian spices and then roasted in a hot oven with butter, potatoes, and small onions. It's a beautiful fusion of East and West, traditionally served at Christmas banquets, though it's delicious any time of the year. The recipe comes from Kevin Peterson, who lives in Kuala Lumpur, Malaysia, but learned how to cook the dish when he lived in Georgetown, his hometown.

MAKES 4 SERVINGS

1 whole free-range chicken, 3 1/2 pounds
(1.4 kilograms)

1/3 cup (2 1/2 fluid ounces/75 milliliters) soy
sauce

2 tablespoons double-black soy sauce (page
87)

1 teaspoon Worcestershire sauce

3 bay leaves

2 pieces cinnamon stick, each 4 inches
(10 centimeters) long

6 whole cloves

5 small red or yellow onions (about 1
pound/455 grams total), each no more than
2 1/2 inches (6 centimeters) long, halved

1 1/2 teaspoons coarsely crushed black pepper

2 tablespoons unsalted butter, softened

1 1/2 pounds (680 grams) small potatoes such
as Yukon Gold, Peruvian blue, or Maine, no
more than 1 1/2 inches (4 centimeters) in
diameter

1. Remove and discard the fat inside the chicken (reserve the head and feet to use in stock if they were attached). Rinse the chicken and thoroughly pat it dry inside and out with paper towels. Tuck the wingtips behind the shoulders.

2. Place the chicken in a bowl large enough to hold it comfortably. Pour both soy sauces and the Worcestershire sauce over it. Add the bay leaves, cinnamon sticks, cloves, and onions. Using your hands or a large spoon, turn the chicken a few times, making sure that some of the liquid, spices, and a few onion halves are slipped inside the cavity. Rub the inside and outside of the chicken with the pepper. Let the chicken marinate, uncovered, at room temperature for 1 to 2 hours. Turn the bird over every 15 minutes or so to distribute the marinade evenly. Its skin will darken a few shades from the soy sauces.

3. Toward the end of the marinating, preheat the oven to 450°F (220°C).

4. Place the chicken, breast side up, in a shallow roasting pan. Scatter the onions around the chicken, making sure that 1 or 2 halves remain inside the cavity. Rub the chicken inside and out with the softened butter. (I like to rub some underneath the breast skin as well, which helps make the breast meat juicier.) Pour the remaining marinade over the chicken, placing the cinnamon sticks and a few of the cloves inside the cavity. Cover the pan loosely with aluminum foil.

5. Roast the chicken for 20 minutes, then turn it over. Tilt the pan toward you and, using a large spoon or baster, baste the chicken and its cavity with the pan juices. Cover the pan once more with the foil and continue roasting for another 20 minutes.

6. Meanwhile, scrub the potatoes but don't peel them. Fill a 3-quart saucepan three-fourths full with water and bring to a boil over high heat. Add the potatoes and cook at a rolling boil until they are just tender when pierced with a fork, 5 to 10 minutes. Drain the potatoes well in a colander.

7. Add the cooked potatoes to the roasting pan. Combine them gently with the onions already in the pan and baste them well with the pan juices. Turn the chicken over again (it should be breast side up this time) and baste it once more. Continue roasting the chicken, uncovered now so that it can brown just a bit, until it's cooked. The total cooking time will range from 1 hour and 10 minutes to 1 1/2 hours. To test for doneness, using a fork, pierce the skin at the thigh joint and press down gently. The juices should have only the faintest tinge of pink. Or, you can insert an instant-read thermometer into the thickest part of the thigh, not touching the bone. The chicken is ready when the thermometer registers 170°F (75°C).

8. Place the chicken on a serving platter. Pour half of the pan juices over it and allow the chicken to rest for at least 10 minutes before carving (this allows time for the juices to be absorbed by the flesh). Place the potatoes and onions around the chicken or in a serving bowl. Pour the remaining pan juices over the potatoes and onions. This chicken is best when served slightly warm. The flavors will be more pronounced and the flesh juicier.

MENU SUGGESTIONS

Kevin Peterson suggests serving this chicken as you would an English holiday roast, with boiled peas and roasted beets, or serving it Malaysian style, with steamed white rice, a soupy, coconut-milk–based vegetable curry, such as Green Beans with Coconut Milk (page 216); Nyonya Sambal (page 120); and Sweet-Sour Cucumber and Carrot Pickle with Turmeric (page 130). Either way, it's stunning.

JAVANESE GRILLED CHICKEN

Ayam Panggang Jawa
(CENTRAL JAVA, INDONESIA)

Similar to chicken teriyaki, this Javanese dish gets its complex taste from its unconventional cooking method: the chicken is first simmered in a broth infused with garlic, coriander, *daun salam* leaves, and galangal, then marinated, and finally grilled. It's important not to overcook the chicken when simmering it. Your aim is to flavor it, not cook it completely. By the time it reaches the table, the chicken has taken on three enticing layers of flavor: the coriander-based broth, the sweet soy marinade, and the smoke of the grill. Although grilling over an outdoor fire will render a more intense-tasting dish, oven broiling works fine, too. Ibu

Suparman, a home cook from Yogyakarta, Central Java, gave me this recipe in exchange for bay leaves and oregano, two exotic ingredients she was having a hard time finding in Java and that I mailed to her as soon as I got home. It was perhaps the best swap I've ever made.

MAKES 4 SERVINGS

FOR THE BROTH

4 cups (32 fluid ounces/1 liter) water

3 cloves garlic, peeled and bruised until juicy with the flat side of a knife

7 whole *daun salam* leaves (page 64; optional)

2 tablespoons coriander seeds

1 piece fresh or thawed, frozen galangal, 2 inches (5 centimeters) long, peeled and cut into slices 1/4 inch (6 millimeters) thick (about 2 tablespoons; optional)

2 teaspoons kosher salt

1 whole free-range chicken, 3 to 3 1/2 pounds (1.4 to 1.6 kilograms), or 3 pounds (1.4 kilograms) free-range chicken wings, thighs, and/or drumsticks

FOR THE MARINADE

1 tablespoon coriander seeds

2 cloves garlic, coarsely chopped

2 tablespoons peanut oil

1/2 cup (4 fluid ounces/125 milliliters) Indonesian sweet soy sauce (page 72)

4 tablespoons water

1. To make the broth, in a 3- or 4-quart (3- or 4-liter) saucepan, Dutch oven, or soup pot, combine the water, garlic, *daun salam* leaves (if using), coriander seeds, galangal (if using), and salt. Bring to a boil over high heat, reduce the heat to medium, cover, and simmer intensely for 10 minutes to allow the flavors to develop.

2. Meanwhile, rinse the chicken under cold running water and pat it dry with paper towels. If using a whole chicken, cut it into 10 pieces. (For instructions on how to do this, see page 50.) If using precut chicken parts, you can leave them whole.

3. Add the chicken pieces to the pan, raise the heat to medium-high, and bring to a boil. Immediately reduce the heat to medium-low and simmer the chicken gently, stirring occasionally, until it's three-fourths cooked, about 30 minutes. It should be tender and just no longer raw, but not mushy or falling off the bone. Keep in mind that it will be grilled or broiled later.

4. While the chicken is simmering, make the marinade. Place the coriander in a small food processor. Pulse until it's ground to a dusty powder, about 2 minutes. Add the garlic, oil, sweet soy sauce, and water to the coriander. Pulse until the garlic is pulverized, about 2 minutes. No shards or slivers should be visible.

5. Using a slotted spoon, transfer the chicken pieces from the pan to a large nonreactive bowl. Pour the marinade over the hot chicken, making sure that every piece is well coated. Allow the chicken to marinate, uncovered, at room temperature for 30 minutes to 1 hour, turning the chicken pieces every 10 minutes to make sure they are evenly covered with the marinade. (Alternatively, you can marinate the chicken overnight, covered, in the refrigerator. Bring the marinated chicken to room temperature before proceeding to the next step.)

6. **To cook the chicken on a grill,** first prepare a medium-hot charcoal fire and oil the grill rack liberally. When the fire is ready (it may take up to 20 minutes), using tongs or 2 forks, place each chicken piece, fleshy side up (or fleshier side up if using drumsticks and wings), on the grill rack 5 to 7 inches (13 to 18 centimeters) from the fire and baste each piece with about 1 tablespoon of the marinade. Don't discard the marinade. Grill the chicken until each piece is crisp and nicely charred, about 5 minutes. Turn each piece with the tongs or forks and baste again; discard any unused marinade. Continue grilling the chicken until the second side is crisp and charred, an additional 5 minutes.

   To cook the chicken in a broiler, position a rack so that the chicken will be 3 inches (7.5 centimeters) from the heat source and preheat the oven for at least 5 minutes. Line a half-sheet pan with aluminum foil and place each piece of chicken fleshy side up (or fleshier side up if using drumsticks and wings) on the pan. Don't discard the marinade. Slide the pan under the broiler. Broil until the chicken begins to brown and to develop charred spots, 4 to 5 minutes. Baste each piece with about 1 tablespoon of the marinade. Continue to broil until each piece is deep reddish brown and crispy, another 2 to 5 minutes. Turn each piece with tongs or 2 forks and repeat the same process: broil, baste, and broil again, until each piece is deep reddish brown, crispy, and lightly covered with charred spots. The timing should be about the same. You should have finished all of the marinade; if not, discard the rest.

7. Using tongs, transfer the chicken pieces to a serving dish and allow them to rest for at least 10 minutes before serving—if you can wait that long.

MENU SUGGESTIONS

This sweetish, mild grilled chicken complements a number of dishes in this book. Consider serving it along with Sweet-Sour Cucumber and Carrot Pickle with Turmeric (page 130); a brothy dish, such as Javanese Spiced Oxtail Stew (page 312); and any of the rice dishes, including Celebration Yellow Rice (page 178). It also makes excellent picnic fare. You can prep and marinate it at home and then grill it at the picnic site.

GRILLED COCONUT CHICKEN WITH LEMON BASIL
Ayam Panggang Sulawesi
(SULAWESI, INDONESIA)

⤚

This is a rich variation on Javanese Grilled Chicken (page 289), perfect for summertime grilling. A cut-up chicken is precooked in a currylike coconut-milk broth seasoned with ginger, turmeric, chiles, kaffir lime leaves, and lemon basil. The broth is reduced to a thick paste, then used to baste the chicken as it grills. Though cooking chicken by this method appears throughout Indonesia and Malaysia, this particular combination of ingredients comes from Manado, the capital of North Sulawesi, Indonesia, the large crab-shaped island due east of Borneo. Manado's cuisine is marked by an almost religious devotion to ginger, lemon basil, and lemongrass.

MAKES 4 OR 5 SERVINGS

FOR THE FLAVORING PASTE

8 shallots (about 6 ounces/170 grams), coarsely chopped

5 cloves garlic, coarsely chopped

2 to 6 fresh red Holland chiles or other fresh long, red chiles such as Fresno or cayenne, stemmed and coarsely chopped

5 to 15 fresh green Thai chiles, stemmed and coarsely chopped (optional, but use them if you like heat)

6 candlenuts (page 48) or unsalted macadamia nuts

1 piece fresh or thawed, frozen turmeric (page 92), 4 inches (10 centimeters) long, peeled and coarsely chopped (about 1 1/2 tablespoons), or 2 teaspoons ground turmeric

1 piece fresh ginger, 4 inches (10 centimeters) long, peeled and thinly sliced against the grain (about 3 1/2 tablespoons)

4 tablespoons peanut oil

2 thick stalks fresh lemongrass, each tied into a knot (page 76)

8 whole fresh or thawed, frozen kaffir lime leaves

1/2 cup (scant 1/2 ounce/15 grams) loosely packed fresh lemon basil (page 74), Thai basil, or Italian basil leaves, coarsely chopped

1 1/2 cups (12 fluid ounces/375 milliliters)
  unsweetened coconut milk

3/4 teaspoon kosher salt

1 whole free-range chicken, 3 to 3 1/2 pounds
  (1.4 to 1.6 kilograms), or 3 pounds (1.4 kilo-

grams) free-range chicken wings, thighs,
  breasts, and/or drumsticks

3 tablespoons fresh lime juice

1. To make the flavoring paste, place the shallots, garlic, red chiles, green chiles (if using), candlenuts, turmeric, and ginger in a small food processor. Pulse until you have a smooth paste the consistency of creamy mashed potatoes.

2. Heat the 4 tablespoons oil in a 12-inch (30-centimeter) skillet (nonstick works best) over medium-low heat. Test to see if the oil is the right temperature by adding a pinch of the ground paste. The paste should sizzle slightly around the edges, not fry aggressively or sit motionless. When the oil is ready, add all the paste and sauté, stirring as needed to prevent scorching, until the shallots and garlic no longer smell raw and the paste begins to separate from the oil, about 5 minutes. Add the lemongrass, lime leaves, and basil and sauté, stirring often, until a lemony aroma rises above the pan, 2 to 3 minutes.

3. Add the coconut milk and salt and stir well to combine with the flavoring paste. Raise the heat slightly and let the coconut milk come to a steady simmer. Reduce the heat to medium-low and continue to cook at a steady, gentle simmer, stirring occasionally, until the flavors begin to meld, about 10 minutes. Taste the broth. It should be spicy and rich. Add a pinch more salt if needed.

4. While the broth continues to simmer, rinse the chicken under cold running water and pat it dry with paper towels. If using a whole chicken, cut it into 10 pieces. (For instructions on how to do this, see page 50.) Alternatively, you may quarter the chicken and cut it into smaller pieces for serving after it has been grilled, or serve the quarters whole if the chicken is small enough. If using precut chicken parts, you can leave them whole. Poke the chicken all over with the tines of a fork, which will allow the flavors of the coconut-milk broth to penetrate the flesh more deeply.

5. Add the chicken to the coconut-milk broth and raise the heat slightly to bring it to a steady simmer. Reduce the heat to medium-low and cook the chicken at a slow, even simmer, stirring every 5 minutes to prevent scorching, until it's three-fourths cooked, 30 to 40 minutes. It should be tender and no longer raw, but not mushy or falling off the bone. Since the liquid may not be deep enough to cover the chicken, you'll need to turn the chicken a few times to ensure that it's evenly cooked. Be careful not to let the coconut milk come to a vigorous boil, or it may curdle. Using a slotted spoon, transfer the chicken to a bowl and set aside. The coconut-milk broth will have thickened substantially by this point.

6. Now, thicken the coconut-milk broth even more so that you can use it to baste the chicken as it grills or broils. Raise the heat slightly and bring the liquid to a vigorous simmer. Cook, stirring every 30 seconds to prevent sticking and scorching, until there is only 1/2 to 3/4 cup (4 to 6 fluid ounces/125 to 175 milliliters) remaining in the pan, 10 to 20 minutes. The final consistency of the liquid should be similar to thick pea soup—it must be thick enough to cling easily to the chicken as it broils or grills. Remove the pan from the heat and discard the lemongrass and lime leaves. If there's too much oil for your liking on top, skim some of it off. Add the lime juice and stir well to combine.

7. **To cook the chicken on a grill,** prepare a medium-hot charcoal fire and oil the grill rack or a grilling basket (the implement of choice in Sulawesi) liberally. Baste the fleshy side of each piece of chicken with the reduced coconut-milk broth, using 1 tablespoon for each piece. Place each chicken piece, fleshy side up (or fleshier side up if using drumsticks and wings), on the grill rack 6 inches (15 centimeters) from the fire. Don't discard the broth. Grill until they begin to pick up a few toasty brown spots, about 5 to 10 minutes; the timing will depend on how hot the fire is. Using tongs or 2 forks, turn them carefully so as not to disrupt the already-grilled side (or turn the grilling basket, if using), and baste again, using up all the remaining coconut-milk broth. Continue grilling the chicken until the second side has picked up a few toasty brown spots, about 5 to 10 minutes longer.

To cook the chicken in a broiler, position a rack so that the chicken will be 3 inches (7.5 centimeters) from the heat source and preheat the oven for at least 5 minutes. Line a half-sheet pan with aluminum foil and place each piece of chicken, fleshy side up (or fleshier side up if using drumsticks and wings), on the pan. Place about 1 tablespoon of the reduced coconut-milk broth over the top of each piece of chicken. Don't discard the broth. Slide the pan under the broiler. Broil until the flesh begins to turn golden brown and develops a few crusty brown spots, about 7 to 10 minutes. Using tongs or 2 forks, gently turn each piece over, being careful not to disturb the already-broiled side, and repeat the same process, generously basting each piece with the remaining coconut-milk broth until it's all used up and broiling until each piece is similarly browned, about 7 to 10 minutes longer.

8. Transfer the chicken to a serving dish and let rest for at least 10 minutes before eating.

MENU SUGGESTIONS

Steamed rice (page 173), Javanese Cucumber and Carrot Pickle (page 132), Stir-fried Asian Greens with Garlic and Chiles (page 205), and Spice-Braised Tuna (page 242) are good accompaniments.

NYONYA DUCK SOUP WITH SALTED MUSTARD GREENS
Itek Tim
(MALAYSIA AND SINGAPORE)

—

This rejuvenating duck soup, made with tomatoes and seasoned with ginger, nutmeg, salted mustard greens, brandy, lime juice, and chiles, is from the meticulously inscribed recipe journals of Charlie Chua, the father of my friend Josephine of Malacca, Malaysia. It's a deliciously balanced dish, the sharp seasonings harmonizing perfectly with the mellow, meaty duck. You'll need a Long Island duck, preferably one that hasn't been frozen. *Itek tim* (*itek* means "duck" in Malaysian, *tim* means "to simmer meat until tender") is intended to be sipped in between bites of other dishes, like a classic Chinese soup. It's never eaten as an appetizer, though you could serve it that way along with bread. Traditionally, the broth, with its tomatoes and pieces of salted Chinese mustard greens, rather than the duck meat, is the star. Guests are invited to pick the meat as they like from the quartered duck pieces in the tureen (much as diners pick the flesh from a whole steamed fish). If you prefer to cut the duck into smaller pieces (10 would be best) so that guests can be served bone-in pieces, follow the instructions on page 50 for cutting up a chicken.

Chinese preserved salted plums (known as *tam pai mui* and *li hing mui* in Cantonese) are available in Chinese supermarkets, usually in the section devoted to preserved fruits or at the checkout counter. They come in small plastic packages, usually 20 or 30 small, unseeded salted plums to a package (Chinese plums are much smaller than plums found in North America). Sometimes the plums are dry and encrusted with chile powder and salt, and other times they're slightly moist. Either is fine. If you can't find the Chinese version of salted plums, Japanese salted plums, known as *umeboshi*, make a good substitute. They are available in health-food stores and in Japanese and Korean markets.

MAKES 5 SERVINGS

1 whole Long Island duck, 4 to 5 pounds (1.8 to 2.2 kilograms)

2 tablespoons kosher salt

4 tablespoons brandy or Cognac

1 pound (455 grams) whole salted Chinese mustard greens (see Cook's Note, page 297)

2 3/4 quarts (2.75 liters) water, preferably spring water or filtered tap water (see Cook's Notes, page 274)

6 Chinese preserved salted plums or Japanese *umeboshi* (see headnote; optional)

1 whole nutmeg, cracked open with a nutcracker or a heavy, blunt object such as
the bottom of a glass measuring cup

3 pieces *asam gelugor* (page 43; optional)

1 piece fresh ginger, 2 inches (5 centimeters)
long, peeled and bruised until juicy with a
heavy, blunt object such as the bottom of
a glass measuring cup

1/2 teaspoon freshly ground black pepper

1 teaspoon sugar

4 firm, ripe small tomatoes such as Roma
(about 12 ounces/340 grams total), cored
and quartered

2 tablespoons fresh lime juice

3 to 6 fresh green Thai chiles, stemmed and
sliced in half lengthwise (optional, but
imparts a wonderfully fiery finish)

1. Rinse the duck and pat it dry with paper towels. Using a large chef's knife or a sharp pair of poultry or kitchen shears, quarter the duck. Leave the back intact, as it will help flavor the stock. Remove any excess fat from what was the cavity and from underneath the neck flap. Cut off the tail and about 1 inch (2.5 centimeters) of the area surrounding it. Rub the salt into the flesh and skin of the duck and allow the duck to rest for a few minutes. Rinse the pieces in cold running water and pat dry. (The salt and subsequent rinsing help remove any gamy taste, a piece of Nyonya cooking wisdom.)

2. Place the duck quarters in a large nonreactive bowl and pour 2 tablespoons of the brandy over them. Massage the brandy into the flesh and set the duck aside to marinate, uncovered, at room temperature until you're ready to add it to the soup.

3. Meanwhile, discard most of the leafy, dark green ends of the salted mustard greens (they are chewy and not as flavorful as the stalk portions) and cut the stalks into chunky pieces 2 to 2 1/2 inches (5 to 6 centimeters) long. Place the pieces in a colander and rinse them under cold running water for 2 minutes to reduce their saltiness. Squeeze them dry.

4. Add the water to a 4-quart (4-liter) saucepan, Dutch oven, or soup pot and bring to a boil over medium-high heat. Reduce the heat to medium and add the mustard greens, preserved plums (if using), nutmeg, *asam gelugor* (if using), and ginger. Cover and cook at a very lively simmer for 15 minutes.

5. Add the duck and ground pepper to the liquid. Raise the heat slightly and bring the liquid to a boil. Reduce the heat to medium-low, cover, and simmer at a steady, low bubble until the duck is cooked through and tender, about 1 1/2 hours. The drumstick meat should be just beginning to pull away from the bone. Don't let the stock come to an aggressive boil, which may cause the duck to toughen. If there's more than a tablespoon or two of rendered fat floating on the surface, skim it off; this dish shouldn't be greasy.

6. Add the sugar and tomatoes and let the stock simmer until the tomatoes are just fork-tender but not falling apart or mushy, 2 to 3 minutes. Taste for salt; you may need to add a pinch, though the salted mustard greens and plums are likely to have provided enough saltiness. Remove and discard the ginger and the *asam gelugor* (if used).

7. Transfer the soup to a large serving bowl or tureen and add the remaining 2 tablespoons brandy, the lime juice, and the chiles (if using). Stir gently to combine, being careful not to break up the tomatoes as you do so. Serve warm or hot, ladling the broth into small individual soup bowls (see Menu Suggestions for other serving ideas).

COOK'S NOTE

Salted mustard greens (called *sayur asin* in Indonesia, Malaysia, and Singapore) are forest green, brine-pickled whole sections of Chinese mustard greens. They're not to be confused with Sichuan pickled turnip (which is encrusted with chile paste) or other chopped fermented Chinese vegetables. They're an important ingredient in Nyonya cooking for their delightfully tart flavor, which is somewhat reminiscent of sauerkraut. Look for salted mustard greens in all Chinese markets, where they are sometimes labeled sour vegetable. Most salted mustard greens are imported from China. They're available three ways: in small vacuum-sealed plastic bags, in cans, or in plastic tubs in the vegetable section of the market. Read the labels of the greens packed in vacuum-sealed bags or in cans, avoiding those that contain sugar, which can make the mustard greens too sweet. Store leftover mustard greens in a tightly sealed plastic container or glass jar in the refrigerator. They'll keep for up to a month.

MENU SUGGESTIONS

Like *soto* (page 271), the Javanese chicken soup to which this dish is distantly related, *itek tim* can be eaten as a first course or as a one-dish meal, with or without rice. My favorite way to serve it is with steamed rice (page 173); Nyonya Sambal (page 120); Stir-fried Water Spinach, Nyonya Style (page 213); and Chile Omelet (page 334)—all dishes that won't detract from its delicately sour-spicy taste.

ABOVE LEFT: *Hasnah and Mat, the bride and groom at the wedding in Kampong Bukit Bangkong, Malaysia, where the feast included Beef Rendang (page 304).*

ABOVE CENTER: *A room in the bride's home, where Hasnah and Mat will greet well-wishers.*

ABOVE RIGHT: *After the water buffalo was slaughtered, the male wedding guests cut it into small pieces for cooking.*

12. FOODS OF CELEBRATION: BEEF, GOAT, AND PORK

For four days, I'd been staying in the small village of Kampong Bukit Bangkong, a couple of hours south of Kuala Lumpur, Malaysia. The sweltering heat was enervating, even for me, a lifelong lover of warm weather. Afternoon temperatures held in the upper nineties, refusing to budge; the 80 percent humidity level made things even worse. Vegetable gardens drooped. Cats hid in the shade. Everyone I met commented, listlessly, on how unusually hot it was. There was *always* a late-day rainstorm to cool the air at this time of year, they said, yet there had been no rain for weeks.

I was in Kampong Bukit Bangkong because Sharifah, a Malaysian acquaintance, wanted me to see this part of the country, the coastal flatlands of Negeri Sembilan state. I would have preferred to be in Kuala Lumpur, watching television in an air-conditioned hotel, but she'd already planned my trip. I was to stay with the village headman, Haji Basir (*haji* is the term for a man who has made the haj, the pilgrimage to Mecca), who ran a guesthouse in his home. As a lure, Sharifah told me, "Haji Basir's wife is a fan-*tas*-tic cook," emphasizing the word *fantastic* as though she were trying to hypnotize me.

Sharifah had been right. Rosniza, a short, olive-skinned woman in her fifties, *was* a fantastic cook. Her elaborate meals, which she prepared with her two pretty teenage daughters in a small outdoor kitchen, showed off the full range of traditional Malay cooking, from rich stews to citrusy salads called *kerabu*. Rosniza graciously allowed me into her kitchen, letting me watch her at work as much as I wanted. "I enjoy being a teacher," she told me as she plucked a stalk of lemongrass from a small garden out back.

One morning, there was a knock at my door. It was Rosniza, fanning herself. "Would you like to join my husband and me at a wedding party?" she asked. "There will be all sorts of food. We'll go in half an hour." Before I could respond, she'd walked away.

Thirty minutes later, I was in a jeep, trundling down a red-dirt road with Rosniza, Haji Basir, and their daughters. As we approached the bride's family home, I could see this was going to be nothing like the prim wedding receptions I'd attended back home. Despite the heat, several hundred villagers had turned out. Cars and motorcycles were parked three deep, teetering near grassy ditches. Families strolled down the road toward the bride's house, a small wooden structure built on stilts. Everyone was dressed to the hilt. Sarongs and tunics in orange, fuchsia, red, and chartreuse green made the gathering seem like a Peter Max painting come to life. Outside the house, a small gamelan ensemble was playing under the shade of a canvas tent.

"The people of Kampong Bukit Bangkong, me included, came from Central Java many generations ago," Haji Basir said half in Malaysian and half in English as we began to wind our way through the crowd. "Land in Java was scarce, so we came to Malaysia seeking more room to farm." He was a short man with a bristly, well-groomed mustache. In his crisp, white tunic and hand-knitted skullcap, he looked like he was born to be village chief. People parted the way for us, bowing their heads out of respect for him. "In our tradition, a wedding lasts for at least three days," Haji Basir continued.

"Three days?" I stammered, as I imagined camping out in this heat for that long.

"Sometimes longer," he replied. "The bride and groom, Hasnah and Mat, are considered holy deities during the wedding time. They are thought to bring good luck to everyone who catches a glimpse of them."

Haji Basir led me to a table and introduced me to Khairy, his second cousin who, he explained, spoke English more fluently than he did. Khairy and I sat down on folding chairs under a coconut palm and drank rose-syrup cordials that had been handed to us by the bride's father. The beverage was intensely sweet and perfumed; it was like drinking a rose itself. Khairy was a lanky man in his late forties. He worked at a bank in Kuala Lumpur, a four-hour round-trip from Kampong Bukit Bangkong, and had been to New York the previous November. "It's a big place!" he said. "And it's much cooler than Malaysia!" In front of us, I noticed a large water buffalo tethered to a tree, eating from a pile of rice stalks and hay. The buffalo snorted in satisfaction as he ate.

"It appears as though he's enjoying his last meal," said Khairy. I looked at him askance, but I could tell he wasn't joking: the buffalo was destined to become our dinner. Khairy explained that weddings were an auspicious time for sacrificing animals, that the animal's death symbolized a sharing of bounty. "Buffalo is always served at our wedding celebrations. It is the most luxurious food," he said. "It would be unfavorable to serve fish—that's a food for nonspecial days."

The gamelan musicians soon put their instruments down. A tall, dour man approached the buffalo, running his hand along the length of its hide. This, Khairy said, was the executioner. He untied the rope and escorted the buffalo to an area a few yards away from the party. A small crowd of men gathered and formed a loose circle. Khairy and I joined them. An imam (a Muslim priest), dressed in a white tunic, stepped forward and recited a quiet, quick prayer. In moments, the buffalo was no more, slain by a few deft blows to its throat.

"The Prophet Mohammad said that the knife that kills our livestock must be as sharp as possible," Khairy whispered when it was over. "There should never be discomfort for the animal that is killed." A few strong men propped up the buffalo on its hind legs against a tree so that, in accordance with Islamic dietary law, it could be drained of its blood before being butchered.

After a time, most of the men at the wedding party gathered under two large tents that had been set up behind the bride's home. They sat at long wooden tables, each covered with plastic tablecloths. Their task was to cut the meat of the butchered buffalo into two sizes: larger, bone-in pieces for a stew; smaller, boneless pieces for a *rendang*. It was one of the strangest sights I've ever seen: fifty smartly dressed wedding guests carefully cutting away at the meat of a whole buffalo as if it were the most normal thing in the world. A woman in her seventies in a red sarong—she was in charge of cooking the meat for the feast, Khairy explained—walked between the tables to scrutinize what the men were doing. Once cut, the meat was piled high into two large, white enamel bowls according to the dish in which it would be used.

"Won't you join us?" Haji Basir asked, indicating an empty seat next to him at one of the tables. I declined. I wanted to see what was going on at the rest of the party. I walked over to a shady area on the other side of the bride's house where several women were sitting on rattan mats on the ground prepping the rest of the feast. I found Rosniza in front of a large bowl filled with bulbs of garlic and asked her what was on the menu.

"First, we are making *sop buntut*, a stew from the tougher pieces of buffalo meat, including the tail," she answered as she broke the bulbs into cloves. "It will be flavored with ginger, garlic, galangal, nutmeg, cinnamon, pepper, and cloves." A woman sitting next to Rosniza was busy pounding spices and shallots in a large mortar. The fragrance was clean and sharp. As soon as the woman finished grinding, she transferred the paste to a plate and started over again.

"Next, there will be *rendang*," Rosniza said. For *rendang*, a dish that originated in West Sumatra, Indonesia, the primary ingredient, often beef and in this case water buffalo, is braised in an intensely spiced coconut-milk curry for hours until all the liquid has evaporated, producing a lusciously rich dish. Rosniza told me that the stew and the *rendang* would be accompanied by a fresh pickle of cucumber and pineapple called *acar nenas*, potato fritters, an assortment of multicolored sticky-rice sweets, and, of course, plenty of freshly steamed white rice. My mouth watered in anticipation. Then I asked, "Is it normal for guests to be part of the food preparation of every wedding party? The food isn't cooked ahead of time?"

"For us, cooking is part of the celebration," Rosniza replied.

I looked around and saw what she meant. By now everyone, except kids under ten, most of whom were playing an enthusiastic game of tag, was joining in to make the feast. Off to the side, five immense woks sat on just as many crackling fires. Three women were their guardians, watching over them like hawks. When the woks were sufficiently hot, the women began sautéing massive handfuls of flavoring paste in hot coconut oil. As soon as the flavoring paste began to separate from the oil, the buffalo meat was added, followed by the cooking liquids—water for the *sop buntut*, fresh-pressed coconut milk for the *rendang*. The cooks gently turned and nudged the food, stopping only to wipe the sweat from their foreheads. The fragrance of meat and spice was everywhere, wafting, I was sure, over the entire country. I half expected all of Malaysia to show up later for the feast.

After about three hours, the cooking was complete. When the dishes had cooled a bit, a group of women, including Rosniza, ladled them into individual small serving bowls, which were carefully arranged on large enamel platters along with big bowls of rice.

Once again, the gamelan ensemble paused, signaling to guests that it was time to eat. People began to gather at every available space—at tables, on mats, on folding chairs, wherever they might squeeze in. There were so many guests that we had to eat in two shifts. Those who could stand to wait for the second shift were obliged to serve the first. I, alas, couldn't wait. I found a seat next to Khairy and Haji Basir and readied myself to gorge. It was a meal without equal. The *rendang* was lush and moist, the *sop buntut* bold and fresh. I was so engrossed in the feast that I'd forgotten why we'd all gathered in the first place: the wedding of Hasnah and Mat. I was brought back to reality when I noticed a commotion up the road. I stopped eating and asked Khairy what was going on.

"Hasnah and Mat are newlyweds. They've just been married by the imam," he said. "They're making their way back to the house." Khairy explained that it was customary for the marriage vows to be conducted in private, with only the immediate families of the bride and groom present.

I caught a glimpse of the young couple and let out a gasp. Both in their early twenties, they were walking slowly up the road, surrounded by well-wishers. They wore matching black and gold silk sarongs that scattered flecks of light on everything nearby. Just then, a thunderbolt cracked overhead. Hot rain began pelting the ground. Someone quickly hoisted colorful fringed umbrellas over the newlyweds.

Within moments, the air was cool, as though God had suddenly switched on the air-conditioning. It was the first rain in weeks, a favorable omen for the new couple. The crowd laughed. Hasnah and Mat smiled like the deities that they were, at least for that day.

Beef, goat, and pork dishes have a revered place on Indonesian, Malaysian, and Singaporean tables. Because meat is a luxury, it's generally reserved for special occasions, such as when there's a wedding couple to fete, a deity to appease, or a family ceremony to mark the passing of a child into adolescence. But although meat dishes aren't commonplace, home cooks are well versed in their preparation (celebrations occur often and are usually a neighborhood affair, so cooks have plenty of opportunity throughout the year to hone their skills). They lavish meat with spices, braise it for hours until it's juicy and tender, and stew it in extravagantly aromatic broths. Meat dishes are rarely austere, so they allow a cook's artistry to shine, showcasing her prowess at orchestrating all the varied elements of local cooking.

Water buffalo are traditionally regarded as valuable beasts of burden and thus aren't raised for consumption. Instead, these docile animals spend their lives tromping through rice paddies, until they're too old to work and are slaughtered. While water buffalo meat is lusciously gamy, beef, which is popular in Malaysia but less so in Indonesia, makes a fine substitute. Beef Rendang (page 304), the West Sumatran classic that I ate at Hasnah and Mat's wedding in Malaysia made with water-buffalo meat instead, is perhaps the most outstanding meat dish of the region. Another dish traditionally made with water buffalo is Malaccan Beef and Vegetable Stew (page 309), a Malaysian recipe seasoned with star anise and cinnamon that may remind you of a European stew.

Most Indonesians and Malaysians are devout Muslims, so pork is *haram* (forbidden) according to their dietary laws. However, there is a long tradition of eating pork among the Malay Archipelago's Christians, Hindus, Nyonyas, and ethnic Chinese. Of the hundreds of pork dishes Nyonya cooks prepare, Spiced Braised Nyonya Pork (page 307), a slow-cooked cousin of beef *rendang*, is my favorite. Its harmonious sweet-sour-spicy flavor comes from vinegar, sugar, cinnamon, and star anise.

In Indonesia and Malaysia (though not in Singapore, with its predominantly Chinese population), goat meat is even more popular than water buffalo, beef, and pork. Goats are a fixture in Southeast Asia: rare is the village landscape that doesn't include a flock of these wiry-haired animals nibbling on virtually anything they come across. Goat meat, ideal for curries, is prized for its deep, layered taste and supple tenderness. A standout recipe is Acehnese Goat Curry (page 314), a rich dish usually served at weddings. You could substitute lamb, but I encourage you to try it with goat. This versatile meat is available year-round in North America in Latin and South Asian markets, and at Italian and Greek butchers during the Easter season.

BEEF RENDANG
Rendang Daging Sapi
(WEST SUMATRA, INDONESIA)

⸺

This extravagantly rich, dry-braised beef curry is a signature dish of the Minangkabau highlands of West Sumatra, Indonesia. It's a triumph of flavor, with lime leaves, nutmeg, and cloves. The dish is cooked by a process that inverts normal braising. The beef is slowly simmered in a spiced coconut-milk broth until the broth evaporates and the meat is left to sauté in the intensely flavored rendered coconut and beef oils left in the pot.

This recipe comes from Rohati, my cooking guru in Padang, West Sumatra. She offered me a few sage words of advice when she gave it to me. First, she said, allow plenty of time to make it. *Rendang* has its own lethargic cooking rhythm, so that the more you try to rush it, the longer it seems to take. I know what she means: I've often underestimated how long it takes to cook and have left hungry dinner guests waiting while it continued slowly to simmer away. Second, she said, use a shallow, wide pan, such as a skillet, rather than a deep soup pot. The less enclosed the cooking space, the easier it will be for the liquid to evaporate—in other words, the opposite of how you want to cook a curry. And third, Rohati advised me always to use the best-quality beef I can get. In America this means avoiding precut stewing beef, which is of inconsistent quality. Instead, choose boneless chuck or bottom round laced through with bright white fat and cut it into cubes yourself.

"*Rendang* is sacred food in West Sumatra," Rohati said. "If you skimp on ingredients, you risk upsetting Allah."

If you decide to use the maximum number of chiles this recipe calls for, you may need to use a standard-sized food processor, rather than a small one. An excellent garnish for this dish (and for the other two *rendang* dishes, on pages 223 and 278), is a tablespoon of very finely sliced fresh or thawed, frozen kaffir lime leaves. Be sure to remove the center stem of each leaf before slicing it.

MAKES 4 TO 6 SERVINGS

FOR THE FLAVORING PASTE

1 whole nutmeg, cracked open with a nutcracker or a heavy, blunt object such as the bottom of a glass measuring cup

5 whole cloves

6 shallots (about 5 ounces/140 grams total), coarsely chopped

3 cloves garlic, coarsely chopped

5 to 20 fresh red Holland chiles or other fresh long, red chiles such as Fresno or cayenne, stemmed and coarsely chopped

1 piece fresh or thawed, frozen turmeric (page 92), 2 inches (5 centimeters) long, peeled and coarsely chopped (about 2 teaspoons), or 1 1/2 teaspoons ground turmeric

1 piece fresh ginger, 2 inches (5 centimeters)

long, peeled and thinly sliced against the grain (about 2 tablespoons)

1 piece fresh or thawed, frozen galangal, 2 inches (5 centimeters) long, peeled and thinly sliced against the grain (about 2 tablespoons; optional)

5 candlenuts (page 48) or unsalted macadamia nuts

2 pounds (900 grams) well-marbled boneless beef chuck or bottom round, cut into 2- to 2 1/2-inch (5- to 6-centimeter) cubes

2 1/2 cups (20 fluid ounces/625 milliliters) unsweetened coconut milk

3 thick stalks fresh lemongrass, each tied into a knot (page 76)

1 piece cinnamon stick, 4 inches (10 centimeters) long

7 whole fresh or thawed, frozen kaffir lime leaves

5 whole *daun salam* leaves (page 64; optional)

1 teaspoon kosher salt

1 tablespoon very finely shredded fresh or thawed, frozen kaffir lime leaves (optional)

1. To make the flavoring paste, place the nutmeg and cloves in a small food processor and pulse until ground to a dusty powder, about 2 minutes.

2. Add the shallots, garlic, chiles, turmeric, ginger, galangal (if using), and candlenuts to the ground spices. Pulse until you have a chunky-smooth paste the consistency of cooked oatmeal.

3. In a 12-inch (30-centimeter) skillet (nonstick works best), mix the beef and the flavoring paste until well combined. Add the coconut milk, lemongrass, cinnamon, whole lime leaves, *daun salam* leaves (if using), and salt. Stir well to combine and bring to a gentle boil over medium heat. Immediately reduce the heat to medium-low and simmer uncovered at a slow, steady bubble, stirring every 10 to 20 minutes with a spatula to prevent the meat and coconut milk from sticking and scorching. You'll probably need to adjust the heat periodically to maintain an even simmer.

4. The meat, coconut milk, and flavoring paste will now go on a fascinating journey. At first, the broth will be thin and gorgeously bright orange. As it cooks, the coconut milk will reduce, its fats (as well as the fat the meat renders) separating from the solids. It will become progressively thicker and darker, eventually turning brown. Continue to

simmer gently until the liquid has reduced by about 95 percent, stirring every 15 minutes or so to prevent sticking. Only the meat, oils, and a bit of very thick sauce will remain in the pot. This will take anywhere from 2 to 3 hours, depending on the skillet that you use, how hot the fire is, and the richness of the coconut milk. Test the meat; it should be tender enough to poke easily with a fork. Taste some of the liquid for salt, and add a pinch more if needed.

5. When all the liquid has evaporated, reduce the heat to low (the meat and the remaining sauce are prone to burning) and allow the beef to brown slowly in the rendered fat. (The fat may be foamy at this point, but it will settle down when the cooking stops.) Stir every 5 minutes or so to prevent sticking and scorching, being careful not to break the beef apart. Continue sautéing the beef until it's the color of roasted coffee beans, 5 to 10 minutes longer. The surface of the beef should be barely moist and have an appetizing oily sheen. (If there is too much oil in the pan for your liking, skim some of it off with a spoon and set aside for later use; it's wonderful for sautéing potatoes.)

6. Remove and discard the cinnamon, lemongrass, lime leaves, and *daun salam* leaves (if used), and then transfer the beef to a serving dish. (Alternatively, serve this dish with all the aromatics, for a more rustic presentation.) Garnish with the shredded lime leaves, if using. Allow the beef to rest for at least 30 minutes before serving. Slightly warm room temperature will best show off its intensely aromatic flavors. This dish will taste even better the next day.

MENU SUGGESTIONS

Though this dish is traditionally paired with rich West Sumatran foods like Fern Curry with Shrimp (page 226) and Padang Fish Curry (page 244), I prefer it with lighter dishes, such as Javanese Cucumber and Carrot Pickle (page 132), Stir-fried Asian Greens with Garlic and Chiles (page 205), Fragrant Fish Stew with Lime and Lemon Basil (page 240), and Tofu and Summer Vegetables in Coconut Milk (page 327). Celebration Yellow Rice (page 178) is also an excellent accompaniment. Because the crusty pan bits that accompany the meat are so fantastically spiced, you don't need to serve a sambal with this dish.

SPICED BRAISED NYONYA PORK
Seh Bak
(MALAYSIA)

⟶

This is a Nyonya pork dish from Malaysia so tender that you can eat it with a spoon. It calls to mind an Asian sauerbraten, but it takes only hours, not days, to make. This recipe, spiked with star anise, cloves, cinnamon, galangal, and vinegar, comes from gifted cook Jennifer Kuan, a native of Malacca, Malaysia. She makes it around Christmas, a holiday that she celebrates because she's Catholic, and serves it with plenty of hot steamed white rice. "Oh, *seh bak* is the best," she once said stirring a big, bubbling pot of the dish. "It tastes like a great, big hug."

The key to its success, Jennifer told me, is to use the best piece of pork shoulder, sometimes called Boston shoulder or pork butt, you can find, preferably one with the skin still attached. The deep striations of fat in pork shoulder are what make the cut so delicious. A Chinese, Latin, or specialty butcher will be your best bet for finding it. You could substitute a leaner pork, but the results won't be as delectable.

MAKES 4 TO 6 SERVINGS

12 shallots (about 10 ounces/285 grams total), coarsely chopped

2 tablespoons peanut oil

1 piece fresh or thawed, frozen galangal, 3 inches (7.5 centimeters) long, peeled, thinly sliced with the grain, and cut into wide matchsticks about 1 inch (2.5 centimeters) long and 1/4 inch (6 millimeters) thick (about 3 tablespoons)

2 pieces cinnamon stick, each 4 inches (10 centimeters) long

4 whole cloves

2 whole star anise

2 pounds (900 grams) boneless nonlean pork such as Boston shoulder, cut into 1 1/2- to 2-inch (4- to 5-centimeter) cubes

1 cup (8 fluid ounces/250 milliliters) water

3 tablespoons palm, cider, or rice vinegar

2 tablespoons double-black soy sauce (page 87)

2 tablespoons sugar

2 fresh red Holland chiles or other fresh long, red chiles such as Fresno or cayenne, stemmed, seeded, and cut into fine matchsticks (for garnish; optional)

1. Place the shallots in a small food processor and pulse until you have a smooth paste. If the shallots won't purée properly and repeatedly creep up the side of the processor

instead of grinding, add up to 2 tablespoons water, 1 tablespoon at a time, periodically turning the processor off and scraping the unground portions down toward the blade. Set aside.

2. Heat the oil in a 3- or 4-quart (3- or 4-liter) saucepan, Dutch oven, or soup pot over medium heat. Add the galangal and cook, stirring frequently with a spatula or spoon, until each piece is golden around the edges and a gingery-green fragrance rises above the pan, 2 to 3 minutes. Add the shallot paste and sauté, stirring often, until the paste no longer smells raw and is lightly golden, 3 to 4 minutes. (Take care not to overbrown the shallot paste, which will give this dish an inappropriately musky taste. Reduce the heat if the paste begins to scorch, or remove the pan from the heat altogether and allow it to cool for a few seconds before proceeding.) Add the cinnamon, cloves, and star anise and sauté until their combined fragrances waft up from the pan.

3. Add the pork cubes and sauté them on all sides until each piece begins to pick up brown spots, 5 to 10 minutes. If the pieces are crowded in the pan, work in 2 batches. Add the water, vinegar, soy sauce, and sugar and stir well to combine, bringing up all the tasty bits at the bottom of the pan. Bring the mixture to a steady, bubbly boil. Immediately reduce the heat to low.

4. Cover partially and continue cooking at a steady, very gentle simmer, stirring occasionally, until about three-fourths of the liquid has evaporated and the meat offers little resistance when poked with a fork, about 2 hours. Don't cook the meat until it's mushy or falling apart. You'll probably need to raise and lower the heat a few times during this period to maintain a steady, very gentle simmer.

5. Remove the lid and raise the heat to medium. Bring the liquid to a rapid simmer (but not a boil), stirring often but gently to prevent sticking and being careful not to shred or break the meat. Continue cooking until nearly all the liquid has simmered away, leaving only a thick, chocolate brown reduction clinging to the meat. This will take roughly 30 minutes, depending on how much liquid was remaining in the pan. There may be an excessive amount of rendered fat in the pan by the time the liquid has simmered away. You can remove up to half of it with a spoon, or you can enjoy its rich, spice-infused taste over rice. (It's incredibly delicious.)

6. Transfer the pork to a serving dish and allow it to rest for at least 30 minutes, which will allow its flavors to intensify. Since this dish is monochromatic in appearance (but not taste!), you may want to brighten it up with a garnish of chiles. Serve warm or at room temperature. This dish tastes even more wonderful if it's chilled and then reheated.

MENU SUGGESTIONS

Try serving this comforting dish with bright-tasting ones that will complement its richness. Good choices would be South Indian–Style Eggplant Pickle (page 133), Indian-Style Fish Stew with Okra (page 249), and Nyonya Shrimp Curry with Fresh Pineapple and Tomatoes (page 260).

MALACCAN BEEF AND VEGETABLE STEW
Semur Daging Lembu
(MALAYSIA)

⁓

Katherine Lazaroo, a Malacca housewife whose husband is Portuguese Malay, showed me how to make this spicy, dryish (though succulent) beef stew, a Malaysian comfort food. It's a classic dish, the result of cooking methods inherited from Portuguese colonizers in the sixteenth century. Subtract its Asian spices and double-black soy sauce and it looks (and tastes) like it comes straight from a Lisbon stove top. Make it on a dreary winter day, when its spicy aroma will perfume your home and lift your sprits. Cooking the vegetables separately and adding them to the stew when it's done is a clever way to ensure that they won't be overcooked.

MAKES 4 TO 6 SERVINGS

1 1/2 pounds (680 grams) well-marbled boneless beef chuck or bottom round, cut into 2-inch (5-centimeter) cubes

10 shallots (about 7 1/2 ounces/215 grams total), coarsely chopped

4 tablespoons peanut oil, plus more for frying

1 whole star anise

2 green cardamom pods, cracked open with the flat side of a knife (page 49)

4 whole cloves

1 piece cinnamon stick, 4 inches (10 centimeters) long

2 tablespoons double-black soy sauce (page 87)

1 teaspoon freshly ground black pepper

1 tablespoon all-purpose flour

2 cups (16 fluid ounces/500 milliliters) water

1 medium-sized red onion (about 6 ounces/170 grams), cut lengthwise into 8 wedges

1 medium-sized carrot (about 4 ounces/115 grams), peeled and cut on the diagonal into slices 1/4 inch (6 millimeters) thick

1 cup (about 5 ounces/140 grams) fresh or frozen shelled peas

2 medium-sized waxy potatoes (about 8 ounces/225 grams total) such as Maine or Yukon Gold, or 5 small waxy potatoes, no more than 1 1/2 inches (4 centimeters) in diameter

2 teaspoons palm, cider, or rice vinegar

Kosher salt (optional)

1. Place the beef cubes in a nonreactive bowl and pour the soy sauce and sprinkle the ground pepper over them. Use your hands or a spoon to massage the seasonings into every nook and cranny. Allow the beef to marinate, uncovered, at room temperature for 30 minutes to 1 hour, stirring every 10 minutes or so to distribute the soy sauce evenly.

2. Meanwhile, place the shallots in a small food processor and pulse until you have a smooth paste. If the shallots won't purée properly and repeatedly creep up the side of the processor instead of grinding, add up to 2 tablespoons water, 1 tablespoon at a time, periodically turning the processor off and scraping the unground portions down toward the blade. Set aside.

3. Heat the 4 tablespoons oil in a 3- or 4-quart (3- or 4-liter) saucepan, Dutch oven, or soup pot over medium-low heat. Test to see if the oil is the right temperature by adding a pinch of the shallot paste. The paste should sizzle slightly around the edges, not fry aggressively or sit motionless. When the oil is ready, add all the paste and sauté, stirring as needed to prevent scorching, until the paste is lightly golden and no longer raw, 3 to 4 minutes. (Take care not to overbrown the shallot paste, which will give this dish an inappropriately musky taste. Reduce the heat if it begins to scorch, or remove the pan from the heat altogether and allow it to cool for a few seconds before proceeding.) Add the star anise, cardamom, cloves, and cinnamon and sauté, stirring constantly, until their combined fragrances waft up from the pan, about 2 minutes.

4. Meanwhile, remove the beef from the marinade (don't discard the marinade) and dredge the cubes in the flour, making sure that they are lightly but evenly covered. Add the beef to the pan, raise the heat slightly, and sauté until the beef begins to pick up brown spots, about 7 minutes. If the pieces are crowded in the pan, work in 2 batches. Add the water and the reserved marinade and stir to combine, scraping up any flavorful bits from the bottom of the pan. Raise the heat to high and bring the mixture to a lively simmer. Immediately reduce the heat to medium-low and cook at a slow simmer, uncovered and stirring occasionally, until the beef is very tender, about 2 1/2 hours. Take care not to let the liquid boil, or the beef will toughen. (If the liquid begins to dry up before the beef is tender, add up to an extra 1 cup/8 fluid ounces/250 milliliters water.)

There should be 3/4 to 1 cup (6 to 8 fluid ounces/175 to 250 milliliters) liquid in the pan when the beef is fully cooked.

5. While the beef is cooking, prepare the vegetables. Fill a 2-quart (2-liter) saucepan with water and bring to a rolling boil. Add the onion and cook until just tender, about 1 1/2 minutes. Using a slotted spoon, transfer the onions to a colander to drain and then set aside. Add the carrots to the same boiling water and boil until fork-tender, about 2 1/2 minutes. Using the slotted spoon, transfer the carrots to the colander to drain and then set them aside with the onions. Finally, add the peas to the boiling water and boil until tender, about 15 seconds if using frozen peas and about 2 minutes if using fresh. Drain them in the colander and set them aside with the onions and carrots.

6. Next, prepare the potatoes. Peel the potatoes, trimming away any bruised or green spots. If using medium-sized potatoes, cut each potato in half lengthwise, and then cut each half lengthwise into fourths, yielding 8 wedges from each potato. If you're using small potatoes, just halve them lengthwise. Pour oil to a depth of 1 inch (2.5 centimeters) into a 2-quart (2-liter) saucepan and place over medium to medium-high heat. When the oil is hot but not smoking (about 365°F/185°C), spear a potato wedge onto a fork and dip a corner of the wedge into the oil. If the potato begins to fry immediately, the oil is ready. With a slotted metal spoon, carefully add the potatoes in small, manageable batches of no more than 8 wedges at a time. Fry the potatoes, turning the wedges frequently with the spoon to prevent them from sticking together, until they're lightly golden on all sides, about 4 minutes total. To test if they're cooked through, pierce a wedge with a fork. It should puncture the wedge with only slight resistance. Using the slotted spoon, transfer the potatoes to paper towels to drain. Don't allow the potatoes to become too brown; the longer they fry, the hotter the oil will become, and some of the wedges may become too brown before becoming fully cooked. Take care to raise and lower the heat occasionally if you see that the potatoes are either sitting limply in the oil or are frying too violently. They'll come out too greasy or darkly colored otherwise.

7. Add the vinegar to the beef and stir well to combine. Taste the stew for salt, and add a pinch if needed. The double-black soy sauce may have provided enough salt. Transfer the stew to a bowl and allow it to rest for at least 20 minutes to give the flavors time to develop. If desired, remove and discard the whole spices.

8. Using a large spoon, gently fold the boiled vegetables and fried potatoes into the stew, mixing them in well. Transfer to a serving dish and serve at warm room temperature to best display the stew's deep, zesty taste. This dish is even better the next day.

MENU SUGGESTIONS

Because this dish is similar to a European-style beef stew (though it has slightly less liquid), it goes well with crusty bread. But if you want to serve it as it's traditionally eaten, accompany it with plenty of steamed rice (page 173), Nyonya Sambal (page 120), Sweet-Sour Cucumber and Carrot Pickle with Turmeric (page 130), and Stir-fried Water Spinach, Nyonya Style (page 213).

JAVANESE SPICED OXTAIL STEW
Sop Buntut
(JAVA, INDONESIA)

Like Malaccan Beef and Vegetable Stew (page 309), this robust, homey Dutch Javanese dish combines European and Southeast Asian cooking styles, making it true fusion food. Although reminiscent of a soupy American stew, its flavorings of ginger, galangal, nutmeg, cinnamon, and cloves are strictly Javanese. Another thing it shares with the Malaccan beef stew is that the vegetables are cooked before they're added to the stew, which allows the cook to control their doneness better. The nutmeg, cracked open and allowed to season the stock gently, rather than being grated into it, lends a hauntingly spicy note. Fried shallots and garlic and Chinese celery greens, sprinkled on top just before serving, marry all the flavors.

In the past, oxtail came from an ox, hence its name. Nowadays it's more likely to be a beef tail. It's easy to cook, and its rich, concentrated flavor is the essence of beef. It's widely available in Asian and Latin markets and specialty meat markets. If it has not already been cut into pieces between the vertebrae, ask your butcher to cut it for you.

Beef short ribs are a good substitute for the oxtails in this recipe. Though a bit fattier, they have a similarly rich, beefy taste and will yield an excellent dish.

MAKES 4 TO 6 SERVINGS

1 1/2 pounds (680 grams) oxtail, cut crosswise into chunks 1/2 to 1 inch (12 millimeters to 2.5 centimeters) thick, or beef short ribs, cut into 1- to 1 1/2-inch (2.5- to 4-centimeter) pieces

2 1/2 quarts (2.5 liters) water, preferably spring water or filtered tap water (see Cook's Notes, page 274)

1 piece fresh ginger, 1 inch (2.5 centimeters) long, peeled and bruised until juicy with a heavy, blunt object such as the bottom of a glass measuring cup

1 piece fresh or thawed, frozen galangal, 2 inches (5 centimeters) long, peeled and bruised until juicy with a heavy, blunt object such as the bottom of a glass measuring cup (optional)

2 tablespoons Crisp-Fried Shallots (page 84)

2 tablespoons crisp-fried garlic slices (see Crisp-Fried Shallots, page 84)

1 piece cinnamon stick, 4 inches (10 centimeters) long

7 whole cloves

1 whole nutmeg, cracked open with a nutcracker or a heavy, blunt object such as the bottom of a glass measuring cup

1 teaspoon freshly ground black pepper

1 tablespoon sugar

1 1/2 teaspoons kosher salt

3 medium-sized carrots (about 10 1/2 ounces/300 grams), peeled and cut on the diagonal into slices 1/4 inch (6 millimeters) thick

Peanut oil for frying

3 medium-sized waxy potatoes (about 12 ounces/340 grams total) such as Maine or Yukon Gold, peeled and cut into 1-inch (2.5-centimeter) cubes

4 Chinese chives (page 55) or scallions (both white and green parts), tops and roots removed and cut into 1-inch (2.5-centimeter) lengths

2 tablespoons finely chopped Chinese celery greens (page 55) or regular celery leaves

1. Combine the meat and water in a 4-quart (4-liter) soup pot or Dutch oven and bring to a rolling boil over high heat. Using a large metal spoon, skim off the foam that rises to the surface and then reduce the heat to medium-low. Add the ginger and galangal (if using), cover, and simmer for 1 hour. Be careful not to let the liquid come to a boil during this time, or the meat will toughen—adjust the heat as necessary.

2. While the meat is simmering, fry the shallots and garlic and set aside.

3. After the hour has passed, add the cinnamon, cloves, nutmeg, pepper, sugar, and salt to the pot and continue to simmer, covered, until the broth is intensely flavorful and aromatic, about 30 minutes longer. The oxtail pieces (or short ribs) should be butter-tender and just coming away from the bone.

4. While the meat continues to cook, prepare the vegetables. Fill a 2-quart (2-liter) saucepan with water and bring to a rolling boil. Add the carrots and boil until fork-tender, about 2 1/2 minutes. Drain them into a colander and set aside.

5. Next, fry the potatoes. Pour oil to a depth of 1 inch (2.5 centimeters) into a 2-quart (2-liter) saucepan and place over medium to medium-high heat. When the oil is hot but not smoking (about 365°F/185°C), slip a potato cube into the pan. If the potato

begins to fry immediately, the oil is ready. With a slotted metal spoon, carefully add the potatoes in small, manageable batches. Fry the potatoes, turning the cubes frequently with the spoon to prevent them from sticking together, until they're lightly golden on all sides, about 4 minutes total. To test if they are cooked through, pierce a cube with a fork. It should puncture the cube with only slight resistance. Using the slotted spoon, transfer the potatoes to paper towels to drain.

6. Take a sip of the stew and taste for salt, adding more if needed. Remove the pot from the heat and allow the stew to cool for 10 minutes, then add the boiled carrots and fried potatoes and stir well to combine.

7. Transfer the stew to a soup tureen or large, shallow bowl. Garnish with the Chinese chives, celery greens, and fried shallots and garlic. Serve promptly.

MENU SUGGESTIONS

In Java, this stew is eaten with steamed rice (page 173) and Javanese Sambal (page 119), Stir-fried Asian Greens with Garlic and Chiles (page 205), Green Beans with Coconut Milk (page 216), and Javanese Grilled Chicken (page 289). You can break with tradition, though, and eat it out of soup bowls with crusty bread.

ACEHNESE GOAT CURRY

Kare Kambing

(NORTH SUMATRA)

⁓

I got the recipe for this rich, golden coconut-milk curry from Sarah, a friend from Jakarta. Sarah was born in the Indonesian capital, but her family is originally from Aceh, the province at the northern tip of Sumatra known more recently for political turmoil and natural disasters than for its rich history as a center of spice trade. When I first met Sarah she was making a trip to her ancestral homeland in hopes of finding an Acehnese husband. As transient as Indonesians are, they are clannish when it comes to marriage. Husbands and wives traditionally come from the same ethnic line, even though they may have been settled far from home for generations. When I saw Sarah on her return to Jakarta, it was a mission unaccomplished, but she did come back with this recipe, an Acehnese classic, from a favorite aunt. It's usually served at weddings and for Lebaran, the feast celebrating the end of Ramadan.

Lamb shoulder or shanks can be substituted for the goat, but goat tastes richer. Goat leg, available at South Asian, Latin, and Greek butchers, is the best (and most common) cut to use. Ask the butcher to hack it into 1 1/2-inch (4-centimeter) chunks for you, though that may have already been done, as it is normally sold cut up. Sometimes the meat will be frozen, sometimes not, depending on the butcher. If it's frozen, allow it to thaw in the refrigerator for a few hours. But frozen or not, cook it within a day of buying it.

MAKES 4 TO 6 SERVINGS

1 cup (3 ounces/85 grams) Toasted Grated Coconut (page 59)

2 tablespoons Crisp-Fried Shallots (page 84; optional)

FOR THE FLAVORING PASTE

2 teaspoons cumin seeds

2 teaspoons black peppercorns

2 tablespoons coriander seeds

5 shallots (about 3 3/4 ounces/110 grams total), coarsely chopped

3 cloves garlic

3 to 8 fresh red Holland chiles or other fresh long, red chiles such as Fresno or cayenne, stemmed and coarsely chopped

3 tablespoons peanut oil

About 25 fresh curry leaves (page 63; optional)

1 piece fresh ginger, 2 inches (5 centimeters) long, peeled, thinly sliced with the grain, and cut into fine matchsticks (about 2 tablespoons)

1 thick stalk fresh lemongrass, tied into a knot (page 76)

2 whole star anise

1 piece cinnamon stick, 4 inches (10 centimeters) long

4 whole cloves

1 1/2 pounds (680 grams) goat leg or lamb shoulder or shanks, preferably bone in, cut into 1 1/2-inch (4-centimeter) chunks

2 1/4 cups (18 fluid ounces/560 milliliters) unsweetened coconut milk

3/4 cup (6 fluid ounces/175 millilters) water

3/4 teaspoon kosher salt

1 tablespoon fresh lime juice

1. Prepare the toasted coconut and the fried shallots (if using) and set aside.

2. To make the flavoring paste, place the cumin, peppercorns, and coriander in a small food processor. Pulse until ground to a dusty powder, about 2 minutes.

3. Add the shallots, garlic, and chiles to the ground spices and pulse until you have a smooth paste the consistency of creamy mashed potatoes. If the paste doesn't purée

properly and repeatedly creeps up the side of the food processor instead of grinding, add up to 2 tablespoons water, 1 tablespoon at a time, periodically turning the processor off and scraping the unground portions down toward the blade as you go. Set aside.

4. Heat the oil in a 3- or 4-quart (3- or 4-liter) saucepan, Dutch oven, or soup pot over medium heat. When it's hot—it should appear slightly shimmery—add the curry leaves (if using) and sauté them until they've picked up translucent blotches, about 30 seconds. Remove the pan from the heat for 30 seconds to allow it to cool slightly.

5. Return the pan to medium-low heat. Test to see if the oil is the right temperature by adding a pinch of the ground paste. The paste should sizzle slightly around the edges, not fry aggressively or sit motionless. When the oil is ready, add all the paste, ginger, lemongrass, star anise, cinnamon, and cloves. Sauté, stirring as needed to prevent scorching, until the paste begins to separate from the oil and the aroma of the spices takes over, 5 to 7 minutes. Add the toasted coconut and stir well to combine.

6. Add the meat and stir well to combine, making sure that the meat is well covered in the toasted coconut and flavoring paste. Raise the heat slightly and sauté the meat, stirring constantly to prevent scorching, until the meat has just begun to pick up brown spots, 3 to 5 minutes. It will resemble meat coated in fine bread crumbs. If the meat is crowded in the pan, work in 2 batches.

7. Add 3/4 cup (6 fluid ounces/175 milliliters) of the coconut milk, the water, and the salt and stir well to combine. Bring to a gentle boil, immediately reduce the heat to medium-low, and cook uncovered at a gentle simmer, stirring every 15 minutes or so to prevent sticking, until the goat is fork-tender and cooked through, 1 1/2 to 2 1/2 hours; the timing will depend on the toughness of the meat. (You may need to raise and reduce the heat periodically to maintain the simmer. Be careful not to allow the liquid to boil aggressively, which will toughen the meat and potentially curdle the coconut milk.) If the liquid starts to reduce until there is only about 1 cup (8 fluid ounces/250 milliliters) left, add up to 1 more cup water, 1/4 cup (2 fluid ounces/60 milliliters) at a time, until it is the consistency of a thick curry.

8. Add the remaining 1 1/2 cups (12 fluid ounces/375 milliliters) coconut milk and taste for salt, adding more if needed. Bring the mixture to a gentle simmer and immediately turn off the heat (the idea is to heat the coconut milk you have just added, not to cook it). You can skim off some of the oil on top if it is more than you like, but remember how flavorful it is, and don't skim off all of it.

9. Transfer the curry to a serving bowl and allow it to rest at room temperature for at least 15 minutes. Add the lime juice and stir well to combine. (The lime juice helps brighten

the dish and emphasize all its complex flavors.) Garnish, if using, with the fried shallots. Serve slightly warm.

MENU SUGGESTIONS

Serve this luxurious dish with rice, Malaysian Spiced Pineapple Pickle (page 136), Ching Lee's Braised Lemongrass Long Beans (page 218), Pan-Seared Tamarind Tuna (page 254), Mien's Garlic Fried Chicken (page 283), and Chile Omelet (page 334).

ABOVE LEFT: *Fresh-made tempeh, originally invented in Java, is a staple food throughout the Indonesian islands; the ingredient is used in everyday favorites such as Garlic-Marinated Tempeh (page 322).*

ABOVE CENTER: *Rooftops in Central Java.*

ABOVE RIGHT: *Tofu was introduced to the people of the Malay Archipelago by Chinese spice traders and quickly became a local favorite.*

13. TEMPEH, TOFU, AND EGGS

Rahmat's thoughts never seem to stray far from soybeans. Although he may be busy fishing in the stream behind his house or watching the latest ghost-story DVD from Hong Kong with his son, his mind will likely turn to the burlap-wrapped satchel of soybeans that arrived on his doorstep that morning. Soybeans, after all, are at the center of Rahmat's life. For most of his fifty-eight years, he has overseen his family's tempeh-making business in Yogyakarta, Indonesia. "Tempeh is a good life," he said to me one afternoon as he dipped his hands into a sack of soybeans and let them run through his fingers. They clinked together like pearls. "And without soybeans, there is no tempeh."

I had come to meet Rahmat because I have a thing for tempeh, the savory, spongy cakes made of boiled soybeans. From the moment I first ate a real Indonesian dish based on it, the ingredient went on my short list of favorite foods. But I'll admit that the first time I tasted tempeh in America in the late 1970s, when it was all the rage among people who shopped at health-food stores in the San Francisco Bay Area, I wasn't so convinced. As delicious (and nutritious) as it was, American cooks didn't seem to know what to do with it. Should they braise it like a piece of beef? Should they fry it like a French fry? Despite my own misguided attempts to cook it, I was still drawn to its earthy sweetness. But in Indonesia, where tempeh had been invented centuries ago by the Javanese, there was no confusion about how to cook it. Tempeh appeared at nearly every meal I ate. It was drizzled with a palm sugar–based reduction. It was simmered in delicate coconut-milk curries. It was cut into hefty chunks, marinated in garlic, and then fried until golden brown and crisp. It was treated like the sophisticated ingredient I always suspected it could be.

When I began exploring markets in Indonesia, I invariably looked forward to visiting the merchants who sold tempeh. They didn't offer the thin, plastic-wrapped version I knew from back home. Instead, what they sold came in thick, round-edged chunks wrapped in fresh, glossy banana leaves. Each parcel seemed like a gift. I would ask the merchant to peel back the leaf so that I could see the pillowy, golden tempeh inside. It smelled of the earth, and of mushrooms. I had heard that Rahmat was one of the few producers in the area who insisted on making tempeh the old-fashioned way—slowly and always using banana leaves, not plastic, for wrapping and curing it—so I sought him out soon after I arrived in Yogyakarta. I wanted to learn how tempeh is made.

When the taxi dropped me off in front of Rahmat's factory, I thought the driver had made a mistake. It was little more than a cinderblock addition to a small village house, rather than the factory complex that I'd been expecting. I checked the address again—we were in the correct place—and paid the driver. A small metal door slowly creaked open, and Rahmat greeted me. He was a short man with a few long strands of gray hair standing in for a beard.

"Welcome to the house of tempeh," he said in Indonesian, smiling warmly.

Inside, Rahmat's factory was considerably more factory-like, with every inch of space filled with activity. In the dim light, Rahmat began to show me around. "The first step in making every batch of tempeh is to remove the skin from each soybean," he said, slapping a fifty-pound bag of dried soybeans. We walked to two industrial-sized pots that were heating over gas burners. About fifty pounds of soybeans were boiling away in the pots. "The beans are boiled for thirty minutes until they have just softened, and then they're soaked in water overnight," Rahmat explained.

In another area, soybeans that had been boiled the previous day were being hand milled by a woman in a bright red T-shirt. She shook the beans between two small framed screens, prying loose the thin, skinlike membrane surrounding each bean to reveal two uniform golden halves. The woman was Malia, Rahmat's cousin. The soybean skin, she told me, would be set aside and sold at the market for use in a Central Javanese dish called *limba kulit kedelai*.

"The next step is to boil the halved beans for another thirty minutes. Then," Rahmat said, raising his eyebrows to heighten the drama of his story, "comes the heart of the tempeh-making process." He introduced me to Ronny, his brother-in-law, whose job it was to oversee the actual making of the tempeh. Ronny sprinkled *ragi tempe*—the white, powdery yeast culture that forms the whitish bloom (called *jamur*) binding the soybeans together in the final product—into two stainless-steel vats. He then stirred the beans with a large wooden spoon to make sure they were well mixed with the yeast.

Once that was accomplished, Ronny carefully placed small portions of the cultured soybeans inside narrow strips of banana leaf. He folded the strips over into long, neat packages that looked like they'd been wrapped at a department store. These were the beautiful parcels that I knew so well from Indonesian markets, except the tempeh had not yet developed to its full size. "Many people who make tempeh nowadays use plastic wrap to shape their tempeh," Rahmat said as he watched Ronny placing the tempeh parcels on a rack to cure. "But plastic has no taste. The banana leaf gives the tempeh flavor."

The rest of the tempeh-making process is left to nature. For the next two days, the parcels sit in the warmest part of the room. As they ripen, the cottony, Camembert-rind-like *jamur* grows around each soybean, making the tempeh cake. Ronny showed me some tempeh parcels that had only been curing for a day. Inside the banana leaf were soybeans covered with a white yeasty paste. At this midway point, Ronny explained, the tempeh, known as *tempe koro*, is not yet ready for eating.

On another rack were tempeh parcels that had reached maturity. Rahmat unfolded one for me. It was as puffy as cotton and had a clean, sweet aroma. "This will keep for two days without refrigeration, which is how long I have to sell it at the market," he said. Just then, Malia brought over a plate of battered and deep-fried tempeh that she had just cooked. I tasted a piece. It was warm and mellow, with a pure taste of soybeans. She smiled broadly as I asked for another helping.

———

Foods made from tempeh, tofu, and eggs are integral to the cuisines of the Malay Archipelago. It's not uncommon for a cook to prepare two or three dishes based on these ingredients for a family supper. Comforting and rich—and universally affordable—they're regarded as foods almost as essential as fish and vegetables. On any table, here or in Asia, they are a delicious substitute for fish, chicken, or meat.

The dishes in which tempeh are used are surprisingly filling, but that's because the ingredient is so rich in protein. And it's made richer in flavor by the many cooks who believe it must always be deep-fried until golden brown, a process that unleashes the full depth of its taste. With its nutty, soothing flavor, tempeh is a perfect backdrop for bright seasonings. Tempeh Sambal with Lemon Basil (page 324) and Caramelized Tempeh with Chiles (page 325) are two Indonesian classics that elevate the humble ingredient to glorious heights, while simple Garlic-Marinated Tempeh (page 322) reveals its quiet beauty. Any of the tempeh recipes in this chapter, served with rice and a vegetable dish, should make a satisfying meal for two or three guests. (For information about buying tempeh, see page 90.)

Tofu (*tahu*) is a refined cousin of tempeh, introduced to Indonesia, Malaysia, and Singapore by Chinese traders who came to the region, probably about the third century. Made of the milky liquid extracted when mashed soybeans are mixed with warm water, it's a smooth, pure ingredient without the earthy quality of tempeh. Cooks prize the clean taste of tofu and its ability to absorb the flavors of the dishes in which it is used. They favor firm tofu (soft or silken varieties are never selected) and, as with tempeh, always deep-fry it before using it, which gives it an appealing golden crust. The ingredient is a big player in the vegetable curries of the region, such as Tofu and Summer Vegetables in Coconut Milk (page 327) from Malaysia. It's occasionally cooked using methods associated with chicken, such as Twice-Cooked Tofu with Coriander (page 330), an Indonesian favorite in which the tofu is simmered in a sweet herbal broth to boost its flavor, then fried. (For information about buying tofu, see page 91.)

Eggs (*telur ayam*) are the not-so-secret ingredient that cooks use to extend meals. A welcome by-product of the chicken flocks that freely roam through the villages of the Malay Archipelago, eggs show up in all sorts of guises to which we in the West are unaccustomed, such as hard cooked in curries, scrambled into stir-fries, and even fried and crowning a plate of fried rice. Eggs also appear in fluffy omelets studded with chiles (Chile Omelet, page 334) and are fried until crisp and then swaddled in sautéed aromatics (Fried Eggs with Garlic, Shallots, Chiles, and Ginger, page 332). But perhaps my personal favorite is the way they're prepared and sold at hawker stalls all over Malaysia and Singapore: soft boiled and topped with soy sauce and finely chopped chiles (Kopi Tiam Soft-Boiled Eggs, page 333). This simple yet flavorful dish is one of the great eating delights of Southeast Asia.

GARLIC-MARINATED TEMPEH
Tempe Goreng
(INDONESIA)

⎯

Here's an everyday Indonesian method for preparing tempeh. First, the tempeh is cut into squares, scored lightly, and marinated in garlicky salted water. The tempeh is then fried until crisp and golden. This dish is as basic to the Indonesian kitchen as steamed rice. Indeed, the cooks who have shown me how to make it would smile to see it in print. Some of you may balk at the idea of deep-frying tempeh, but Indonesian cooks believe it's the only way to give it the depth and crispness it deserves.

MAKES 4 SERVINGS

8-ounce (225-gram) piece tempeh

2 teaspoons kosher salt

5 cloves garlic, peeled and bruised until juicy
  with the flat side of a knife

1 1/2 cups (12 fluid ounces/375 milliliters) water

Peanut oil for frying

1. With a sharp knife, cut the tempeh into 2-inch (5-centimeter) squares about 1/3 inch (9 millimeters) thick (slightly thicker is fine). Lightly score both sides of the tempeh with

4 diagonal cuts: 2 cuts in one direction, and then 2 cuts in the opposite direction. Don't score deeply; the slashes should be about 1/8 inch (3 millimeters) deep. (Be extra careful not to cut all the way through, or the tempeh may fall apart when fried.) Why score? It allows the marinade of garlic, salt, and water to better penetrate the interior.

2. Combine the salt, garlic, and water in a large, shallow bowl. Stir until the salt is completely dissolved. Place the tempeh in the garlic water and marinate, uncovered, at room temperature for 15 minutes, turning the tempeh every so often to make sure it absorbs the marinade evenly.

3. Remove the tempeh from the marinade and gently pat it dry with paper towels. You don't want it to be completely dry, but you don't want it to be so wet that the hot oil will splatter when the tempeh is put in it. Set aside.

4. Pour oil to a depth of 1/2 inch (12 millimeters) into a 12-inch (30-centimeter) skillet and place over medium to medium-high heat until hot but not smoking. To test if the oil is the right temperature (it should be about 365°F/185°C), spear a square of tempeh onto a fork and slip a corner of the square into the oil. If the oil is ready, it will immediately bubble vigorously around the tempeh. Gently slide as many of the tempeh pieces into the hot oil as will fit without touching, working in 2 batches if the pan isn't big enough to accommodate them all at once. Fry the squares, turning them often with 2 forks or tongs, until they're uniformly golden and crispy, 2 to 3 minutes; the timing will depend on the thickness of the tempeh and how hot the oil is. Be sure not to fry the tempeh beyond the point at which it is just golden, or it will taste bitter. You may need to adjust the heat periodically: if the oil is too hot, the tempeh will likely overbrown in spots; if it's too cool, the tempeh will likely come out greasy. Using the forks or tongs, transfer the tempeh squares to paper towels to drain.

5. Arrange the tempeh on a plate and serve warm or at room temperature.

MENU SUGGESTIONS

This dish is a ubiquitous accompaniment to meals in Indonesia, where cooks often make it in lieu of putting together a more elaborate dish. There are few savory foods in this book that it doesn't complement. Try it with Lemongrass-Scented Coconut Rice (page 176), Javanese Sambal (page 119), Chopped Vegetable Salad with Coconut and Lime Leaf Dressing (page 156), and Javanese Chicken Curry (page 275).

TEMPEH SAMBAL WITH LEMON BASIL
Sambal Tempe
(BALI, INDONESIA)

⟋

The fragrance of lemon basil infuses every bite of this beautiful dish of deep-fried tempeh pieces slathered in a ruby red sambal. It's important that the lemon basil only be added at the last possible moment—you want it to be kissed by the warmth of the sambal, not cooked. I got this recipe at a simple *warung* (eating stall) many years ago in Denpasar, Bali.

MAKES 4 SERVINGS

1 recipe just-cooked Garlic-Marinated Tempeh (page 322)

3 tablespoons peanut oil

1 teaspoon dried shrimp paste (page 65), pressed into a disk 1/4 inch (6 millimeters) thick

4 shallots (about 3 ounces/85 grams total), coarsely chopped

3 cloves garlic, coarsely chopped

10 fresh red Holland chiles or other fresh long, red chiles such as Fresno or cayenne, stemmed and coarsely chopped

1 teaspoon palm sugar (page 79), thinly sliced, or dark brown sugar

1/4 teaspoon kosher salt

1 cup (about 1 ounce/30 grams) loosely packed fresh lemon basil (page 74), Thai basil, or Italian basil leaves

1. Prepare the tempeh and set aside.

2. Heat the oil in a 12-inch (30-centimeter) skillet (nonstick will work best) over medium heat. Add the shrimp paste disk and sauté it, turning it over a few times with a spatula, until both sides have golden brown spots around the edges, 2 to 4 minutes. Don't worry if the shrimp paste crumbles as you're sautéing it. If it does break apart, just continue sautéing until all the pieces are golden brown. Using a slotted spoon, remove the shrimp paste from the skillet and allow it to cool for 1 minute. Set the skillet aside with the oil in it.

3. Place the sautéed shrimp paste, shallots, garlic, chiles, palm sugar, and salt in a small food processor. Pulse until you have a chunky-smooth paste the consistency of cooked oatmeal.

4. Reheat the oil in the skillet over medium-low heat. Test to see if the oil is the right temperature by adding a pinch of the ground paste. The paste should sizzle slightly around

the edges, not fry aggressively or sit motionless. When the oil is ready, add all the paste and sauté, stirring as needed to prevent scorching, until most of the liquid from the chiles and shallots has evaporated and the paste begins to separate from the oil, about 9 minutes. Taste for salt, and add a pinch more if needed. Remove the pan from the heat and allow the paste to cool for a few minutes until it is warm, not hot.

5. Add the Garlic-Marinated Tempeh and lemon basil leaves to the paste. Gently fold the tempeh into the paste until the pieces are evenly coated and the leaves are evenly distributed, being careful not to break up the tempeh. Transfer to a serving dish and serve at once.

MENU SUGGESTIONS

Partner this sweet-and-hot dish with rice, Padang Fish Curry (page 244), Sautéed Cabbage with Ginger and Crispy Indian Yellow Lentils (page 209), and Javanese Grilled Chicken (page 289). You don't need to include a sambal, as this dish itself serves as one.

CARAMELIZED TEMPEH WITH CHILES
Tempe Kering
(CENTRAL JAVA, INDONESIA)

Ibu Kuncoro, a cook in Yogyakarta, Central Java, made this for me one afternoon with fresh tempeh from Rahmat's factory. It's a remarkable dish, with crisp tempeh coated in an appealingly sticky-sweet sauce made of palm sugar, chiles, *daun salam* leaves, galangal, garlic, and shallots. Its name means "dry tempeh," and it often accompanies *tumpeng*, the cone-shaped yellow rice dish (Celebration Yellow Rice, page 178) eaten in Indonesia on ceremonial occasions. It's also excellent when served as a part of an everyday meal.

MAKES 4 SERVINGS

1 tablespoon tamarind pulp, plus 3/4 cup (6 fluid ounces/175 milliliters) very warm water to make extract

1 pound (455 grams) tempeh, cut on the diagonal into slices 2 1/2 inches (6 centimeters) long and 1/4 inch (6 millimeters) thick

Peanut oil for frying

2 cloves garlic, thinly sliced

2 shallots (about 1 1/2 ounces/40 grams total), thinly sliced

2 to 5 fresh red Holland chiles or other fresh long, red chiles such as Fresno or cayenne, stemmed and very thinly sliced on the diagonal

6 to 9 tablespoons (85 to 130 grams) palm sugar (page 79), thinly sliced, or dark brown sugar

1/2 teaspoon kosher salt

5 whole *daun salam* leaves (page 64; optional)

1 piece fresh or thawed, frozen galangal, 1 inch (2.5 centimeters) long, peeled and thinly sliced with (not against) the grain (about 1 tablespoon; optional)

1. Place the tamarind pulp in a small nonreactive bowl and mix it with the warm water. Let the pulp rest until it softens, 10 to 15 minutes. Squeeze and massage the softened pulp through your fingers, loosening the fruit's auburn pulp from the shiny black seeds, brittle brown skin shards, and sinewy bits of string. With your fingers, remove all the solid pieces from the liquid and discard them. All that will remain is the caramel-colored extract. This tamarind extract will be thinner than most of the other tamarind extracts in this book. Set the extract aside.

2. Next, deep-fry the tempeh. Pour oil to a depth of 1/2 inch (12 millimeters) into a 12-inch (30-centimeter) skillet and place over medium to medium-high heat until hot but not smoking. To test if the oil is the right temperature (it should be about 365°F/185°C), slip a piece of tempeh into the oil. If the oil is ready, it will immediately bubble vigorously around the tempeh. Gently slide as many of the tempeh slices into the hot oil as will fit without touching, working in 2 batches if the pan is not big enough to accommodate them all at once. Fry the slices, turning them often with a slotted spoon, until they are uniformly golden and crispy, 2 to 3 minutes; the timing will depend on the thickness of the tempeh and how hot the oil is. Be sure not to fry the tempeh beyond the point at which it is just golden, or it will taste bitter. You may need to adjust the heat periodically: if the oil is too hot, the tempeh will likely over-brown in spots; if it's too cool, the tempeh will likely come out greasy. Using the slotted spoon, transfer the tempeh slices to paper towels to drain. Set the pan aside on a cool place on the stove and allow the oil to cool for a few minutes.

3. Pour off all but about 3 tablespoons of the frying oil and return the pan to medium-low heat. When the oil is hot, add the garlic and shallots and sauté, stirring constantly, until they've softened and are beginning to turn translucent, about 2 minutes. Don't let the garlic and shallots change color. Add the chiles and palm sugar (add the larger amount if you want a sweeter dish) and sauté, mashing the sugar with a spatula or the back of a spoon, until the palm sugar has melted, about 2 minutes.

4. Add the tamarind extract, salt, and the *daun salam* leaves and galangal (if using). Stir well to combine and raise the heat slightly. Bring the liquid to a vigorous simmer. Reduce the heat slightly and cook the liquid at a simmer until it is reduced by almost two-thirds and is the consistency of thin honey, about 10 minutes. It may look a bit foamy. Don't worry, it will settle as it cools.

5. Turn the heat off and remove and discard the *daun salam* leaves and galangal (if used). Gently fold the fried tempeh into the reduced liquid, coating each piece evenly with the sticky-sweet sauce. Be careful not to break up the tempeh as you stir—the sauce is viscous, and the tempeh quite fragile.

6. Transfer the tempeh to a serving dish and serve promptly.

MENU SUGGESTIONS

Although this dish of royal lineage is often paraded out at elaborate feasts and served alongside Celebration Yellow Rice (page 178), it's also good at everyday meals. Serve it with an array of dishes that aren't as sweet, such as plain steamed rice, Grilled Coconut Chicken with Lemon Basil (page 292), Stir-fried Bean Sprouts with Chinese Chives (page 208), and Malaccan Beef and Vegetable Stew (page 309).

TOFU AND SUMMER VEGETABLES IN COCONUT MILK
Sayur Lodeh
(MALAYSIA)

❧

This lovely dish of deep-fried tofu, carrots, green beans, and cabbage in a pale yellow coconut-milk broth is a Malaysian family favorite. A large quantity of candlenuts in the flavoring paste lends the broth its body and richness. Deep-frying tofu gives it a pillowy, spongelike texture that helps it absorb flavors more readily. This dish is often served for breakfast with sliced *lontong*, rice that has been boiled in bamboo cylinders until it forms tight, compact cakes. It can just as easily be served for lunch or dinner with plain steamed rice. You can omit the dried shrimp paste for a vegetarian version.

MAKES 4 SERVINGS

FOR THE FLAVORING PASTE

1 1/2 tablespoons dried shrimp paste (page 65)

6 shallots (about 5 ounces/140 grams total), coarsely chopped

2 cloves garlic, coarsely chopped

4 to 10 small dried red chiles such as árbol, stemmed and coarsely chopped

1 piece fresh or thawed, frozen turmeric (page 92), 2 inches (5 centimeters) long, peeled and coarsely chopped (about 2 teaspoons), or 2 teaspoons ground turmeric

7 candlenuts (page 48) or unsalted macadamia nuts

4 tablespoons peanut oil, plus more for frying

1 piece fresh or thawed, frozen galangal, 2 inches (5 centimeters) long, peeled and bruised until juicy with a heavy, blunt object such as the bottom of a glass measuring cup (optional)

1 cup (8 fluid ounces/240 milliliters) unsweetened coconut milk

3 cups (24 fluid ounces/750 milliliters) water

30 green beans, stemmed and sliced on the diagonal into 1 1/2-inch (4-centimeter) lengths (about 1 1/3 cups/6 ounces/170 grams)

2 medium-sized carrots, peeled and cut into thick matchsticks 1 1/2 inches (4 centimeters) long by 1/3 inch (9 millimeters) wide (about 2 cups/7 ounces/200 grams)

1 tablespoon sugar

3/4 teaspoon kosher salt

8 ounces (225 grams) firm fresh tofu (two 4-inch/10-centimeter squares), each square halved on the diagonal into triangles 1/2 inch (12 millimeters) thick

1/4 small head green cabbage, cored and cut into 1-inch (2.5-centimeter) squares (about 2 cups/8 ounces/225 grams)

1. To make the flavoring paste, place the shrimp paste in the center of a 5-inch (13-centimeter) square of aluminum foil. Fold the edges of the foil over to form a small parcel, and press down with the heel of your hand to flatten the shrimp paste into a disk 1/4 inch (6 millimeters) thick. Heat a gas burner to medium-low or an electric burner to medium-high. Using a pair of tongs or 2 forks, place the sealed parcel directly on the heat source. Toast until the paste begins to smoke and release a burning, shrimpy smell, about 1 1/2 minutes. With the tongs or forks, turn the parcel over and toast the other side for another 1 1/2 minutes, then turn off the burner. Again using the tongs or forks, remove the parcel and let cool for 30 seconds to 1 minute. Carefully unwrap the foil; the edges of the disk should be black-brown and toasty and the center should be golden with some black-brown patches. Using a spoon, scrape the toasted shrimp paste into a small bowl and allow it to cool for another 30 seconds. Discard the foil.

2. Place the toasted shrimp paste, shallots, garlic, chiles, turmeric, and candlenuts in a small food processor. Pulse until you have a smooth paste the consistency of creamy

mashed potatoes. If the paste won't purée properly and repeatedly creeps up the side of the processor instead of grinding, add up to 2 tablespoons water, 1 tablespoon at a time, periodically turning the processor off and scraping the unground portions down toward the blade.

3. Heat the 4 tablespoons oil in a 4-quart (4-liter) saucepan, Dutch oven, or soup pot over medium-low heat. Test to see if the oil is the right temperature by adding a pinch of the ground paste. The paste should sizzle slightly around the edges, not fry aggressively or sit motionless. When the oil is ready, add all the paste and sauté, stirring as needed to prevent scorching, until the shallots and garlic no longer smell raw and the paste begins to separate slightly from the oil, 5 to 7 minutes. Be careful not to let the flavoring paste cook for too long. It should be limp and silken, not golden and crusty.

4. Add 1/2 cup (4 fluid ounces/120 milliliters) of the coconut milk and all the water. Raise the heat to medium and bring the liquid to a steady simmer, stirring constantly. Add the green beans, carrots, sugar, and salt and stir to combine. Reduce the heat to medium-low and let the vegetables simmer gently uncovered, stirring occasionally, until they are fork-tender and only slightly crunchy, about 15 minutes. (Don't let the liquid boil, or the coconut milk may curdle. You may need to adjust the heat periodically if the simmer becomes too vigorous or too slow.)

5. Meanwhile, deep-fry the tofu. Dry the tofu triangles thoroughly with paper towels. Pour oil to a depth of 1 inch (2.5 centimeters) into a 1 1/2- to 2-quart (1.5- to 2-liter) saucepan and place over medium to medium-high heat until hot but not smoking. To test if the oil is the right temperature (it should be about 365°F/185°C), spear a piece of tofu onto a fork and slip a corner of the piece into the oil. If the oil is ready, it will immediately bubble vigorously around the tofu. Using 2 forks or a pair of tongs, add the tofu pieces in small batches (crowding will cool the oil down and make the tofu greasy). Fry the tofu pieces, turning them often with a slotted spoon, until they're uniformly golden and crispy, 3 to 5 minutes. Be sure not to fry the tofu beyond the point at which it is just golden, or its texture will be tough, its taste bitter. Using the slotted spoon, transfer the tofu pieces to paper towels to drain.

6. Add the fried tofu and cabbage to the simmering coconut-milk broth and continue to cook uncovered, stirring occasionally, until the cabbage is wilted and beginning to turn translucent, about 10 minutes. Do not let the cabbage overcook and become mushy.

7. Add the remaining 1/2 cup (4 fluid ounces/120 milliliters) coconut milk and allow it to heat through, about 2 minutes. Taste for salt, and add a pinch more if needed. Remove and discard the galangal.

8. Transfer the tofu, vegetables, and broth to a shallow serving bowl and allow the dish to rest for at least 15 minutes before eating. It will taste best when slightly cooled.

MENU SUGGESTIONS

I like to serve this mild, soupy dish along with steamed rice (page 173) and dryish dishes, such as Stir-fried Shrimp Sambal (page 262), Grilled Coconut Chicken with Lemon Basil (page 292), Beef Rendang (page 304), and Chile Omelet (page 334).

TWICE-COOKED TOFU WITH CORIANDER
Tahu Goreng Bacem
(CENTRAL JAVA, INDONESIA)

Twice-cooking, an Indonesian technique, is beloved by the cooks of Central Java. This recipe from the city of Solo involves simmering tofu—tempeh or bone-in chicken pieces are sometimes substituted—in a sweet-salty marinade until the marinade is completely reduced (it's partially absorbed by the tofu, partially evaporated by cooking). The tofu is then deep-fried until golden brown and crisp. It's an unusual blend of savory and sweet, with the warm taste of Indonesian sweet soy sauce and coriander seeds reigning. *Tahu goreng bacem* is a traditional component of a *nasi liwet* meal, which also includes Lemongrass-Scented Coconut Rice (page 176) and *gudeg*, a dryish curry made with young, unripe jackfruit. Serve this dish slightly warm, with plenty of steamed white rice. It makes excellent leftovers.

MAKES 4 SERVINGS

FOR THE MARINADE

1 teaspoon tamarind pulp, plus 3 tablespoons very warm water to make extract

2 tablespoons coriander seeds

2 cloves garlic, coarsely chopped

2 shallots (about 1 1/2 ounces/40 grams total), coarsely chopped

1 piece fresh or thawed, frozen galangal, 1 inch (2.5 centimeters) long, peeled and thinly

sliced against the grain (about 1 tablespoon; optional, but traditional)

2 tablespoons Indonesian sweet soy sauce (page 72)

2 tablespoons palm sugar (page 79), thinly sliced, or dark brown sugar

1 cup (8 fluid ounces/250 milliliters) water

1 pound (455 grams) firm fresh tofu (four 4-inch/10-centimeter squares), each square halved on the diagonal into triangles 1/2 inch (12 millimeters) thick

Kosher salt (optional)

Peanut oil for frying

1. To make the marinade, place the tamarind pulp in a small nonreactive bowl and mix it with the warm water. Let the pulp rest until it softens, 10 to 15 minutes. Squeeze and massage the softened pulp through your fingers, loosening the fruit's auburn pulp from the shiny black seeds, brittle brown skin shards, and sinewy bits of string. With your fingers, remove all the solid pieces from the liquid and discard them. All that will remain is a thick caramel-colored extract. Set the tamarind extract aside.

2. Place the coriander seeds in a small food processor and pulse until ground to a dusty powder, about 2 minutes. Add the tamarind extract, garlic, shallots, galangal (if using), sweet soy sauce, palm sugar, and water to the ground coriander. Pulse until everything is well puréed, about 2 minutes.

3. Transfer the marinade to a 12-inch (30-centimeter) skillet (nonstick will work best). Add the tofu and bring to a gentle simmer over medium heat. Taste a bit of the marinade for salt, and add a pinch more if needed (the sweet soy sauce will probably add sufficient saltiness). Reduce the heat slightly and let simmer, uncovered and turning the tofu often to make sure all sides are covered in the marinade, until all of the liquid has evaporated, 30 to 45 minutes. Be careful not to let the tofu get stuck to the bottom of the pan while the liquid is evaporating. Remove the tofu triangles from the pan and set them aside until they are cool enough to handle.

4. Now, deep-fry the tofu. Dry the tofu triangles thoroughly with paper towels. The tofu doesn't need to be completely dry—bits of the marinade clinging to the surface are fine—but if it's very wet it will splatter when placed in the hot oil. Pour oil to a depth of 1 inch (2.5 centimeters) into a 1 1/2- to 2-quart (1.5- to 2-liter) saucepan and place over medium to medium-high heat until hot but not smoking. To test if the oil is the right temperature (it should be about 365°F/185°C), spear a piece of tofu onto a fork and slip a corner of the piece into the oil. If the oil is ready, it will immediately bubble vigorously around the tofu. Using 2 forks or a pair of tongs, add the tofu pieces in small batches (crowding will cool the oil down and make the tofu greasy). Fry the tofu pieces, turning them often with a slotted spoon, until they're golden brown and crispy, 3 to 5 minutes. It's fine if small portions of the tofu pick up dark spots (the sugars in the marinade that remain on the surface scorch easily). Using the slotted spoon, transfer the tofu pieces to paper towels to drain.

5. Transfer the tofu to a serving plate and serve warm or at room temperature.

MENU SUGGESTIONS

Pair this enticingly sweet concoction with such dishes as Lemongrass-Scented Coconut Rice (page 176), Javanese Chicken Curry (page 275), and Acehnese Goat Curry (page 314). Make sure that its companion dishes don't use palm sugar as a dominant flavoring.

FRIED EGGS WITH GARLIC, SHALLOTS, CHILES, AND GINGER
Telur Mata Sapi Bumbu
(INDONESIA)

This chile-hot fried-egg dish turns up on tables as an accompaniment to rice-based meals, not for breakfast. It's simple to make. Fry a few eggs (Indonesians like their fried eggs—which they call *mata sapi*, or "eye of the buffalo," for their appearance—on the crispy side, and so do I), then top them with the sautéed aromatics, which include ginger, chile, shallots, and garlic. A splash of vinegar added to the aromatics binds all the flavors. My thanks to the Djulinas family in Padang, West Sumatra, for this recipe.

MAKES 3 SERVINGS

3 tablespoons peanut oil, plus more as needed

3 eggs

Kosher salt

3 cloves garlic, thinly sliced lengthwise

2 shallots (about 1 1/2 ounces/40 grams total), thinly sliced lengthwise

2 to 3 fresh red Holland chiles or other fresh

long, red chiles such as Fresno or cayenne, stemmed and thinly sliced on the diagonal

1 piece fresh ginger, 1 inch (2.5 centimeters) long, peeled, thinly sliced with the grain, and cut into fine matchsticks (about 1 tablespoon)

1 teaspoon palm, cider, or rice vinegar

1. Heat the 3 tablespoons oil in a 12-inch (30-centimeter) skillet (nonstick will work best) over medium heat. When it's hot—it should appear slightly shimmery—crack an egg into it. Season the top of the egg with a pinch of salt. When the white is just beginning to turn brown and crispy around the edges, carefully turn the egg over with a spatula. Sauté until the yolk is set, about 1 minute. You want the surface of the egg to be golden and the yolk to be fairly firm. Transfer the fried egg to a serving plate with the spatula and set aside. Fry the remaining eggs in the same manner, setting them all

aside on the serving plate and always leaving the oil behind in the pan. Add more oil to the pan if the eggs threaten to stick. Allow the pan to cool for a few minutes before proceeding to the next step.

2. Return the pan with its oil to medium-low heat. When it's hot, add the garlic, shallots, chiles, ginger, and vinegar and sauté, stirring often, until the garlic and shallots are just beginning to wilt and turn translucent, 3 to 4 minutes. Don't let the garlic and shallots brown.

3. Evenly ladle the sautéed ingredients over the fried eggs and serve at once.

MENU SUGGESTIONS

This easy-to-make dish can be served alongside rice, Javanese Cucumber and Carrot Pickle (page 132), Fern Curry with Shrimp (page 226), and Padang Fish Curry (page 244). Alternatively, you can pair it with a light Western-style salad and crusty French or Italian bread. Or, eat the eggs as you would fried eggs at breakfast, though they'll be considerably more potently flavored than what you're accustomed to!

KOPI TIAM SOFT-BOILED EGGS
Telur Setengah Masak
(MALAYSIA)

～

Small open-air coffee shops, called *kopi tiam* or *kedai kopi*, are a fixture in all Malaysian cities (and Singapore, too). Workingmen and -women launch their days in these humble establishments over tea sweetened with condensed milk (Hawker's Tea, page 354) and thick slices of white bread toasted over open coals. The toast is typically accompanied by soft-boiled eggs topped with a few red chile slices, a dusting of pepper, and a splash of soy sauce. This simple combination of flavors is the essence of Malaysia.

MAKES 1 SERVING

2 large eggs

Soy sauce

A few very thin slices fresh red or green Thai chile

Freshly ground black or white pepper

1. Pour water to a depth of 3 inches (7.5 centimeters) into a 2-quart (2-liter) saucepan and bring to a rolling boil over high heat. One at a time, gently lower the eggs into the water with a spoon and then reduce the heat slightly. Cook the eggs until they're soft-boiled to your liking; 2 to 3 minutes is standard for large eggs.

2. When the eggs are ready, immerse them in cold water for a few seconds and then crack them into a small serving bowl, discarding the shell. Serve immediately garnished with a splash of soy sauce, the chile slices, and a grind or two of pepper.

CHILE OMELET

Telur Dadar Pakai Cabai

(INDONESIA, MALAYSIA, AND SINGAPORE)

⏤

Studded with slivers of bright red chiles, this golden omelet is the perfect choice if you need a simple-to-make dish to round out a menu. You're likely to have all the ingredients on hand and it only takes a few minutes to make, start to finish. Don't roll or fold the omelet. Instead, serve it flat on a large, round plate, to show off the pretty random pattern of chile slices speckling its surface.

MAKES 2 TO 4 SERVINGS

3 large eggs

Pinch of kosher salt

2 tablespoons peanut oil

2 fresh red Holland chiles or other fresh long, red chiles such as Fresno or cayenne, stemmed and very thinly sliced on the diagonal

Indonesian sweet soy sauce (page 72) for serving

1. Break the eggs into a bowl and add a pinch of salt. Beat the eggs with a fork until they're just blended. Don't overbeat them: You want only to mix the whites and yolks together.

2. Heat the oil in a 12-inch (30-centimeter) nonstick skillet over medium heat. When it's hot—it should appear slightly shimmery—add the sliced chiles. Sauté the chiles, stirring them constantly with a spatula, until they just begin to go limp, about 1 minute. Leave the chiles in the pan.

3. Raise the heat to medium-high. Allow the oil to heat for a few seconds, then pour the blended eggs over the chiles. Very quickly spread the chiles out with a spatula so that they're evenly distributed throughout the omelet and not settled into clumps. Immediately start shifting the pan around the heat, to prevent the edges of the omelet from sticking to the sides of the pan.

4. After about 1 minute (the time will vary according to the thickness of the pan), the omelet should be almost three-fourths set (the center should still be creamy). Slide the spatula under the omelet, simultaneously shaking the pan with a circular motion to loosen any portions of the omelet that are stuck to the bottom of the pan. Lift and flip the omelet with a smooth motion. (This is going to take some practice; I still occasionally fail, even though I've made omelets like this one hundreds of times.) The cooked side should be flecked with golden spots.

5. Turn the heat off and cook the omelet for another 30 seconds in the heat remaining in the pan, continuing to move the pan in a circular motion until the second side is just set.

6. Flip the omelet over directly onto a large, round serving plate. The side you cooked last should be face up. Do not fold or roll it; it should remain flat.

7. Serve promptly with a bottle of sweet soy sauce on the table—this omelet's penultimate condiment.

MENU SUGGESTIONS

There are few foods this dish won't welcome. For starters, try rice, Sweet-Sour Cucumber and Carrot Pickle with Turmeric (page 130), Gado-Gado (page 154), Potato Rendang (page 223), and Indian-Style Fish Stew with Okra (page 249).

ABOVE LEFT: *Nutmeg is ground by hand with a grater.*

ABOVE CENTER: *A spice cake cooking in a home kitchen in Indonesia; in most kitchens there, ovens are heated not by gas or electricity, but by coconut shells.*

ABOVE RIGHT: *Ali, a farmer in Indonesia's Spice Islands, with a glass of Cinnamon Tea (page 353) to cool him from the afternoon heat.*

14. SWEETS AND BEVERAGES

I was wandering through the streets of Bandung, in West Java, Indonesia, in the sweltering noonday sun. It was the first week of Ramadan, the Islamic fasting month, and the city was at a standstill. Restaurants were shuttered, satay pushcarts idle. A few office workers on their lunch hour strolled around aimlessly, unsure what to do with themselves now that lunch or snacking or even having a glass of tea wasn't an option. A group of crows circled overhead, vulturelike.

This was the second time I'd been in Bandung during Ramadan. The first time, though I'd tried hard to observe the fast out of consideration for others, I didn't make out well. I hoarded crackers and cookies in a locked cupboard, sneaking them throughout the day. Now, a few years later, I didn't want to be excluded from the communal spirit of the month. It's a festive period, a time of bonding and friendliness and joy, when old scores are settled and weary souls recharged. I was determined to be part of it. The rules were simple, and they were ingrained into me: from sunrise to sunset, no eating, no drinking beverages of any kind, no sexual activity, and no angry or aggressive language (or thoughts). I could handle all that. But then as I stared at a mound of perfect oranges in the window of a fruit shop, I wasn't so sure. I sighed, thinking about how I'd fared the last few days. The first day of the fast had been sheer torture, the second day slightly less so. By the third day, I was starting to experience a strange, delirious enjoyment in being famished. I was beginning to learn to rise above the hunger rather than succumb to it. As someone who usually plans his every waking moment around food, it was nice to have a break. Still, I couldn't help but imagine how satisfying popping open one of those oranges would be, its sweet, clear juice filling my parched mouth.

That afternoon I had extra incentive to resist the temptation to eat. I'd been invited to celebrate *berbuka puasa*, the breaking of the fast, at the home of Mami (pronounced Mommy). She was the mother of Juanda, an Indonesian diplomat I'd met in Jakarta. "My mother is one of Bandung's best Sundanese cooks!" Juanda said, barely able to control his enthusiasm. The term *Sundanese* referred to his West Javanese ethnic group, known for its rich artistic traditions and graceful cuisine. I was determined to be as hungry as I could when I arrived at Mami's house.

I continued walking in the heat, ducking under awnings and trees for shade every chance I got. I took in a faint smell of butter and caramelized sugar, the universal aroma of sweets being baked. I kept walking until I found the source of the fragrance: a large old-fashioned bakery with a hand-painted sign identifying it as Sumber Hidangan, which roughly translates to The Source of the Repast. Maybe, I thought, I'd buy some sweets to take to Mami.

Inside, clerks in starched white uniforms padded softly across the black-and-white tiled floor as ceiling fans whirred overhead. The fragrance was overwhelming. My stomach growled. A smiling young clerk approached me. "What would you like?" she asked, her eyes twinkling. I scanned the display cases. There were carefully crafted European-style baked goods, including cakes, fruit tarts, and more varieties of butter cookies than I'd ever seen. "Everything!" I blurted out.

From previous visits, I knew that the people of Bandung appreciate all kinds of sweets but have a special affinity for those made with butter, flour, and sugar, rather than only the classic Indonesian types made with rice flour and palm sugar. Such European-style confections are a legacy of the four hundred years that Dutch colonizers spent in Bandung. Though rarely eaten as desserts following a meal, these sweets are prized as late-afternoon tea snacks or, most especially, during Ramadan, as a way to celebrate *berbuka puasa*.

After a millisecond of indecision, I ordered a pound of butter cookies, two loaves of puffy white bread, and a few imported Droste chocolate bars—perfect for Mami, I hoped.

A few hours later I was in a rickety taxi on my way to meeting Mami. We passed a busy vegetable market, with heaps of carrots and cabbages sprawled out in the bright sun. In the distance I could make out emerald green tea plantations on the high mountain slopes just outside the city. Finally, I reached Mami's house. It was a grand place, a sleek art deco mansion, probably built in the 1930s, with stylish, slatlike windows all around and extensive grounds overgrown with tropical foliage. I paid the taxi driver and walked up the winding driveway. The front door was ajar.

"Mami?" I called out. There was no answer. I waited a moment, then entered. Two large rooms flanked a long hallway. On the right was the dining room, an elegant table filling its length. On the left was a sitting room with an assortment of high-backed chairs, antique Chinese chests, and a large collection of old, dusty West Javanese *wayang* marionettes, arranged as if in conversation with one another. I called out again. A girl who appeared to be about fifteen emerged. I identified myself, and she silently led me through the house.

Mami sat in the shade in a high-backed rattan chair overlooking a backyard garden bursting with pink bougainvillea. She appeared to be in her midseventies and wore a lemon yellow sarong that billowed around her bare feet. Her mostly gray hair, slick with coconut oil, was pulled back into a bun.

"Mami," I said. "It's James, Juanda's acquaintance." She slowly turned toward me. She had the drawn but clear-eyed look of someone who'd been fasting. "I brought you something," I continued, handing her the bag of goodies from Sumber Hidangan. She took the bag and inhaled deeply. Her face softened.

"Sumber Hidangan," she said, looking up at me. "It's the best bakery in Bandung." I felt proud that I had won Mami's approval. "You'll have to forgive that I am not better dressed," she continued. "When you're as old as I am, the fast is not easy." She clapped her hands together, and a servant came running. "*Teh manis*," she said to the girl, ordering me a glass of sweet tea.

"Mami," I said, "I'll wait for sundown. I'm fasting, too."

She looked at me quizzically, then after a moment said, "I'll get you a tea."

"No, thank you, Mami. I'll wait."

The corners of her kohl-rimmed eyes crinkled slightly. Who exactly is this unfamiliar American in front of me and why is he fasting? she seemed to be asking. After a few moments she spoke softly. "Everything is Allah, including your thoughts," she said. "They'll give you the strength to endure the fast." She stood up, balancing herself on the edge of the chair. "Come. I'll show you how I get *my* strength."

Mami led me through the garden. We entered the house, walking down a long corridor into a large, brightly lit, airy kitchen. Four cooks were hard at work preparing that night's feast.

"They are making *spekkuk* now," Mami said. I knew *spekkuk*, the Dutch Indonesian spice cake commonly served during Ramadan. It was one of my favorite local sweets, often prepared in multiple thin layers, sometimes as many as twenty. Approaching a young girl who was creaming a bowl full of butter, Mami sniffed the contents of the bowl. "I want to see if the butter is nice," she said. "During the fast, tasting the food is not allowed, not even a little."

I'd never thought of that aspect of fasting before. What a challenge it must be to cook without tasting! "Not even a little pinch?" I asked.

"Not even a little pinch," she confirmed. "Allah sees everything."

Another servant sifted flour into the creamed butter. The flour had been seasoned with freshly ground cinnamon, cloves, and nutmeg, and their aroma rose up all around in a sweet cloud. "If you skimp on spice, the cake will not be—how should I say?—*enak*," Mami said, using the Indonesian word for delicious. She paused and gave a few brief instructions to another cook who was busy making *kolak*, a liquidy coconut-milk sweet with ripe plan-tains and palm sugar.

"Come, my new friend," Mami said. "I want to show you something special."

She led me deeper into the house, past more rooms filled with handsome antiques, until we entered a small, dark room at the end of a hall. She flicked on an overhead light. Boxes and stacks of books filled every bit of the space. Mami reached up to a shelf and pulled down a wooden box. "These are all my old recipes—all of the boxes in this room contain them," she said, carefully opening it. "I have collected them since I was a young girl, when I first got married, many, many years ago." She handed me a small stack of papers, each apparently handwritten in stylish cursive. She picked up a sheet of paper and leaned closer to the light to read it. "Oh, this one," she said, exhaling. She held it as if it were a long-lost love letter. "It's really *enak*." She handed me the recipe—it was for pineapple tarts—and slowly stood up. "I'm going to go nap," she said. "Why don't you stay here and have a look at these while I sleep? You can write down those you like."

She closed the door behind her. For the next two hours, I sat on the floor poring over as much as I could. The recipes were like pressed flowers in a diary, each revealing some moment in Mami's past. There were recipes for classic Indonesian desserts like *onde-onde*, poached dumplings made of sticky-rice flour and filled with palm sugar. "Made this for Mery's 2nd birthday, 1959," said a handwritten note in the margin. There were recipes for Western-style sweets, like lemon pie ("Must use lime juice for lemons," Mami wrote), and recipes that were equal parts Indonesian and Western, like Dutch-style butter cookies with nutmeg ("Juanda loves these"). Although I'd just met Mami, her recipes made me feel as though I'd known her for years.

After an hour or so—I'd lost track of time—there was a knock at the door. It was Mami. She'd changed from her sarong into an elegant orange Sundanese batik threaded with gold. She carried an old delft serving plate with the freshly baked *spekkuk* arranged neatly on it. She smiled. "It's after six o'clock now. The fast is over for today," Mami said, offering me a slice. "You can have a piece. It will make you feel better." I held the still-warm cake in my hands. "It is even more *enak* than a recipe," she added as I bit into it.

—

The people of Indonesia, Malaysia, and Singapore are passionate about their *kueh-kueh* (spelled *kuih-kuih* in Malaysia and Singapore), or "sweets." They're an essential part of everyday life, and they're eaten throughout the day, not just paraded out after dinner or on special occasions. For many people in the region, especially the residents of Java and Bali, sweets are powerful symbols. They represent the riches the world has to offer, and are used extensively in village celebrations and Hindu temple offerings. This may partly explain why it's a long-standing custom to honor guests, who are viewed as living, breathing incarnations of gods, with a plate of sweets as soon as they walk through the door. I can't recall ever going into someone's home and not being welcomed with a slice of freshly baked cake or a sticky-rice treat—with something, anything sweet. I can get used to being treated like a god!

The recipes in this chapter include three popular categories of sweets. The first is made up of moist, fluffy cakes (often called *kek*) and crispy cookies (called biscuits in Malaysia and Singapore). They're similar (and in certain cases identical) to those we know in the West. They're made of wheat or rice flour, eggs, cow's milk or coconut milk, and often, but not always, butter and a leavening agent such as baking powder. But the similarities to Western sweets stop there. Indonesian, Malaysian, and Singaporean cooks ingeniously flavor their cakes and cookies with local ingredients, such as mangoes, and an array of spices. The two recipes I've chosen to represent this category are Mami's Indonesian Spice Cake (page 342), a spicy spin on an old-fashioned Dutch-style butter cake, and Nutmeg Tea Cookies (page 344), a Ramadan favorite.

Puddings and sweet compotes enriched with coconut milk (called *pengat* in Malaysia and Singapore and *kolak* in Indonesia) make up the second category. They are served as a mid-morning or late-afternoon pick-me-up and also appear at *berbuka puasa* feasts. Cooks like to serve them right after the day's fast ends as they quickly help raise blood-sugar levels depleted from fasting. As too much heat mutes their delicate taste, they're brought to the table slightly warm but never hot. Because these dishes are easy to make and so tasty, I've included three recipes here. Among them is Sweet Spiced Mung Bean Porridge (page 346), which combines mung beans, coconut milk, spices, and sugar. It's traditionally eaten in the morning, as a hearty breakfast snack, but it translates brilliantly as an after-dinner dessert. Another luscious treat is Purple Rice Pudding with Coconut Milk (page 345). It consists of sweetened, sticky purple rice simmered to a puddinglike thickness and topped with coconut milk (a touch of salt in the coconut milk subtly emphasizes the sweetness of the dish). This spare dish is a personal favorite. I like the way the earthy, sticky rice contrasts with the sweet, rich coconut milk. Plantains with Coconut Milk and Palm Sugar (page 347) is the third recipe in this category.

The final category is *jajan pasar*, or "market sweets." These classic Southeast Asian treats are prepared from sticky-rice or taro flour or, sometimes, from sticky rice itself. Recognizable by their firm, gelatin-like consistency and neon-bright colors, they are crafted in an assortment of whimsical shapes, such as diamonds, scrolls, triangles, ovals, and flowers. The Nyonyas of Malaysia and Singapore excel at *jajan pasar*. They create their versions, flavored with *daun pandan* leaves and a range of floral essences and extracts, in multicolored layers, including purple, pink, green, yellow, orange, red, and blue (the colorings are traditionally derived from flowers and herbs). They require an artisan's hand to make, and most home cooks buy them from market vendors who specialize in them. But I wanted to include a not-too-difficult *jajan pasar* recipe that I think you'll enjoy: Sweet Rice Dumplings with Palm Sugar and Coconut (page 349). These petite dumplings—they're the size and shape of large grapes—are filled with palm sugar that melts into a delicious, caramel-like syrup as the dumplings cook.

INDONESIAN SPICE CAKE
Spekkuk
(INDONESIA)

—

This butter-rich spice cake, flavored with cinnamon, nutmeg, and cloves and known as *spekkoek* (the Dutch spelling) or *spekkuk*, is an inheritance from Holland's four-century colonization of Indonesia. The recipe was given to me by Mami, my friend in Bandung, Indonesia, who is an expert in all things sweet. Because butter is a rare commodity in Indonesia, especially outside of big cities, many cooks substitute margarine. Mami wouldn't dream of doing that. "*Spekkuk* is a special-occasion cake. It deserves a splurge," she says. She usually makes this cake when important guests come calling, or for her *berbuka puasa* (literally, "opening the fast") feasts during Ramadan. Essentially a pound cake baked in a tube, or Bundt, pan, it has a golden, faintly crisp exterior and a shamelessly rich, velvety interior. There are few things more satisfying than eating a warm slice of *spekkuk* along with sweetened tea (the traditional accompaniment) or icy cold milk (my favorite accompaniment).

Lapis legit (literally "layered stickiness") is a *spekkuk* constructed of up to twenty-five layers, each no thicker than 1/8 inch (3 millimeters). The more layers you make, the more grand the cake. It's made by spreading successive thin layers of batter, one layer at a time. As each layer is added, it's baked until it's cooked through, usually five to ten minutes, and then another layer is spread on top. The process is repeated until all of the batter is used up. Some cooks alternate white, spice-free batter with golden brown spice-laced batter for a variegated effect. Other cooks make *lapis legit* with ten thicker layers, as opposed to twenty-five thin ones. Though these multilayered cakes are lovely to look at, they taste no different than a single-layered *spekkuk*.

Have all of your ingredients at room temperature and this cake will go together easily.

MAKES ONE 9-INCH (23-CENTIMETER) TUBE CAKE

2 cups (8 1/4 ounces/235 grams) sifted cake flour, plus more for dusting

1/2 teaspoon baking powder

1 teaspoon freshly grated nutmeg

1/2 teaspoon ground cloves

4 teaspoons ground cinnamon

Pinch of kosher salt

1 1/2 cups (12 ounces/340 grams) unsalted butter (3 sticks), at room temperature, plus more for greasing

1 2/3 cups (13 ounces/370 grams) granulated sugar

4 large eggs, at room temperature

3 large egg yolks, at room temperature, lightly beaten

2 teaspoons vanilla extract

1 tablespoon powdered sugar (optional)

1. Position a rack in the middle of the oven and preheat the oven to 325°F (165°C). Grease and lightly flour a 9-inch (23-centimeter) tube pan with 3 1/2-inch (9-centimeter) sides (or, my preference, use a nonstick pan of the same size but don't grease and flour it).

2. Resift the sifted flour along with the baking powder, nutmeg, clove, cinnamon, and salt into a bowl. Now, resift the flour mixture and then set it aside.

3. In another bowl, using an electric mixer on high speed, beat the butter until it's soft and very pliant, about 1 minute (or 4 to 6 minutes by hand with a wooden spoon). Gradually add the granulated sugar and beat on high speed until the mixture is pale and fluffy, 3 to 5 minutes (or 6 to 8 minutes by hand).

4. One at time, add the 4 whole eggs and beat on high speed until the mixture is light and fluffy, about 2 minutes (or 5 minutes by hand).

5. Add the flour mixture to the butter mixture in 3 equal parts, beating on low speed or stirring with the wooden spoon until the batter is smooth and the flour is well combined with the butter mixture. Add the egg yolks and vanilla and continue to beat or stir until they're well mixed into the batter.

6. Pour the batter into the prepared pan, smoothing the surface. Place on the middle oven rack and bake until a toothpick inserted into the thickest part of the cake comes out clean, about 1 hour (though I'd recommend checking it after 45 minutes).

7. Remove the pan from the oven and let the cake cool in the pan on a wire rack for 10 minutes. If necessary, carefully run a thin knife around the perimeter and the inner rim of the cake to help loosen it from the pan. Invert the pan onto the rack and lift it off of the cake. Turn the cake right side up and let it cool on the rack.

8. Transfer the cake to a serving platter. Using a fine-mesh sieve, dust the top with the powdered sugar, if desired.

NUTMEG TEA COOKIES
Kue Kering
(INDONESIA)

———

Like Indonesian Spice Cake (page 342), these delicious little butter cookies, fragrant with vanilla and a pinch of nutmeg, are a legacy of Dutch rule. This recipe is adapted from one from Mami, my sweets expert in Bandung, Indonesia. Her special touch is the nutmeg, which she adds for its warm aroma. As with the spice cake, have all your ingredients at room temperature to streamline making the cookies.

MAKES ABOUT 45 SMALL COOKIES

8 ounces (1 cup/225 grams) unsalted butter (2 sticks), at room temperature

3/4 cup (5 1/2 ounces/155 grams) sugar

1 teaspoon vanilla extract

1 large egg, at room temperature

2 1/2 cups (12 1/2 ounces/355 grams) all-purpose flour, sifted

Pinch of kosher salt

1/4 teaspoon freshly grated nutmeg

1. In a bowl, using an electric mixer on high speed, beat together the butter and sugar until pale and fluffy, about 3 minutes (or 4 to 6 minutes by hand with a wooden spoon). Beat in the vanilla and egg until they're well combined.

2. In a large bowl, stir together the flour, salt, and nutmeg with a wooden spoon. Gradually add the flour mixture to the butter-egg mixture and stir by hand just until combined.

3. Divide the dough into 4 equal portions. Place 1 portion on a sheet of plastic wrap on a work surface. Using your hands and the plastic wrap, roll the dough into a log 1 inch (2.5 centimeters) in diameter, making sure that the plastic wrap covers the entire length and diameter of the roll. Gently flatten the ends of the log by gently tapping them on the work surface, and then fold the plastic wrap over the ends. Roll the log a few more times to make it as smooth and evenly cylindrical as possible. The smoother and more even the log, the rounder and more uniform your cookies will be. Wrap the log in an additional sheet of plastic wrap. Repeat with the remaining 3 dough portions. Lay the 4 logs flat in the refrigerator and chill until firm, at least 2 hours or up to overnight.

4. Position a rack in the middle of the oven and preheat the oven to 350°F (180°C). Have ready 2 ungreased baking sheets.

5. Remove 2 logs from the refrigerator and unwrap them. (Keep the remaining 2 logs in the refrigerator until you're ready to use them.) Using a sharp knife, cut each log into slices 1/4 inch (6 millimeters) thick. Work quickly, as this dough softens rapidly. (Chill the dough in the freezer for about 5 minutes if it becomes so soft and droopy that you can no longer easily manage the cookies.) Place the slices on 1 of the baking sheets, spacing them about 1 inch (2.5 centimeters) apart (they spread as they bake).

6. Place the baking sheet on the middle oven rack and bake the cookies until their edges are golden and their tops are a very pale gold, about 10 minutes. Remove from the oven and let the cookies cool on the baking sheet on a wire rack for 3 minutes. Then, using a spatula, transfer the cookies to 1 or more wire racks to cool completely.

7. Repeat the cutting, baking, and cooling with the remaining 2 logs and the second baking sheet. (If you can't accommodate all the cookies on the 2 baking sheets and need to reuse 1 sheet to bake the balance of the cookies, be sure to let the sheet cool completely before you put the cookies on it.) The cookies will keep in a tightly covered container in the refrigerator for up to 1 week.

PURPLE RICE PUDDING WITH COCONUT MILK
Pulut Hitam
(INDONESIA, MALAYSIA, AND SINGAPORE)

⟶

Purple sticky rice, which is sometimes called black sticky rice, is dark brown to purple when raw and turns a deep purple as it cooks. It's related to white sticky rice and is available in all Chinese and Southeast Asian markets, often in 8-ounce (225-gram) bags. Its nutty taste is complemented by sugar, as this spare but delicious dessert—one of the easiest recipes in this book—demonstrates. To make the pudding, you boil the rice until it's tender and puddinglike, spoon it while it's still warm into cups or bowls, and then drizzle it with lightly salted coconut milk, which helps pacify its sweetness. The combination is irresistible.

MAKES 4 SERVINGS

1 cup (7 ounces/200 grams) purple sticky rice (see headnote)

6 1/2 cups (52 fluid ounces/1.6 liters) water

2/3 cup (5 ounces/140 grams) sugar

1 cup (8 fluid ounces/250 milliliters) unsweetened coconut milk

1/4 teaspoon kosher salt

1. Place the rice in a 3- or 4-quart (3- or 4-liter) saucepan. Fill the pot halfway with cold water. If any rice hulls or small twigs float to the surface, scoop them aside with your hand and discard them. Gently swirl your fingers through the rice for about 20 seconds. Be careful not to massage the rice aggressively. You don't want to crack or break the grains. Allow the rice to settle for a few seconds. Tilt the pot over a sink and drain out all the water, cupping the rice with your hand to prevent it from spilling out of the pot. Repeat this process with 2 more changes of water. Leave the rinsed rice in the pot.

2. Add the water and sugar to the rinsed rice, stirring well to combine. Place the pan over high heat and bring the water to a rolling, noisy boil. As soon as it boils, reduce the heat to medium-low. Simmer, partially covered, until the grains have split open and the rice is tender and the liquid has thickened to the consistency of a thickish pudding, 50 minutes to 1 1/4 hours. You'll need to stir the rice periodically and even more toward the end of cooking—as the mixture thickens, it becomes heavy and prone to scorching and sticking. Taste some. It should be soft, with just a hint of chewiness, when it's done. If the rice is not yet tender and has begun to run out of water, add more water 1/2 cup (4 fluid ounces/ 125 milliliters) at a time. Set the pan aside and allow the rice to cool until it's warm.

3. In a small bowl, combine the coconut milk with the salt and set aside at room temperature.

4. Spoon the warm rice into 4 serving bowls. Drizzle an equal amount (4 tablespoons) of the coconut milk over each serving. Serve warm.

SWEET SPICED MUNG BEAN PORRIDGE
Bubur Kacang Padi
(INDONESIA AND MALAYSIA)

—

This sweet breakfast porridge is enriched with coconut milk and made aromatic by cinnamon and ginger. While it's a wonderful way to start the day (or even end it), it can also be eaten for dessert after a meal. Mung beans, the olive-colored green beans that, when left to sprout, become mung bean sprouts, are often regarded as a sweet in Southeast Asia. Their likable texture and gentle taste provide a perfect backdrop for the flavorings of this dish. Fragrant *daun pandan* leaves are traditionally added, but they aren't necessary, as the vanilla compensates for their taste. This recipe is from Rohati, my cooking friend in Padang, West Sumatra, who often serves it after early morning trips to her local market.

MAKES 4 SERVINGS

1 cup (about 7 ounces/200 grams) mung beans

4 1/2 cups (36 fluid ounces/1.1 liters) water

4 fresh or thawed, frozen *daun pandan* leaves (page 64), each tied into a knot (optional)

1 piece cinnamon stick, 4 inches (10 centimeters) long

1 piece fresh ginger, 2 inches (5 centimeters) long, peeled and bruised until juicy with a

heavy, blunt object such as the bottom of a glass measuring cup

1 1/2 cups (12 ounces/340 grams) sugar (or slightly less to taste)

1/4 teaspoon kosher salt

1 teaspoon vanilla extract

1 cup (8 fluid ounces/250 milliliters) unsweetened coconut milk

1. Rinse the mung beans in a few changes of cold water, picking through them to remove stones and grit. Place the beans in a 2-quart (2-liter) saucepan and add the water, *daun pandan* leaves (if using), cinnamon, and ginger. Bring the beans to a rolling boil over high heat, using a large spoon to skim off any foam that appears on the surface. Immediately reduce the heat to medium-low and cover the pan. Cook at a gentle simmer, stirring occasionally, until the beans are cracked open but not mushy, 35 to 40 minutes. Taste the beans. They should be soft and tender and not at all crunchy.

2. Raise the heat to medium and return the beans to a simmer. Add the sugar, salt, and vanilla, stirring well to combine. Continue to simmer, stirring occasionally to prevent scorching, until the sugar is thoroughly dissolved, about 3 minutes.

3. Reduce the heat slightly and stir in the coconut milk. Cook until the coconut milk is just heated through, 2 to 3 minutes. Remove from the heat and allow the dish to cool slightly. Remove and discard the *daun pandan* leaves (if used), cinnamon, and ginger.

4. Divide the mung beans and sauce evenly among 4 bowls. Serve barely warm. If the beans are too hot, you won't taste the spices as clearly.

PLANTAINS WITH COCONUT MILK AND PALM SUGAR
Kolak or *Pengat Pisang*
(INDONESIA, MALAYSIA, AND SINGAPORE)

On the last day of Ramadan, after the imams (Muslim priests) have interpreted the moon's position and proclaimed the month-long fast over, chants praising Allah ring out from the loudspeakers of local mosques. The atmosphere everywhere is electric. In Indonesia, this time is known as Lebaran and lasts up to fourteen days, while in Malaysia and

Singapore, where the holiday is kept shorter because of the demands of modern life, it's called Hari Raya, or the Great Day. Lebaran and Hari Raya are like New Year's Day, Christmas, and Easter all rolled into one. After four challenging weeks of self-reflection and physical limitations (not only is food forbidden during Ramadan's daylight hours, so is drinking beverages, including water!), people are both spent and exhilarated. "Let the party begin" is the universal sentiment. And begin it does, with more eating and merriment than seems humanly possible.

A few years ago during Lebaran, I was in Padang, in West Sumatra, Indonesia, in the home of my friend Hasan. On the morning of the first day, thousands of townspeople gathered at the grounds of the governor's palace for a massive communal prayer. Afterward, Hasan and I stopped by his sister Ari's home. She greeted us with a warm smile and bowls filled with this sweet, rich classic: ripe plantains simmered until just tender in palm-sugar–sweetened coconut milk.

Bananas can't really be substituted in this dish—they'll turn to mush. Fortunately, ripe plantains are easy to come by in Latin and Asian markets and in many supermarkets. Be sure to select plantains that are fully ripe, almost uniformly black, but not mushy. Alternatively, allow them to ripen for a few days in a paper bag. Anything less than very ripe plantains will make this dish taste inappropriately sour.

MAKES 4 SERVINGS

1 1/4 pounds (570 grams) very ripe, deep yellow to black plantains (3 or 4 medium sized; see Cook's Note, page 163), peeled and cut on the diagonal into slices about 1/4 inch (6 millimeters) thick

1 1/2 cups (12 fluid ounces/375 milliliters) unsweetened coconut milk

1 1/2 cups (12 fluid ounces/375 milliliters) water

4 1/2 tablespoons palm sugar (page 79), thinly sliced, or dark brown sugar

2 fresh or thawed, frozen *daun pandan* leaves (page 64), each tied into a knot (optional)

1/4 teaspoon kosher salt

1. Place the plantain slices, coconut milk, water, palm sugar, *daun pandan* leaves (if using), and salt in a medium-sized saucepan and stir well to combine. Don't worry if the palm sugar doesn't dissolve instantly. It will do so as it cooks.

2. Place the pan over medium-high heat and bring to a gentle boil, stirring frequently. Immediately reduce the heat to low and let the liquid simmer gently until the plantains are fork-tender, 3 to 6 minutes. (Don't let the coconut milk boil for more than a few seconds, or it might curdle.) Test a plantain slice. It should be soft and tender but still hold its shape. It shouldn't be mushy, falling apart, or ragged around the edges, nor

should it be firm. Continue to cook for a few minutes if the plantains aren't yet done. Otherwise, remove the pan from the heat and set aside to cool until the liquid is warm.

3. Ladle equal amounts of the plantains and coconut milk into 4 bowls and serve while still slightly warm. In Indonesia, Malaysia, and Singapore, this dish is commonly ladled into a punch bowl from which guests serve themselves.

SWEET RICE DUMPLINGS WITH PALM SUGAR AND COCONUT
Onde-Onde
(INDONESIA, MALAYSIA, AND SINGAPORE)

I remember the first time I encountered *onde-onde* (sometimes called *klepon*), a sweet sticky-rice dumpling eaten throughout Indonesia, Malaysia, and Singapore. It was part of a lavish buffet at the Jakarta home of my friend Tanya Alwi. Dusted in lacy strands of grated coconut, these dumplings were unfamiliar but inviting, so I bit into one. The filling—made of palm sugar, which melts into a luscious caramel-like syrup as the dumplings poach—burst gently in my mouth, like a juicy grape. I was instantly hooked. The dumpling portion is made of glutinous rice flour (called *tepung ketan*) flavored with vanilla and *daun pandan*. The flour, which forms the basis of many sweets, makes a dough that is appealingly chewy when cooked. The *daun pandan* flavoring—created by pulverizing *daun pandan* leaves in water until it has absorbed their flavor—is not essential but adds a subtle herbal note. (I don't recommend substituting the *daun pandan* extract available in many Chinese and Southeast Asian stores. It tastes too artificial.) However, soft, sweet freshly grated coconut *is* essential. Grated dried coconut is too hard and flavorless to use in this dish (also don't use baker's coconut, which is far too sweet). Preparing *onde-onde*, while not effortless, is not as difficult as it might seem, though it's much easier if you can get someone to help you: one person can roll the dumplings and the other can be in charge of poaching them and then dredging them in the grated coconut as they come out of the boiling water.

MAKES ABOUT 44 DUMPLINGS

7 fresh or thawed, frozen *daun pandan* leaves (page 64; optional)

1 cup (8 fluid ounces/250 milliliters) plus 3 tablespoons water

6 drops green food coloring (optional, but it will give the dumplings a festive color)

4 1/2 tablespoons palm sugar (page 97), thinly sliced, or dark brown sugar

2 1/3 cups (7 ounces/200 grams) finely grated fresh coconut (page 58)

1/4 teaspoon kosher salt

2 1/2 cups (1 pound/455 grams) glutinous-rice flour (see Cook's Note, page 351)

1 teaspoon vanilla extract

1. If you're using the *daun pandan* leaves, cut them into 2-inch (5-centimeter) pieces and place them in a small food processor along with the water. Pulse until the leaves are well pulverized and the water has absorbed their flavor, about 30 seconds. Pour the mixture through a fine-mesh sieve into a bowl, squeezing the pulverized leaves until they no longer contain any liquid. Discard the leaves. Add the food coloring (if using) and stir well to combine. Set aside.

2. Measure 1/4 teaspoon of the palm sugar and roll it into a ball; repeat with the rest of the sugar. (These balls will be stuffed inside the sticky rice later.) Set aside.

3. In a small bowl, combine the grated coconut and salt and set aside.

4. Place the flour in a bowl. If you made the *daun pandan*–flavored water, add it to the flour along with the vanilla. If you're not using *daun pandan*–flavored water, add the plain water to the flour along with the vanilla and the food coloring (if using). Stir until there are no more lumps and you have a thick, smooth batterlike dough. It should appear glossy. Test a bit to see if you can roll it in your hands without it sticking. Add a bit more water, a teaspoon at a time, if the dough is too dry, or flour, also a teaspoon at a time, if it's too sticky.

5. Fill a 3-quart (3-liter) saucepan with water and bring it to a rolling boil over medium-high heat.

6. Initially, you'll be making and cooking 1 dumpling at a time. To form a dumpling, measure 1 1/2 teaspoons of the dough and roll it into a ball between your palms. With your little finger, make a small depression in the center of the ball of dough and fill it with a ball of palm sugar. Pinch the dough around the palm sugar to seal it inside. Gently roll the dough between your palms once more, smoothing the surface into a round ball and making sure that the palm sugar is well sealed inside the dumpling. You don't want the palm sugar to leak out when the dumpling cooks.

7. Immediately add the dumpling to the boiling water; it will start to sag and lose its round shape if you delay. Poach, stirring gently with a spoon, to prevent the dumpling from sticking to the bottom of the pot, until the dumpling rises to the surface, 3 to 5 minutes.

8. With a slotted spoon or tea strainer, immediately transfer the dumpling to the bowl containing the grated coconut and, using 2 spoons, roll the dumpling in the coconut until it's evenly coated. Transfer to a plate to cool.

9. Continue forming and poaching 1 dumpling at a time. Eventually you'll be able to make several at a time, but start out slowly until you get the hang of it. Discard any dumplings that burst open during the poaching.

10. Serve the dumplings soon, at room temperature. If there are leftover dumplings, cover them with plastic wrap and store them at room temperature for no longer than 2 days. Chilling these dumplings will make them hard and unpalatable.

COOK'S NOTE

Glutinous-rice flour, also called sweet-rice flour and sticky-rice flour, resembles cornstarch. It's available in Asian markets, usually in clearly labeled 1-pound (455-gram) bags imported from Thailand. Don't confuse glutinous-rice flour with regular rice flour, which doesn't have the same sticky quality. Store glutinous-rice flour as you would wheat flour: in a cool, dark place for up to 1 year.

A NOTE ON DURIANS

Because of their temperate climates and plentiful rainfall, Indonesia, Malaysia, and Singapore are home to a year-round bounty of tropical fruits. Markets are filled with beautiful heaps of golden mangoes, vanilla-scented bananas, and exotic citrus fruits. But my favorite is the durian, a much-lauded (and often feared) spiky-skinned fruit. In his seminal natural-science book *The Malay Archipelago* (1869), naturalist Alfred Russel Wallace described the taste of a durian: "A rich butter-like custard highly flavored with almonds gives the best general idea of it, but intermingled with it comes wafts of flavor that call to mind cream cheese, onion sauce, brown sherry, and other incongruities."

I just call durians delicious, but I'll admit that I was more than a little unsure the first time I tasted one. I was in Singapore, and though I'd already traveled widely in Indonesia and Malaysia, I'd successfully avoided eating this odd-smelling fruit. Curiosity got the better of me one hot day in the city's Chinatown. Durians were in season, and there were vast piles of them for sale everywhere I looked. With their prickly skins, they resembled medieval torture devices, but the time had come. I knew I had to try one. An old Chinese vendor, tickled pink at the idea of a Westerner taking interest in the fruit, whacked one open for me with a cleaver. I sat down in the shade and took a cautious bite. It not only smelled strange, but it also tasted strange. But by the third bite, I was hypnotized by its complex taste and custardlike consistency.

In the years since, I've become a durian acolyte, and when I learn that someone is cut from the same cloth, I ask that person to join me in a feast. My favorite such indulgence was in Padang, West Sumatra, Indonesia. My friend Hasan and I had a serious durian jones one afternoon, so we drove a few hours south of town to an area of virgin jungle famous for its wild durians. There, locals forage the rain forest for the best fruits, which have fallen to the ground, and sell them on the roadside. We bought a half dozen. And despite our sincere intention to wait until we got home to eat them, appetite intervened. We ate all six on the roadside, barely stopping to breathe between bites. It was durian heaven.

A decade ago it was difficult to partake of my fondness for durians when I was at home in the United States. Nowadays it's easy. Frozen whole durians imported from Thailand are widely stocked in North America's Chinese and Southeast Asian markets (durians that have not been frozen are available in Canada). Although they lack the deeply layered taste of unfrozen durians, they can be excellent. Choose small fruits that are heavy for their size. Those with the strongest aroma—a cross between very ripe mango and pineapple, with subtle notes of alcohol and sulfur (my apologies to Sir Wallace's colorful description)—will taste best. If a durian is frozen, thaw it at room temperature before eating. It may take up to 3 hours if the fruit is heavier than 4 pounds (1.8 kilograms). I find that durians are too rich to top off a meal. They're best enjoyed in midafternoon, around the same time you would take tea.

BEVERAGES

Although Java is one of the world's most important coffee-growing regions (which is why coffee is colloquially known in North America as java), tea is the real drink of choice in Indonesia, Malaysia, and Singapore. You won't find a *kampong* (village) street corner or a big-city high-rise complex where there aren't at least a few people chatting in a communal space as they sip glasses of sweetened *teh* (tea). The best variety in Indonesia is a lightly cured orange pekoe, which has a soft, slightly herbal taste. It is widely grown in the volcanic highlands of Java and Sumatra, where it thrives at altitudes of three thousand to six thousand feet. But there are hundreds of tea varieties grown and processed, including uncured green teas (*teh hijau*) and smoky-tasting deeply cured teas that are similar to Lapsang souchong. Teas that have been mixed with flowers and herbs are also popular. Among them are *teh wangi* (fragrant tea) from Indonesia, a blend of orange pekoe and whole jasmine flowers. It is often served iced and copiously sweetened with sugar. Malaysia's best teas come from the Cameron Highlands, a tea- and vegetable-growing region a few hours north of Kuala Lumpur, the capital city. The most popular brand from the Cameron Highlands is Teh Boh, a hearty, robust, Assam-like orange pekoe cultivated on a plantation established by the British in the early 1900s. It is increasingly available in sachets in many Asian supermarkets in North America; buy some if you see it.

I've included two methods for making black tea in this chapter: Cinnamon Tea (below), a Spice Islands specialty, calls for using cinnamon-infused boiling water rather than plain water, and Hawker's Tea (page 354), a favorite in Malaysia and Singapore, is made rich and irresistible with sweetened condensed milk.

Cordials (*stroop*) made with still or sparkling water and fruit syrups are also drunk in the region. Serving them is a common way to greet guests on their arrival. Although most cooks today use commercially produced syrups, the best are still made at home. Lime-Cordial Syrup (page 356), from the father of my friend Josephine Chua, is an excellent example.

CINNAMON TEA
Teh Kayu Manis
(SPICE ISLANDS, INDONESIA)

This aromatic tea is a specialty of Banda, a mini-archipelago in the Spice Islands where spices seem to find their way into everything that is drunk or eaten.

MAKES 4 SERVINGS

4 pieces cinnamon stick, each 4 inches (10 centimeters) long

5 cups (40 fluid ounces/1.25 liters) water, preferably spring water or filtered tap water (see Cook's Notes, page 274)

2 tablespoons loose black tea such as Ceylon or Assam

Sugar

1. Combine the cinnamon sticks and water in a medium-sized saucepan and bring to a rolling boil over high heat. Reduce the heat to medium and allow the water to simmer until the fragrance of cinnamon wafts above the pan and the spice thoroughly infuses the water, about 3 minutes.

2. Place the loose tea in a teapot or nonreactive container and pour the simmering cinnamon-flavored water over it. Allow the tea to steep until it's the strength you desire; best is about 2 minutes.

3. Strain the tea into teacups or glasses and serve hot. Let guests add sugar to taste.

HAWKER'S TEA
Teh Tarik
(MALAYSIA AND SINGAPORE)

—

Black tea tempered with sweetened condensed milk is hugely popular in Malaysia and Singapore. It's a milky, sweet adaptation of the way tea is drunk in India, and I urge you to try it. In both countries, *mamak* (Muslim Indian) street-food vendors specialize in making this tea in a truly theatrical fashion. They pour the tea, already mixed with the milk, from glass to glass, often from a distance of more than three feet, resulting in a frothy, lattelike beverage. Here's how to do it in your own home.

MAKES 1 SERVING

1 teaspoon loose black tea such as Ceylon or Assam

3/4 cup (6 fluid ounces/175 milliliters) boiling water, preferably spring water or filtered tap water (see Cook's Notes, page 274)

About 1 1/2 tablespoons sweetened condensed milk

1. Place the tea in a teapot or nonreactive container and pour the boiling water over it. Let it steep until deep brown and quite strong, about 3 minutes.

2. Strain the tea into a large cup. Add the condensed milk (adjust the amount to how sweet you like your tea) and stir to combine.

3. Working at a distance of about 18 inches (45 centimeters), pour the tea back and forth 2 or 3 times from the original cup to another large cup. This cools the tea while also making it delectably frothy. It takes practice to master, but after a few attempts you'll be as skilled as the best *mamak* in Malaysia.

4. Transfer the tea to a teacup or glass and serve immediately, before the layer of foam on top collapses.

WARM SPICED LIMEADE
Bandrek

(NORTH SUMATRA, INDONESIA)

Petronius, the first-century Roman author, called cinnamon the "child of a distant soil that makes one forget the rose's scent." This recipe, from my friend Kois, who comes from Aceh, Indonesia, makes the fragrant assets of the spice stand out. Usually drunk warm on chilly nights in the North Sumatran highlands, this sweet beverage is restorative if you're feeling under the weather, yet is equally delicious served over ice.

MAKES 3 SERVINGS

3 thick stalks fresh lemongrass, each tied into a knot (page 76)

2 pieces cinnamon sticks, each 4 inches (10 centimeters) long

3 whole cloves

1 piece fresh ginger, 2 inches (5 centimeters) long, peeled and bruised until juicy with a heavy, blunt object such as the bottom of a glass measuring cup

4 1/2 cups (36 fluid ounces/1.1 liters) water, preferably spring water or filtered tap water (see Cook's Notes, page 274)

5 tablespoons palm sugar (page 79), thinly sliced, or dark brown sugar, or more to taste

3 tablespoons fresh lime juice, or more to taste

A few sprigs fresh mint and ice (optional)

1. Combine the lemongrass, cinnamon, cloves, ginger, and water in a medium-sized saucepan and bring to a rolling boil over high heat. Reduce the heat to medium, cover partially, and allow the water to simmer until the fragrance of the seasonings wafts above the pan and the seasonings thoroughly infuse the water, about 7 minutes.

2. Add the 4 tablespoons of palm sugar and stir until it's dissolved. Remove the pan from the heat, add the 3 tablespoons lime juice, and stir well to combine. Taste the beverage. It shouldn't be overly sweet or overly sour. Adjust accordingly, adding a teaspoon or so more lime juice to bring up the tartness, or 2 or 3 teaspoons more palm sugar to make it sweeter.

3. Remove and discard the seasonings (leave the cinnamon sticks, if you like), divide the limeade among 3 glasses or cups, and serve hot. You can also serve this beverage over ice, garnished with mint sprigs, if desired.

LIME-CORDIAL SYRUP

Sirop Air Limau

(MALAYSIA)

—

Charlie, the father of my friend Josephine Chua, was a soft-spoken Malaysian business-man who passed away a few years ago. He collected recipes in journals and on scraps of paper, in the same fashion as my friend Mami in Bandung. This simple method for lime syrup for cordials is one such recipe. It's excellent drizzled over shaved ice, to make a cooling snow cone, or added to still or sparkling water for a fast limeade (see the last step of the recipe for the proper ratio of syrup to water).

Kasturi limes are the most commonly used variety in Malaysia and Singapore. Slightly smaller than Ping-Pong balls, they have smooth yellow-green rinds, a sweet-tart taste with hints of tangerine, and lots of seeds that require intensive plucking. (For more information about *kasturi* limes, see page 76.)

MAKES ABOUT 4 CUPS (32 FLUID OUNCES/1 LITER) SYRUP

5 1/2 cups (2 pounds, 6 ounces/1.1 kilograms) sugar

3 cups (24 fluid ounces/750 milliliters) water, preferably spring water or filtered tap water (see Cook's Notes, page 274)

1 1/2 cups (12 fluid ounces/375 milliliters) fresh *kasturi* lime juice (page 76) or Persian lime juice

Still or sparkling water and ice (optional) for making cordials

1. Bring the sugar and 3 cups water to a rolling boil in a medium-sized saucepan, stirring to dissolve the sugar. Reduce the heat to medium-low and continue to stir until the sugar dissolves completely. Add the lime juice and simmer gently until the liquid begins to thicken, about 10 minutes. Remove from the heat, let cool for a few minutes, and then pour through a fine-mesh sieve into a clean bottle. The syrup will keep, tightly covered, in the refrigerator for 1 month.

2. To make 1 cordial, combine 1 tablespoon lime syrup with 1 1/2 cups (12 fluid ounces/375 milliliters) cold still or sparkling water and stir well to combine. Serve at once, neat or over ice.

SINGAPORE SLINGS

(SINGAPORE)

Alcoholic beverages are not widely consumed in Indonesia and Malaysia. Not only do they not mix well with the pervasive equatorial heat, they are considered *haram* (taboo) in Islam, the predominant religion. Singapore, with its mostly non-Muslim Chinese population, is another story. Though the Singapore sling is more of a tourist favorite than a popular local drink, it's nevertheless delicious *and* truly Singaporean. Reportedly first made in the early 1900s by Ngiam Tong Boon, a bartender at Singapore's Raffles Hotel, its balance of sweet, sour, and abrasive flavors is immensely appealing. Make one and imagine that you're Somerset Maugham sipping it under the cool shade of a frangipani tree.

MAKES 2 SERVINGS

2 1/2 fluid ounces (75 milliliters) gin

1 fluid ounce (30 milliliters) cherry brandy

1/2 fluid ounce (15 milliliters) Benedictine

1/2 fluid ounce (15 milliliters) Cointreau or kirsch

8 fluid ounces (250 milliliters) unsweetened pineapple juice

1 fluid ounce (30 milliliters) fresh lime juice

1/2 fluid ounce (15 milliliters) grenadine

A few drops Angostura bitters

Ice cubes

2 thin, triangular slices fresh pineapple (for garnish; optional)

2 maraschino cherries (for garnish; optional)

1. Pour the gin, cherry brandy, Benedictine, Cointreau, pineapple juice, lime juice, grenadine, and Angostura bitters into a cocktail shaker. Add a few ice cubes, cover, and shake vigorously for a few seconds.

2. Fill 2 tall glasses (a Collins glass is traditional) with ice, and strain the contents of the cocktail shaker into the glasses. Garnish each glass with a slice of pineapple and a maraschino cherry, if desired.

SELECTED BIBLIOGRAPHY AND READING LIST

Alford, Jeffrey, and Naomi Duguid. *Hot Salty Sour Sweet: A Culinary Journey Through Southeast Asia.* New York: Artisan, 2000.

Anderson, Benedict. *The Spectre of Comparisons: Nationalism, Southeast Asia and the World.* New York: Verso, 1998.

Corn, Charles. *The Scents of Eden: A History of the Spice Trade.* New York: Kodansha America, Inc., 1998.

Cost, Bruce. *Bruce Cost's Asian Ingredients.* New York: William Morrow and Company, 1988.

Deane, Shirley. *Ambon: Island of Spices.* London: The Travel Book Club, 1979.

Echols, John M., and Hassan Shadily. *Kamus Indonesia Inggris: An Indonesian-English Dictionary.* 3rd ed. Jakarta: Penerbit PT Gramedia, 1989.

———. *Kamus Inggris Indonesia: An English-Indonesian Dictionary.* Jakarta: Penerbit PT Gramedia, 1975.

Eliot, Joshua, Liz Capaldi, and Jane Bickersteth, with David Woodley and Jasmine Saville. *Indonesia Handbook.* London: Footprint Handbooks, 2001.

Hannah, Willard A. *Indonesian Banda: Colonialism and Its Aftermath in the Nutmeg Islands.* Indonesia: Yayasan Warisan dan Budaya Banda Neira, 1991.

Ho, Alice Yen. *At the South-East Asian Table.* Singapore: Oxford University Press, 1995.

Hor, Fatihah Seow Boon, and Nor Zailina Nordin. *The New Malaysian Cookbook.* Kuala Lumpur: Preston Corporation, 2001.

Hutton, Wendy. *Tropical Fruits of Indonesia.* Hong Kong: Periplus Editions, Ltd., 2000.

———. *Tropical Herbs and Spices of Indonesia.* Hong Kong: Periplus Editions, Ltd., 1997.

———. *Tropical Vegetables of Indonesia.* Hong Kong: Periplus Editions, Ltd., 1996.

Jelani, Rohani. *Homestyle Malay Cooking.* Singapore: Periplus Editions (HK) Ltd., 2002.

———. *Malaysian Hawker Favourites.* Singapore: Periplus Editions (HK) Ltd., 2001.

Kasper, Lynne Rossetto. *The Splendid Table.* New York: William A. Morrow, 1992.

Lee, Geok Boi. *Asian Rice Dishes.* Singapore: Periplus Editions (HK) Ltd., 2002.

———. *Nonya Favourites.* Singapore: Periplus Editions (HK) Ltd., 2001.

Marks, Copeland. *The Exotic Kitchens of Indonesia: Recipes from the Outer Islands.* New York: M. Evans and Company, Inc., 1989.

Miller, George. *To the Spice Islands and Beyond: Travels in Eastern Indonesia.* London: Oxford University Press, 1996.

Miller, Mark, and John Harrison. *The Great Chile Book.* Berkeley, California: Ten Speed Press, 1991.

Milton, Giles. *Nathaniel's Nutmeg.* New York: Farrar, Straus and Giroux, 1999.

Mowe, Rosalind, ed. *Southeast Asian Specialties.* Cologne: Konemann Verlagsgesellschaft mbH, 1999 (English edition).

Owen, Sri. *Classic Asian Cookbook.* New York: D.K. Publishing, Inc., 1998.

Rombauer, Irma, Ethan Becker, and Marion Rombauer Becker. *The All New Joy of Cooking.* New York: Scribner, 1997.

Sahni, Julie. *Classic Indian Cooking.* New York: William A. Morrow, 1980.

Solomon, Charmaine, and Nina Solomon. *Charmaine Solomon's Encyclopedia of Asian Food.* New York: Tuttle Publishing, 1998.

Steinberg, Rafael, and the editors of Time-Life Books. *Foods of the World: Pacific and Southeast Asian Cooking.* Alexandria, Virginia: Time-Life Books, 1970.

Stella, Alain. *The Book of Spices.* New York: Flammarion, 1998.

Stevens, Molly. *All About Braising.* New York: W. W. Norton, 2004.

Tan, Su-Lyn, and Mark Tay. *World Food: Malaysia and Singapore.* Footscray, Australia: Lonely Planet Publications Pty. Ltd., 2002.

Tan, Sylvia. *Singapore Heritage Food: Yesterday's Recipes for Today's Cook.* Singapore: Landmark Books, 2004.

Tarling, Nicholas. *The Cambridge History of Southeast Asia.* Vol. 1, *From Early Times to c. 1500.* London: Cambridge University Press, 1999.

Tim Tujuh Sembilan Tujuh. *Aku Cinta Makanan Indonesia.* Jakarta: Penerbit PT Gramedia Pustaka Utama, 2000.

Trang, Corinne. *Essentials of Asian Cuisine: Fundamentals and Favorite Recipes.* New York: Simon & Schuster, 2003.

Tropp, Barbara. *The Modern Art of Chinese Cooking.* New York: William A. Morrow, 1982.

Winneke, Odilia, and Rinto Habsari. *Bumbu Indonesia.* Jakarta: Penerbit Gramedia Utama, 2001.

Witton, Patrick. *World Food: Indonesia.* Footscray, Australia: Lonely Planet Publications Pty. Ltd., 2002.

Wong, Julie. *Nonya Flavours: A Complete Guide to Penang Straits Chinese Cuisine.* Kuala Lumpur: Star Publications (Malaysia) Berhad, 2003.

Young, Grace. *The Breath of a Wok: Unlocking the Spirit of Chinese Wok Cooking Through Recipes and Lore.* New York: Simon & Schuster, 2004.

SOURCES

BANGKOK CENTER GROCERY
104 Mosco Street
New York, New York 10013
Telephone: 212-349-1979
www.thai-grocery.com
A friendly New York store selling mail-order
  sweet soybean paste, Thai *hom mali* (jasmine
  rice), Mae Ploy coconut milk, dried and fresh
  chiles, fresh galangal and kaffir lime leaves,
  and frozen *daun pandan* leaves.

D'ARTAGNAN
280 Wilson Avenue
Newark, New Jersey 07105
Telephone: 800-327-8246
Fax: 973-465-1870
www.dartagnan.com
Organic free-range chicken, Muscovy and
  Long Island ducks, and goat.

CROSS COUNTRY NURSERIES
P.O. Box 170
199 Kingwood-Locktown Road
Rosemont, New Jersey 08556
Telephone: 908-996-4646
Fax: 908-996-4638
www.chileplants.com
A New Jersey nursery that specializes in chile
  plants, with hundreds of varieties that can
  be shipped to your door.

EARTHY DELIGHTS
1161 East Clark Road, Suite 260
DeWitt, Michigan 48820
Telephone: 800-367-4709 or 517-668-2402
Fax: 517-668-1213
www.earthy.com
Fiddlehead ferns and baby fingerling potatoes.

EVERGREEN Y.H. ENTERPRISES
P.O. Box 17538
Anaheim, California 92817
Telephone: 714-637-5769
www.evergreenseeds.com
A good Asian-produce seed source, including
  seeds for lemon basil, long beans, *choy sum*,
  and Japanese eggplants.

GOURMETSLEUTH
P.O. Box 508
Los Gatos, California 95031
Telephone: 408-354-8281
www.gourmetsleuth.com
Tamarind, woks, and hard-to-find spices.

IMPORTFOOD.COM
P.O. Box 2054
Issaquah, Washington 98027
Telephone: 888-618-8424 or 425-687-1708
Fax: 425-687-8413
www.importfood.com
Fresh galangal and lemongrass.

INDOMART
25608 Barton Road
Loma Linda, California 92354
Telephone: 909-796-4000 or 909-799-7215
Fax: 909-799-7265
www.indomart.us
North America's only Indonesian supermarket, with a thriving online business where you'll find shrimp chips, dried shrimp paste, Indonesian sweet soy sauce (including the excellent Cap Bango brand), palm sugar, and frozen tempeh.

KALUSTYAN'S
123 Lexington Avenue
New York, New York 10016
Telephone: 800-352-3451 or 212-685-3451
Fax: 212-683-8458
www.kalustyans.com
A New York shop offering fine spices, fresh turmeric and curry leaves, and a wide variety of Asian ingredients.

MELISSA'S/WORLD VARIETY PRODUCE, INC.
P.O. Box 21127
Los Angeles, California 90021
Telephone: 800-588-0151
www.melissas.com
An excellent online produce merchant carrying lemon basil, baby potatoes, fresh banana leaves, kaffir lime leaves, long beans, chiles (Fresno, Thai, and Holland when available), and an assortment of Asian greens.

NIMAN RANCH
1025 East 12th Street
Oakland, California 94606
Telephone: 866-808-0340
Fax: 510-808-0339
www.nimanranch.com
Naturally raised beef (including oxtails and beef short ribs) and pork (including boneless pork shoulder).

PATEL BROTHERS
42-92 Main Street
Flushing, New York 11355
Telephone: 718-661-1112
Fax: 718-661-2076
www.patelbrothersusa.com
A chain of Indian, Pakastani, and Bangladeshi supermarkets that also offers online sales. At the stores, you'll find wonderful Asian produce, including fresh turmeric and curry leaves, and some of the freshest spices available in North America.

PENZEYS SPICES
P.O. Box 933
Muskego, Wisconsin 53150
Telephone: 800-741-7787 or 414-679-7207
Fax: 262-785-7678
www.penzeys.com
Top-quality spices, such as green cardamom pods and whole cassia sticks from Sumatra.

TEMPLE OF THAI
P.O. Box 112
Carroll, Iowa 51401
Telephone: 877-811-8773
www.templeofthai.com
Tamarind, purple sticky rice, and dried shrimp.

THAI HERBS & SPICES
P.O. Box 151835
Austin, Texas 78715
Telephone: 512-507-0981
www.thaiherbs.com
A wonderful nursery specializing in Asian vegetables and aromatics. Small plants shipped to your door, including lemon basil, lemongrass, curry leaf, *daun pandan*, and turmeric.

UWAJIMAYA
600 Fifth Avenue South
Seattle, Washington 98104
Telephone: 206-624-6248
www.uwajimaya.com
A celebrated Seattle Asian supermarket with a range of perishable and nonperishable Indonesian, Malaysian, and Singaporean ingredients available online.

ACKNOWLEDGMENTS

I had long heard that adage about books taking more than one person to write, about how creating them is really more a communal effort than a solitary one. Boy, is that ever true.

First and foremost, I want to thank Darrell Hucks, my partner. More often than not, his devotion to making this book come to life surpassed even mine. He shopped for fresh turmeric to test recipes, ground flavoring pastes to amazing smoothness, and pored over every last word of the manuscript more times than I can count, bettering it with each pass. This book would not exist were it not for his efforts. I also want to thank my mom, Bernice Oseland, who offered both editorial wisdom and emotional support, and Pete and Sam, whose companionship and good humor pulled me through many distracted moments.

My editor, Maria Guarnaschelli, championed this book from the moment she received the proposal. The intensity with which she turned to making it the best book possible was truly inspiring. I shall be forever grateful.

The warm support of my agent, Doe Coover, was a source of constant comfort throughout the four-year gestation of this book, from my staring (initially) at a blank computer screen to the final proof. Doe's office staff, including Frances Kennedy and Colleen Mohyde, was equally invaluable.

My dear friend Kay Blumenthal read through both the proposal and the manuscript with extraordinary care. Her notes were remarkable not only for their intelligence but also for their generosity. The same sentiment applies to Pamela Kaufman of *Food and Wine*; Pamela Renner; Thor Stockman; and Constance Monaghan, who has been an encouraging friend since the days when we worked at *L.A. Weekly*, many years ago.

The fine folks at W. W. Norton—particularly Debra Morton Hoyt, Andrew Marasia, Eleen Cheung, Erik Johnson, Nancy K. Palmquist, Susan M. Sanfrey, Robin Muller, Star Lawrence, Karen Walker, Wanda Bazemore, and Aaron Lammer—made putting this book together both easy and fun. Sharon Silva was a fabulous copy editor; I am indebted to her for catching so many errant words and numerical loose ends. The designer, Iris Weinstein, created a lean, smart look that put a smile on my face the instant I saw it. And Justin Morrill's maps—and his wily sense of humor—are things of real grace.

My good friends at *Saveur* over the years are this book's godparents. Christopher Hirsheimer, one of the magazine's founding editors, not only sent me out to write stories in Malacca, Malaysia, and Padang, Indonesia—assignments that eventually became this book's spiritual backbone—but also shot the exquisite plated color food photographs that adorn its pages. I offer her my deepest thanks. My editors at the magazine, including Colman Andrews, Kathleen Brennan, Caroline Campion, Melissa Hamilton, Dorothy Kalins, Amy Lundeen,

Judith Sonntag, and Margo True, provided guidance and wisdom over the course of my writing many other stories about Southeast Asia.

For their recipe-testing skills—and their kindness—I am indebted to Aileen Donovan, Jan Novello, and Michele Bonds.

Very special thanks go to Rick Smilow and Liz Young of the Institute of Culinary Education; to Todd Coleman, formerly of ICE; and to the hundreds of marvelous students I have taught at the school over the past few years.

Warm thanks to Sarah Ross; Irene Khin Wong; Daniel Scharfman; Cynthia Eddy; Regina Ross; Rinaldi Joi and his wife, Ibu Suzan; Alesia Exum; Sherry Russell; Jill Goodman; Cathy Cavender; Jim Chew; Grace Chew; Emilya Cachapero; Cristina Sales; Irene Sax; Margie Schnibbe; Kok Choo Heng; Suansee; Helen Tong and Tong Kok Kiang of Taste Good Restaurant in Queens, New York; Tom, Jenna, Diane, John, and Clu Gulanger; Lonnée Hamilton; Darwin Harjono; Datin Amy Hamidon; Shivani Vora; Rati Lohtia; George and Mike Kuchar; Gary Goldberg of the New School; Denise Maher; M. P. Radhakrishnan; Marilyn Welch; Sreelesh V. K.; Sreenivasan; Timothy Fox of Fox Global Communications; Vijayan Swami; the friendly people of Melissa's Variety Produce; and Mary Scully and Encik Rahim of Tourism Malaysia in New York City.

In Indonesia thanks are due to the Alwi family: Tanya; Om Des; Mira; Ramon; Mien; Ibu Tuti; and Ibu Ann and Karma, both of whom passed away during the past two decades. I am also indebted to the following: Amalia Pulungan; Dian Afriani; Inam; Siti; Hasanuddin Mahyudin and his wife, Nanik; Pak Arzein; Misran Ali; Dr. Wiendu Nuryanti; Hasrin Mansyur; Nasrul and Warisah (and their children Sias, Sei, Ides, Imus, and Rian), in Air Hangat; the late Pak Djuanda and his mother, Mami, and his sister, Merry; Om Paul, in Makassar; Pak Achson, in Lamongan, and his wife, Ibu Renny; Tamalia Alisjahbana; Sasmiyarsi Sasmoyo and her husband, Aristides Katoppos; Arfian; Gatot Wibowo; Ibu Rohati and her daughter, Dewi; Pak Dede, in Banda; and Pak Muhammad and his brother Pak Budi, in Bau-Bau.

In Malaysia and Singapore, my deepest gratitude is owed to Josephine Chua and her husband, Keong, and her son, Daniel; Jenny Kuan and her husband, Gerard Fernandis; Mohammad Khairy Ishak; Ibu Lila; Elaine Thong; Goh Mai Loon; Julie Wong of *Flavours* magazine; Kok Sia; Ng San Fatt; Tong Ming Hui; Joe and Katharine Lazaroo; Sharifah Loon Syed Danial; Alan Ng; Roselan Hanafiah Al-Idrus; Haji Basir B. Wagiman; Zaharah Adam and her daughter Yuni; Bruno M. Dedual of Y.T.L. Hotels; Dato Mary Ritchie; Encik Kamal; Mat Daud bin Mat Ali; Kevin Peterson of Kevin Peterson Sdn. Bhd.; Ng Kin Lam; Jenny Gau; Ken Ho; Goh Ching Lee; Adele Chung; and Sylvia Tan.

Most of all I want to thank the hundreds of home cooks and street hawkers of Indonesia, Malaysia, and Singapore who have allowed me into their kitchens over the past twenty-four years with natural warmth, grace, and selflessness that continue to astonish me. Many of them are named in this book; just as many are not. Either way, I hope that I have honored them as best as I can.

In late December 2004, as I was finishing the second draft of this book, an underwater earthquake off the coast of northwestern Sumatra unleashed a tsunami of catastrophic proportions. In the minutes, weeks, and months afterward, some 169,000 Indonesians, most of them from the Sumatran province of Aceh, died. A number of people who contributed to this book were directly affected, including Cut Siti Sarah, who lost eight family members in Banda Aceh, the capital city of Aceh, and Pak Kois Affasia, an Acehnese friend who lost nearly as many. I send a special prayer to Sarah and Kois and to the millions of people throughout the world touched by that tragedy.

INDEX

Page numbers in **boldface** refer to recipes themselves; page numbers in *italics* refer to photographs.

Kevin's Spiced Roast Chicken with Potatoes, Penang Style, 35, 117, 123, 158, 216, **287–89**
Kikkoman soy sauce, 88
king crab:
   Black Pepper Crab, 37, **264–65**
   Ketam Lada Hitam, 37, **264–65**
kingfish:
   about, 68, 238
   in *Asam Pedas,* 47, 63, 239, **249–52**, 309, 335
   in Indian-Style Fish Stew with Okra, 47, 63, 239, **249–52**, 309, 335
   as substitute in *Chuan-Chuan,* 80, 156, 213, 239, **252–53**
   as substitute in Pan-Seared Mackerel with Chiles and Garlic, 80, 156, 213, 239, **252–53**
KitchenAid Chef Series Food Chopper, 108
kitchen shears, 107
Knife peanut oil, 78–79
knives, 106–7
Kokita sweet soybean paste, 89
Kolak, 79, 163, 341, **347–48**
kolak. See compotes
Koon Chun soy sauce, 88
Kopi Tiam Soft-Boiled Eggs, 37, 322, **333–34**
kosher salt, 82, 83
kresik. See Toasted Grated Coconut
krupuk udang. See shrimp chips
kueh-kueh. See sweet(s)
Kue Kering, 341, **344–45**
kuey teow. See noodles, fresh
kuih-kuih. See sweet(s)
kunn choy. See Chinese celery greens
kunyit. See turmeric
Kwong Hung Seng Sauce, 89

labu, 202
lada kering. See chile(s), red, dried
lada merah. See chile(s), red Holland
lamb:
   as substitute in Acehnese Goat Curry, **314–17**, 315
   as substitute in *Kare Kambing,* **314–17**, 315
lan jiang. See galangal
laos. See galangal
lapis legit, 342
lauk pauk, 111
lemon basil, 32
   about, 74–75
   Ayam Panggang Sulawesi, 34, 104, 135, 218, 252, 270, **292–94**, 327, 330
   in Chopped Vegetable Salad with Coconut and Lime Leaf Dressing, 33, 74, 79, 112, **156–58**, 323
   Fragrant Fish Stew with Lime and Lemon Basil, 48, 64, 70, 74, 112, 232, 239, **240–42**, 247, 281, 306
   Grilled Coconut Chicken with Lemon Basil, 34, 104, 135, 218, 252, 270, **292–94**, 327, 330

Grilled Whole Fish with Lemon Basil and Chiles, 33, 69, 74, 239, **256–59**
   in Herbal Rice Salad, 73, 81, 173, **186–89**
   Ikan Kuning, 48, 64, 70, 74, 112, 232, 239, **240–42**, 247, 281, 306
   in *nasi kerabu,* 73, 81, 173, **186–89**
   in *Nasi Ulam,* 73, 81, 173, **186–89**
   Pepes Ikan, 33, 69, 74, 239, **256–59**
   Sambal Tempe, 229, 244, 278, 321, **324–25**
   substitutes for, 75
   Tempeh Sambal with Lemon Basil, 229, 244, 278, 321, **324–25**
   in *Urap,* 33, 74, 79, 112, **156–58**, 323
lemongrass:
   about, 75–76
   Ching Lee's Braised Lemongrass Long Beans, 37, 205, **218–20**, 246, 274, 317
   in curry, 34
   in Ginger-Scented Coconut Rice, 36, 176, **178**
   in Herbal Rice Salad, 73, 81, 173, **186–89**
   Kacang Panjang Belacan, 37, 205, **218–20**, 246, 274, 317
   Lemongrass and Shallot Sambal, 33, 117–18, **122–23**
   Lemongrass-Scented Coconut Rice, 64, 109, 118, 120, 132, 133, 147, 173, **176–78**, 179, 209, 263, 285, 323, 330, 332
   in *nasi kerabu,* 73, 81, 173, **186–89**
   in *Nasi Lemak,* 36, 176, **178**
   Nasi Uduk, 64, 109, 118, 120, 132, 133, 147, 173, **176–78**, 179, 209, 263, 285, 323, 330, 332
   in *Nasi Ulam,* 73, 81, 173, **186–89**
   Sambal Serai, 33, 117–18, **122–23**
Lemongrass and Shallot Sambal, 33, 117–18, **122–23**
Lemongrass-Scented Coconut Rice, 64, 109, 118, 120, 132, 133, 147, 173, **176–78**, 179, 209, 285, 323, 330, 332
lengkuas. See galangal
lentils, yellow. *See* yellow lentils
lettuce, in Gado-Gado, 86, 118, 128, 140, 141, 142, **154–56**, 229, 335
limau. See lime(s)
lime(s), 202. *See also* kaffir lime leaves
   about, 76
   Bandrek, 110, **355**
   in Chicken Curry Noodle Soup, Kuala Lumpur Style, 36, 189, **195–99**
   Fragrant Fish Stew with Lime and Lemon Basil, 48, 64, 70, 74, 112, 232, 239, **240–42**, 247, 281, 306
   Ikan Kuning, 48, 64, 70, 74, 112, 232, 239, **240–42**, 247, 281, 306
   in *Kare Laksa,* 36, 189, **195–99**
   Lime-Cordial Syrup, 353, **356**
   in Nyonya Sambal, *114,* 116, 117, **120–22**, 191, 255, 262, 283, 285, 289, 297, 312
   in *Sambal Belacan, 114,* 116, 117, **120–22**, 191, 255, 262, 283, 285, 289, 297, 312

Sambal Goreng Buncis, 22, 23, 27, 123, **216–18**, 285, 289, 314

Sambal Mangga Muda, **123–24**, 242, 255

Sambal Serai, 33, 117–18, **122–23**

Sambal Tempe, 229, 244, 278, 321, **324–25**

Sambal Udang, 79, 102, 156, 180, 225, 239, 252, **262–63**, 278, 330

Sambal Ulek, 118, **119–20**, 178, 197, 207, 285, 314, 323

Stir-fried Shrimp Sambal, 79, 102, 156, 180, 225, 239, 252, **262–63**, 278, 330

Tempeh Sambal with Lemon Basil, 229, 244, 278, 321, **324–25**

Sambal Bajak, 118, **119–20**, 178, 197, 207, 285, 314, 323

Sambal Belacan, 114, 116, 117, **120–22**, 191, 255, 262, 283, 285, 289, 297, 312

Sambal Goreng Buncis, 22, 23, 27, 123, **216–18**, 285, 289, 314

Sambal Mangga Muda, **123–24**, 242, 255

Sambal Serai, 117–18, **122–23**

Sambal Tempe, 229, 244, 278, 321, **324–25**

Sambal Udang, 79, 102, 156, 180, 225, 239, 252, **262–63**, 278, 330

Sambal Ulek, 118, **119–20**, 178, 197, 207, 285, 314, 323

sambar, 211

satays:

Beef Satay, 125, 128, 133, 142, **144–47**

Chicken Satay, 32, 62, 112, 125, 128, 133, 142, **147–50**, 180

Sate Ayam, 32, 62, 112, 125, 128, 133, 142, **147–50**, 180

Sate Sapi, 125, 128, 133, 142, **144–47**

Shrimp Satay, 85, 112, 142, **150–53**, 196, 244

Sate Ayam, 32, 62, 112, 125, 128, 133, 142, **147–50**, 180

Sate Sapi, 125, 128, 133, 142, **144–47**

sauces, 118

dipping. See dipping sauces

Javanese Peanut Sauce, 118, **128–29**, 141, 147

Saus Kecang Tanah, 118, **128–29**, 141, 147

Saus Kecang Tanah, 118, **128–29**, 141, 147

Saus Lado, **127**, 163

Sautéed Cabbage with Ginger and Crispy Indian Yellow Lentils, **209–11**, 252, 325

Savoy cabbage, about, 212

sayur asin. See mustard greens, salted

Sayur Lodeh, 118, 123, 132, 178, 306, 321, **327–30**

sayur sawi. See choy sum; mustard greens

sayur sawi putih. See bok choy

sea salt, 82

Seh Bak, 122, 209, 242, 303, **307–9**

seledri. See Chinese celery greens

Semur Daging Lembu, 255, 303, **309–12**, 312, 327

serai. See lemongrass

sereh. See lemongrass

serrano chiles:

as substitute for fresh green Thai chiles, 54

as substitute for Holland chiles, 54

sha he fen, 190

shallots, 202

about, 83–85, 202

Crisp-Fried Shallots, 70, **84–85**, 272, 275, 313

Fried Eggs with Garlic, Shallots, Chiles, and Ginger, 322, **332–33**

Kentang Balado, 32, 98, 112, 200, 202, **221–23**, 246

Lemongrass and Shallot Sambal, 33, 117–18, **122–23**

in Malaccan Beef and Vegetable Stew, 255, 303, **309–12**, 312, 327

Rohati's Crisp-Fried Potatoes with Chile and Shallot Sambal, 32, 98, 112, 200, 202, **221–23**, 246

Sambal Serai, 33, 117–18, **122–23**

in Seh Bak, 122, 209, 242, 303, **307–9**

in Semur Daging Lembu, 255, 303, **309–12**, 312, 327

in Spiced Braised Nyonya Pork, 122, 209, 242, 303, **307–9**

Telur Mata Sapi Bumbu, 322, **332–33**

Shanghai choy (Shanghai bok choy), 45

about, 206

in Mee Goreng Tauceo, 89, 112, 122, 127, 189, **191–93**

in Stir-fried Asian Greens with Garlic and Chiles, 43, 112, 120, 125, 126, 127, **205–7**, 223, 225, 249, 253, 255, 262, 278, 283, 294, 306, 314

in Stir-fried Chinese Egg Noodles with Shrimp and Asian Greens, 89, 112, 122, 127, 189, **191–93**

in Tumis Sayur, 43, 112, 120, 125, 126, 127, **205–7**, 223, 225, 249, 253, 255, 262, 278, 283, 294, 306, 314

shellfish. See crab; shrimp; squid

shrimp:

about, 85, 238, 239

in Char Kuey Teow, 35, 127, 189, 190–91, **193–95**

dried. See dried shrimp; dried shrimp paste

Fern Curry with Shrimp, 203–4, 205, 223, **226–29**, 306, 333

Gulai Paku, 203–4, 205, 223, **226–29**, 306, 333

Mee Goreng Tauceo, 89, 112, 122, 127, 189, **191–93**

Nyonya Shrimp Curry with Fresh Pineapple and Tomatoes, 36, 48, 121, 220, 239, **260–62**, 309

in Penang-Style Stir-fried Kuey Teow Noodles, 35, 127, 189, 190–91, **193–95**

Sambal Udang, 79, 102, 156, 180, 225, 239, 252, **262–63**, 278, 330

Shrimp Satay, 85, 112, 142, **150–53**, 196, 244

Stir-fried Chinese Egg Noodles with Shrimp and Asian Greens, 89, 112, 122, 127, 189, **191–93**

Stir-fried Shrimp Sambal, 79, 102, 156, 180, 225, 239, 252, **262–63**, 278, 330

Stir-fried Tamarind Shrimp, 102, 122, 183, **255**

Udang Asam, 102, 122, 183, **255**

Udang Masak Nenas, 36, 48, 121, 220, 239, **260–62**, 309